EVANGELISM IN THE EARLY CHURCH

EVANGELISM
IN THE
EARLY CHURCH

by

MICHAEL GREEN

Principal of St. John's College, Nottingham

WILLIAM B. EERDMANS PUBLISHING COMPANY
GRAND RAPIDS, MICHIGAN

For Crispin and Gill Joynson-Hicks
who, like the early Christians, use
their home, their opportunities and
their friendships to share with others
the Good News of Christ.

Biblical quotations are generally taken from the
Revised Standard Version or The New English
Bible; patristic citations generally from the Ante
Nicene Library or the Loeb Library.

PREFACE

There were two considerations which induced me to write this book. The first was that the whole subject of evangelism in the early Church has been unaccountably neglected in recent years. Nothing substantial has been written in English directly on this topic since Harnack's great book, *The Mission and Expansion of Christianity*, was translated. Harnack, though brilliant as a writer and encyclopaedic as a scholar, lived a long time ago. Our conception of the nature of the gospel has changed a good deal since the hey-day of Liberal Protestantism which he represented. Moreover, men like C. H. Dodd and Roland Allen have made significant contributions to different aspects of the subject. There seemed, therefore, to be room for a book which tried to reappraise some of the main aspects of evangelism in antiquity in the light of recent study, and to do some fresh research and thinking on the whole problem.

The second consideration was a more personal one. Most evangelists are not very interested in theology: most theologians are not very interested in evangelism. I am deeply committed to both. So the study of this subject was particularly congenial to me.

I have deliberately refrained from defining the scope of this study too precisely. It concentrates on the New Testament period both because of its normative importance for all subsequent evangelism, and also because it happens to be the sphere in which I am least ignorant. But I felt that it would be a mistake to leave the matter at the end of the New Testament period. I have, therefore, carried it through until about the middle of the third century, taking in roughly the 200 years stretching from St Paul to Origen. The book does not attempt to give an exhaustive or even chronological examinaton of the second or third century evidence: the treatment is topical and necessarily selective. I have, however, cited a good deal from the primary sources, in order to allow the men of the early Church to speak for themselves on the gospel and how it spread.

Neither do I make any attempt here to give a comprehensive account of the mission of the Church in the broad sense. This is ground which has been often and ably traversed. I have tried to stick closely to evangelism in the strict sense of proclaiming the good news of salvation to men and women with a view to their conversion to Christ and incorporation into his Church. There is, accordingly, little about pre-evangelism and the infiltration of pagan society by

7

Christian influence and ideals; little on the social and political implications of the gospel; and little on the catechesis of the early Christians as they followed up their evangelistic outreach and consolidated the ground gained.

However, I believe that a study of evangelism even in this restricted sense is of real significance for our day. If it can help us to understand afresh the gospel these early Christians preached, the methods they employed, the spiritual characteristics they displayed, the extent to which they were prepared to think their message through in the light of contemporary thought forms, to proclaim it to the utmost of their power, to live it, and to die for it, then a study such as this might, perhaps, be of some service towards recalling the Church in our own day to her primary task.

I would like to take this opportunity of expressing my deep gratitude to the Council of the London College of Divinity for allowing me a sabbatical term in the summer of 1968, and to the Tyndale Fellowship for Biblical Research for allowing me free residence, during that term, at Tyndale House Library, Cambridge, whose Librarian, Mr Alan Millard, has constantly been willing to lay his own work aside in order to help others. I am very grateful to Dr J. M. C. Toynbee and Professor H. E. W. Turner for their help with different aspects of the book. I owe more than I can acknowledge to Dr Dacre Balsdon, of Exeter College, Oxford, and to Dr Henry Chadwick, then of Queens' College, Cambridge, who respectively gave their pupil a love for the classics and theology. I am particularly grateful to the latter, and to Professor Maurice Wiles, of London, for reading through this manuscript and making many helpful suggestions and corrections. Mr Edward England has been the most courteous and encouraging of publishers. I want to thank two colleagues, Mr Stephen Travis and Mr Franklyn Dulley, for their help, together with Dr Timothy Mimpriss and Mr Grahame Humphries for assistance with the tedious task of indexing. The efficiency of my secretary Judith Berrill and the long suffering of my wife and children have been an enormous support during a particularly busy period preparing for the College's move to Nottingham in 1970. And I am thankful to the students of many universities in this country and overseas for driving me, through the challenge of leading university missions, to get back to first principles and examine afresh the bearing of evangelism in the early Church on the task of making Christ known today.

E. M. B. Green,
The London College of Divinity,
September, 1969.

CONTENTS

ILLUSTRATIONS

[1] The British Museum
[2] The Mansell Collection, London
[3] Professor Enzo Crea and Fratelli Alinari, Instituto di Edizioni Artistiche, Roma

The author wishes to acknowledge his indebtedness to the above for permission kindly given to reproduce their photographs.

The line drawing on p. 174, from *The Crucible of Christianity* (ed. Arnold Toynbee), is reproduced by kind permission of Messrs. Thames and Hudson.

1

PATHWAYS FOR EVANGELISM

IT WAS A small group of eleven men whom Jesus commissioned to carry on his work, and bring the gospel to the whole world.[1] They were not distinguished; they were not well educated; they had no influential backers. In their own nation they were nobodies and, in any case, their own nation was a mere second-class province on the eastern extremity of the Roman map. If they had stopped to weigh up the probabilities of succeeding in their mission, even granted their conviction that Jesus was alive and that his Spirit went with them to equip them for their task, their hearts must surely have sunk, so heavily were the odds weighted against them. How could they possibly succeed? And yet they did.

It is almost impossible to exaggerate the obstacles that lay in their way; some of them will be considered in the next chapter. But it is equally true to recognize that probably no period in the history of the world was better suited to receive the infant Church than the first century A.D., when, under an Empire which was literally world-wide, the scope for the spread and understanding of the faith was enormous. The interplay of Greek, Roman and Jewish elements in this *praeparatio evangelica* is well known, but is worth looking at afresh if this study is to be put in its proper perspective. In the earliest account we have of the spread of Christianity, the Acts of the Apostles, the debt owed to Greece, Rome and Jewry is plain on almost every page. By the second century Christians were becoming more reflective and self-conscious about the background into which the Church was launched,[2] and began to argue that it was a divine providence which had prepared the world for the advent of Christianity. Not all their arguments are of equal value,[3] but that the first century did provide invaluable pathways for the spread of the gospel it is idle to deny.

ROMAN PEACE

First and foremost was the *pax Romana*. The spread of Christianity would have been inconceivable had Jesus been born half a century earlier. As it was, the new faith entered the world at a time of peace unparalleled in history. The whole known world was for the first time under the effective control of one power—Rome. To be sure, that situation had almost been reached over a century earlier when, after the victorious conclusion of the Third Punic War, Rome found herself the dominant power in the Mediterranean basin. She had introduced, by force of arms and good colonial administration, a political unity such as Alexander the Great had only dreamed of. Polybius wrote his *History*, covering the years 220–145 B.C., in order to record for posterity how "the Romans in less than fifty-three years succeeded in subjugating nearly the whole world to their sole government—an achievement unexampled in history". But this position was short-lived. Mistress of the world, Rome was not mistress of herself. Within a few years of the destruction of Carthage in 146 B.C. a would-be Roman reformer, Tiberius Gracchus, was clubbed to death in a riot led by the ex-consul, P. Scipio Nasica. His death initiated an internal struggle which led to a hundred years of civil wars. Marius, Sulla, Pompey, Crassus and Julius Caesar, to mention only some of the more famous participants in this century of carnage, all took up arms against their fellow-countrymen and embroiled the whole world in their disastrous struggle for power. When Julius Caesar was struck down by the daggers of Brutus and Cassius in 44 B.C., it must have seemed that one more nail was being driven into the coffin of the Roman *imperium*, despite the claim of the conspirators that they acted only in order to kill a tyrant and revive the Republic. The outcome was a further bloody struggle, between the Triumvirate consisting of Marcus Antonius, M. Aemilius Lepidus and the dead Caesar's grand-nephew, Caius Octavius, on the one hand, and Brutus and Cassius on the other, which was settled at the battle of Philippi. This in turn was followed by the eclipse of Lepidus, a titanic struggle between Antony and Octavius which culminated in the battle of Actium (31 B.C.) and, a year later, the death of Antony and his mistress, Cleopatra, coupled with the Roman annexation of Egypt.

Octavius's supremacy was now undisputed. The weary nations turned in gratitude to their deliverer from a century of war, and acclaimed him with the utmost sincerity as "saviour of the world" [4] The poets, Virgil and Horace, proclaimed the beginning of a new era; "*redeunt Saturnia regna*".[5] For the first time for two centuries the temple of Janus had its great doors closed as a sign of peace and in 17 B.C. Augustus (as a grateful Senate had entitled him a decade earlier, in return for his having, in appearance at any rate, restored Republican government)[6] celebrated the *Ludi Saeculares* in which Horace sang the achievement of the "son of Anchises and Venus"[7] and the peace, plenty and happiness of his principate. Perhaps more impressive than this official piece of propaganda are inscriptions from all over the ancient world which show the gratitude of ordinary people for the Roman peace Augustus had inaugurated. For instance, one inscription, dating from about 6 B.C. in Rome, records the eulogy of a sorrowing husband for his dead wife. In it he not only talks of their forty-one happy years of marriage, their children and his wife's virtues, but he goes out of his way to pay tribute to the *pax Augusta*. "It was since the pacification of the universe and the restoration of the Republic that, at length, happy and quiet times came our way."[8]

Augustus maintained this peace by means of the army. This was, broadly speaking, stationed around the boundaries of the Empire so that, with the frontiers firmly garrisoned, citizens could sleep in peace. Gaul had been conquered by Julius Caesar, Asia Minor by Pompey, and Augustus took pains to advance frontiers to the Rhine and Danube. These were picketed by legions and patrolled by naval detachments. In the East, he gained diplomatic successes against the Parthians (whom, for geographical and cultural reasons, it would have been impracticable to include within the Empire) and established the frontier on the Euphrates. All within that area was pacified and Romanized. There was no fear of civil strife arising again because, by an astute division of territory between himself and the Senate, Augustus ensured that he would keep control of all those provinces which needed a military presence. By the time of his death only a single legion was to be found in a senatorial province—that in Africa. Under such circumstances internal and external peace seemed assured. Tacitus makes no exaggeration when he reports "sensible men" as saying: "the Empire was hedged in by sea, ocean or long rivers throughout. Legions, fleets, provinces—all was fitly linked together."[9] Augustus had succeeded in creating a corporate unity of the whole of the civilized world.

The development of the road system went on apace: Augustus took a special interest in roads and made their upkeep, the *cura viarum*, an imperial responsibility, administered by a board of senior senators. The reason for this is obvious enough. It not only enabled speedy movement of troops to take place for police activity or military operations, but facilitated the swift transmission of news through the official post, the *cursus publicus*, which Augustus set up. A veritable network of roads radiated out from the Golden Milestone in Rome to all parts of the Empire, and they were kept in good repair. This road system had other great advantages,[10] notably the encouragement of trade and the fostering of travel and social intercourse between different nationalities of the Empire, thus forging an increasingly homogeneous civilization in the Mediterranean world. The possibilities of spreading the gospel afforded by this swift and safe method of travel were fully exploited by the early Christians, and both the New Testament and the literature of the second century simply take for granted journeys of enormous length which would scarcely have been possible after the fall of the Empire until modern times. One oft-quoted inscription found at Hierapolis in Asia Minor on the tomb of a merchant records that he travelled to Rome no less than seventy-two times.[11] He needed no passport anywhere in the Empire. Provided he did not bring merchandise with him, he would have to pay no customs duty, though he was liable to pay a small tax for using the road. It is clear from the pages of the Acts that Christians made the maximum use of the Roman road system, and that it formed an unconscious directive to their evangelism. What a merchant could do for financial advantage, a Christian could do in the cause of the gospel.

GREEK CULTURE

Greek Language

Greece, too, made signal contributions to the spread of Christianity. Perhaps the most important was the Greek language itself. This was now so widely disseminated through the Mediterranean basin that it acted as an almost universal common tongue. Captive Greece captured her conquerors, as Horace complained; and from the second century B.C. when she fell under Roman control, the Greek language rivalled Latin. The conquests of Alexander had already made Greek the common language of the East more than a century before, and now the West followed suit, though Spain remained Latin-speaking. As early as 242 B.C. Livius Andronicus, a Greek slave, was brought to Rome, freed, and became a master of Greek and Latin literature. From then on it was normal for Roman education to be conducted in Greek. Greek tutors, many of them distinguished captives or, like Polybius, political deportees, tended to be so self-satisfied about their superior culture and language that, like the English after them, they did not take the trouble to learn other languages well. They taught in Greek: and the Romans not only put up with it, they liked it.[12] Such patriots as the Scipios and Cicero were expert in Greek: the earliest Roman historians like Fabius Pictor, wrote in Greek. Quintilian, the celebrated educationalist of the first century A.D., insisted that a boy should begin by learning Greek,[13] and many of the official Roman inscriptions that

16

century are in Greek. Fifty years earlier Cicero had observed that Greek was read by practically the whole world, while Latin was confined to its own territory. The satirists, Juvenal and Martial, scornfully pointed out that even the womenfolk did their love-making in the Greek tongue![14] It was, therefore, quite natural that Paul the Jew should address the Latins of Rome in Greek, or that Irenaeus, himself a native of Asia Minor, should write in Greek as he conducted his missionary and apologetic work in France in the second century. Interestingly enough, it was in Greek that the Roman captain, Claudius Lysias, asked the apostle Paul, whom he suspected of being an Egyptian brigand, "Do you know Greek ?"[15] The advantages for the Christian mission of having a common language can hardly be overestimated. It did away with the necessity for missionary language schools. Missionaries using it would incur none of the odium that English-speaking missionaries might find in some of the underdeveloped countries; for Greek, the language of a captive people, could not be associated with imperialism. Moreover, it was a sensitive, adaptable language, ideally suited for the propagation of a theological message, because for centuries it had been used to express the reflections of some of the world's greatest thinkers, and thus had a ready-made philosophical and theological vocabulary. The lack of this specialist vocabulary in Latin led to difficulties some 250 years later, when Latin replaced Greek as the common language of the Western Empire.

Greek Thought

The Greek language cannot be separated from Greek thought. Through it Greek literature was opened up and served as the model for Roman writers. Thus Virgil's *Aeneid* was inspired both in form and content by Homer's *Odyssey* and, in part, *Iliad*: Catullus and Horace copied the Lesbian poetry of the sixth century B.C., and so forth. The poets were the theologians of the day; and the common people derived their conception of the gods and their activities from the Homeric sagas. Indirectly, therefore, this popularizing of theological mythology was a real preparation for the gospel. Thoughtful people reflected on the cruelties, adulteries, deceits, battles and lies attributed to the gods, and they were repelled. It was not the Christians who first mounted an attack on the crude anthropomorphic polytheism of the masses. It had been exposed by Greek philosophers long before. Nobody had been more forthright in exposing the unworthy actions of the traditional gods than Plato,[16] and his attacks were popularized through the teaching of the sophists.[17] These men were to be found in all the main cities of the ancient world; in the open air as freely as indoors they functioned, teaching whoever would pay them. Plato's *Protagoras* gives an idea of the attractiveness, the adroitness and the shallowness of these men and an impression of their influence. The Greek sophists had as great a power over the common people as the Reformation preachers. Their ridicule of the gods must in no small degree have prepared the way for the Christian message. At all events, the Apologists of the second century built upon the foundations they had laid, and often used the weapons of the Greek philosophers in order to denounce the Greek gods. A glance through the *Apology* of Aristides or the *Address to the Greeks* of Justin will show the Christians using this method of attack; a great deal of material came to their hand, for not only Plato but also the Stoics, Epicureans and Cynics had preceded Christianity in this attack. Rigorous Greek thought, honest Greek seeking after truth made men impatient of the worthless deities they had traditionally worshipped. It has been well said of the Greeks that it was not that men became so depraved that they abandoned their gods, but rather that the gods became so depraved that they were abandoned by men.

Not only was there a movement away from polytheism in the Graeco-Roman world of the first century (though it is easy to over-emphasize this: paganism was still a force to be reckoned with in the fourth century A.D.), but a tentative move towards monotheism can be discerned. The problem of the One and the Many had long fascinated Greek thinkers and they were not prepared to accept an account of the universe which did not give a satisfactory account both of its unity and its diversity. As early as Xenophanes in the sixth century B.C. thinking men were not only attacking the Homeric legends which made the gods act dishonourably[18] and adopt human shape, but were groping their way towards a single supreme Deity, who governs the whole universe through thought. Such sayings of his as "there are many gods according to custom, but only One according to nature" or "there is one God, the greatest among gods and men, unlike mortals in appearance, unlike in thought"[19] had considerable influence on Greek religious thought. Even the common people, who still believed in a multitude of gods, often tended to regard Zeus, the king of the gods, as the fount of godhead, the "Father of gods and men" as Homer called him.[20]

Plato and Aristotle both provided impetus for this movement towards monotheism. The former gave as the highest of his Ideas the Idea of Goodness, which he identified with God; and this God was personal.[21] He was the Demiurge, the one who imprinted on the flux of formless matter the ideas which we find copied in the world of appearance in which we live. The process of creation is described in the *Timaeus*, and it is clearly attributed to the goodness of God.[22] Aristotle also inclined heavily towards monotheism. Such subsidiary gods as there may be are banished into inter-stellar space; within our sphere, there is the Prime Mover, who, although he did not create the world (which is eternal), nevertheless forms it by thought. Above change and decay, he is ceaselessly at work and yet perfectly at rest. This God is immaterial; indeed, Aristotle calles him self-subsistent thought, *noēsis noēseōs*.[23] But, whilst successfully avoiding the anthropomorphism of the poets, Aristotle removes his God from any personal relationships with men, if indeed his God is personal at all.[24] Such a deity as he conceives is a cold, mathematical Final Cause. In the *Magna Moralia* he expressly says that it is quite wrong to think that there could be any friendship between men and God.[25] For we could not be said to *love* God in any case, and God could not return our love.

It is clear that the God posited by these Greek philosophers is neither entirely self-consistent, nor by any means to be confused with the personal, redeeming Creator God of the Judaeo-Christian tradition. Nevertheless the general movement towards some sort of monotheism or monism among the intelligentsia of the day (with the exception of the Epicureans and Sceptics) proved an important *praeparatio evangelica*, and one on which the Christians were not slow to build. Admittedly one early Christian attitude to pagan culture was that of utter rejection. Tertullian is, perhaps, the most extreme example of it. "What has Athens to do with Jerusalem?" he asked. "What concord is there between the Academy and the Church? . . . Away with all the attempts to produce a mottled Christianity of Stoic, Platonic, and dialectic composition! We want no elaborate disputation after possessing Jesus Christ, no inquisition after enjoying the gospel. With our faith we desire no further belief."[26]

That was certainly one early Christian attitude. It was shared by Tatian[27] and many early Christians. But it was impossible to maintain consistently. Greek thought had penetrated the whole ancient world too thoroughly to be exorcized by simply shutting one's eyes to it. Accordingly, in the New Testament itself we find Paul and other Christian missionaries making use of what is true and useful in paganism;[28] in the second century this procedure was developed with enthusiasm. It was called "spoiling the Egyptians", and was used with great effect by Justin, Aristides, Athenagoras, Theophilus and the great Alexandrians, Clement and Origen. Plato and Aristotle, the Stoics, and even Euripides are called to the bar to defend

Christian doctrines of God. Examples like the following from Justin could be multiplied: "If on some points we teach the same things as the poets and philosophers whom you honour, and on other points are fuller and more divine in our teaching, and if we alone afford proof of what we assert, why are we unjustly hated more than all others? For while we say that all things have been produced and arranged into a world by God, we shall seem to utter the doctrine of the Stoics. And while we affirm that the souls of the wicked, being endowed with sensation even after death, are punished, and that those of the good being delivered from punishment spend a blessed existence, we shall seem to say the same things as the poets and philosophers. And while we maintain that men ought not to worship the works of their hands, we say the very things that have been said by the comic poet Menander."[29] That is a representative example of how the Christians made use of the preparation for the gospel afforded, so they believed, by Greek religion.

Enthusiastic Cults

But Plato's Form of the Good, or Aristotle's Unmoved Mover, must have provided little to satisfy the religious instincts of the volatile Greeks. Similarly, the Romans with their cold state religion, and their exceedingly limited family religion,[30] catering as it did for neither ethics nor worship, were wide open to influence from emotional, enthusiastic cults which claimed to help men with their daily problems, to give them immortality, and to enable them to share their lives with the god. What is more, these cults had the appeal of esoteric clubs, whose devotees were initiated into the ultimate riddles of the universe, and whose cults were never allowed to be divulged. By the first century A.D. the Graeco-Roman world was inundated with mystery cults of this sort. The most prominent among them were the worship of Cybele or the Great Mother from Asia Minor, Dionysus from Greece, Isis, Osiris and Serapis from Egypt, Mithras from Persia, and into the same category the Roman would add Judaism and Christianity. These were all Hellenistic *superstitiones*, private religious cults, and Rome was reluctant to ban them unless their adherents proved guilty of some offence against morality or the State. They provided an outlet for the emotional and religious feelings of the people, particularly of the common people whose needs were not met by the cold, clever dialectic of the philosophers.[31] For the lower classes, the early Empire could be a lonely place, and these cults afforded companionship, common cult meals in the temple of the patron deity, often followed by dancing girls and a wild party. A slave in such surroundings would find a measure of liberty, a freed man equality, a soldier refreshment, and women had a full place: indeed, in the Isis cult, women took the most prominent part. The enthusiasm engendered by these cults was great; they were led by professional priesthoods which explained the meaning of the ritual to the initiates, and they were not state-aided, but entirely supported by the contributions of their devotees—and people always value most what they pay for. Apart from the sense of brotherhood engendered by these cults, and the promise they gave of a proper burial,[32] they offered three particular attractions.

First, they promised to deal with guilt. It is a mistake to suppose that a sense of sin was unusual in the ancient world. Quite the reverse. From the time of *The Oresteia* of Aeschylus in the fifth century B.C., and even earlier,[33] Greek thought had had deeply impressed upon it the truth that wrongdoing must be punished, that guilt must be expiated, that men are responsible for their actions. In the first century this sense of the link between wrongdoing and punishment was heightened by the civil wars; manifestly, men concluded, this must be punishment for the religious negligence and unworthy lives of the citizens. On the State level Augustus sought to rectify this by staging a religious revival; on the literary level sensitive writers like Virgil and Seneca evidenced a real sense of sin; whilst the man in the street, wanting something that applied more personally to himself, joined one of the mystery religions. It does not take much imagination to conjure up a picture of the lasting effect the initiation ceremony into the Cybele cult, for instance, must have produced. Here the initiate was placed under a grill, above which the throat of a bull or a ram was cut. He was drenched in the blood, symbolizing both the piacular and the energizing power of the animal, and emerged crying out that he was born again for eternity, *renatus in aeternum*.[34]

The quest for security was even greater than the search for cleansing. And here again the Mysteries offered an answer which was to be taken up and greatly deepened by Christianity. The world was a dangerous place. One has only to read the Epistles of Paul to the Romans, Galatians and Colossians or any of the Apologists to see how gripped men were by fear of the *daimonia*, spiritual forces (usually of evil) which influenced their lives. At the mercy of the demonic, men felt themselves also to be the playthings of Fate. This came about through the rise and great popularity of the pseudo-science of astrology in the last century B.C. A man's destiny was fixed according to the pattern of the stars when he was born—and the astrologers claimed to know the secret. The Emperor Tiberius was greatly under the influence of one such astrologer, Thrasyllus, and Claudius and Nero fell under the spell of his son, Tiberius

Claudius Balbillus. That no less persons than the Emperors should have been taken in by these men shows the compelling appeal of astrology. But the darkest side of the picture was the sense of determinism under which folk laboured, the feeling that nothing could deliver them from the jaws of unfeeling Fate. That is precisely where the Mysteries came in. The Isis cult, for one, prided itself on offering to its initiates power over Fate, a way of escaping from chill Destiny. When Lucius, in Apuleius's *Golden Ass*, is about to become a devotee of Isis, and is weighed down by being at the mercy of blind Fate, he is promised "the day of deliverance awaits you".[35] Isis is greater than Destiny.

The sense of union with the delivering god or goddess was expressed in different ways. It might be by an orgiastic ecstasy, as in the Dionysiac cult; it might be by means of a sacred meal, as in the worship of Serapis, or perhaps, as in the *Satyricon* of Petronius, it might be through some repulsive phallic rite. But, irrespective of the details of the ritual, the quest for union with the god underlay them all; for it is thus that security was to be found.

Cleansing, security, and immortality. This was the third hunger of the human heart to which the state religion had nothing to say, and which refused to be silent. Most of the mystery religions promised men immortality; those of Cybele, Dionysus, Mithras and Isis certainly did. Hence their greatest appeal. The immortality that the philosophers argued over, that the literary men sighed for,[36] the Mysteries actually demonstrated in their cult, often through graphic symbolism. Thus, to return to the *Golden Ass*, Apuleius tells how Lucius was dressed in twelve stoles to symbolize the twelve celestial spheres through which he passed during his initiation into the Isis cult. Of his climactic experience he says, "I penetrated to the boundaries of death. I trod the threshold of Proserpina, and after being borne through all the elements, I returned again to earth . . . having been in the presence of the gods below and the gods above, and having done them obeisance."[37]

It was along the pathways of the Greek language, Greek thought and Greek cults that the Christian gospel travelled in the early days. It made excellent progress.

Romans and Jews

But by far the broadest avenue for the advance of Christianity was afforded by Judaism. The Jews had spread far beyond the confines of Palestine long before the first century; and everywhere they went, they took their religion with them. The dissemination of Jews in the East dates from the fall of the Northern Kingdom of Israel in the eighth century B.C. when the ten "lost tribes" were deported. It was accelerated in the Hellenistic period by the voluntary migration of Jews to the new towns of the Levant in pursuit of trade, Egypt, Syria and Asia Minor being the three favourite areas.[38] By the mid-second century B.C. the Jews were significant enough to warrant friendly letters on their behalf from the Roman Senate to the Ptolemy of Egypt, and the "kings" of various Asiatic places such as Pamphylia, Rhodes, Cyprus and Cyrene.[39] Another glimpse of the spread of Judaism is given us in the list in Acts 2, where places as diverse as Crete and Arabia, Parthia and Egypt, Persia and Pamphylia are mentioned as sending representative pilgrims up to Jerusalem for the Feast of Pentecost. Josephus tells us that as many as 10,000 Jews were slaughtered one day in Damascus during Nero's principate,[40] and that the Jewish people were thickly spread all over the world, but especially in Antioch and Syria.[41] Philo tells us that there were over a million Jews in Egypt in his day,[42] about the time of Christ; thus they formed about an eighth of the population. Their prevalence in Greece and Asia Minor is made abundantly plain by the Acts of the Apostles. And there was a large and often troublesome colony of them in Rome.

The first contacts we know of between Rome and the Jews took place in the time of the Maccabees; Judas Maccabaeus in 168 B.C., and later Jonathan Maccabaeus, sent embassies to Rome to establish friendly relations.[43] A third such embassy in 139 B.C. resulted in a treaty with Rome, and this is probably the occasion referred to by the historian Valerius Maximus,[44] who says the Jews were sent home for trying to corrupt Roman customs with the cult of Jupiter Sabazius. Although he has muddled up their worship of Yahweh Sabaoth with that of Jupiter Sabazius (a Phrygian deity), this early mention by a pagan historian points to two features about Judaism which remained constant: their strict monotheism, and their proselytizing zeal. But apart from this tenuous link, the Romans had little to do with the Jews until Pompey's wars in the East. The tiny kingdom of Judaea got tossed like a cork in the maelstrom of the civil wars, and Aristobulus played his cards wrong with the result that Pompey captured Jerusalem in 63 B.C. He was determined to enter the temple and see what was in the Holy of Holies, which was surrounded with so much mystery. Despite the cries of "Sacrilege!" he went in, and found to his amazement precisely nothing! The Romans could not get over this. That there should be no image of the god in his inmost shrine seemed to them fantastic, and was one of the reasons why they tended ever afterwards to regard the Jews as atheists. "Their sanctuary was empty; their mysteries meaningless," wrote Tacitus.[45]

Thousands of Jews were brought to Rome in Pompey's triumphant procession. But the Romans found them very inconvenient slaves on account of their peculiar religious habits, and, according to Philo, most of them were released from servitude, and even gained Roman citizenship.[46] They formed a colony in the Trastevere suburb of Rome, where they grew and flourished.

The Romans never understood the Jews. But they were extremely fair and tolerant towards them. The reason for this is that the Jews had backed a winner in Julius Caesar; they had soldiered with him and supported him loyally. He showed his gratitude by allowing them remarkable privileges, which were confirmed by statute. Josephus proudly gives a whole list of these enactments in his *Antiquities of the Jews*.[47] The Jews must not be hindered by anybody from carrying out their sacrifices and other religious duties. They were not to be compelled to break the Sabbath, even when on military service. They were not conscripted for the army: Dolabella expressly exempted them from military service.[48] Their high priesthood was guaranteed, their food laws respected. In the big cities like Rome, Babylon, Alexandria and Antioch they had their own *gerousia* or senate, headed by an ethnarch who was an important civic figure. They had their own courts of justice which could not only exact fines but inflict scourgings. Indeed, their protected position was very enviable, as is clear from the continued riots in Alexandria which their presence provoked. So advantageous was it, that later on in times of persecution against Christians, Jewish believers in Christ were tempted to apostatize for the sake of the social and economic benefits possessed by Jews.[49]

The Appeal of Judaism

The Jews were not popular, but they were influential; and their influence could be felt in the highest échelons of society. Shortly after the death of Jesus the Royal Family of Adiabene on the Tigris came over to the Jewish faith. Josephus himself was an honoured Roman guest of three Emperors. Poppaea Sabina, the mistress of Nero, was a Jewish sympathizer, and she seems to have intervened with Nero on behalf of the Jews.[50] In the lower reaches of society Jewish influence, though less well-documented, must have been considerable. An inscription survives of a Jerusalem captive who was slave to Claudius;[51] Augustus's wife, Livia, had a Jewish servant, Akme,[52] and Juvenal three times mentions (with distaste) the unique peculiarities of the Jews.[53] There can be no doubt that they made a great impression. Even Tacitus, who has almost nothing good to say of them, is impressed by their monotheism. "The Jews acknowledge one God only, of whom they have a purely spiritual conception. They think it impious to make images of gods in human shape out of perishable materials."[54] This lofty monotheism, this worship of the one Creator God who will be the Judge of men, exercised a powerful appeal in the ancient world which was, as we have seen, for all its overt polytheism, moving in the direction of the worship of one supreme being. And, unlike the semi-monotheism of some of the philosophers, this faith was held and no doubt disseminated by the humblest, most untaught of Jews: it did not need the advocacy of a Philo or a Josephus to gain a hearing.

Moreover, whereas the philsophers could say little about the high God towards whom they were fumbling, there was no such difficulty for the Jew. Plato had said, "To find the Maker and Father of the Universe is a hard task; and, when you have found him, it is impossible to make him known to all the people."[55] But the Jew was conscious of having found the one true God—or rather of being found by him. God had not left men to grope after him in the dark; he had revealed himself in the history of Israel and the Scriptures. These Scriptures had long been available for Greeks as well as Hebrews to read. To meet the needs of the Hellenistic Jews of Alexandria the Septuagint had been produced. Here a man could learn about God, if he was a serious seeker after truth, though he would have difficulty with the barbarous Greek translation! Here was the oldest book in the world; here were the oracles of God. As for Greek and Roman knowledge, it all derived from the books of Moses. This line of argument can be seen in Josephus, *Against Apion*, and it was taken over by Christian Apologists.

Together with the Septuagint went the habit of regular worship, either in a synagogue or in an open air meeting place. Prayer, psalm singing, Scripture reading, together with the exhortation based upon it—this type of service was unique in ancient religion. It was far more interesting than attendance at a temple ceremony to watch the *haruspices* examine the entrails. It was as much reminiscent of a philosophical school as a religious activity, and it appealed to people. Josephus tells us that in Antioch, for instance, where there were so many Jews, a large number of Greeks were attracted to the services, and became in some sense a part of the Jewish community.[56] This is obvious enough from the pages of the New Testament. Full-blooded Jews, proselytes (duly circumcised), and God-fearers (the uncircumcised but devout worshippers) were all to be found in the synagogue.

It is interesting that the congregation included, on occasion, military men from the Roman occupying forces, like Cornelius. So impressed was another officer with the religion of Israel where he was on active service, that he had a synagogue built for them at Capernaum.[57]

But the very gradation of Jews, proselytes, God-fearers and plain Gentiles was an indirect preparation for the gospel. For no man could be a "son of Abraham" in the fullest sense unless he was born a Jew. The Mishna says that the proselyte should pray in synagogue "O God of *your* fathers";[58] he is not, and never can be, on a par with them. Indeed, even the Jew of the Dispersion sank in status when he was out of the Holy Land, for there were some points of his religion, notably sacrifice, which he could not carry out. Women and children, too, were less than full citizens of Israel, at least in the sight of the Jewish male, who thanked God daily that he was not born a woman! All such class distinction was done away within Christianity, and this gave the new religion a flying start on Roman soil: after all, however much he admired the Jewish religion and ethics, it was hard for a Roman citizen to demean himself by becoming a second class citizen of a despised and captive Oriental nation. But this was not necessary in order to become a Christian, where all men were brothers, and distinctions of race, sex, education and wealth meant nothing. Furthermore, whilst retaining all the attractions of Judaism, Christianity dispensed with those two great Jewish stumbling-blocks, as they appeared to the Graeco-Roman world, circumcision and food laws. Food laws the Gentiles thought simply laughable. Circumcision was much worse: it was mutilation—the sort of thing you might expect from wild, exotic sectaries like the devotees of the Cybele cult, and quite definitely non-Roman. The substitution of baptism for circumcision gave Christianity an enormous advantage over Judaism, for baptism seemed in line with the lustrations to which pagans were accustomed.

There was another respect in which the Jews provided a preparation for the gospel; they accustomed the ancient world to the idea of proselytism, of conversion to an exclusive monotheistic religion. Apart from Judaism, there was no other religion in the world of the day which would not make room for other faiths. "Live and let live" was the motto of antiquity about gods. After all, it could be very inconvenient inadvertently to offend some powerful deity of another nation! Although, astonishingly, it has excited some scepticism among scholars, the practice and success of Jewish proselytism during this period is well attested, notably in the non-Jewish literature. Horace[59] and Juvenal[60] speak cynically of the proselytizing zeal of the Jews. Josephus refers to the great zeal for Jewish worship

26

displayed throughout the Empire, to the conversion of many of the Greeks, and to the quantity of treasure supplied to Jerusalem by the half-shekel Temple tax levied among proselytes.[61] Matthew's "They compass sea and land to make one proselyte" is no exaggeration.[62] There existed a whole range of missionary literature such as the *Sibylline Oracles* (Jewish propaganda in pagan dress), designed to bring pagans to the faith.[63] This was a natural outcome of his faith for the better type of Jew; convinced as he was of the superiority of his religion, he wanted to share it. Many of the rabbis encouraged this missionary concern. Hillel said, "Be one of the disciples of Aaron, following after peace, loving mankind and drawing them to the Law."[64] And Rabbi Eleazar went as far as to say, "God scattered Israel among the nations for the sole end that proselytes should wax numerous among them."[65] Of course, this attitude cooled a good deal when the persecution of the Jews began in real earnest. It was a different story after the fall of Jerusalem and later the crushing of the Great Rebellion under Hadrian. But for most of the first century of our era there can be no doubt that proselytism was proceeding apace.[66] Too fast for the Roman officials, who recognized the legal position and privileges of the Jews, but did not like their proselytizing. Time and again we read of their expulsion from Rome under successive emperors because their numbers were increasing so fast.[67] What spurred them to this missionary endeavour? Paradoxically, it was their exclusivism. The more seriously one believed (and men did believe it with increasing conviction from the days of Antiochus Epiphanes onwards) that Israel was what mattered to God, while the nations were, as the writer of *2 Esdras* engagingly puts it, "like unto spittle", the more one was bound to try to rescue some brands from the burning. We have then, a chain reaction. Persecution led the Jews along the paths of Apocalyptic, according to which, in the coming Messianic Kingdom, all wrongs would be righted, Israel would be vindicated, and the ungodly Gentiles crushed. This in turn led to proselytizing, for one could not with an easy conscience reflect on the fewness of the saved and the multitudes of the lost and do nothing about it. Hence the growing concern to bring Gentiles under the wing of the people of God.

It is of course, dangerous to generalize about so variegated a faith as Judaism. Literary and archaeological discoveries during the last fifty years have revealed the bewildering complexity of faith and practice that went to make up Israel. Heterodox and syncretistic groups flourished throughout the Levant; Hellenistic and Persian thought had penetrated even into the most conservative circles within Judaea itself. Nevertheless these elements of ethical monotheism, circumcision, synagogue worship, Scripture reading and proselytism figured prominently in most circles that called themselves Jewish. And in all these ways Judaism prepared the way for Christianity.

The Christian faith grew best and fastest on Jewish soil, or at least, soil that had been prepared by Judaism. The spread of the Jews, their monotheism, their ethical standards, their synagogues and Scriptures, and not least their concern for conversion all were major factors in the advance of the Christian faith. As Harnack says, "The amount of this debt is so large, that one might almost venture to claim the Christian mission as a continuation of the Jewish propaganda."[68] Almost, but not quite. For that would be to leave Jesus Christ out of account.

2

OBSTACLES TO EVANGELISM

IN VIEW OF the undeniable advantages, outlined in the previous chapter, which the early Christian missionaries enjoyed, it is dangerously easy to underestimate the magnitude of their achievement. Those who have never lived in a society which has been won over from paganism by Christianity find it hard to imagine how extensive are the obstacles presented to the Christian faith by religion, vice, custom and sheer *laissez-faire*. Moreover, we tend to assume that it was much easier for the earliest disciples in the unsophisticated days in which they lived to evangelize their fellows; whereas today in the highly complex society in which we live the task appears to us to be much harder.

Whilst it is entirely fruitless to speculate on the comparative difficulty of preaching the gospel in different ages, there can be no doubt that it was an exceedingly difficult operation in the conditions and circumstances of the first century. Wherever they went, Christians were opposed as anti-social, atheistic and depraved. Their message proclaimed a crucified criminal, and nothing could have been less calculated than that to win them converts. To the Greeks such a story showed how ridiculous the new faith was; to the Romans how weak and ineffective it was; while the Jews could not bring themselves to stomach it at all. To Jew and Gentile alike Christians were offensive, on account both of the doctrines and the behaviour credited to them. All this they had to live down if they were going to win anybody at all for Jesus Christ.

JEWISH OBSTACLES TO THE GOSPEL

The Stumbling-block of Christ

It has never been easy to win Jews to the Christian religion, and it was not easy in the first century, despite the fact that Christianity was born in the matrix of Judaism.

First and foremost among the difficulties the early missionaries encountered was the fact that they were nobodies. A handful of men without formal rabbinic training were attempting to correct the theology and belief, let alone the religious practices, of properly qualified, professional religious leaders: men, moreover, who stood in a tradition of oral instruction which was supposed to reach back to Moses.[1] What impertinence! No wonder the high priestly party regarded them with a mixture of wonder and contempt as "untrained laymen".[2] But it was no laughing matter when these same ignorant laymen started attracting a sizeable following (including some priests)[3] and set about stirring up a hornet's nest round the ears of the religious authorities, accusing them of judicial murder. The movement must be nipped in the bud.

But this is precisely what proved impossible. The Christians could not be so easily disposed of. And so the Jews had to come to terms with the message these men preached. Almost every item of it was an affront to Judaism. Christians claimed, first and foremost, that Jesus was the Messiah—the acme and culmination of all the hopes of Israel, however variously these hopes had been expressed. Whether or not Jesus claimed the title Messiah for himself is disputed, but there can be no doubt that it was as Messianic pretender that he was executed and that after his death he was forthwith proclaimed as Messiah by his followers. Acts 2:36 represents the thrust of much early preaching, "Let all Israel then accept as certain that God has made this Jesus, whom you crucified, both Lord and Christ." So central was this emphasis on the Messiahship of Jesus that within a few years "Christ" (the Greek for Messiah) had ceased to designate Jesus's function and had come to be a sort of surname. Now all this was peculiarly offensive to the Jew. It was not easy to think of a carpenter-teacher as the summit of Israel's development. It was not easy to think of someone so recent as embodying a wisdom greater than that of Moses long ago. It was not easy to believe that an unordained rabbi who often came into conflict with the official exponents of the Torah could be the divinely authenticated teacher of Israel. This was why in his lifetime so few of the religious leaders had any faith in him.[4] But, after his execution, it was not merely difficult, it was preposterous to think of him as Messiah. By definition the Messiah was a deliverer, a conqueror. Typical of the hopes of the time is the seventeenth *Psalm of Solomon*, written perhaps half a century B.C.:

"Behold, O Lord, and raise up for them their king, the son of David
Ready for the time which thou, O God, choosest for him to begin his reign over Israel thy servant,
And gird him with strength to shatter unrighteous rulers,
And to purge Jerusalem from Gentiles that trample her down to destruction."

The psalm certainly goes on to speak of more "spiritual" qualities in the Messiah: sinners would be expelled, pride rebuked, and Israel's glory enhanced. But the political side of the Messiah's work was primary. So long as God's Holy Land languished under the domination of a foreign yoke, God himself was affronted every day. Deliverance must include political independence. And this Jesus manifestly failed to bring. His death upon the cross marked him out as a blatant failure, so far as any claim to Messiahship were concerned. So far from conquering, he was conquered. Why follow such a man?

Worse still, this worship of a crucified Messiah was distinctly blasphemous. The Old Testament made it perfectly plain that anyone hanged on a stake was resting under the curse of God.[5] How could God's Chosen One possibly have been exposed in the place of cursing? We know this constituted an almost insuperable problem to the Jew. Time and again in the Acts, and again in the letters of both Paul and Peter it is referred to: with good reason. Both of them had found the doctrine of a crucified Messiah a tremendous stumbling-block, until they came to understand its depth of meaning.[6] The problem persisted for most Jews. Justin has to deal with it at length in his dialogue with the Jew Trypho: "Be assured," Trypho remarked, "that all our nation waits for Christ. And we admit that all the Scriptures which you have quoted refer to him. But whether Christ should be so shamefully crucified, this we are in doubt about. For whosoever is crucified, is said in the Law to be accursed, and I am exceedingly incredulous on this point. It is quite clear, indeed, that the Scriptures announce that Christ had to suffer; but we wish to learn if you can prove it to us whether it was by the suffering cursed in the Law."[7] That was the problem which any Christian had to solve who wanted to make converts among the Jews.

It would not have been so bad if Christians had contented themselves with asserting that Jesus was the Messiah. But they went much further. The earliest baptismal confession[8] that we can trace is the short assertion that "Jesus is Lord".[9] It must be remembered that "Lord" was the particular name for God in the Old Testament: in the LXX it translates *Adonai*. There could be no mistake about the matter. Jesus himself, followed by the early Christians, made great play with Psalm 110:1 in which David addresses "my Lord". This was interpreted as referring to Jesus, who was thus David's Lord.[10] Is it any wonder that the Jews thought Christians were preaching a second God? How could they, in their pure monotheism, have any truck with such blasphemy? The whole central portion of the *Dialogue with Trypho* is taken up with discussion of the Christian claim that Jesus is divine. It is clear that any suggestion of apotheosis, and any hint of incarnation, are quite unacceptable to a Jew. As for the virgin birth, it was seen by the Jews as a revolting slur on God, a story such as the Greeks told of Zeus and Danaë;[11] its supposed backing in the Isaiah text, "A virgin shall conceive and bear a son" was based on a misunderstanding of the original;[12] and it was more probable, if there was anything unusual about the birth of Jesus, that he was the child of an unmarried mother.[13]

The Stumbling-block of the Church

It was not only the Christology of the Christians which excited such passionate reactions among the Jews: their ecclesiology was just as provocative. Some of them, like Stephen, appeared to speak slightingly about the temple and its ritual. Indeed, the building of the temple was all a great mistake: "David found favour with God, and desired to find a tent for the God of Jacob. *But Solomon built him a house!* However," continued Stephen, "the Most High does not live in temples made with hands . . ."[14] It is not surprising that this sort of preaching made the Jews wild, and resulted not only in the death of Stephen but the first of the anti-Christian persecutions engineered by the Jews.

It was not long before the Christians were saying that the Law was too hard for any man to bear.[15] It did not matter what food a man ate: God was not concerned with such things. When one considers the almost divine place given to the Law in Judaism it can readily be seen that the diminution of even the ceremonial part of it would irrevocably alienate the Jews. Worse still, the sacred rite of circumcision was soon left behind by this new movement. The very sign of the people of God which had stood from the days of Moses, indeed of Abraham, was impiously banished to the scrap heap. Entry to the people of God was now offered on equal terms to Greeks and barbarians alike, without any insistence on the costly repentance involved in the symbolic cutting away of Gentile impurity in circumcision. This was truly appalling. Instead of devotion to God's age-old Torah, this new cult taught worship of a second God, born of a virgin and executed as a criminal. Instead of the Sabbath, the first day of the week was kept for worship and called, impertinently, the Lord's Day—as if it was not the seventh day which God had specially set aside. How could such a people, so manifestly disobedient to the commands of God, have any claim to be his representatives?

The Jewish feelings on this matter can be grasped the more effectively by reading the very first charge which Trypho[16] brings against the Christians: "This is what we are most at a loss about:

that you, professing to be pious, and supposing yourselves better than others, are not in any particular separated from them, and do not alter your mode of living from the nations, in that you observe no festivals or sabbaths, and do not have the rite of circumcision; and, further, resting your hopes on a man that was crucified, you yet expect to obtain some good thing from God, while you do not obey his commandments. Have you not read that the soul shall be cut off from his people who shall not have been circumcised on the eighth day ?"[17]

The Jewish faith was never monolithic. Great varieties of belief and practice were tolerated in worldwide Jewry: they were not, it seems, at first unduly disturbed by the synagogues of the Nazarenes meeting separately, as was the custom among many synagogues with particular axes to grind. But the more they learned about Christianity, the more clear it became that the new religion was utterly incompatible with the religion of Israel, and must be eliminated root and branch. Hence the riots that ensue in the pages of the Acts of the Apostles as the gospel is preached by the early missionaries in the synagogues. Hence the persecution of the Christians at the hands of Jews in Jerusalem in the time of Stephen,[18] in Damascus under Saul of Tarsus,[19] in the Asian cities in the time of the Apocalypse,[20] and in the burning of Polycarp, where it was the Jews who egged on the proconsul.[21] It was perfectly understandable. Quite apart from the question of their heterodoxy, the Christians constituted a menace, for they created riots wherever they went. The life of the Jews was quite precarious enough in the midst of a heathen environment without gratuitous irritations like that. Why should they be inconvenienced by these Christian disturbers of the peace ?[22] The London Papyrus of Claudius[23] shows what trouble the Jews had with the pagans in Alexandria; and there may be a hint of Christian trouble-making in the reference Claudius makes to troublesome Jews who "sail down from Syria and Egypt and stir up, as it were, a common plague throughout the world."[24] Suetonius's famous assertion that Claudius expelled the Jews from Rome because they were causing excessive riots at the instigation of one Chrēstus (i.e. Christ) is evidence, albeit garbled, that Christians were causing trouble in the ghetto.[25] And in the *Antiquities of the Jews*, after giving his celebrated though short account of the Christians, Josephus continues, "About the same time also *another* sad calamity put the Jews in disorder."[26] It is clear that he regards Christianity as just such another unfortunate menace to Jewry. After all, Judaism was a *religio licita*.[27] They were a nation whose right to its worship was recognized at Rome. Why should they tolerate Christians spreading heresy under their auspices ? Why should their hard-won protection be extended to these miscreants who were no nation but rather a mixed bag of renegade Jews and credulous Gentiles ? Had they lifted a finger to help the national cause of Israel in the dark days of the Jewish Revolt (A.D. 66–70) or of the Great Rebellion under Hadrian ? No. Then they would utterly disown the Christians. Indeed, they would denounce them in their public worship.[28] The split between the Church and the Synagogue had become complete.

GRAECO-ROMAN OBSTACLES TO THE GOSPEL

In order to appreciate the problems of evangelism among pagans in the early days of the Empire, a number of different factors have to be borne in mind.

Private Belief and State Religion

First, there is the religious aspect. The Romans made a fundamental distinction between *religio* and *superstitio*. *Religio* meant the state religion, primarily the Roman state religion; it was the formal link between men and the gods. In Rome's case this was conceived of as originating in a contract between Numa, the first priest-king of Rome, and Jupiter, king of the gods. Under the terms of this contract the god would look after Rome's security and progress, while the state would look after the god's needs by supplying the proper sacrifices and worship. Such was the agreement. And the prime cause of the troubles in the century preceding Augustus lay just here: the state had ceased to bother about the gods. By way of punishment, therefore, the gods had allowed the state to go to rack and ruin in the civil wars. Hence the (somewhat short-lived) religious revival that was an important plank in Augustus's platform. He revived the ancient priesthoods and the Vestal Virgins. He headed the state cult himself as *pontifex maximus* after the office fell vacant in 12 B.C., and the importance he attached to it is shown by the appearance of the title on his coinage. The *Ludi Saeculares*, celebrated in 17 B.C., were intended to mark the inauguration of a new era when religion and morality would once again characterize Rome. In the *Res Gestae*[29] he boasts of having repaired "no less than eighty-two temples in Rome, leaving none out". Once again, Rome was paying due regard to the gods; it was to be expected that the gods would once again offer their protection to the state.[30]

It was not necessary that men should *believe in* the ancient gods. Belief was a private matter. But they were expected to participate in the state cult. Worship was a public matter, and the safety of the state depended upon it. Thus, Juvenal recounts his preparations for

34

sacrifice with charm and enthusiasm, but it is enthusiasm for the country life which the animals and the place of sacrifice conjure up —not for the gods.[31] Of them and their doings he wrote elsewhere, "These things not even boys believe, except such as are not yet old enough to have paid their penny for a bath."[32] Even a man like Lucretius, sworn enemy as he was of religion, which he attacked relentlessly in his *De Rerum Natura*, was well-known for his regular participation in the worship of the gods. Belief was unimportant; but the ceremonial and the offerings must go on. Such an attitude may seem utterly inconsistent, but it was deeply rooted in the ancient world. Plato, in the fourth century B.C., when arguing for theism, says to his young agnostic friend, "I can tell you that no one who has taken up in youth the opinion that the gods do not exist ever continued in the same till he was old," and counsels him meanwhile, though still an agnostic, to make sure that he offers sacrifice and prayer and to beware of committing any impiety against the gods![33] As far back as one likes to go, the cult was the important thing.

In their approach to the religions of other nations, the Romans showed great respect. They were not going to wage war on anyone's gods. So they tended to identify the foreign deity with a god of their own who performed the same function or, if there was no obvious candidate, they simply added the god in question to their pantheon. Mutual recognition marked the attitude of Romans and other nations to each other's gods, and this worked well until they met the Jews. These exclusive monotheists refused to allow Yahweh to be added to the pantheon or to be identified with Jupiter. He was the God of the whole earth, and they would worship him alone. This seemed very odd and narrow-minded to the Romans but they were a practical people, adaptable and tolerant in religion, as in so much else. They allowed the Jews to be an anomaly and to worship God in their own way, so long as they would offer prayer for the Roman state. Matters became more strained between them as time went on and, after the fall of Jerusalem in A.D. 70, the temple tax paid by worldwide Jewry was diverted to Jupiter Capitolinus and so, in effect, the Jews became the only nation in the Empire who were taxed for their religion. But still they were not persecuted for their faith.[34]

Why, then, was it that the Romans turned against the Christians? Why did they not offer their customary religious toleration to the new faith? The answer lies in the distinction between *religio* and *superstitio* mentioned above. Christianity was not a *religio*. It could not be described as a link binding any particular nation to the gods. For Christianity was a faith which embraced men of all races and backgrounds, barbarian as well as civilized. It was a *superstitio*, a private belief, coming from none too savoury a quarter at that; it must be judged, like other *superstitiones*, on its merits.

The Roman attitude to private religious convictions, *superstitiones*, was once again entirely tolerant, so long as public decency and order were not outraged by the cult in question. The Eastern mystery religions were looked down on as proletarian and "enthusiastic" by the cultured classes in Graeco-Roman society, but they were not outlawed. Some of their wilder manifestations might have to be Romanized, perhaps. Thus the cult of Cybele was, under Claudius, rendered more acceptable by the banning of the frenzied emasculation of its priests which had shocked sensitive Romans like Catullus and Lucretius. In future the high priest, the *archigallus*, would have to be a Roman citizen and must not be a castrated man.

Other cults came under a temporary ban if their behaviour warranted it. There was the notorious case of Paulina, a Roman lady of distinction in the time of Tiberius, who was raped by an admirer under the guise of the god Anubis in the temple of Isis. This could not be tolerated, despite the fact that the Isis cult had a considerable following in Rome.[35] Tiberius had the priests concerned in this intrigue crucified, the temple destroyed, and the image of the goddess thrown into the Tiber.[36] Yet it was not Isis worship as such, but its misdemeanours, which evoked the wrath of officialdom. The cult survived this setback, and continued to flourish.

There was, however, one class of *superstitiones* which Rome would not tolerate, those whose proceedings necessarily involved anti-social or criminal behaviour. Thus, the Senate crushed the Bacchanals as early as 186 B.C. not only because of the excesses involved in their orgies, but also because of the prejudice done to Roman religion by this foreign cult.[37] Tiberius made magic an actionable offence;[38] this included knowledge of the black arts as well as exercise of them. It was reasonably supposed that a man could not know about magic without making use of that knowledge. The other example we have of the outlawing of a *superstitio* is that of the Druids. They were violently anti-Roman and were supposed to commit human sacrifice; accordingly, they were progressively persecuted. Under Augustus no Roman citizen might belong to them. Tiberius suppressed the Druid priesthood, and Claudius rooted out the cult altogether.[39] At least, this was the theory of the thing. In practice it was not wholly effective. The cult of Bacchus flourished in the early centuries A.D. and frescoes of a Bacchic orgy have been found on the walls of Pompeii; magic continued to be widely practised, and there is a lot about it in the second century *Golden Ass* of Apuleius; as for the Druids, they were busy fanning revolt in Germany a quarter of a century after the death of Claudius.⁴⁰ It was much the same with Christianity. In A.D. 64 Christians were believed to be guilty of arson, and were cruelly tortured in Nero's gardens.⁴¹ Thereafter, membership of a society reputed to be criminal and anti-social might at any time be sufficient grounds for official punitive action. But this was sporadically applied and Rome no more succeeded in outlawing Christianity than she did the other three proscribed cults mentioned above. However, it can hardly have helped the cause of the gospel in the Roman world that it was commended by a group of people whose beliefs rendered them liable to persecution. Within thirty years of the founding of the new faith, to join the Christians meant to court martyrdom.

Three Factors which aided Christians

There were, however, three factors which combined to give Christianity growing room. The first was that the Romans had no hard and fast legal rules governing provincials. The administration of justice overseas was vested in the proconsul or procurator governing the province, and he was not required either to refer matters to Rome or to be bound by Roman custom. Further, in Rome itself there was no specific procedure for dealing with the majority of offences. What was called the *ordo judiciorum publicorum*, or "List of National Courts",⁴² covered some of the major crimes and related especially to high society, but the offences of the common man were dealt with by the city prefect or the annually-elected praetors. In any case, religious offences did not come within the *ordo* and, accordingly, they would be settled by the magistrate as he thought fit. "They dispensed justice by personal *cognitio*, and they determined their own punishments."⁴³ This meant that, in the absence of a general law proscribing Christianity throughout the Empire,⁴⁴ there was a great lack of uniformity in the way in which Christians were treated. Pliny might use his legal position to take cognizance of the Christians: Gallio might, with equal propriety, use his to decline to hear the case. The matter lay within his sole discretion. That is why, for instance, Tertullian addresses his plea to Scapula, Proconsul of Africa, and not to the Emperor.⁴⁵ It lay within the *arbitrium* of the governor to remedy the situation.

The second factor which protected the Christians was that the power to try cases and to pronounce capital sentence lay with the proconsul alone in the provinces of the Empire.⁴⁶ This was an authority which could not be delegated, though the proconsul might select a body of provincials to assist him in the administration of justice.⁴⁷

Thirdly, the process of prosecution in Roman law favoured the Christians. There was no public prosecutor. Charges had to be brought and sustained by a private accuser. Although for a period during the principate of Tiberius and Domitian anonymous information was tolerated, this was so unpopular and essentially un-Roman that it was swiftly swept aside by Trajan. He expressly told Pliny, who had written to ask his direction on the Christian affair, that no anonymous allegations were to be admitted as evidence.[48] It was a serious matter to lay an official accusation before the proconsul. If it was proved to be vexatious, heavy penalties could follow. These factors combined to protect the majority of Christians long enough for the Church to become settled throughout the length and breadth of the Empire.

Such, in outline, was the official position. But in practice it was complicated by a number of factors. For one thing, the Christians were often confused with the Jews, from whom they had sprung, and who were officially protected by the state. It is almost certain that the riots in the Jewish quarter mentioned by Suetonius[49] under Claudius as occurring *impulsore Chresto* were in fact the result of the growing self-consciousness of the Christian Jews in Rome. Claudius's stern denunciation of trouble at Alexandria due to the arrival of Jews from Egypt and Syria may well reflect a similar confusion between Christianity and Judaism.[50] Although one would have thought that the Fire of Rome made quite clear the distinction between Jews and Christians (particularly with Poppaea at hand to clarify the Jewish differentia), nevertheless as late as A.D. 70 Titus could reflect that to destroy the temple at Jerusalem "would be an invaluable way of doing away with both the Christian and Jewish religions for, although mutually inimical, these two faiths had sprung from the same root—the Christians had arisen from Judaism—and, once the root was dug up, the stem would soon perish".[51] Such was the hope of a general well-versed in the Jewish question—a vain hope as it turned out. The fall of Jerusalem had no effect on the spread of Christianity, at least in the pagan world. But, if such an expert could be so far out, it is hardly surprising if many less experienced governors supposed that Christianity was a branch of Judaism and, as such, entitled to imperial toleration.[52] While this confusion did not add to the popularity of the Christians, it did make for their protection.

Three Factors which told against Christians

However, other considerations worked in the opposite direction. First and foremost were the crimes, real or imaginary, which were associated by the common people with the Christian cause. They were accused of atheism, as were the Jews before them, because they did not do honour to the customary gods.[53] As we have seen, this was regarded not only as impiety but as disloyalty to the state. The Jews were a licensed exception, but one could not have people from every nation joining in this public repudiation of the gods. Atheists were dangerous to the welfare of the community.

Then, in addition to their atheism, common rumour had it that they were guilty of both incest and cannibalism; Christians had constantly to refute such rumours. The well-informed knew quite well that they were false: thus Pliny[54] could discover nothing depraved in the deaconesses he found taking part in the Christian assemblies, and declared himself impressed that the Christians "bound themselves by an oath (*sacramento*) not to commit any crime, be it adultery, robbery or brigandage". He records that, when they met for a meal—the Agape, no doubt—the food they consumed was "of an ordinary kind and quite innocent".[55] However, those who were prepared simply to go on hearsay believed the Christians could be guilty of anything. One can understand how it arose. The Christians met in secret; they used realistic language about feeding on Christ in the Eucharist, and they spoke of loving fellow-Christians, whom they called brothers and sisters in Christ. Gossiping lips and dirty minds did all the rest. There was some justification for this slander. Incest, immorality and the consumption of idol-meats occurred in the Corinthian church about A.D.50. It is clear from both Clement of Alexandria and Irenaeus[56] that heretical cults using the Christian name were guilty of the most terrible obscenities. Allegations such as the following by Caecilius may well have been a gross caricature of orthodox Christianity, but were painfully near the mark as a description of some deviationist Christian behaviour: "After much feasting, when the fellowship has grown warm, and the fervour of incestuous lust has grown hot with drunkenness, a dog that has been tied to the lampstand is provoked, by throwing a small piece of offal beyond the length of a line by which he is bound, to rush and spring; and, thus, the conscious light being overturned and extinguished in the shameless darkness, the connections of abominable lust involve them in the uncertainty of fate. Although not all in fact, yet in consciousness all are alike incestuous, since by desire of all of them everything is sought for which can happen in the act of each individual."[57] That is the sort of reputation Christians enjoyed with the mob.

Whether or not the Christians merited these three charges of atheism, incest and cannibalism is beside the point.[58] They were universally regarded as the sort of people who might be guilty of crimes like these. Their early press is uniformly bad. Tacitus calls them "hated by the populace for their crimes" and "both guilty and deserving of the severest penalties", though he does not believe they set fire to Rome. Suetonius accuses them of a "novel and pernicious *superstitio*", the pompous upper-class Pliny of "a depraved and excessive *superstitio*". They were deemed to hate the whole world,[59] on account of their secretiveness, cohesiveness and withdrawal from so much of social life because it was contaminated by idolatry. Professor E. M. Blaiklock[60] has drawn attention to the frequency with which the word "plague" is applied to Christians: in the Tacitus account, in the Claudius rescript, in Pliny's letter and in Tertullus's speech.[61] He suggests that a passage in Plato gives the key to the way Christians were thought of as social misfits "unable by temperament or unwilling by conviction to participate in the common activities of a group or community". Plato wrote: "Any man incapable of participating in mutual respect and law must be put to death as a social plague."[62]

How much of a misfit in society Christians were, it is easy to imagine. It appears in the Apocalypse, where unwillingness to recognize the Lordship of Domitian involved Christians in social ostracism and economic boycott.[63] Unable to attend the Imperial Games or, it would seem, even use the Imperial coinage, they suffered great hardship in resolutely "coming out of the world". This tendency was the prevailing one in the second century, though there were notable exceptions to it. We see it at its height in Tertullian. His *De Spectaculis*, *De Corona* and *De Idolatria* show how riddled with idolatry the social life of the time was, and how the sensitive (perhaps hypersensitive) Christian conscience reacted to it. Thus, the Christian would not attend gladiatorial shows or games or plays. He would not read pagan literature. He would not enlist as a soldier, for then he would come under orders that might conflict with his standards and with his loyalty to Jesus Christ. He would not be a painter or sculptor, for that would be to acquiesce in idolatry. Nor would he be a schoolmaster, for then he would inevitably have to tell the immoral stories of the pagan gods. The Christian had better steer clear of business contracts, because these required the taking of oaths, which the Christian abjured. They had better keep out of administrative office because of the idolatry involved . . . and so on. Is it any wonder that the Christians with standards like this appeared to be "united in the hatred of the human race"?

Indeed, Christians seemed so odd and socially unprofitable in pagan eyes that Tertullian as late as the end of the second century had to stress that they are of the same flesh and blood as other men:

"We live among you, eat the same food, wear the same clothes, have the same habits and the same necessities of existence. We are not Indian Brahmins or Gymnosophists, who dwell in the woods and exile themselves from ordinary human life . . . We sojourn with you in the world, abjuring neither forum, nor shambles, nor bath, nor booth, nor workshop, nor inn, nor market . . . We sail with you, we fight with you, we till the ground with you, we join with you in business ventures."[64] One doubts whether the pagans were impressed by this oratory. They had seen too much evidence to the contrary.[65]

It was not only in public life that Christians excited so much suspicion and hostility. Imagine what it would have been like in a family where one member was a Christian married to a pagan. Tertullian graphically describes a divided house, and gives us a vivid insight both into the problems of a Christian wife and into what the pagan husband must have thought of his wife's Christian activities:[66] "On all the memorial days of demons . . . she will be agitated by the smell of incense. And she will have to go out by a gate wreathed with laurel and hung with lanterns, as from some new consistory of public lusts; she will often have to sit with her husband in club meetings and taverns." What husband will put up with her Christian work and worship? "If there is a morning service to be attended, her husband makes an appointment to meet his wife at daybreak at the baths. If there is a fast to be observed, the husband that same day arranges a supper party. If a charitable journey has to be made, never is family business more pressing. For who would allow his wife, on the pretext of visiting the brethren, to go round from street to street to other men's homes, and, worst of all, to the poorer cottages? Who will willingly put up with her being away from his bed at nightly meetings? Who will, without anxiety, endure her absence all night long at the Easter Vigil? Who will, without suspicion, send her off to attend that Lord's Supper of which so many defamatory things are said? Who will allow her to creep into prison to kiss a martyr's bonds? Who will allow her to meet any of the brethren to exchange the kiss?" There was no getting away from the fact that the Christians were different. Harnack made an interesting study of the growing self-consciousness among the Christians, and awareness among the pagans, that Christians constituted a *tertium genus*, a third type of person in the world alongside Romans and Jews.[67] This was all very disturbing, and took a lot of living down for the Christian who was anxious to introduce his pagan friends to Christ.

As if to confirm the worst suspicions entertained by the Roman world of the anti-social proclivities of the Christians, it became increasingly plain that they would not take any part whatever in the Imperial cult. The growth and significance of ruler worship in the Roman world is a vast and intricate subject,[68] but the main lines of development are clear enough. In the East, it had long been customary to render divine honours to the king. The house of Antiochus encouraged this by adopting titles like Epiphanes ("God manifest") and having coinage struck of themselves arrayed in the radiate crown of Zeus. When the Roman generals, equally impressive-looking and far more powerful, invaded Asia Minor and humbled these potentates in battle, it was natural for their obsequious subjects to transfer their worship to the goddess Roma and her ambassadors on the spot![69] When Augustus became master of the Empire, it was equally natural to transfer this respect to him. It struck him that here was a most useful tool for drawing together men of differing faiths and cultures in his world dominion and giving them a focus of loyalty in the Emperor himself. It helped, of course, to have a "god" as one's adopted father! What Dr Balsdon[70] has described as "one of the most extraordinary coincidences in history" occurred in 44 B.C. "It had made a god of Julius Caesar. There was happily the firm Republican tradition of Rome's founder, Romulus, becoming the god Quirinus after his death. In July 44 B.C., four months after Caesar's murder, during the very celebration of the games in honour of his victory, an unexpected comet appeared in the sky. It was a prodigy, accepted by the populace as evidence—even before the expertise of the priests had been consulted—that Julius Caesar was now in heaven, a god, Divus Julius."

With such a pedigree, Augustus could look forward to divinization at his death and such, in fact, was accorded to him, and most of his successors. A bystander at the funeral would assert before the Senate that he had seen the soul of the dead leader ascend to heaven as a star, and the Senate would oblige by declaring him divine. This was a harmless conceit, by no means taken seriously by the Roman aristocracy themselves,[71] but useful for forging political links and focussing political loyalties. Though he was never officially worshipped as divine in the West during his lifetime (that would have offended Roman tradition), temples were consecrated to "Rome and Augustus" or to the *genius Augusti*, while in the East he was worshipped as a god outright. The cult was regulated by zealous provincial officials, and refusal to worship the Emperor could have fatal consequences, particularly under Emperors like Gaius, Nero or Domitian who took their divinity seriously. Christians, accordingly, appeared most dangerous people; they would not share in this basic pledge of loyalty to the state. Of course, on their principles, they could not. Jesus had laid the foundation of the distinction between the realm of God and Caesar in his answer about the tribute money, and his followers pursued this line of demarcation.[72] Caesar should be honoured[73] but not worshipped. They would not bow the knee or sprinkle incense to Caesar. How could they? They belonged to another *divi filius*; they owed allegiance to another *imperator*; they were securely related to God through another *pontifex maximus*. Both Christ and Caesar claimed world dominion. A Christian could not consistently say "Caesar is Lord" if he professed "Jesus is Lord". The reason is obvious enough, and compelling; but the impression given could not but be one of political disloyalty. And, as Pliny's letter to Trajan makes plain, when a man persisted in refusing to make the customary gesture to the traditional gods and the imperial statue, then he was clearly actionable for *contumacia*, criminal obstinacy. This was, to Pliny's experienced legal mind, eminent justification for the death penalty.[74]

Intellectual and Cultural Objections to Christianity

We have seen some of the political, religious and social obstacles in the way of Christian advance in the first century. There were plenty of others—economic, ethical, cultural and intellectual—to which brief allusion must be made.

On the intellectual plane, Christianity suffered from most of the objections which the ancient world raised against Judaism, to which three additional charges could be made. In the first place, Christianity was new and almost by definition nothing new could be true.[75] Christians, accordingly, had to argue that not only did Christianity have a very ancient origin, being derived from Judaism, itself so ancient that pagan philosophers drew their wisdom from it;[76] but also that, being the very truth of God, all men everywhere who had attained to the truth in any measure had been uttering what was compatible with and contained in Christian doctrine.[77]

Not only was it new, Christianity was ridiculous; for it proclaimed that the wisdom of God was exhibited in the cross of Jesus. Now it stood to reason to anyone brought up in or even slightly influenced by the Platonic tradition of Greek thought, that truth and wisdom did not reside in particulars, but in universals such as the Theory of Forms postulated. The claim that a particular birth, and a recent one at that, coupled with a particular death, and a sordid one at that, were the key to the wisdom of the ages was utterly laughable. As early as 1 Corinthians (chapters 1 and 2) and Colossians (chapter 1) we find Paul asserting that Jesus is not just a particular, but the embodiment, revealed in time, of the eternal Cosmic Wisdom, and

43

this method of apologetic had a long history subsequently among the Apologists.

But the circumstances of Jesus's death made the Christian claim even more unacceptable. One might argue with at least a semblance of reason that some ultimate truth about the universe and the human soul was disclosed by the dying hours of Socrates, as with great dignity he discoursed about life and death, and then drank hemlock. But what possible claim had the execution of a criminal on a horrid Roman cross to exhibit the rationale of the universe ? To the Roman such a death was a demonstration of servility, of weakness, of inferiority and guilt. To the Greek it was all of this and folly as well. No wonder the story went round that the Christians worshipped an ass's head,[78] or their own virilia. The worship of neither would be more obscene and revolting than the worship of a recently condemned convict on that lowest of all scaffolds, the cross. It went without saying that the Christians who believed such foolish things were thought of as being hopelessly anti-intellectual, a suspicion which some Christian apologetic as well as behaviour did a lot to substantiate.[79]

Christians were despised, furthermore, for their cultural inferiority. They appealed to the simple, unlettered lower classes for the most part. Such was the situation in first century Corinth, where "few men of wisdom by any human standard, few powerful or high born" figured among the Christian community.[80] And such continued to be the general trend for some time to come, though with notable exceptions. Celsus charged the Christians with being "the uninstructed, the servile and the ignorant", who "repel every wise man from the doctrine of their faith, and invite only the ignorant and vulgar". In so doing, Celsus believes, Christians admit that only such individuals are worthy of their God, and "they manifestly show that they desire and are able to gain over only the silly, the mean and the stupid, with women and children".[81] We have already seen that upper class Romans tended to regard all *superstitiones* as appropriate only for the lower classes, and especially despised Oriental cults, even with as high an ethic, as sublime a monotheism and as ancient a pedigree as Judaism. How could they be expected to follow a *superstitio* from which even the Jews were at pains to dissociate themselves ? Not that the Christians minded: the very reverse. They gloried in the fact that their message had been revealed by God in his wisdom not to the intelligent and highly placed, but to humble believing people. Paul rejoiced in this truth in 1 Corinthians 1 and Athenagoras gave eloquent expression to it in chapter 11 of his *Embassy for Christians*. "Among us you will find uneducated people, and artisans, and old women who, if they are unable in words to prove the benefit of our doctrine, yet by their deeds they exhibit the benefit arising from their persuasion of its truth. They do not rehearse speeches, but exhibit good works; when struck, they do not strike again; when robbed, they do not go to law; they give to those that ask of them, and they love their neighbours as themselves." But all this could not mask the lowliness of their origin and of their social station. When Paul addressed Christians as belonging to the Imperial Household in Rome, it was not to Caesar that he wrote, but to the slaves of one of his executed freedmen![82] Christianity was a *superstitio* that belonged to the dregs of society.

Ethical and Social Stumbling-blocks in Christianity

As such, its ethical standards must have been an enormous obstacle to its progress. The pages of Tacitus, Suetonius, Martial, Juvenal, Petronius and other writers of the period show how far Rome had fallen from the days when she was a virtuous, rustic people. In high society and in the slave community alike, we read of prostitution, adultery, homosexuality, child exposure, concern only for "bread and circuses", for gladiatorial shows and wild beast fights, for money and for power over others at any price. It is all too easy to blacken any period in history, and no doubt Tacitus's picture of Tiberius's age is unduly influenced by his experiences under Domitian, but there can be no doubt that imperial Rome of the first century was exceedingly depraved. None of the mystery religions demanded a radically different ethic[83] of their members. But Christianity, like Judaism, did. It demanded a standard as rigorous as the highest ideals of the Stoics, and went far beyond them in making love for one's neighbour rather than cold duty the norm for behaviour. The Apologists are full of the change that comes over the life of a man converted to Christ. Here is a typical example from Justin: "We who formerly delighted in fornication now embrace chastity alone; we who formerly used magical arts, dedicate ourselves to the good and unbegotten God; we who valued above all things the acquisition of wealth and possesions, now bring what we have into a common stock and share with everyone who is in need; we who hated and destroyed one another and, on account of their different customs would not live with men of a different race, now, since the coming of Christ, live on excellent terms with them and pray for our enemies and endeavour to persuade those who hate us unjustly to live conformably to the good precepts of Christ to the end that they may become partakers with us of the same joyful hope of a reward from God the ruler of all."[84] Such a revolution in life

45

and values has indeed an attraction, but it also commonly puts off those who, as Paul expressed it, "not only commit [*sc.* evil things] but have pleasure in those who do them".[85] The "world" does love its own, and it does hate those whose standards show it up; particularly is this the case when the standards of pagan society are unusually low, and those of the Church unusually high, as in the first and second centuries they were. All this made for a definite break with the past once a man became a Christian; but the very magnitude of the change was a formidable obstacle.

The last difficulty in the way of Christianity in the pagan world that we shall mention concerned the trade guilds.[86] Clubs were extremely popular in the artisan classes of the Roman world at this time. There were clubs for sport, clubs to foster social life, burial clubs and clubs composed of men belonging to the same trade. They would meet, usually in the temple of the god of their trade, and enjoy mutual companionship, feasting and entertainment. But they easily became centres for political agitation, as they were quite unsupervised in their internal affairs. This accounts for the stringent restrictions placed upon their multiplication by successive emperors and the almost pathological phobias of Trajan on the subject. He unwillingly agrees that a confederate city like Amisus in Bithynia can hardly be deprived of the Benefit Societies there, which have been guaranteed by statute, but he warns Pliny not to encourage such guilds in other cities.[87] He wanted them prohibited because the contributions ostensibly made for the poor and needy were often used to instigate riot and faction. We see this happening in many places in the New Testament—at Ephesus and at Corinth for example.[88] It is not altogether surprising that Trajan refused to allow Pliny to authorize a fire brigade of 150 members at Nicomedia because "it is to be remembered that this sort of society has greatly disturbed the peace of your province . . . and whatever title we give them, and whatever our object in giving it, men who are banded together for a common end will all the same become a political association before long".[89] There is some evidence that this ban on free association unless specifically authorized was used as a handle against the Christians in the first century. Pliny himself tells Trajan that the Christians had ceased to meet after he had forbidden it under the terms of an edict precluding political associations.[90] The early Christians would constantly have had to run the risk of arrest for illicit assembly.

But this was not the only problem posed by the existence and prevalence of the guilds. There were at least two others. On the one hand, the guild itself might be organized against Christianity, which was deemed to be injurious to its interests. The classic instance of this is the riot at Ephesus provoked by the silversmiths, when they found that conversions to Christianity caused a fall off in their sales. One suspects that something similar must have happened in Bithynia towards the end of the first century, for Pliny tells us that the "contagious superstition" of Christianity had spread not only to the towns but to the villages and rural districts, and that the temples had been almost deserted; as a result there had been no demand (until the officious Pliny came on the scene to put things right) for sacrificial animals "which for some time past have met with few purchasers". Evangelism on the scale presupposed by that statement could hardly have been conceivable without the organized opposition of guilds with vested interests in the pagan cult. When men's livelihood and their beliefs are both challenged by some new movement, the reaction is usually sharp. Tertullian's short treatise *De Idolatria* goes into this subject in detail and shows the variety of trades associated in varying degrees with idolatry, which a Christian must on no account practise.

But, even if he stayed within his guild, the Christian was not free of problems. The cult meals in the idol's temple,[91] which was one of the main functions of the guild; the temple prostitutes,[92] who were one of their main attractionshow c—ould he contract out of these things? The problem is acute from the days of 1 Corinthians onwards. How far was a Christian likely to get in his trade, or how was he to influence his workmates for Christ if he did not join with them in their convivialities? If he did, his influence for Christ was compromised. This was the problem that exercised the Asian churches at the time of the Apocalypse,[93] a problem to which John and the Nicolaitans returned different answers.

At whatever level in society it was attempted, evangelism in the early church was a very daunting undertaking. It was a task involving social odium, political danger,[94] the charge of treachery to the gods and the state, the insinuation of horrible crimes and calculated opposition from a combination of sources more powerful, perhaps, than at any time since. We must go on to examine the core of the message which they proclaimed, the message which turned even the Roman world upside down.

3

THE EVANGEL

CHRISTIANITY BURST ON the world with all the suddenness of good news: good news proclaimed with great enthusiasm and courage by its advocates, and backed up by their own witness and experience. It was the fruit of their conviction that God had transformed the apparent defeat of Good Friday into the supreme victory of Easter Day.[1]

The precise nature of this proclamation in the early church has been much discussed in recent years, particularly since the publication in 1936 of C. H. Dodd's *The Apostolic Preaching and its Developments*. But there has been undue concentration on what has become technically known as the "kerygma", which is supposed to have been a fairly fixed body of preaching material common to the early missionaries. We shall examine this contention later on, but at this point it is worth noting that it is all too easy to be beguiled by particular words into building a theological superstructure upon them which they were never designed to bear, as James Barr has pointed out powerfully in his *The Semantics of Biblical Language*. In the New Testament the *kērussein* root (to "proclaim") is by no means primary. It is just one of the three great words used for proclaiming the Christian message, the other two being *euaggelizesthai* (to "tell good news") and *marturein* (to "bear witness"). In the course of this chapter we shall examine each of these three concepts in turn, and it may well be that a broader-based understanding of the early Christian gospel will emerge. The gospel is good news; it is proclamation; it is witness.

GOOD NEWS

Messianic Good News

It was no ordinary good news that rocked Palestine around the year A.D. 30. It was no mere message about a carpenter-teacher who had been executed under the Roman procurator. It was nothing less than the joyful announcement of the long awaited Messianic salvation, when God had come to the rescue of a world in need. Small surprise, then, that the content of their message became known as *to euaggelion,*[2] *the* good news. Only later was this term used of the documents in which the story came to be recorded, the written gospels. Primarily it was applied to the events themselves, and to the act of announcing them.[3]

St Luke traces it all back to the occasion in his own home synagogue in Nazareth when Jesus read the lesson from Isaiah 61. "The Spirit of the Lord is upon me, because he has anointed me to preach the good news to the poor. He has sent me to proclaim release to the captives, and recovering of sight to the blind, to set at liberty those who are oppressed, to proclaim the acceptable year of the Lord." Jesus shut the book, and astonished his hearers by calmly informing them, "Today this scripture has been fulfilled in your hearing."[4] The passage in Isaiah was highly significant. It refers to the return from Exile; and the messenger, anointed with God's own Spirit, announces God's signal victory, his kingly rule. It is nothing less than the dawn of a new age, and one from which the heathen are not excluded. The days of salvation have arrived; the people of God are ready and waiting for him like a bride for her husband, their unworthiness covered by a robe of righteousness, their relationship with their God established by an everlasting covenant. Joy will be the order of the day; Zion will be rebuilt, and God will cause righteousness to spring forth for the Gentiles. All that, and more, is contained in the chapter of Isaiah from which Jesus read. All that he claimed to fulfil. When he had died in agony, shame and apparent failure on the cross, his disciples must have thought that they had been mistaken, and that he was a fraud. The resurrection came to them as God's vindication of the claims Jesus had made. They saw that he was "designated Son of God in power by his resurrection from the dead".[5] And they proceeded to announce these joyful tidings with tireless zeal and boundless enthusiasm. It spread like wildfire precisely because the first hearers well understood that this was the Messianic salvation which was at issue. It was not merely a matter of the atoning death of a great man: since the days of the Maccabees they had understood that the death of a hero for his people might have expiatory significance.[6] Nor was the resurrection, by itself, the fundamental thing. John the Baptist was rumoured to have risen from the dead;[7] Jesus himself had on occasion, it appears, raised folk from the dead without anyone supposing that there was anything Messianic about them.[8] But when Jesus, Jesus who had claimed to bring in the eschatological salvation, rose from the tomb, that was a different matter. It was, as they put it, seen to be "according to the scriptures".[9] It was the vindication of the Suffering Servant, the ascension in glory of the Son of Man, the fulfilment of the prophecy to David through Nathan long ago that "He shall build a house for my name, and I will establish his kingdom for ever. I will be his father and he shall be my son."[10] And that was something to shout about. That was good news.

Accordingly, it is not surprising that we find the early Christians making tremendous play with the words *euaggelizomai* and *euaggelion*. They are very much more frequent than the "kerygma" root, which has become a theological technical term in our day, though it clearly was not in the first century.

The Messianic good news begins with the Messianic forerunner, John the Baptist. He exhorted and preached good news to the people.[11] The good news begins with his repentance preaching and announcement of the coming kingdom.[12] His story is, in fact, the beginning of the gospel.[13]

John's promised "mightier one" was not long in coming on the scene. And when he did, it was to give the glad tidings of the advent of the kingdom for those who would repent and believe the good news.[14] And when, subsequently, John temporarily lost faith in him, Jesus sent him this reassuring reply: "The blind see, the lame walk, lepers are cleansed, and the deaf hear, the dead are raised up and the poor have the good news preached to them."[15] Once again Isaiah 61:1 appears on our Lord's lips in this reply, coupled on this occasion with Isaiah 35:5, in order to stress the theme of fulfilment. God had kept faith; his promised deliverer had come. So John could take courage. The new age had dawned; there was no place now for looking back in doubt. And throughout his ministry Jesus carried out this programme of preaching, healing, exorcizing and integrating spoiled specimens of humanity. He had come to bring the Messianic *Shalom*[16] to all and sundry: "He preached peace to you who were far off and peace to those who were near."[17] That had always been envisaged as the function of the Messiah. It was, therefore, hardly surprising that the angels in heaven should announce to the shepherds at his birth, "I bring you good news of great joy; for to you is born this day in the city of David a Saviour, who is Christ the Lord."[18]

There was no less joy on earth after the resurrection had set God's seal on the authenticity of Jesus. His disciples audaciously and exultantly spread this good news of a Saviour. The verb is very frequent in the New Testament. Sometimes it is used absolutely:[19] sometimes we read that they spread the good news *to* people, Jew and Samaritan, Greek and Roman, bond and free.[20] Sometimes the hearers are the object of the verb; as we say, they evangelized people.[21] But most frequently the content of their news is hinted at by some accompanying word or phrase; and the variety and yet homogeneity of the contents ascribed to the evangel are interesting. The Christians "proclaimed the good news" of "the gospel", or of "the faith".[23] More specifically, they proclaimed the good news about "the kingdom",[24] as Jesus had done. But this could very easily be misunderstood in the Roman Empire, as it was, for instance, at Thessalonica;[25] so it is not surprising to find them more frequently preaching simply the person and achievement of Jesus as the good news. And yet it *is* surprising; it is fantastic! The one who came preaching the good news has become the content of the good news! What clearer evidence could there be that the earliest Christians regarded Jesus with the highest possible respect, as embodying in his person and achievement the kingly rule of God himself? It was Origen who said Jesus was the *autobasileia*, the kingdom in person;[26] but the idea was there in the apostolic proclamation of Jesus. So we find them spreading the good news that Jesus is Messiah, or that through him the ancient promises have been fulfilled.[27] We find them proclaiming the good news of peace through Jesus,[28] of the Lordship of Jesus,[29] of the cross of Jesus,[30] of the resurrection of Jesus[31] or simply of Jesus himself.[32] Nothing more was needed. For however expressed, whether as the Messiah of Old Testament expectation, as Lord over the demonic powers or whatever other category of interpretation was employed, the early preachers of the good news had one subject and one only, Jesus. This was their supreme concern. This was their "word" which they broadcast so assiduously.[33] We shall, in this chapter, be concentrating on the good news preached by the earliest Christians, but it is not without significance that 150 years later we find the same enthusiastic assessment of and love for the gospel in this broadest of senses in a writer like Origen. He gives an extensive survey of the meaning of "gospel" as he understands it, in the first part of Book One of his *Commentary on John*.[34] The gospel is good news about Jesus, first and foremost. Not only a recital of what he said and did, though this, too, is "gospel" (and it is "the office of an evangelist . . . to narrate how the Saviour cured a man who was blind from birth, or raised up a dead man who was already stinking"): not only "such discourse also as is not narrative but hortatory and intended to strengthen belief in the mission of Jesus". No, the supreme significance of "gospel" is good news about Jesus. "We must say that the good things the Apostles announce in this Gospel are simply Jesus." To be sure, the good news has specific and varied content. "One good thing is life: but Jesus is the life. Another good thing is the light of the world, when it is true light, and the light of men: and all these things the Son of God is said to be." The same may be said of the truth, or the way that leads to truth, the door, or the resurrection. "All these things the Saviour teaches that he is." Origen goes on to show that the gospel was latent in the Old Testament, and alludes to Philip's proclaiming it to the eunuch by means of Isaiah 53. It is present in the teaching of Jesus: "The apostles . . . who sought to preach the good tidings, could not have done so had not Jesus himself first preached the good tidings to them." He reiterates the Christocentric nature of the proclamation both to the original apostles and to others through their agency: "Jesus himself preaches good tidings of good things, which are none other than himself: for the Son of God preaches the good tidings of himself to those who cannot come to know him, through others." Thus, Origen continues, is fulfilled the prophecy of Isaiah 61:1ff. which Jesus quoted in Luke 4:18f. at the outset of his ministry; a passage which we have already considered. And the purpose of the whole evangelistic enterprise he summarizes succinctly: "to perpetuate the knowledge of Christ's sojourn upon earth, and to prepare for his second coming, or to bring it about as a present reality in those souls which were willing to receive the Word of God as he stood at the door and knocked and sought to come into them."

So much for Origen: he provides evidence enough to show that the primitive understanding of the gospel was not lost by the third century. Let us now return to the first century and see how they thought of the *euaggelion*.

Mark's Good News

Our earliest gospel, St Mark's, has some very important light to shed on the way in which the good news was understood in primitive Christianity. It is a curious fact that whereas Mark uses the noun eight times, but never the verb, Luke reverses the process, and uses the verb very freely both in the gospel and Acts, but the noun only twice, when he is purporting to give the words of others in the speeches.[35] This may be because, as we shall see, the noun meant a good deal in the contemporary pagan world, but the verb was not used to any significant degree; the verb, however, derives from Hebrew usage, Deutero-Isaiah in particular, but the Jews made no great use of the noun.[36] Luke, it would seem, for all his universal concern, is more at home in the Hebrew thought at this point than Mark, who is concerned to make the gospel meaningful in Rome. However that may be, what Mark says about the gospel is important.

In the first place, it is a message with a quite specific content. It is always *to euaggelion, the* gospel. It is a recognizable message which a man can proclaim[37] and believe in.[38] It can be called the good news of God's kingly rule,[39] or simply of the one who inaugurates that rule, Jesus.[40] He is in fact identified with "the gospel" in two places in Mark, and intimately connected with it in another.[41] Thus the centrality of Jesus within the good news is studiously maintained in this Gospel. It may be that early second century tradition is right in seeing a strong link with Peter in St Mark's Gospel:[42] it may be that the Form Critics are right in stressing the pre-Marcan independent circulation of a great many of the stories in Mark's Gospel. In either case we are taken behind the evangelist to an earlier period in the first three decades of the church's life.[43] During those decades Jesus's central place in the gospel was not in dispute.

But we can go further. This good news covered the period from the baptism of John, which is where Mark begins, assuring us that this is the beginning of the gospel of Christ,[44] until the resurrection, with which he abruptly closes his story.[45] Within this framework Mark makes it clear that, the good news centres on the redemptive death of Jesus. The prediction of the passion enshrined in the incident of the woman of Bethany who came and anointed his head with unguents makes that very clear. "She has done what she could," says Jesus, "she has anointed my body beforehand for burying. And truly, I say to you, wherever the gospel is preached in the whole world, what she has done will be told in memory of me."[46] This verse leads us on to another point in the gospel as understood by Mark. It is intended for the whole world, not merely Jews, thus carrying out the highest ideals of Jewish universalism. The gospel of God's kingly rule proclaimed to the Jews is meant for the Gentiles too: "The gospel must first be preached to all nations."[47] The equivocal attitude towards the Gentiles taken up by the Old Testament and rabbinic Judaism had been resolved by Jesus.[48] Whilst he limited himself almost entirely to Israel during his ministry,[49] he was nevertheless the bearer of salvation. And in the age of salvation it was well understood that the *Goyyim*, "the nations", would come and share in the Messianic kingdom.[50] But how could they come without hearing? That is a question Paul posed and answered in Romans 10:13ff.; it is a question which drove the earliest Jewish Christians out to evangelize the Gentiles. The Marcan continuator[51] was quite right in his emphasis in 16:15, "Go into all the world and preach the gospel to the whole creation." He probably took it from Matthew 28:18–20, where this universal note makes a fascinating climax to what is in many ways a very particularlist Gospel.

But although it is absolutely universal in its offer, Mark knows that the good news is only effective among those who repent, believe, and are prepared to engage in costly, self-sacrificial discipleship.[52] Only the man who is prepared to lose his life for the sake of

Christ and the gospel can find it; for it was only by losing his life for the sake of others that Christ could offer new life to men, the new life proclaimed in the gospel.

Paul's Good News

If we turn to Paul, the other main New Testament writer who uses the noun "gospel" a great deal, we find much the same picture. Again "the gospel" has a clearly defined content; so much so that in about half his references it stands by itself without qualification. You can spread the good news of it,[53] teach it,[54] announce it,[55] chatter it,[56] make it known,[57] or put it forward for discussion.[58] Similarly, it could be heard,[59] received,[60] accepted as reliable tradition[61] and so on. There was a recognizable shape to it.

The shape appears to have been very much like that of the good news in the Gospel of Mark, though it is formally different in a number of places. It is called "God's good news" time and again,[62] and though it is never called by Paul "the good news of the kingdom", this may be fortuitous for he often speaks of the kingdom of God in contexts where he has just been talking of the gospel.[63] It may, on the other hand, be partly, at any rate, deliberate; owing to the political overtones involved in preaching a *kingdom* Paul wisely preferred for the most part to translate what he had to say into other categories, such as eternal life, salvation, or justification.

Furthermore, as in Mark, the gospel is equated with Jesus.[64] Once again the cross[65] and resurrection[66] are central. One need hardly point out the universalism so strongly present in the preaching of the Apostle to the Gentiles; Paul knows his good news is meant for the Jew first and also for the Greek.[67] He, too, is challenged by the need to reach men with this saving gospel. That is why he is not ashamed of it: that is why he fulfils his call to spread it.[68] He regards the discharge of this duty as a priestly service and a sacred trust.[69]

It is the same gospel the world over, to Jew and Greek alike, though it may be couched in different terms and even thought forms. A great deal has been made by continental scholars of the contradiction between Paul's statement of the gospel in 1 Corinthians 15:1ff. together with his claim that he got it by tradition from the earliest disciples, and his passionate disclaimer of any reliance on man for his gospel which we find in Galatians 1:18ff. But the contrast is more formal than material. What Paul is saying in these two passages amounts to this. The form of his gospel is indeed similar to that of the Jerusalem church—indeed, he says as much in Galatians 2:2, a verse often overlooked in this discussion; nevertheless the dynamic for his preaching, the authorization for it, the conviction about it, came not from any mere knowledge of the events, not from any recitation of the Jerusalem *credo*, but from an encounter with the risen Christ himself.[70] *This* was the source of his conviction that there was good news to proclaim to a world in need, a gospel of universal validity.

Mark's final points about the gospel are also prominent in the teaching of Paul. Repentance and faith are the essential human conditions,[71] though Paul prefers to use synonyms for repentance such as dying to sin and putting off the old man. And finally, Paul is just as clear as Mark that response to the gospel will involve a life of dedicated toughness. It will be costly. Men must make sacrifices for it.[72] Its furtherance is a task in which all Christians must be involved,[73] an athletic contest, so to speak, in which all Christians are required to take an active part.[74]

In all these respects Paul's gospel and Mark's are substantially identical; they are the only two New Testament writers who use the noun to a significant extent. To be sure, Paul adds some apparently distinctive characteristics. He stresses that the good news is according to the Scriptures:[75] the work of Jesus fulfils the purposes of God and is not to be set in opposition to the Old Testament. But so does Mark,[76] in effect, by saying that the good news accords with the prophecies of Isaiah and Malachi. Paul lays stress on the theme of judgment implicit in the gospel; if men do not accept it they will be held accountable.[77] Noticeably enough the only other two mentions of *euaggelion* in the Epistles make this very same point,[78] an emphasis which comes through loud and clear in the preaching of the second century.[79] Mark would not quarrel with this; the correlative of losing your life for Christ's sake and the gospel's is trying to hang on to it, and that, Mark knows, is to lose it irretrievably.[80] Paul stresses the *dunamis* of the gospel,[81] its power of moral reformation, breaking the shackles of evil; but why did Mark constantly refer to acts of *dunamis* by Jesus if he did not mean to make precisely the same point?

The genuinely distinctive elements in Paul's gospel-preaching seem to have been as follows. First, he used the forensic language of justification,[82] especially in contexts where Jewish good works were thought of as meriting divine favour; he did so in order to safeguard God's initiative in providing salvation. Second, he stressed the final and absolute nature of the gospel; it is the gospel of truth, of hope, of power, of immortality, of the glory of God immanent within our world.[83] It is, in short, *the* mystery of God, the truth once hid and now revealed to men, nothing less than the wisdom of God.[84] Thirdly, Paul stressed the ethical implications of the gospel. If a man is subject to the gospel of God, it means that he has the divine grace at work within him.[85] It is, therefore incumbent upon him to live his daily civilian life in a way that is worthy of the gospel he professes.[86]

The Aptness of the Term

Such is "the good news" as it was understood and propagated by two early Christian writers. It was a happy choice of word, for "good news" had, apart from its general appeal, specific overtones both in Jewish and pagan circles, which made it particularly significant.

The noun, which, as we have seen, is frequently used by Paul and Mark in the New Testament, had little by way of Old Testament background. But it meant much to the Greek world. It was the word used *par excellence* to announce victory,[87] victory over hostile forces, and, derivatively, of the thank-offerings given to the gods in gratitude for such victory.[88] It was used, too, of communications from the gods,[89] usually by oracles: these were "good news"—or so one hoped! But supremely the word was used in the Imperial Cult.[90] The announcement of the Emperor's birth was "good news": the celebrated Priene inscription reads "The birthday of the god was the beginning, for the world, of the joyful tidings which have gone out because of him."[91] The coming of age of Caligula, for instance, was (ironically, as it later proved) hailed as the good news of salvation and good fortune.[92] The accession of the *princeps* was traditionally thought of as good news and was celebrated with joy and sacrifices by a people genuinely grateful for the measure of salvation the Empire had brought them.[93]

Now this language has obvious affinities with the New Testament. It may well be that St Mark is deliberately contrasting the Christian good news with its imperial counterpart in Rome. Both speak of salvation, but the Christian *sōtēria* is far more profound than the imperial: it embraces rescue from sin and death as well as political liberation. Both speak of the good news of a ruler born, come of age, enthroned; but the Christian *euaggelion* is far more profound than the imperial: her ruler sits on the throne of the universe, not merely of the Empire, and his birth is a real incarnation of the only God, not the mock deity of the imperial dynasty.[94] Friedrich puts it well. "The N.T. speaks the language of its day. It is a popular and realistic proclamation. It knows human waiting for and hope of the *euaggelia*, and it replies with the *euaggelion*, but with an evangel of which some might be ashamed, since it is a stumbling-block. The gospel means for men salvation—but salvation through repentance and judgment. For many this gospel may be ironical when they hear it (cf. Acts 17:32). But it is real joy; for penitence brings joy and judgment, grace and salvation. Caesar and Christ, the emperor on the throne and the despised rabbi on the cross, confront one another. Both are evangel to men. They have much in common. But they belong to different worlds."[95] I suspect it was just this contrast with the imperial cult which Paul and Mark were seeking to bring out when they used the word *euaggelion*. This was the background against which they wrote.

Luke's Good News

With Luke it was different. He used not the noun but the verb. And whereas the noun has no specific Old Testament significance the verb has enormous importance, particularly in Deutero-Isaiah. Conversely, while the noun is important in secular usage the verb is rare and insignificant. Luke appears to take over the Hebrew substantive participle, which comes frequently in 2 Isaiah, and is translated by the *euaggelizomai* root in the LXX: for he preserves this Semitic background in·his frequent use of the participle *euaggelizomenos*, where a noun would have been more natural. We have already seen something of the significance of this good news proclaimed by the prophet in Isaiah 61:1ff. Similar concepts are to be found in Psalm 96, one of the great enthronement psalms. To quote Friedrich again, "The close connection between this whole circle of thought and the N.T. is evident. The eschatological expectation, the proclamation of the kingly rule of God, the introduction of the Gentiles into salvation history, the rejection of the ordinary religion of cult and Law (Psalm 40) and the link with the terms 'righteousness' (Psalm 40:9) 'salvation' (Isaiah 52:7, Psalm 95:1) and 'peace' (Isaiah 52:7)—all point us to the New Testament."[96] Nor was this Messianic conception of the good news forgotten by later Judaism. For instance, Rabbi Jose, at the end of the first century A.D., said, "Great is peace, for when the king, Messiah, will reveal himself to Israel, he will begin only with peace, for it is written, 'How beautiful on the mountains are the feet of him who bringeth glad tidings, who publisheth peace'." Or, as the Midrash on Psalm 147:1 reads, "Isaiah said: How beautiful on the mountains are the feet of those who proclaim good news. When the Holy One, blessed be He, will be King, they will all be messengers bearing good news, as it is said, 'He who declares good things causes peace to be heard'."[97] There is a great deal more among rabbinic writings in this vein. It helps us to understand the impact made by the good news when the Christians began proclaiming it. In both Jewish and Gentile backgrounds alike, the word was electric. The Christian evangel came like a spark to the tinder of ancient society.

The Word Kērussō and its Usage

The second of the great words widely used in the New Testament to define the evangelism of the early Christians is the *kērussein* root. It means, basically, to proclaim like a herald. The noun, *kērux* (herald) is scarcely used, perhaps because of the very specific Greek background to the term.[98] For the herald was important in himself, an inviolable person on whom nobody might lay hands with impunity; and that the Christian evangelist emphatically was not. The word *kērugma*, proclamation, is infrequent, too, which is surprising in view of the fact that it has become anglicized (kerygma) as a technical term for the early preaching. Apart from the "preaching of Jonah"[99] however, the only man to use the word in the New Testament is Paul, and then only half a dozen times. It is clear from Romans 16:25f. that Paul understands it as identical with the *euaggelion*; it is specifically equated with "gospel" in that verse, and in the context themes like the fulfilment of the Scriptures, the advent of Jesus the Christ, the universal relevance of the message, the need for obedient faith and the power of this message to establish men once they receive it, all confirm this identification.

In 1 Corinthians Paul asserts that his *kērugma* is entirely different from the proclamations made by the contemporary sophists, or travelling lecturers, who often thought of themselves as messengers of the gods;[100] they tried to make the content of their proclamation as impressive as could be, and its form as cultured as possible. Paul disclaims any such aim. He proclaimed a message which, so far from looking like "wisdom", was sheer folly. Where is the wisdom, where the universal significance of a man executed in humiliating circumstances on a cross?[101] Nor did he seek to cover up the scandalous nature of his message by couching it in the fine phrases of Greek philosophy: "My speech and my message [*kērugma*] were not in plausible words of wisdom, but in demonstration of the Spirit and of power, that your faith might not rest in the wisdom of men but in the power of God."[102] In both form and content (as well as aim) his proclamation stood in striking contrast to that of the sophists. But of course men could not be experiencing the power of God in their lives if they did not believe in the resurrection of Jesus, through which God's power was let loose in human lives. That is why Paul reasserts in 1 Corinthians 15:14 that without faith in the resurrection, the proclamation he has been making is an empty shell, void of power and dynamic; nothing better than the moralizing tales the sophists tell.

And that is all Paul tells us about the *kērugma*, except for the two passages in the Pastorals[103] where he claims that it is a sacred trust committed to him, and that therefore he must take every opportunity to proclaim it, even using his appearance in the dock before Nero as a chance for announcing his herald's message.[104]

When we turn to the verb "to proclaim" (*kērussō*) we find that it is almost exactly as frequent as *euaggelizomai*. It is used in much the same way, too; either absolutely, or with a dative (of the people to whom proclamation is made) or with an accusative denoting the content of what is proclaimed. Its use is admittedly wider than the other verb. It is not always "the good news" that is proclaimed. The famous crux of 1 Peter 3:19 probably means not that Jesus proclaimed the gospel to the spirits in prison, but merely that like a herald he announced his victory to them. Certainly in Luke 12:3 we have the secular heraldic use of the word coming through, with no overtones of the gospel: "What you have whispered in private rooms shall be proclaimed upon the housetops"; and in verses like "you who preach against stealing, do you steal?"[105] it is equally plain that the meaning is simply a public announcement of whatever nature, such as a herald might give. Again, there is no "gospel" about Acts 15:21, "Moses has in every city those who preach him." Nevertheless it remains true that for a great many of its occurrences in the New Testament, *kērussō* means precisely the same as *euaggelizomai*. Its two most common usages make this perfectly plain. Twelve times "preach the good news" is rendered by *kērussein to euaggelion*, thus bringing both roots into juxtaposition; and on nine occasions we read of people preaching Christ or Jesus (*kērussein ton Iēsoun*), just as we read of them telling the good news of Jesus (*euaggelizesthai ton Iēsoun*). From this the same two points emerge that we noted earlier about the good news, namely the absolute centrality of Jesus in what was proclaimed, and the broadly identifiable nature of the proclamation.

If we ask how it comes about that *kērussō* and *euaggelizomai* are so often identified in the New Testament, the answer is, I think, to be found in Isaiah 61:1f. This passage was, as we saw, basic to their understanding of "the good news" and its preaching;[106] but it also contains a twofold reference to *kērussein*. "He has sent me to proclaim release to the captives . . . to proclaim the acceptable year of the Lord." Professor Friedrich in the Kittel *Wörterbuch*, too preoccupied with existentialist interpretation of the word to notice its signal conjunction with *euaggelizesthai* in this crucial passage where Jesus interprets his ministry, nevertheless has this splendid comment: "He proclaims, like a herald, the year of the Lord, the

Messianic age. When heralds proclaimed the year of jubilee through-out the land with the sound of the trumpet, the year began, the prison doors were opened, and debts were remitted. The preaching of Jesus is such a blast of the trumpet."[107] With this background then, in Jesus's own understanding of his mission, it is not surprising to find the identification of the proclamation with the good news in strata of the New Testament as varied as Matthew, Mark, Luke and Paul. It was the announcement of the climax of history, the divine intervention into the affairs of men brought about by the incarnation, life, death, resurrection and heavenly session of Jesus of Nazareth.

Was there a fixed Kerygma?

This is a question which demands to be put, since we have noticed that both "the good news" and "the proclamation" had an identi-fiable form. It is a question which has split the scholarly world since the publication of C. H. Dodd's *The Apostolic Preaching and its Development*. This maintained that an examination of 1 Corinthians 15, the speeches in Acts, the shape of St. Mark's Gospel and certain other passages in the New Testament warranted the conclusion that there was a fixed pattern in the evangelistic preaching of the early Church; that it contained, in fact, the following six points. The Age of fulfilment has dawned. This has taken place through the ministry, death and resurrection of Jesus. By virtue of the resurrection, Jesus has been exalted to the right hand of God, as Messianic head of the new Israel. The Holy Spirit in the Church is the sign of Christ's present power and glory. The Messianic Age will shortly reach its consummation in the return of Christ. And finally, the kerygma always closes with an appeal for repentance, the offer of forgiveness and the Holy Spirit, and the promise of salvation, that is, the life of the Age to Come to those who enter the community.

This view of the matter has won wide acceptance in the English speaking world,[108] the more so since Martin Dibelius, working from quite different premisses, had come to much the same conclusion in his book, *From Tradition to Gospel*.[109] Footnotes to Dodd have been added in plenty, of course: A. M. Hunter sees a basically three point gospel throughout the New Testament, as does C. T. Craig, only unfortunately the three points are somewhat different![110] Floyd Filson and T. F. Glasson both contend for a five point kerygma,[111] though here again their five points are not identical. Gärtner sug-gests a seven point message,[112] and Geweiss gives a detailed expo-sition of the united kerygma of the early Church.[113] Recently Neil Alexander[114] has written an interesting essay on "The United Character of the New Testament Witness to the Christ event", where he maintains that fulfilment, newness, finality and a transcendental claim are the four recurring features in every variety of the apostolic preaching, with the sole exception of the Epistle of James.

Opposition to this whole approach has been evident on the Continent and in America for many years. Sometimes it springs from existentialist presuppositions, dominated by the thinking of Rudolf Bultmann,[115] and perpetuated even by disaffected members of his "school" such as Ulrich Wilckens of Berlin,[116], Hans Conzelmann of Göttingen[117] and Ernst Käsemann of Tübingen.[118] On this view, it is the encounter with Christ in the preaching of the kerygma which elicits faith, not any series of doctrinal assertions about a peasant rabbi of Nazareth. The gospel is God's summons, through the act of preaching, to the listener to make the decision which will usher him into a new dimension of existence. Those who hold this view make much of the notion that the kerygma is something revealed directly by God, according to Galatians 1:11–17; just as Dodd and his followers had made much of the notion that the kerygma is a series of assertions about Jesus handed down from the very earliest days of the Church, according to 1 Corinthians 15:3–8. Both positions tend to soft-pedal the evidence which is inconvenient to them, and William Baird is perhaps right in suggesting that both are right in what they affirm and wrong in what they deny: "Dodd points to the importance of history for the gospel; Bultmann to the importance of the gospel for faith."[119]

But it is not only the existentialist theologians who are unconvinced by the evidence for a heavily stylized pattern of the gospel. H. J. Cadbury wrote a good many years ago, "Neither in his day [Luke's] nor previously is the content of the apostolic preaching static or monolithic. It is a message in process—what in another connection Paul calls 'the progression of the gospel'."[120] He is unimpressed by the arguments for a fixed kerygma. Quite apart from the variety in the kerygmas which different scholars reconstruct, the probabilities of the situation would militate against undue fixity in the presentation of the message. It would inevitably be determined to a large extent by the background and understanding of the listeners. This is the approach of Professor C. F. D. Moule in his *The Birth of the New Testament*. He takes very seriously the variety of situations in which the early Church was called upon to explain itself and its Master. If we ask what is the unifying factor in all this, his reply is, "In a word, the apostolic proclamation about Jesus."

Eduard Schweizer writes along similar lines. In an essay in *Current Issues in N.T. Interpretation*, he compared and contrasted two creedal formulae, 1 Corinthians 15:3–5 with 1 Timothy 3:16.

Whereas both centre unambiguously on Jesus Christ, the first is composed against a background, (we may call it Hebraic) where man was conscious of his sin, and of the problem this would cause before a holy God at the last judgment. It assures him that "Christ died for out sins and God accepted this by raising him from the dead. Therefore sin and death lost their power; the eschatological day has broken."[121] The second creed is composed against a background (we may call it Hellenistic) where the problem is not sin but a terrifying sense of the loneliness of man imprisoned in a hostile world and at the mercy of implacable Fate. Under these circumstances the creed, which does not so much as mention the cross of Jesus, stresses his deity (not mentioned in the first creed) and assures the believer that Jesus is Lord, that he (and not Fate) holds the world in his mighty and merciful hands, and that through what he has done access to the heavenly realm is open to the Christian.

Schweizer has elsewhere given other examples of this varied proclamation of the unique and always central Christ.[122] He takes Romans 1:1–4 as an early Palestinian creed contrasting the earthly limitations of Jesus with his post-resurrection power and dignity. He was Son of David while on earth, in accordance with the Nathan prophecy of 2 Samuel 7, but he was "adopted"[123] as Son of God at the resurrection, thus fulfilling the eschatological and cosmic dimensions of the Nathan prophecy which had seemed to have been precluded by Jesus's death on the cross: the resurrection was seen, he thinks, as a sort of second stage in Jesus's Sonship.

Not so the conception of "Son of God" found in Paul and John. Here the background is not Palestinian Judaism with its Davidic hope, but the liberal Judaism of Egypt with its Wisdom-Logos ideology; and the Christian assertion is that this, too, is fulfilled not in some academic timeless Wisdom speculation but in the eternal, preincarnate Son of God who was born at a specific time and place as the Jesus of history. This conception inspired the language of John's prologue, of Hebrews 1:1ff., Galatians 4:4, John 3:16 and so on.

These two approaches to the same term represent two quite different understandings of "Son of God". The one sees Jesus "adopted" as Son of God since the resurrection; the other as the pre-existent divine being. Formally so different, in reality their content is, Schweizer maintains, much the same. The "Palestinian" creed said: "In Jesus Christ God acted decisively, fulfilling 2 Samuel 7: the New Age dawns with the resurrection, the accession of Jesus to the Lordship of the universe." The "Hellenistic" creed said, "In Jesus Christ God has encountered the world not casually but definitely and finally. The dominance of the law and of the forces of evil has been overthrown through the Son of God."

Others, such as Ralph Martin,[124] Walter Hollenweger,[125] and W. Manson[126] have adopted a somewhat similar approach to the variety-in-unity of the kerygma; and, though one might question the passion for discovering pre-Pauline and other early creeds everywhere in the New Testament (since the ingenuity of their discoverers is matched only by the highly subjective nature of the enterprise), there is obviously a great deal to be said for their main point, which is what one would in any case have expected. All Christians were convinced that Jesus Christ was God's last word to man, the one who brought as much of God to us as we could appreciate in the only terms we could take it in, the terms of a human life; the one who in dying and rising again was manifestly vindicated in his claims and achievement. This they all believed in common: their modes of expressing it depended to a large extent on their own intellectual and spiritual background and on that of their hearers.

Another way of coming at this whole question is suggested by Form Criticism. Developed by Schmidt, Dibelius and Bultmann in the second two decades of this century, it was an attempt to get behind the sterilities of Gospel Source Criticism (which divided the material into M, L, Q and the rest) and penetrate into the oral period when the good news was not written down, but passed on by word of mouth in the market places, bazaars and wine shops of the ancient world. Though Form Critics are no more united in their reconstruction of the "forms" by which material was preserved which later found its way into the gospels than are Dodd and his followers on the details of the kerygma which later became incorporated in the Acts and Epistles, there is at least this much general agreement. The separate *pericopae,* or short paragraphs in the gospels, originally circulated independently, and each was remembered because it was germane to one of the burning concerns of the early Church, such as catechesis, worship, apologetic or evangelism. To be sure, many Form Critics believe that once they have found this *Sitz im Leben Kirche* they have gone far enough, and that there never was a *Sitz im Leben Jesu*: the story was made up by the early community. That such scepticism is no necessary correlative of the Form Critical method is, however, increasingly widely recognized today. Judgments on content hardly follow from premisses on form! But the quest of the Form Critics for the life situation in which the story would have been useful is an enquiry of the utmost importance. It is, indeed, difficult to think of a more illuminating question to put to the gospel material than: "In what circumstances and for what purpose

63

would that story have been thought so vital by the early Church that they had at all costs to preserve it?" Dr Beasley-Murray addresses himself to this question with great simplicity and realism in a small but important book, *Preaching the Gospel from the Gospels*. In it he shows how the miracles, parables and even the events in the life of Jesus (which Bultmann would never allow had any relation to the kerygma at all) could have served the missionary and evangelistic preaching of the Church. Let us, by way of illustration, take a couple of examples (not used by Beasley-Murray) from St Mark's Gospel, which is widely recognized as kerygmatic through and through; it contains, that is to say, illustrative material for evangelistic preaching —almost every story in it is about Jesus, and almost every story requires a decision. It is interesting that Papias,[127] early in the second century, should have given much the same account of the origin of Mark's material as the modern Form Critics. Mark, he informs us, was not himself an eye-witness of what he records, but was the interpreter of Peter. He wrote down what he remembered of Peter's preaching concerning what the Lord had said or done. He did so accurately, but not in order: Peter himself had composed his addresses in no chronological order, but *pros tas chreias*, in order to meet the needs of the audience. It does not take very much imagination to listen to Peter telling and applying the story of the woman with the haemorrhage, for instance. "Look at her state," he would say. "This flow of blood was only a little thing, but a serious one. It cut her off from her family, her synagogue, and thus from her God, through the ceremonial uncleanness it brought. It gradually weakened her whole constitution as it went on year after year. And, worst of all, it was, humanly speaking, incurable. Is that not the situation you are in? Your sins may not seem large in your eyes, yet they separate you from your family, your fellows, your God. They increasingly grip your life, as you succumb to them time after time; and they are, humanly speaking, incurable. Is that not your plight? Then listen to what I have to tell you. This woman had heard about Jesus; she came up behind Jesus in the crowd, she touched Jesus in faith (though it was a very imperfect faith, full of superstition: it is the object on which faith reposes, not the quality which faith possesses that is important); and at once she was healed. Jesus required her to take her stand publicly as one cured by him: she came in great fear and trembling, and told the whole truth. Then she went away—not only with her feelings to rely on, but with a solid word of Jesus, assuring her of her new relationship with him, and of the peace and healing into which she had entered through faith. Well," Peter would say, "if Jesus could do it for her, he can do it for you. You have heard; you have come up to him hidden in the crowd, perhaps; will you not touch him for yourself? However defective your faith may be, if it is faith in Jesus, it will not be disappointed. You will immediately be put in the right with God, and once you have publicly confessed him, you can enter into the peace and power of the forgiven life: you can be sure of it, not because of your feelings, but because of the Lord's promise." Surely that is the way the story would have been used in the early Church. What else *could* it be used for? If so, then we have an inkling of how the *historia Jesu*[128] was used kerygmatically, of how the early missionaries made their proclamation.

It so happens that we are not reduced to speculation on this point. We have a remarkable example of the way this very story was used in preaching, preserved in a most unexpected place, the writings of an early fourth century monk from the deserts of Egypt, Macarius the Egyptian.[129] These *Spiritual Homilies* of Macarius fall well outside our period, but they enshrine timeless stuff, the simple evangelical preaching full of power and persuasion, which was directed to the ordinary man from the days of the apostles onwards. "And again," writes Macarius, "as the woman who was diseased with the issue of blood, on believing truly and touching the Lord's hem at once found cure, and the flow of the unclean fountain of her blood dried up, so every soul that has the incurable wound of sin, the fountain of unclean and evil thoughts, if it only comes to Christ and implores in true faith, finds saving cure of that incurable fountain of the passions . . . which fails and dries up through the power of Jesus only. Nothing else can cure this wound . . . He came and took away the sin of the world . . . And as that diseased woman spent all that she had upon those who professed to be able to cure her, but could be healed by none until she approached the Lord, truly believing and touching the hem of his garment . . .", so, he argues, nothing availed to cure the sickness of the human soul "until the Saviour came, the true Physician, who cures mankind without cost, who gave himself a ransom for men. He alone accomplished the great saving deliverance and cure of the soul. He set it free from bondage, and brought it out of darkness, glorifying it with his light." Of course, there needs to be a response to the Lord, and Macarius is not slow to stress it. Referring both to the woman, and to the blind man, whom he has been using as another paradigm of salvation, he concludes, "Had not that blind man cried out, had not that sick woman come to the Lord, they would have found no cure. So unless a man comes to the Lord of his own free will, with wholehearted sincerity, and beseeches him with the assurance of faith, he finds no cure."[130]

C

It is moving to reflect that this type of preaching was still to be found in the fourth century Church which in many other ways had deviated so notably from the apostolic pattern.

But to return to St Mark. The same fifth chapter furnishes us with another example of kerygmatic material, the story of the Gerasene demoniac. If the woman with the haemorrhage was used to preach cleansing to those plagued by the guilt of sin, this story was no doubt used to proclaim Christ's deliverance and integrating power in the lives of those who were at the mercy of conflicting emotions and evil powers. Here was a man who saw himself as the prey for a veritable "legion" of disintegrating impulses; he had no shame, no self-control, no social life. He was at home, poor man, only in a living death among the tombs. He, too, met with Jesus. And the Son of God (significant title here) showed himself Lord of the evil spirits, and cast them out, once the man had surrendered to him by giving him his name (which was of course to Hebrew man no mere label but the key to the character and the personality). There would no doubt be a good laugh among his fascinated listeners, as the evangelist related the fate of the pigs—they had no business to be keeping swine in the semi-Jewish country of Transjordan. Serve them right! I cannot think that humour was excluded from effective gospel preaching then any more than it is now. But after their laugh they would be brought back to the point; and this concerned the fate of the man, not the pigs. He was to be found sitting at the feet of Jesus instead of hacking himself to pieces in the tombs; he was clothed before Jesus, instead of rushing around naked and dead to shame; he was in full control of himself, instead of being at the mercy of the evil forces which had ruled his life. Surely here was superb illustrative matter to preach the earliest Christian creed: *Kyrios Jesus*, Jesus is Lord. The challenge implicit in such a story would need no underlining.

Such, in broadest outline, was the proclamation of the early Christians: united in its witness to Jesus, varied in its presentation of his relevance to the varied needs of the listeners, urgent in the demand for decision. But was the proclamation as varied as we have made out? What are we to make, if so, of the sermon material included in the Acts?

The Evangelistic Sermons in Acts

However incomplete Dodd's assessment of the early kerygma may have been, it showed that there is a very high degree of uniformity running through the speeches or sermons attributed to Peter in the early part of the Acts. More recent study has only served to underline this fact.[131] The question is, does this pattern of gospel preaching go back to the early days of the Jerusalem church, or is it entirely a composition of St Luke's, representing, no doubt, typical gospel preaching of his own day?[132] It is a difficult question to which very different answers are given.

Those who believe that the sermons do not give us a reliable account of early apostolic preaching make the following points, among others.

1. Luke, writing in the manner of a Greek historian, would put into the mouths of his actors what he thought appropriate, not attempt to discover what was actually said. Thucydides is frequently adduced as a pattern.

However, Thucydides, supposing he was Luke's model, did not simply write free composition. He stuck as closely to what was said on the occasion as he could.[133] Furthermore, whilst the speeches in Thucydides were his literary highlight, in Luke they are couched in his worst Greek. The parallel with Thucydides, in fact, is not felicitous.[134] Actually, ancient historians differed widely in their conception of writing history. Some, like Lucian, were at pains to be precise;[135] others, like Thucydides, were primarily interested in providing lessons for future generations;[136] others, like Livy, were very loose with the facts;[137] many, like Cicero, regarded historiography as supremely the art of the orator![138] When we throw in religious historiography like Philostratus's *Life of Apollonius of Tyana* and the Jewish historiography of the Maccabees the picture becomes even more complicated, and it is exceedingly unsafe to argue from other writers as to what Luke could or could not have done in his speeches. We must examine them in the context of his own work.[139]

2. Much is made of the intrinsic improbability of Luke having any record of the early Jerusalem kerygma. But how do we know? Shorthand was available in antiquity: notes might even have been taken of some of the epoch-making addresses of the apostles.[140] There are men alive today who well remember the thrust and general content, as well as some of the particular wording, of Churchill's war speeches nearly thirty years ago. Furthermore, when we recall the extent to which rabbis were trained to learn by heart,[141] it would be very surprising if echoes of the early proclamation of Jesus were not to be found in the Jerusalem community during the two years when Luke, awaiting the outcome of Paul's trial at Caesarea, travelled about Palestine gaining information for his gospel. If we are to argue the matter in intrinsic probability, there is a great deal to be said for the primitive nature of the Lucan sermons.

3. It is further objected that the sermons are too similar: Peter's are too Pauline, and Paul's, especially at Pisidian Antioch (13:16ff.) are too Petrine. Many scholars agree with C. F. Evans[142] that the speeches fit in ill with their contexts and should therefore be regarded as a literary device on the part of Luke.

All of this is, however, open to dispute. There are interesting parallels between the material attributed to Peter in the early speeches of Acts and 1 Peter.[148] It is not true that there are no distinctively Pauline touches in the sermons attributed to him: it is in a Pauline speech that we read of justification and the redemptive nature of Christ's death;[144] and the parallels between his Areopagus address and Romans 1 and 2, or between his Lystra sermon and 1 Thessalonians 1, have often been observed. Furthermore, the extent to which the Petrine and Pauline sermons agree in substance may not be because Luke made them both up; it may equally well be due to the fact, which is asserted both by Galatians 2:1–12 and 1 Corinthians 15:1ff., that both men preached the same gospel. Finally, the superficiality of Evans's complaint that the speeches accord ill with the context in which they are supposed to have been spoken, has been brilliantly shown up by Wilckens, who demonstrates conclusively how closely they are in fact integrated with their context.[145]

It cannot be denied that there are many marks of Luke's hand in the speeches of Acts. But there are several good reasons for believing that he did not make them up, *ex nihilo*, so to speak, but is rather making a conscious attempt at recording the mission-preaching of the earliest community of Christians.

1. The Aramaisms in these sermons are very considerable. These are particularly numerous in chapters 1–3 and 10. Indeed, C. C. Torrey undertook to retranslate them back into Aramaic.[146] His views must be received with caution, in the light of later work;[147] and Sparks[148] could conceivably be right in arguing that Luke is writing in deliberately archaistic, Septuagintal terms at these points. Nevertheless, this does not satisfactorily dispose of the Aramaisms, nor explain why Luke did not archaize elsewhere in the same way. Wilcox in a recent book[149] has shown considerable respect for this belief in an Aramaic substructure to the speeches; and R. P. Martin,[150] in an interesting analysis of the characteristics of translation-Greek, has shown that Aramaic sources do lie behind substantial parts of the Acts speeches. This indicates that Luke was very probably using early traditional material in the composition of his sermons in Acts.

2. The doctrine in these sermons is quite unlike that of Luke him-

self. He certainly did not think of Jesus as simply "a man approved of God", "the prophet", "the righteous one", "the prince (or 'originator') of life".[151] His own theology did not expect "times of refreshing from the presence of the Lord that he may send the Christ appointed for you";[152] his eschatology was of a different order.[153] Long ago Harnack[154] was greatly impressed by the antiquity of the title "servant of God" used of Jesus in the speeches of Acts but nowhere else in Luke, and Cullmann[155] and Jeremias[156] agree with him. The recent attempt by Wilckens[157] to evade this point has been capably refuted by Dupont.[158] Certainly the appearance of a "different" theology in the Acts sermons need not necessarily mean that it is ancient; but when taken with the Aramaisms and the very Jewish nature of the doctrinal formulations concerned, the presumption is strong that we have here something very old.

3. The use of Old Testament *testimonia* in these sermons is very significant. Luke is clear that this was the apostolic method of preaching the gospel to Jews; he does not, apparently, use it himself, nor does he represent it as the normal approach to Gentiles, whether educated, as at Athens, or primitive, as at Lystra. Dodd has shown[159] how closely these quotations from the Old Testament are interwoven with the kerygma which he identified in the sermons, and his case has not been effectively overthrown.[160]

These are some of the reasons for supposing that in the sermons in Acts we have access to a very old stratum of tradition. This is confirmed by two other considerations. The fact that in his Gospel Luke treated the words of Jesus as almost sacrosanct, whereas he felt free to alter their order and setting quite radically from his Marcan source, is an indication that he probably handled the early preaching in much the same way, and that he did his best to reproduce its substance. The survival of eye-witnesses of the events recorded is also an important consideration, not always accorded its full weight. Had Luke been as dependent on his imagination as some scholars suppose for the content of the sermons he gives us in Acts, many an aged Christian who had been present on the day in question, would have protested. Accordingly, we may with some confidence accept the sermons in Acts, not indeed as a transcript of what was said, nor even as a summary of the addresses (so thoroughly has Luke conformed them to his own style) but as a reliable sample of the way in which the earliest Christians set about convincing first the Jews of Jerusalem, then proselytes like Cornelius, then Diaspora Jews and finally Gentiles from varying backgrounds, of the truth of the Christian proclamation.

Both the broad homogeneity of approach to evangelistic preaching suggested by this examination of the sermons in Acts, and the variety indicated by our previous consideration of the problem, must be given due weight. There was enormous scope for versatility in preaching the gospel: there is variety galore in the Acts sermons themselves, variety which Dodd's selective and rather superficial treatment glosses over: taking other passages of the New Testament into account the variety is all the more noticeable. But although Dodd claimed too much, his work is of lasting value in working out in considerable detail the hint given both in Mark and Paul that the gospel had a recognizable shape and content. Christians had a common approach to evangelism, however much they might differ in details and transpose some of the thought forms into other keys: and they did plenty of that as we shall see. There was some sort of "pattern of sound words"[161] and this proved a useful springboard for the memories of the evangelists: it did not serve as a strait-jacket, inhibiting all imagination and initiative on their part.[162]

WITNESS

The third great cluster of words used in the New Testament to describe the evangelistic work of the early Church comes from the *martureō* root. Like the other two, *euaggelizomai* and *kērussō*, this word group also had a history which made it singularly appropriate for their purpose. It is primarily a legal term and was frequently used in Greek to denote witness to facts and events on the one hand, and to truths vouched for on the other. In both cases the personal involvement and assurance of the man making the witness was an important element.

The Old Testament usage has two points of great interest which help us to understand the way the term is used in the New. In the first instance, God himself is frequently the subject of the verb. He bears his witness when he disclosed himself to men; thus a hundred times and more we find reference to the "tent of witness" or the "ark of witness". The tent was the place where God revealed something of his presence as he met with his people; the ark was the box which enshrined the record of his self-disclosure, the Law of Moses (called *ta martyria* in the LXX of Exodus 25:16). God himself bears witness to his own nature—after all, who else is there that can? Accordingly, the New Testament frequently speaks of God or the Spirit or the Scriptures bearing witness.[163] Without his witness there would be no revelation.

Secondly, in Deutero-Isaiah, which so profoundly prepared the way for the Christian understanding of the gospel, God calls on his people to be witnesses for him over against the dumb idols of the heathen. "You are my witnesses, says the Lord, and my Servant whom I have chosen, that you may know and believe me, and understand that I am He. Before me no God was formed, nor shall there be any after me. I, I am the Lord, and beside me there is no saviour. I declared, and saved, and proclaimed, when there was no strange god among you. And you are my witnesses."[164] Or again: "Fear not, nor be afraid; have I not told you from of old and declared it? And you are my witnesses! Is there a God beside me? There is no Rock; I know not any."[165] Here we find the uniqueness, eternity and saving initiative of God stressed over against the impotent gods of the heathen; and the task of the people of God, called his servant in the first passage, is to proclaim this, to bear witness to it. One is reminded of the function ascribed to the Servant in the Servant Songs to bear him witness among the heathen in order to reach the Gentiles with the saving knowledge of God.[166]

When we turn to the New Testament we find a good many occurrences of the ordinary sense of "witness" (meaning to attest facts or assert truths) but it is in Acts and the Johannine writings that we meet it in the special sense of Christian witness.[167] Paul often speaks of God bearing him witness, but he does not use *martus* in this sense of Christian witness and apart from one doubtful example,[168] he does not use *martureō* or *marturia* for this purpose either. This may be because, as we shall see below, the word was specially connected with the first-hand testimony of those who had known the incarnate Jesus; it may also be because he had no need for it, having made such copius use of the other two concepts of proclamation and evangelism.

The Witness in Luke–Acts

What, then, did Luke mean by "witness"? The basic passage[169] is Luke 24:48 where Jesus commissions the disciples to be his witnesses "of these things". What things? The context is rich and quite explicit. It is the identification of Jesus as Messiah, the fulfilment of all the Scriptures in him, his suffering and death, his resurrection, and the proclamation of repentance and faith in his name to all nations, beginning from Jerusalem. That is what they are to bear witness to. And it is just the same in content as the *kērugma* and the *euaggelion* which we have already examined. These are the facts they are to attest. These are the truths they are to assert, on the strength of personal experience. The power to equip them for this task of witness-bearing is promised them in the next verse; and this commissioning and empowering is filled out in the opening verses of the

Acts, where "You shall be my witnesses" is matched by "You shall receive power when the Holy Spirit has come upon you".[170] Not only is the pattern of Isaiah 43 and 44 being fulfilled, but so, once again, are various elements connected with the other two words—the importance of the kingdom,[171] the central place occupied by Christ in the witness,[172] and God's gracious design for Jew and Gentile alike.

The other references in Acts do not add a great deal to the picture. Supremely it is witness to Jesus which is required,[173] and this includes his earthly life, his cross and particularly his resurrection.[174] An important feature is "his exaltation to God's right hand as Leader and Saviour to give repentance to Israel and forgiveness of sins".[175] In this passage the Holy Spirit also joins in the witness-bearing (in the hearts of the crowd), just as in Acts 1:8 and John 15:26f. The apostolic Church were quite clear that God's gift of his Spirit was intended not to make them comfortable but to make them witnesses.

Three points call for discussion in this examination of Christian witness according to St Luke. First, he has a strong tendency to restrict the word "witnesses" to those who had known the incarnate Jesus. This is true of all the references apart from the last three in Acts. The witnesses are the people who have lived through the events of Good Friday and Easter, and who can bear personal testimony both to their historicity and to their interpretation. It is because of this function of the witness to guarantee, so to speak, the continuity between the Jesus of history and the Christ of faith,[176] that Paul has to refer in 13:31 not to "us witnesses" (he was not, in this sense), but to "those who are now his witnesses to the people". But so strongly did the sense of personal encounter with the risen Jesus overshadow the idea of witnessing that by the end of the Acts both Stephen and Paul are called witnesses. Both have a special vision of Jesus. The one sees Christ at his martyrdom,[177] the other at his conversion.[178]

Second, it is interesting that the life of Jesus should be included in the content of the "witness", particularly in view of the contemporary insistence in Germany that the life of Jesus was of no interest to the early Christians[179] (why, then, did they write and read gospels?) and had nothing to do with the kerygma, which apart from asserting the historical "that-ness" of Jesus, concentrated on on his saving significance. So strongly is this felt even by scholars who would no longer subscribe to the views of Rudolf Bultmann, that Ulrich Wilckens is reduced to arguing that Acts 10 is not kerygma at all, but a primitive example of the gospel form of writing.[180] However, Graham Stanton[181] has no difficulty in showing that this chapter is indeed an example of genuine evangelistic preaching to proselytes, and he points out that whereas in the Jerusalem area the person of Jesus and the events of the passion and its sequel would be well known, once you got away to somewhere like Caesarea it would be necessary to explain who Jesus was and what he had done in his life, not merely his death. This does not mean that there is in this address a gradual slipping away from the challenge of the kerygma to mere edifying tales about the life of Jesus; far from it. But it does mean that the proclamation of the atoning death and resurrection of Jesus would be meaningless to all except those who had been closely involved without some reference in the "witness" to the sort of person Jesus was and the sort of life he lived.[182]

Mention of the atoning death of Jesus leads directly on to the third point of significance in the Lucan "witness". The cross of Jesus is indeed part of the message of the Lucan sermons; that is agreed on all sides. But it is not, we are told, given atoning significance by St Luke. This I believe to be too rash a conclusion to draw from the fact that nowhere does Luke specifically say that forgiveness comes to men through the cross *tout simple*.[183] What, then, is the witness to the cross, according to Luke's sermons in Acts? The following seven points are, I think, sufficient indication that though Luke had no distinctive *theologia crucis* his teaching was not substantially different from that of the rest of the New Testament on this important subject.

1. The seriousness of sin is frequently stressed in Acts, in the demand for repentance, the punishment of sinners (such as Ananias and Sapphira, Elymas, Herod and the sons of Scaeva), and the reminders of the last judgment.[184]

2. Men are held responsible for their sinful actions, even when it is specifically noted that God overrules the wickedness of man for his own purposes.[185]

3. Salvation for men comes from God alone:[186] this is repeatedly emphasized, and is also underlined by the fact that Jesus's death is said to be part of the age-long plan of God[187] (no accidental disaster resulting from human wickedness) and that baptism is something done *for* a man not *by* him, thus embodying the objective "givenness" of salvation.

4. When the cross and resurrection are mentioned, they are frequently put into immediate juxtaposition to the offer of divine forgiveness,[188] thus indicating that they were integrally connected in the thought of St Luke.

5. Jesus is several times identified with the Suffering Servant of Isaiah 42 and 53, and always in the context of suffering and vindication.[189] This fact alone makes it very difficult to suppose that Luke

had no clear doctrine of the atonement: for no passage in the Old Testament was more commonly used by the Christians than this to explain their Lord's expiatory death.

6. On one occasion the death of Christ is spoken of as a ransom:[190] the Church has been ransomed with the Lord's own blood (or the blood of the Lord's own).

7. Jesus, it is repeatedly mentioned, died on a tree.[191] This is a plain allusion to Deuteronomy 21:21–23 which explains that anyone who is hung up on a tree in death rests under the curse of God.[192] This could hardly have escaped Luke's attention: it indicates a strongly vicarious understanding of the cross of Christ.

These considerations give pause to the assumption that Luke had no understanding of the atonement, and they explain why he recognizes that the cross as well as the resurrection is a necessary element in the witness which the early Christians made with such joy and confidence.[193]

The Witness in John

The understanding of "witness" in the Johannine writings is rather different; and it is important to remember that he uses this group of words to the exclusion of *euaggelizesthai* and *kērussein*. Why is "the witness" a mode of expression which is so important for him?

The answer lies, I think, in John's deep convictions about the person of Jesus. Few men have understood this better than Søren Kierkegaard. His book *Philosophical Fragments* is one of the shrewdest re-statements of the basic message of St John ever to have been written. He points out that a human teacher, be he as wise as Socrates, can only assist at the birth of truth and knowledge in another person; he can be no more than a midwife, so to speak. The identity of the teacher is as unimportant as the moment when the disclosure is made. For the teacher is a mere midwife; only God can beget. But what if God does beget? What if God comes himself to teach and impart new life? Why then, the Teacher becomes all important, and the moment of illumination or entering on this new life becomes highly significant. This is in fact, John is convinced, what has happened. The Absolute became our Contemporary; God became man for thirty years or so, in order to bring us to a new dimension of life, through knowing him.[194] But how can you demonstrate so staggering a claim? How can you bring it home to others? The answer is, by witness. You can listen to the witness to himself which Jesus, the Teacher, brings; you can allow its inherent truth to convince you, and bring you to faith in him, and so to this new quality of life he came to make available for men. There is, after all, nothing more ultimate than the Divine Teacher to which you can appeal in order to validate his message. What is required is faith in the witness he brings.

That, surely, is why the person of Jesus is brought so strongly into relief as the content of "the witness" in this gospel. Witness is borne to him by the Baptist, true enough,[195] for the Baptist is the last and greatest of God's prophets.[196] But only divine witness can substantiate the claims of a divine person. Accordingly we find Jesus giving witness to his own person and work[197] and when this is rejected by the Jews because it is autonomous, and their Law asserted that only witness supported by at least two people could stand,[198] Jesus points out that he has indeed other supporting and divine witness. The Father bears witness to Jesus,[199] and he does so by attesting the divine words which Jesus speaks[200] and also the divine miracles or signs which Jesus does.[201] Moreover, the God-given Scriptures bear constant witness to Jesus,[202] and to crown all this divine attestation is the internal witness of the Spirit of God in those who accept the testimony.[203] Only God can bear adequate witness to God. And when God did so, some believed; the link between "witness" and "faith" is strongly emphasized in this gospel.[204]

But what could the first generation believers do to share with others who had not been present the new life they enjoyed in Christ? They could bear their witness; that is all. They had two things to say. First, that they had believed, and had found the claims of the divine Teacher to be true in their own lives and experience. Second, they could give the evidence on which they had committed themselves. That is all a historical contemporary can possibly do for later generations or for those who were not there. And that is what John set out to do in his preaching and in his writings. He says time and again that he has believed; and he gives the evidence which led him to that life-changing encounter with Jesus. His Gospel is indeed *marturia*[205] and like all witness to Jesus, it is intended to lead others to faith.[206] The Gospel is so skilfully written that almost all of its main themes have long histories in both pagan and Jewish thought;[207] the author rings every bell he can in the minds of as wide a variety of readers as he can reach. But beneath the ambivalent language, the message is very much the same as we have seen elsewhere in the New Testament. The deity of Jesus is fundamental;[208] he is the Truth, the Light of the world, the Word of God who is himself God.[209] He is also attested in the witness as the Saviour of the world,[210] the Lamb of God who takes away the world's sin,[211] and the one who is filled with God's Spirit and imparts the same to believers.[212] This testimony to Jesus, his incarnation,[213] his real death on the cross,[214] his real resurrection from the tomb[215] is all eye-witness stuff. The disciple who is a contemporary can only do this much for what Kierkegaard calls "the disciple at second hand". But this eye-witnessing to the facts, and this repeated assurance that they work out in experience can lead the "disciple at second hand" to the faith-encounter with Jesus which will produce life; "blessed are those who have not seen, and yet believe."[216] They are blessed, because when they believe they do see! Seeing is not believing, in this Gospel; the reverse is true—believing is seeing.[217] And when you believe the witness and see for yourself, you are no longer a "disciple at second hand"; you are a disciple at first hand, every bit as much in touch with the Divine Teacher as the historical contemporary on whose testimony you believed. "He that believes on the Son of God has the witness in himself."[218]

This is not all the Johannine writings have to say on the subject of witness;[219] but it explains why it occupies such a prominent place, allied as it is to the person of Jesus on the one hand and the faith of the hearer on the other. It is the most profound understanding of the place of testimony in faith to be found anywhere in the New Testament; it answers the questions of those who were not there, "How can I be sure?", a question to which Luke had returned a characteristic and rather simpler answer.[220]

There are, then, good grounds for E. G. Selwyn's words: "I sometimes wonder whether the term 'kerygma' has not been worked too hard, and whether the word *marturia* and its cognates would not describe better the primitive and indispensable core of the Christian message."[221] The justice of his assertion has impressed itself on me strongly; for the very afternoon I wrote these words about the witness in St John, a student came to see me about the Christian faith. He had intellectual difficulties, and lacked any personal encounter with the divine Teacher who became our Contemporary. For him St John's approach was singularly meaningful, whereas other presentations of the Christian message which he had heard had left him cold. He went away to join the ranks of those who, though they cannot see, believe; and believing, he began to see.

This long chapter has not attempted to do more than indicate the main outline of the basic evangel about Jesus in the New Testament period through an examination of the three main word groups for mission preaching. There are of course other words used for this, like *lalein*[222] and *kataggellein*,[223] but none of them rivals any of the main three in significance. There are also other approaches which might have been equally useful: we might have followed the broad sweep of the enquiries made by Neil Alexander[224] and A. M.

Hunter,[225] which provide an excellent indication of the essence of the new preaching. Alternatively, we might have attempted the sort of study adopted by J. N. D. Kelly in the first part of his *Early Christian Creeds*, and seen what happened to this kerygma in the second century; but much of that will emerge in subsequent chapters, and it seemed best to concentrate in this one on the New Testament itself.

Perhaps the only merit of the sketch attempted here has been to avoid the unduly cramping effects of concentrating too much upon the putative contents of a supposedly fairly rigid kerygma. It has also, perhaps, suggested something of the variety among the earliest Christians in their presentation of a gospel which was basically homogeneous; and this is a characteristic which certainly persisted into subsequent generations. In the next two chapters we shall look at some of the ways in which this core of the gospel was adapted to the very differing needs of the Jewish and Gentile environments which it set out to penetrate for Christ.

4

EVANGELIZING THE JEWS

THE CHRISTIAN GOSPEL is good news about a Jew. It was preached by Jews to Jews, in the first instance. And it is the merit of writers such as S. G. F. Brandon,[1] Robert Eisler[2] and H. J. Schonfield[3] to have reminded us of this fact, however bizarre their views may be in other respects. When the first followers of Jesus proclaimed him so enthusiastically as Messiah on the Day of Pentecost, they were talking in terms that made sense to their Jewish hearers, whether or not that message was acceptable. Let us examine the main emphasis of the mission preaching of the Church among the Jews, always remembering that we are not talking about a new religion, at least for a couple of decades after the resurrection, but about a "sect" within Judaism. Moreover, in some places, notably Jerusalem, this remained the state of affairs until about A.D. 85 with the publication of the anti-Christian Benediction.[4] Indeed, the Christians were not finally distinct from Jewry until after the Bar-Cochba Revolt in A.D. 135. Jewish Christians in the early days had no thought of separating themselves from the rest of Israel. They hoped that Israel would come to share their convictions about Jesus, and thus hasten his triumphant return to set up his Kingdom. That is why they preached so boldly and irrepressibly to their Jewish brethren wherever they were to be found. We are not as well informed about the Jewish Mission as we would wish, but the main outlines of their approach can be discerned in the various strata of the New Testament, the Jewish Apocryphal Gospels, and the second century Apologies, together with a certain amount of material provided by orthodox Jewish sources.

THE PROMISES ARE FULFILLED

It has been widely recognized, following C. H. Dodd in his *Apostolic Preaching* and *According to the Scriptures*, that one of the main planks in the Christian platform among the Jews was that the ancient Scriptures had at last been fulfilled, the promises had come true, and that this had been achieved in the person of Jesus of

Nazareth. Accordingly, the approach to the Jew was always made through the Old Testament.

We have already noted that the early creed of 1 Corinthians 15:1ff. laid repeated stress on the contention that both the death and resurrection of Jesus were according to the Scriptures. This emphasis recurs in every strand of the New Testament, with the sole exception of the Epistle of James. It comes in every single evangelistic address in the Book of Acts, with the sole exception of the truncated address of Paul to the Gentiles of Lystra.[5] St Mark's whole presentation of Jesus is governed by the *dei*, the "must" of fulfilled prophecy.[6] Indeed, he lays it down in the first verse of his Gospel that the beginning of the good news is the prophetic testimony, John the Baptist, the fulfilment of the Elijah hope; in the same way, at the Baptism the Old Testament themes of Servant of Yahweh and Son of Man are combined and applied to Jesus. The Transfiguration is another example of this fulfilment theme, indicating that Jesus is the goal of both Law and Prophets. If we look at Matthew, the correlation of the person and work of Jesus with the Old Testament is even more strongly stressed. He has a dozen examples of a fulfilment formula: "This was done that it might be fulfilled which was spoken by the prophet, saying . . ."[7] He builds the discourses of Jesus up into five books (chapters 5–7, 10, 13, 18, 23–5) obviously meant to parallel the five books of the Law; and lest anyone should miss the point, Matthew underlines it with another formula: "And it came to pass when Jesus had finished these sayings . . ." Luke's whole two volume work is one of fulfilment— from the birth and infancy narratives onwards up till the crucial turning to the Gentiles in Acts 13:46ff., which was seen as the fulfilment of the work of the Servant of Yahweh begun by Jesus and continued in his evangelists. The ministry of Jesus begins with Christ's synagogue claim to fulfil the prophecy of Isaiah about the good news of salvation,[8] and closes with Jesus explaining to his disciples after his resurrection that "everything written about me in the Law of Moses, the Prophets and the Psalms, must be fulfilled".[9] In his preface to Theophilus, Luke declares his purpose; and it is nothing less than to show that fulfilment has come through Jesus. Luke 1:1 is normally mistranslated: "Inasmuch as many have undertaken to compile a narrative of the things which have been accomplished among us." What Luke actually wrote was "fulfilled among us".

St John's Gospel has precisely the same thrust. The details of the Passion are shown to be in accordance with the Scriptures; so is the resurrection.[10] During his ministry he had acted and spoken "so that the Scriptures might be fulfilled".[11] The Scripture cannot be broken, and it points to him.[12]

It would be pointless to go through the rest of the New Testament making the same point. It stands out clearly on every page. Origen put it well when he said, "The beginning of the Gospel is nothing but the whole Old Testament."[13] More recently, Hoskyns expressed himself thus: "There is no event or utterance recorded of him which does not proceed from a conception of the Messiahship smelted and sublimed from the ore of the Old Testament Scriptures."[14]

The Appeal to Scripture

This being the case, we are not surprised to find that in the early sermons in Acts this method of arguing from Scripture is everywhere apparent. "This is what was spoken by the prophet" is how Peter begins to set out the significance of Jesus.[15] And this remained the fundamental method of approach to the Jew until the split with the synagogue had become irreversible in the second century. Even after that, Christian apologetic against Jews retained this method, though, regrettably, no longer sought to win the hearers to the faith. The Old Testament was the Bible of the Jew and the Christian alike, and it was, as C. H. Dodd has pointed out "a standing principle of Rabbinic exegesis of the Old Testament that what the prophets predicted had reference to 'the days of the Messiah', that is to say, to the expected time when God, after long centuries of waiting, should visit his people with judgment and blessing bringing to a climax his dealings with them in history".[16] Accordingly whether we are looking at the sermons of Peter, the preaching of Paul in Romans or the *Dialogue* of Justin with Trypho, we find that the matter is argued and settled entirely on the basis of the Scriptures. Do they, or do they not back up the claims the Christians are putting forward in the name of Jesus? That is the issue.

We can get a closer look at the content of those claims from a fascinating passage in Acts 26:23. Paul is defending himself in front of Agrippa, but his concluding words look as if they had often been used as headings in synagogue discussions with the Jews. "I stand here testifying to small and great, saying nothing but what the prophets and Moses said would come to pass, that (literally "*if*") the Messiah must suffer and, by being the first to rise from the dead, should proclaim light both to the people and to the Gentiles." It seems as though the suffering of the Messiah, his resurrection, and his fulfilment of Isaiah 49 both for Jews and Gentiles, were major topics for discussion between Christians and Jews.

These discussions might take place anywhere: in open-air preaching, in front of the sanhedrin, in the home of a godfearer, in the chariot of a proselyte, in front of a petty princeling, or in a private house.[17] They might take place in the course of an afternoon walk, as between the old man and Justin.[18] This must have been how the gospel spread most effectively among the Jews. Justin was certainly not the first to discover that the Scriptures and the words of Jesus "possess a terrible power in themselves" and also "a wonderful sweetness" which makes its own indelible impression. "Straightway a flame was kindled in my soul, and a love of the prophets and of those men who are friends of Christ, possessed me," he wrote.[19] Cleopas and his companion had a similar experience on the road to Emmaus as Jesus gave them a never-to-be-forgotten Scripture lesson. " 'O foolish men, and slow of heart to believe all that the prophets have spoken! Was it not necessary that the Messiah should suffer these things and enter into his glory?' And beginning with Moses and all the prophets, he interpreted to them in all the Scriptures the things concerning himself."[20] It is not surprising that they said to one another, rather like Justin subsequently, "Did not our hearts burn within us while he opened to us the Scriptures?" Many a Jewish heart burned within him as he heard the apostolic preaching of Jesus, matched it up with the Old Testament, and found it fitted. We can well imagine the searching of the Scriptures which must have ensued in synagogue after synagogue as Paul and the other missionaries made a start there. For of all the methods of approach of the Christians to the Jews, that of synagogue preaching was most important. Here not only the Jews themselves, but the very fertile soil of the Godfearers was to be found. No wonder, then, that Christians made a bee line for the synagogues and preached Jesus as Messiah, according to the Scriptures. It was in the synagogue that Stephen argued the Messiaship of Jesus so powerfully that though they "arose and disputed with him . . . they could not withstand the wisdom and the Spirit with which he spoke."[21] It was in the synagogues that Paul and Apollos spoke to such effect after their conversion, confounding the Jews by proving that Jesus was the Messiah[22] and confuting the Jews in public, showing by the Scriptures that the Messiah was Jesus.[23] We read of the Beroeans receiving the news with all eagerness and searching the Scriptures daily to see if these things were so.[24] The Western text of 18:5 makes this very reasonable addition to Paul's testimony that the Messiah is Jesus: "There was much speaking and interpretation of Scriptures." Of course there was. Sometimes people would come back in large numbers next week; sometimes whole days would be spent on discussions of this sort.[25] Sometimes the discussions would be courteous and friendly, as in Justin's dialogue with Trypho, where the Jew professed himself very grateful for the discussion, having found in it far more than he had expected. "If we could do this more frequently," he said, "we should be much helped in the searching of the Scriptures themselves. But since you are on the eve of departure, do not hesitate to remember us as friends when you are gone."[26] Justin ends by recommending once again Jesus as God's Messiah, and prays that Trypho may come to put his faith in him.

But often the discussions must have been much more acrimonious than this. The riots that ensued time and again in the Acts as the missionaries were angrily thrown out of the synagogues and sometimes stoned give eloquent proof of the divisive nature of this preaching of Jesus as Messiah. It was the most explosive topic imaginable in the political situation of the first century, particularly in the decades leading up to the Great Revolt of A.D. 66–70. And as we shall see below, the Messiah the Christians preached was by no means to every Jew's liking.

Of course, some believed, wherever the message travelled. It might be a visiting proselyte like the Ethiopian eunuch, who put his faith in the one who had fulfilled the prophecy of the Suffering Servant; it might be a sector of the Corinthian synagogue which was so convinced by what they heard that they started a rival establishment next door! But everywhere there was joy among the believers; everywhere there was the same desire to spread this message of the Messiah.

It is just the same today when a Jew accepts Jesus as Messiah. I recall talking to a most intelligent graduate overseas who was interested in Christianity because her friends appeared to have "got something". She came on a Christian houseparty, and the quality of the fellowship there brought her to discuss the whole Christian case with me. I showed her from the Old Testament Scriptures how closely Jesus had fulfilled the varied hopes of the prophets. She believed, and was baptized. Father (a rabbi) was persuaded to come to the baptism, but has been in irreconcilable opposition ever since. Her sister also came, and is a believer now, though not allowed by the father to meet with any other Christians or attend Christian worship. This pattern of acceptance and rejection within the very same family must have been repeated time and again in the early days. And the zeal of my friend to reach others with the good news she had come to recognize for herself is no less reminiscent of the Acts of the Apostles. She is studying Greek and Hebrew, and intends to work full time among Jews. "You know," she wrote recently, "it is so blatantly clear that Jesus died for our sins on the cross and rose from the grave—I just long to get it across to others, especially to my own people. I am longing to work among them and show them their Messiah."

A fascinating example of how this argument from prophecy was actually carried out in antiquity is given to us by Origen. He remarks, commenting on Isaiah 53, "I remember that once in a discussion with some whom the Jews regard as learned (i.e. Rabbis) I used these prophecies. At this the Jew said that these prophecies referred to the whole people as though of a single individual, since they were scattered in the dispersion and smitten, that as a result of the scattering of the Jews among the other nations many might become proselytes. In this way he explained the text: 'Thy form shall be inglorious among men' and 'those to whom he was not proclaimed shall see him' and 'being a man in calamity'. I then adduced many arguments in the disputation which proved that there is no good reason for referring these prophecies about one individual to the whole people. And I asked which person could be referred to in the text: 'This man bears our sins and suffers pain for us' and 'but he was wounded for our transgressions and he was made sick for our iniquities'; and I asked which person fitted the words 'by his stripe we were healed'. Obviously, those who say this were once in their sins, and were healed by the passion of the Saviour, whether they were of the Jewish people or of the Gentiles: the prophet foresaw this, and put these words into their mouths by the inspiration of the Holy Spirit. But we seemed to put him in the greatest difficulty with the words 'because of the iniquities of my people he was led to death'. If according to them the people are the subject of the prophecy, why is this man said to have been led to death because of the iniquities of the people of God, if he is not different from the people of God? Who is this if not Jesus Christ, by whose stripe we who believe in him were healed, when he put off the principalities and powers among us, and made a show of them openly on the cross?"[27]

Messianic Testimonia

So widespread was this method of arguing the Christian case from the Scriptures that it would be reasonable to assign its origin to Jesus even without the specific statement of Luke 24: 25f, 44f. "To account for the beginning of this original and most fruitful process of rethinking the Old Testament we found need to postulate a creative mind. The gospels offer us one. Are we compelled to reject the offer?"[28] Such is Dodd's conclusion of the matter after studying the main *testimonia* used by the early Christians to explain the person of their Master in categories drawn from the Scriptures. It is indeed well based. But his view that the Old Testament quotation of the early Christians was confined to broad tracts of Scripture, not concentrated on particular verses, thus dispensing with the need for postulating an early Testimony Book, is less secure. That the early Christians had some such list of Messianic proof texts is, *a priori*, probable in view of the shortage of written books in the days when there was no printing, the difficulty of finding the place in a large cumbersome scroll, and the fact that the Scriptures were written in Hebrew, a language which had become unfamiliar to a great many Jews. Indeed, it is doubtful whether all synagogues possessed complete copies of the Old Testament Scriptures: many of the smaller ones may well have made do with the set lectionary passages for first and second lessons, from the Law and the Prophets. Under these circumstances, and in times, moreover, when Messianic expectation was white hot, it would be strange indeed if collections of Messianic proof texts did not circulate among the Jews, orally at any rate, but probably in writing. Origen appears to favour such a view when he writes, "I am of the opinion that before the advent of Christ the chief priests and scribes of the people taught that Christ would be born in Bethlehem, on account of the distinct and clear character of the prophecy. This interpretation reached even the multitude of the Jews."[29] Granted that Dodd is right in showing that many of the verses used by the Church in apologetic are but the top of hidden icebergs, pointing us to the context in which they occur in the Old Testament, it is nevertheless undeniable that many of them do nothing of the kind: the Matthaean *testimonia* in particular are highly eclectic and by no means all closely related to their Old Testament contexts. There is, in fact, a whole mass of evidence, ignored by Dodd, but drawn together in B. P. W. Stather Hunt's *Primitive Gospel Sources*, which makes it almost certain that the early Christians did use a collection or collections of Messianic testimonies of this sort, and, moreover, that this pattern continued and was used by the Apologists, culminating in the Testimony Books of Melito of Sardis and Cyprian. Stather Hunt suspected the existence of a pre-Christian collection of this nature, but was not able to point to it. The matter has now however been put beyond dispute, since the discovery of the Messianic collection of proof texts[30] in Cave Four at Qumran dating from perhaps 100 B.C. In one area of Judaism at any rate there were people who collected together Old Testament texts which they used to encourage themselves in their hopes of the coming deliverer.

This collection is of particular interest. It falls into two types.

There is, first and foremost, the simple list of Messianic texts—the prophet like Moses of Deuteronomy 18:18; the Star of Jacob of Numbers 24:15ff., and Jacob's blessing on Levi from Deuteronomy 33:8–11. There can be little doubt that the Qumran sectaries used these Scriptures to bolster up their own expectation of the eschatological age. Apparently they looked for the prophet like Moses[31] to herald in the Messianic Age: indeed, an Aramaic text from Cave Four indicates that he was seen as Elijah *redivivus,* fulfilling the prophecy of Malachi 4.5.[32] The Covenanters seem to have looked for two anointed ones in the Last Day, a Royal Messiah and a Priestly Messiah, alluded to in the "star" and the "Levi" proof texts respectively.[33] The former is, fascinatingly enough, called in *The Community Rule* the Messiah of Israel and the *Nasî,* the Prince—a title derived from Ezekiel's Davidic prince.[34] This should settle conclusively the meaning of Matthew 2:23: whilst there is no Old Testament text stating, "He shall be called a Nazarene," there are several, such as those just cited in Ezekiel, which indicate that the Davidic leader would be *nasî,* prince.[35] The Priestly Messiah would be more important than the Davidic Messiah, partly because the king always was subordinate to the High Priest, in theory at any rate,[36] and partly no doubt because the Covenanters had given up the hope of redemption for the majority of the people; accordingly the figure of a Davidic ruler was not as appropriate as a priestly figure who would usher in peace, brotherhood and righteousness for the covenant society.[37]

The second type of Messianic teaching to be found in the Scrolls is incorporated in the Commentaries. It is known as the *pesher* method, whereby the words of the prophecy are made a peg on which to hang contemporary events. J. M. Allegro has published[38] four documents from Cave Four which belong to this category. The first shows how they interpreted Genesis 49:10. "*There shall not cease a ruler from the tribe of Judah*; when there shall be dominion for Israel there will not be cut off a king in it belonging to (the line of) David. For *the ruler's staff* is the royal mandate; the families of Israel are the *feet. Until* the Messiah of Righteousness *shall come,* the shoot of David, for to him and to his seed has been given the royal mandate over his people for everlasting generations, which has awaited the Interpreter of the Law(?) with the men of the Community . . ." This was a passage which had great vogue in the Apologists; Justin used it no less than four times.[39] The second fragment is no less interesting from the Christian point of view. It is their citation of and comment on the Nathan prophecy of 2 Samuel 7:11f. "*And the Lord tells you that he will build a house for you, and I will set up your seed after you, and I will establish his royal throne for ever. I will be to him as a father and he will be to me as a son.* He is the Shoot of David, who will arise with the Interpreter of the Law, who . . . in Zion in the last days; as it is written, *And I shall raise up the tabernacle of David that is fallen.* That is the *tabernacle of David which is fallen* and afterwards he will arise to save Israel." This shows the men of Qumran not only using the same text which the Christians fastened on to,[40] but also applying it to a personal Messianic figure of their hopes. The fundamental difference of course was this: the Covenanters were still looking for their Messiah or Messiahs—whether they were expecting one, two or even three is much disputed[41]—whereas the Christians were quite sure that the Messiah had come. And so, whereas the Covenanters used these texts for their own consolation, the Christians used them constantly and confidently in confrontation with other Jews. The promises were not meant so much for consolation as for proclamation.

There is no doubt that the first Christians used both these methods of commending Jesus. They took over and adapted lists of Messianic texts[42] such as those found in Cave Four: indeed, there is even an example at Qumran of the composite citations which we find in the New Testament, for the saying about the Prophet like Moses has prefixed to it Deuteronomy 5:28f., without any dividing mark,[43] thus making the words apply not to Moses but to the coming Prophet. Furthermore, the Christians took over the *pesher* method of interpreting the Old Testament. St Matthew's Gospel is a good example of this,[44] but the same technique is employed in the Acts,[45] 1 Peter[46] and St John.[47] Midrashic exegesis, common in Judaism, was also taken over by the Christians; the basic concern was to interpret the text, to draw out the hidden meaning, and apply it to the contemporary scene. St Paul makes considerable use of this method of expounding the significance of Christ.[48] He even makes restrained use of the allegorical method, developed to such a bizarre degree in Philo.[49] The notable thing about the Christian exegesis of the Scriptures is that they began with the person of Jesus himself, who, they were convinced, was God's final Word to man, and sought in the Scriptures (the acknowledged oracles of God) ways of understanding his significance and relating it to the whole of redemptive history. They made little distinction between the different types of Jewish exegesis; they used them all, as occasion served, to point up the revelatory and redemptive function of their Master. They did not, for the most part, make arbitrary use of Old Testament citations that suited them; they could never have sustained an argument with well informed Jews if they had. They made use of and conflated accepted methods of exposition, whilst treating them from an entirely new perspective, that of fulfilment. "In their exegesis," writes Dr Longenecker, "there is the interplay of Jewish presuppositions on the one hand with Christian commitment and practices on the other; which joined to produce a distinctive interpretation of the Old Testament."[50] But whatever types of exegesis were used,[51] and not all of them were sound,[52] there can be no doubt at all that the Bible provided the main road into Judaism for the gospel. Indeed, without exaggeration one could say it was the only road.

THE MESSIAH IS JESUS

Variety in Expectation

Messianic expectation ran high in the first century. There were good reasons for this. The astonishing victories under the Maccabees had led to a resurgence of Jewish confidence and nationalism: the unbeliever had been defeated once—then why not again? If the House of Seleucus had been humbled by the revolt of Judas Maccabaeus, why should not the House of Augustus be cut down to size by the anointed king of God's choosing, when he came? In view of the Old Testament promises about the revival of the House of David and its eternal rule, in view of the affront to God afforded by impious Gentiles holding down the Holy Land, it was a reasonable enough hope, and it was very widely shared by the common man.[53]

What is more, this view gradually gained currency outside the Jewish world, no doubt as a result of the widespread dispersion of the Jews. Suetonius[54] and Tacitus[55] both record the rumours which were circulating in Roman society that the rulers of the world would arise from Judaea. Magical predictions said the same, and this made a great impression on credulous Romans.[56] Moreover, the Jews had seen the value attributed by pagan antiquity to the *Sibylline Oracles*, the prophetic statements of the Cumaean Sibyl,[57] and had cashed in on this type of literature for apologetic purposes. Needless to say, the Oracles began to prophesy the ascendency of the Jews! One Oracle proclaims: "When Rome shall rule over Egypt, which she still hesitates to do, then shall the great kingdom of the immortal King appear among men, and a holy prince [i.e. the Messiah] shall come who shall rule over the whole earth for all ages of the course of time. Then shall implacable wrath fall upon the men of Latium..."[58] Another speaks of a king from the East who would establish universal peace and bring prosperity to the Jewish people which would excite Gentile envy; they would gather against the Jews, and try to destroy both them and their Temple, but would themselves be destroyed by God. This would lead to a widespread flowing of the Gentiles to Zion in conversion.[59] These particular oracles date from the second or first century B.C. and they had wide currency. Similar expectations are to be found in the Pharisaic *Psalms of Solomon*, written about 50 B.C. A Davidic Messiah,[60] raised up by God, would overthrow the Gentile overlords, restore Israel's glory, gather the dispersion, reign from Jerusalem and bring the Gentiles under his sway as he acts as God's vice-regent on earth.

This was the hope most widely shared, no doubt: a political Messiah of David's stock, wielding the weapons primarily of spiritual power, but nevertheless ridding the holy soil of Israel from foreign domination, and ushering in the days of glory of which the prophets had spoken. With this conception the sceptre passage and the Nathan prophecy from Qumran would fit. But there were other views.

We have already noted the prevalence of the hope for two anointed leaders, continuing since the Return from Exile in the sixth century; it is to be found not only in the *Testaments of the Twelve Patriarchs*[61] and at Qumran, but also in Rabbinic literature.[62] Then there was the prophet like Moses, found both at Qumran[63] and among the Samaritans.[64]

The *Parables of Enoch* make great play with the concept of a Son of Man, called the elect one, the righteous one, God's fellow, the light of the Gentiles and so forth. Pre-existent, the Son of Man sits on the throne of God, possesses universal dominion and judges the wicked.[65] The problems of this part of *Enoch* are extremely complex, but there is reason to suppose that it represents one strand of Messianic speculation current in the time of Jesus, however corrupt its Ethiopic text and however real the possibility of its having suffered Christian interpolation. This probability is reinforced by the appearance of the Son of Man in *2 Esdras*.[66]

We find another type of interpretation in *2 Esdras* 7–28f., where the Messiah is seen as Son of God, though the exact meaning of the term is not clear: he is also very human—indeed he dies, and his death ushers in the last judgment. Yet another way of looking at the longed-for deliverance was through the medium not of warfare but of suffering. There are passages in the Scrolls which show that the Covenanters had not only a corporate understanding of the role of the Servant of Yahweh, which they reckoned to fulfil themselves;[67] but also a personal and Messianic interpretation as well. In addition to a disputed verse in the *Community Rule*,[68] the Isaiah Scroll from Cave One reads *mshhty* (anointed) for the M.T. *mshht* (marred) in Isaiah 52:14. The meaning would thus be, "As many were astonished at you: so I anointed his appearance above any man, and his form beyond that of human society", and it would seem likely that the sectaries had identified (in at least one strand of their complicated and unhomogeneous eschatological teaching) the Messiah with the Suffering Servant. In another strand of their writings, they saw themselves as the Suffering Servant of the Lord, the faithful Remnant whose afflictions were redemptive.[69]

Complexity in Fulfilment

With all these conflicting views of the coming Deliverer in circulation, it would be inevitable that when the Christians began to proclaim Jesus as Messiah to the Jews they would encounter not only immense and immediate interest but also intensive interrogation. What sort of a Messiah was he? The answers the Christians gave satisfied some Jews and not others; but at all events they showed that their Jesus did not fit precisely into any of the contemporary strait-jackets of Messianic prediction. He shared features in common with most of these speculations, but was bigger than any and all of them.

Was he Son of David? Yes indeed he was. Son of David, Seed of David, Stock of David, all of that.[70] Hence, of course, the importance of the genealogies in evangelism. But he was more than David's descendant, more than the inheritor of the promises of Amos about the tabernacle of David gaining possession of all nations. He was David's Lord, and that placed important limitations on the sense in which he was his "son".[71] It is the resurrection that vindicates this claim for Jesus. God raised him up: his soul did not stay in Hades, and his flesh did not taste corruption. What was this but David's prophecy about the Messiah long ago in Psalm 16? It could not be about himself that David spoke, because his tomb was still to be seen in the first century, and his flesh assuredly did taste corruption. It must be that he was speaking of the Messiah, and it is important to notice that David called him not "son" but "Lord".[72] It is as Lord that he has ascended into heaven, and now sits in the place of power. Such was Peter's argument on the Day of Pentecost, and it must often have been repeated in discussions about the parentage of Jesus.

Was he a political leader? This must have been one of the most difficult questions for Christians to answer. For on the face of it he had been such, and was a failure. How could he be the Messiah if he ended up on a Roman cross, as a discredited "king of the Jews"?[73] The answer seems to have been that he was indeed a political leader, but once again not quite what was expected. He came preaching the kingly rule of God; he exemplified it in his community of followers, which embraced Pharisees like Nicodemus, Herodians, ordinary patriots like James and John bar Zebedee, collaborationists like the tax collectors Matthew and Zacchaeus, and extreme Zealots like Simon the Zealot, and perhaps Judas Iscariot and Peter.[74] He welded this collection of political irreconcilables into a deep and united fellowship, as a foretaste of what he could do in reconciling political and social tensions anywhere. True he died on the cross; but had the Jew never heard of the birth pangs of the Messianic Age, the place of suffering in victory, the need even for the Servant of Yahweh to suffer before his vindication? To be sure, there is a sense in which Jesus's kingdom is not of this world; yet the day would come when he will restore the kingdom to Israel, when his apostles will rule over the new Israel, when the kingdoms of the world will become the kingdoms of Yahweh and of his Messiah.[75] This hope was not deferred to the indefinite future or spiritualized away in the early preaching to the Jews; even in the second century it was still an earthly kingdom and an earthly millenium that was held out to the faithful.[76] Jewish repentance, Jewish turning to Jesus as Messiah would hasten the advent of the longed for "times of refreshing from the presence of the Lord" when God would "send the Messiah appointed for you, Jesus, whom heaven must receive until the time for establishing all that God spoke through the mouth of his holy prophets of old".[77] Then Jesus would be a political leader all right.[78] And in the meantime, to demonstrate that he is indeed not a deceiver but is in the place of highest honour and power with God, waiting for the right moment in which to exercise his ascendancy over his enemies, there is the presence of his mighty Spirit in the Church, continuing in and through them the *dunameis*, the acts of power, done by Jesus in his lifetime. No, the cross does not mean that Jesus was weak; the very reverse.[79] It was the climax of the mighty acts of God in him; it was triumphantly vindicated as such by the resurrection—of which we are witnesses. This is how the early preachers handled the charge of political weakness arising from the execution of Jesus. There is no doubt that many Jews refused to be convinced that a condemned criminal could possibly be the one Israel was looking for. But there is good evidence that many did believe, and that the speedy growth of the Church in Jerusalem in the earliest days was not a little due to the fact that an imminent return of Christ in power to rule, to defeat the Romans, to consummate what he had inaugurated, was the ardent expectation and hope of the Jewish Christians. Nevertheless, although this political element was undoubtedly of greater significance in the early evangel than it has been given credit for, it must not be overstressed.[80] The Jewish Christians did not take part in the Great Rebellion of A.D.

66–70, when even the Qumran Covenanters were deceived into thinking the day of deliverance had dawned, and perished for their mistake. Nor did the Christians join in the Second Revolt of A.D. 133–135. No doubt they remembered the warnings of Jesus against following false Messiahs.[81] They refused to ally themselves with Bar Cochba whom Rabbi Akiba proclaimed as Messiah; they knew that if Jesus had not brought in the Kingdom, it did not lie in the power of the Son of a Star to do so.

Was Jesus a prophetic, or perhaps a priestly Messiah? Yes, he was both. Everyone recognized Jesus to be a prophet.[82] But even within his lifetime there was a section of the people who regarded him as *the* Prophet who would usher in the end-time.[83] There seems no evidence that Jesus thought of himself in this way, but after his resurrection we are told that the disciples made use of this category of Messianic expectation to draw attention to his significance. Twice in the early sermons in Acts he is described as the Prophet like Moses[84] and this Christology continued within Jewish Christianity, if we may judge from the *Gospel of the Hebrews*[85] and the *Preaching of Peter*.[86] But if this understanding of Jesus lingered on in Jewish Christianity, it also died with it. For good as it was in emphasizing the revelatory function and eschatological significance of Jesus, it made no room for his pre-existence, his parousia or his present enthronement at the right hand of God. All of these points are brought out in the proclaiming of Jesus as priest, which we find in Hebrews. Obviously, this would have a very limited appeal (only to Jews, and among them only to priests in any marked degree)[87] but in circles where there was expectation of a Levitical priest coming as an eschatological figure it would be a useful category in which to explain Jesus. To be sure he was not of the tribe of Levi; but that was a problem which could be circumvented. He was of an entirely different order, instanced by Melchisedek who was priest as well as king, and demonstrated his superiority over the Levitical priesthood by the twofold means of accepting tithes from Levi (in the loins of Abraham!) and blessing him . . . "and it is beyond dispute that the inferior is blessed by the superior".[88] Striding onto the scene in Genesis "without father or mother . . . he has neither beginning of days nor end of life, but resembling the Son of God he continues a priest for ever". That is the priesthood to which Christ belongs;[89] and if the readers, perhaps themselves Levitical priests, felt disposed to dismiss Melchisedek as an early anomaly they find themselves impaled on Psalm 110:4.[90] This psalm, recognized as Messianic, looks to the Messiah as priest for ever, after the order of Melchisedek. And the Messianic priest, Jesus, has many advantages which the writer to the

Hebrews outlines in full, advantages which no human priest can match. He is sinless, he lives for ever, and he has once and for all made the lasting sacrifice for sins, when he took responsibility for them in person on Calvary.[91] Moreover, this priest, unlike any such figure expected in the *Testaments of the Twelve Patriarchs* has no merely earthly function. He has this, and it is stressed particularly in chapters 9 and 10 of the Epistle. But he has also a present role, to intercede for men by his presence at the right hand of God to which he has been exalted; and he has a future role, too, when he comes in judgment at the parousia.[92]

But what of the Son of Man, a Jew might ask: does your Jesus fill this role? Once again the answer is a modified "Yes". Despite learned assertions to the contrary,[93] it seems to me to be beyond all reasonable doubt that Jesus did think of himself as Son of Man;[94] that the ambivalence of the Aramaic *barnasha* which could be either a self-designation or a reference to the Danielic Son of Man was a deliberate gesture on Jesus's part, in line with the ambivalence of his total person. The evangelists make it clear that only Jesus spoke of himself in this way;[95] this was not their Christology—they thought of him as "Lord" or "Christ". But the very fact that they retained this title for Jesus in their gospels suggests that there were areas where this was a particularly attractive understanding of the person and work of Jesus. Lohmeyer has conjectured that Galilee was in all probability such a place:[96] there were, he believed, circles here steeped in Daniel, the *Parables of Enoch*, and the *Apocalypse of Ezra*, the three places in non-Christian literature where the Son of Man is given messianic significance; they would readily understand when Jesus spoke of the eschatological Son of Man who was to come in the clouds of heaven. That was merely a reiteration of their own understanding of the Son of Man. But when Jesus spoke of *himself* as the Son of Man incarnate, the Son of Man embodied in a humble carpenter rather than a heavenly judge—this was news to them. There is nothing about an incarnation of the Son of Man in pre-Christian thought. There was another staggering way in which Jesus modified all previous understanding of the glorious figure of the Son of Man who would come to judge the world. He taught that the Son of Man must suffer, and rise again from the dead; in short, he must fulfil the role of the Suffering Servant, and give his life as a ransom for the many.[97] This was an unheard of thing in Judaism. It may indeed be true, as Jeremias has argued,[98] that in some respects the characteristics of the Servant had been applied in random verses to the Son of Man in Judaism, but never had he been identified with him. The Son of Man represented the highest conception of glorification; the Servant represented the nadir of degradation. It was the genius of Jesus that joined these two conceptions together. He showed by his teaching and his passion the royalty of service, the grandeur of vicarious suffering.

There is evidence to suggest that the Son of Man Christology did not simply die in Christendom. It continued in the understanding of Jesus as the Man, the archetypal man. Such a conception appealed both to intellectual Jews like Philo[99] and also to Hellenistic circles where speculation about the Primal Man[100] was rife. This had the added attractiveness of emphasizing the pre-existence of the Messiah; he was identified with the Adam of Genesis 1:27, the Heavenly Man, ideal as God meant him to be, in contrast to the fallen, earthly, empirical man of Genesis 2:7, in whose humanity we all share. Paul makes use of this terminology,[101] so does John,[102] so does the Epistle to the Hebrews.[103] Interestingly enough, it survived in the pseudo-Clementine *Preaching of Peter*, a second century Jewish-Christian work with Gnostic tendencies. Here the true prophet is identified with Adam, so we have a link with the understanding of Jesus as the Prophet which was also popular in Jewish-Christian circles. It was a valuable tool for explaining Jesus's significance to a wide variety of listeners, particularly those who had come into touch with the speculations of educated, Hellenistic Judaism. The themes of pre-existence, final judgment, and vicarious suffering were united in a single person, Jesus himself. And he was the content of their proclamation.

If there were those[104] who were accustomed to think of the coming deliverer in terms of the Suffering Servant, here again the Christians could make a most imposing case. Their Deliverer fitted to a detail the picture of the Servant of Isaiah, as the Qumran Community did not. Here was one who was utterly sinless, unlike the "house of holiness for Israel, a company of holy of holies for Aaron"[105] which the Covenanters claimed to be. Here was one who could "atone for the land and requite the wicked with their reward" in a way no mere martyr community could;[106] in reality their deaths could no more atone for sins than could the Aaronic sacrifices.[107] Both might be said to remove ceremonial defilement, but could not touch the case of the man who "sinned with a high hand". Deliberate flouting of God had no forgiveness in Jewish thought. But the voluntary death of Jesus was different; it was nothing less than the self-giving of God's Son, and its efficacy was lasting and effective. Philip the evangelist was sure that it was of Jesus that the prophet Isaiah had spoken.[108] It was he alone who fulfilled Isaiah 53: who was so spotless that "he committed no sin, no guile was found on his lips", so patient (in contrast to the warlike musings of the men of Qumran) that "when he was reviled, he did not revile again". Martyred, like some of the Covenanters and the Maccabees, "when he suffered he did not threaten, but trusted to him who judges justly"; moreover he was utterly different in this respect, that "he himself bore our sins in his body on the tree . . . by his wounds you have been healed".

The Death of Jesus

It was with Scriptures like these that Christians argued that the Messiah had to suffer. And many a fair-minded Jew would have granted their point. Thus Trypho, after having had a good dose of such Scripture teaching from Justin, concedes, "It is quite clear that the Scriptures announce that Christ had to suffer . . . We know that he should suffer and be led as a sheep."[110] So much is agreed. But the point of division comes at the manner of Jesus's death, the crucifixion. Trypho was speaking for all Jews when he voiced this objection, "But prove to us whether he must be crucified and die so disgracefully and so dishonourably the death accursed in the Law. For we cannot bring ourselves even to consider this."[111] Two points in particular stuck in their throats.

First, such a death was a stumbling-block because it indicated weakness in the supposed Messiah. We have already seen something of how the Christians handled this charge.[112] So far from being an act of weakness the cross was the supreme act of power in Jesus's life. There he met and defeated the forces of evil: he reigned from the tree as Justin loved to say,[113] and many of the Fathers after him —and though they may have been mistaken in thinking this was the true text of Psalm 96, they were quite right in seeing this as one of the main themes in St John's account of the passion. The cross is the power of God for Paul, too;[114] there Jesus "disarmed the principalities and powers and made a public example of them, triumphing over them in it".[115] But the crowning demonstration that the cross was victory not defeat was provided by the resurrection. That is the whole thrust of the testimony in the early speeches of Acts. "You crucified and killed him by the hands of lawless men. But God raised him up, having loosed the pangs of death because it was not possible for him to be held by it." "He was not abandoned to Hades . . . This Jesus God raised up, and of that we are all witnesses."[116] Such was the apostolic testimony as they rebutted the charge that the cross spelt defeat. God had vindicated his suffering Servant by exalting him to the highest place in the universe in recognition of his faithfulness unto death, even death on a cross; in consequence he has every right to the title of Kyrios, Lord.[117] He fulfils the prophecy of Psalm 110:1, and sits in power on the right hand of God. Justin stresses the power of the cross by a quaint piece of allegorical exegesis of the battle with Amalek when Joshua led the fight and Moses held up his hands outstretched in prayer.[118] He was quick to note the cruciform shape Moses adopted with his arms outstretched. "If he gave up any part of this sign, which was an imitation of the cross, the people were beaten; but if he remained in this form, Amalek was proportionately defeated, and he who prevailed prevailed by the cross. For it was not because Moses so prayed that the people were made stronger, but because, while one who bore the name of Jesus (Joshua) was in the forefront of the battle, he himself made the sign of the cross."[119] Fanciful writing, but it appealed to Jews, many of whom, like Philo, regarded the allegorical meaning the most profound sense of understanding Scripture. And beneath the quaint argument the conviction of the *Christus Victor* theme shines through, as it does in another demonstration of the power of the cross, the brazen serpent on the pole.[120] No, crucifixion does not mean that Jesus was weak and a failure.

The other objection of the Jews to the thought that the Messiah could have died upon a cross lay in the Old Testament assertion that a man whose body was exposed upon a tree lay under the curse of God.[121] How could Messiah be accursed? This was a problem which faced the Christians from the very outset, and it seems that from the outset they began to grope their way to the answer. Both Peter and Paul are represented as preaching that the Jesus who died in the place of cursing on the tree was somehow Saviour.[122] Through his death there, the rescue from sin which the Old Testament longed for had been accomplished. It is not worked out yet in a coherent theology; but they sense that in some way the cross dealt with sin, and that the resurrection of Jesus, which the Jews themselves could not gainsay, showed that the curse had been exhausted. Later they came to understand more fully how this could be. Peter explains[123] that Christ bore *our sins* to that place of the curse, in fulfilment of Isaiah 53. Paul explains that Jesus was indeed suffering in the accursed place, but that the curse he bore belonged rightly to us; for we had broken the law of God and so merited his judicial wrath: "Cursed be everyone who does not abide by all things written in the book of the Law, and do them." That is the situation which led Jesus to the cross for us. "Christ redeemed us from the curse of the law, having become a curse for us—for it is written, 'Cursed be everyone who hangs on a tree'."[124] This must have remained the standard way of[125] meeting the Jewish objection that his death on the cross showed Jesus rested under God's curse. We find it being used in almost Paul's own words by Justin. "For the whole human race will be found to be under a curse. For it is written in the Law of Moses, 'Cursed is everyone that continueth not in all things that are written in the book of the Law to do them.' And nobody has accurately done all—you will not venture to deny this—but some more and some less than others have observed the ordinances enjoined . . . If then, the Father of all wishes his Christ for the whole human family to take upon him the curses of all, knowing that after he had been crucified and was dead, He would raise him up, why do you argue about him, who submitted to suffer these things according to the Father's will, as if he were accursed, and do not rather bewail yourselves?"[126]

The Birth of Jesus

This, then, was the standard way of dealing with the problem which the death of Jesus afforded to Jewish hearers of the Christian gospel. But no less formidable was the issue which surrounded his person and his birth. It is well stated by the Jew Trypho:[127] "Answer me then first, how you can show that there is another God beside the Maker of all things; and then you will show further that he submitted to be born of the Virgin." The deity of Jesus was anathema to the Jews, as it still is;[128] and the thought that God had submitted to be born of a virgin was a blasphemy modelled upon pagan myths about the amours of Zeus with mortal women. This is not the place to give a detailed study[129] of the way Justin seeks to convince Trypho on the matter of the virgin birth, largely by insisting on the "virgin" in Isaiah 7:14 despite Trypho's justifiable complaint that it is a mistranslation of the Hebrew *'almah* which means merely young woman. It is unquestionable that the virgin birth was part of the common creed of Christendom by the time Justin wrote. But it may well not have been in the earlier period. The virgin birth did not figure in the early preaching in Acts: indeed, a Christology verging on adoptionism appears there.[130] There is no evidence that it formed part of the gospel preaching in any part of early Christendom. It is not mentioned in the writings of John, Mark or Paul.[131] It was undoubtedly believed in some areas of Jewish as well as Gentile Christianity: in addition to the birth stories in both Matthew and Luke, Matthew's formula quotation of Isaiah 7:14 may well indicate that the text was used in apologetics before his time. All this does not mean, of course, that Jesus was not born of a virgin; the Jewish evidence, such as it is, supports Matthew and Luke's assertion that Jesus's birth was not like that of other men.[132] But it does mean that the virgin birth was not in the earliest days that crucial item of the creed which later it became. Far more fundamental to the Jew's objection was the Christian belief that Jesus shared the nature of God.

Nowhere in the New Testament is Jesus unambiguously declared to be God. Certain passages, like John 1:1, Colossians 2:9, Hebrews 1:1ff. certainly go near to identifying him with God, but always the Christians are careful to remember the humanity of Jesus and the subordination which that brings with it. However, the earliest and most widespread Christological confession seems to have been "Jesus is Lord";[133] it is anchored firmly in the earliest days of the Aramaic speaking Palestinian Church not merely by the sermons in Acts,[134] which might be disputed, but by the cry *Maranatha* (O our Lord, Come!) used in solemn invocation at the Eucharist,[135] which cannot be denied. Here were Christian Jews applying to a crucified Rabbi the word "Lord" which had been used in the Old Testament as the most frequent title for Yahweh's ineffable name. They justified it by Psalm 110:1, where, in a psalm admitted to be messianic, God calls the Messiah "Lord". They vindicated this claim by pointing to the resurrection: proof positive that Jesus had ascended to the place of power with God designated by the psalm.

But even this confession gave room for the strict Jew to guard the monotheism of his faith, which later Christological definition made more difficult. There was a variety of senses in which one could take *Mar, Lord*—anything from a polite "sir" to the majestic Lord of the Universe.[136] The same applied to "Son of God". This was the burden of the voice at the baptism, we are told—Jesus is the "Son" of Psalm 2:7.[137] This was the burden of Jesus's claim in the story of the wicked husbandmen; "last of all he sent his Son".[138] This was his admission before the High Priest, that he was the glorious Son of Man and the Son of the Blessed.[139] There is nothing improbable in Jesus having made such an admission, as Otto Betz has recently shown.[140] The famous Nathan prophecy envisaged the coming Davidic ruler as "Son" of God: "I will be his Father and he shall be My Son." Blasphemy, the High Priest chose to construe it: the blasphemy lay in a humble carpenter claiming to be the eschatological "Son" both of God and of David, who was about to usher in the everlasting kingdom of 2 Samuel 7:13. But for the Jew who believed that Jesus had done just this, the Jewish Christian in fact, here was a category of Christological understanding which did nothing to disturb his monotheism. Jesus was not "Son" by physical generation, on this view; physically he was Son of David. But he was designated "Son of God" in the sense of author of the eternal

kingdom and occupant of David's throne for ever, by the resurrection.[141] This was very different from calling Jesus "Son of God"
in an ontological sense, a way of interpreting him which always
tended to remain a stumbling-block to the Jew. It might be got over
by identifying Jesus with the pre-cosmic Wisdom or Logos thought
of, since the days of the Wisdom literature, as being God's fellow
and agent in creation; that is the approach both of John's Prologue
and the beginning of Hebrews, and it would make sense to the
educated Jew without any suggestion of ditheism. But the way in
which the Jewish Christian really liked to think of Jesus was the one
in whom the Divine Spirit rested in his fulness, thus fulfilling the
Messianic prophecy of Isaiah 11:1ff. Thus the *Gospel of the Hebrews*
reads, "The whole fount of the Holy Spirit shall descend on him"
and again, "It came to pass that when the Lord was come up out of
the water, the whole fount of the Holy Spirit descended upon him
and rested on him, and He said to him, 'My Son . . . thou art my
rest; thou art my first-begotten Son that reignest for ever'."[142] Again,
the *Gospel of the Ebionites*, written early in the second century,
represented Jesus as "a certain man named Jesus of about thirty
years of age" who was baptized by John, "And as he came up from
the water, the heavens were opened and he saw the Holy Spirit in
the form of a dove that descended and entered into him. And a voice
sounded from heaven that said: Thou art my beloved Son, in thee I
am well pleased."[143] Now this gospel represents a docetic tendency
which soon crept into Jewish Christianity; the advent of the Spirit
here described is not adoption or inspiration but the union of a
heavenly being with the man Jesus, thus producing the Christ, the
Son of God.[144] But the perfectly orthodox Jewish Christian Christology from which it sprang is evident enough. Jesus is the one on
whom the Spirit rested, the one thus marked out as God's Son:[145]
the one whom God uniquely sent, the one who uniquely passes on
God's message, because to him alone God did not vouchsafe his
Spirit in any limited way.[146] This is a Christology which Trypho
would have found it much easier to accept, and one which it is not
too easy to reconcile with Jesus's pre-existence. "Some of your
discourse," says Trypho, "seems to be paradoxical, and wholly
incapable of proof. For when you say that this Christ existed as God
before the ages, then that he submitted to be born and become man,
yet that he is not man of man, this appears to me to be not merely
paradoxical but also foolish."[147] Justin has the grace to admit that it
does look paradoxical, before he sets out to put the Jew right! Had he
been arguing eighty years earlier, he might not have striven so hard
to force Trypho to confess Christ in categories which were obviously

not helpful to him because of the associations that they bore. It is salutary to remember that nowhere in the Acts speeches is Jesus declared to be God, or even Son of God. The approach was more flexible in those days, though the convictions underlying the assertions were much the same: Jesus in the early Acts speeches does things which are attributed to God in the Old Testament. With this more flexible approach to Christology went a success among Jewish listeners which was never to be repeated after the hardening events of the two Revolts and the publication of the Thirteenth Benediction.[148] Insistence on the single-track orthodoxy of incipient Catholicism produced the inevitable Jewish reaction. The Christians were dismissed as impious blasphemers who wanted to assert two Gods, and the supreme calumny of God having union with a woman.

THE LAW IS MODIFIED

The two great divisions between Christians and Jews were whether or not the Messiah had come, and whether or not the Law had to be kept. The first we have considered in some detail, as it was the crucial issue; but the second must be briefly examined even in a study of evangelism among the Jews like this, because the problem of the Law raised an enormous barrier to evangelism.

Israel's Status is Claimed

The Jew would have four main grievances under this head. In the first place, his status as Israel had been appropriated by the Christians.[149] This followed naturally from their convictions about Jesus as Messiah. If he was Messiah, his followers must be the true Israel. It was as simple as that. The Messiah was inconceivable apart from his flock. Jesus fulfilled the prophecies of the Old Testament, and his people were therefore heirs to all its promises. This meant that those Jews who did not put their faith in Jesus were renegades from the true Israel; they might be Jews outwardly, but were not so at heart.[150] There had always been a line of disbelief and apostasy within Israel;[151] often it had been the preponderant part of the nation. So the initial smallness of the Christian community did nothing to deter them from laying claim to be the "Israel of God".[152] They energetically called on the House of Israel to repent of their attitude of hostility to Jesus which had culminated in his execution, and turn back to acknowledge him as Messiah.[153] They did not see themselves as innovators: their doctrine of resurrection was good Pharisaic orthodoxy—it could be found in the Psalms as well. Their doctrine of the Messiah was clearly set out in the Scriptures for all who had eyes to see. Why, then, did the Jewish nation hold back? If they persisted in disbelief and apostasy, God would judge them as he had their disobedient forefathers of old. This is stressed particularly strongly in the Epistle to the Hebrews and the speech of Stephen. He would, as Paul put it, cut out the dead wood from the Olive of Israel, and graft other (Gentile) branches in.[154] Indeed, the refusal of Israel to acknowledge their Messiah was a mark, surely, of divine displeasure and judgment on them; it was evidence of a judicial blindness, such as Isaiah had spoken of long ago. From very early times Isaiah 6:9, 10 was used as a *testimonium* to explain the situation which arose when Jews rejected the gospel. It is found quoted (independently, it would seem) in Matthew, Mark, John, Acts, Paul and Justin.[155] It is probably not true to say that in New Testament days Christians claimed to *be* Israel, as they certainly were claiming by Justin's day;[156] Israel remains the Jewish people, but it is seen as the Jewish people who put their faith in their Messiah—a people in whose lot the believing Gentiles share,[157] and from whose company and title the unbelieving Jews are debarred.[158] As early in the Acts as 2:40, the "crooked generation" of Deuteronomy 32:5 is applied by Peter to that part of Israel which does not acknowledge the Messiah. Here was the beginning of a process which led inevitably to the Church claiming the complete and exclusive right to the place of Israel, thus disinheriting the Jews. The process is in full swing by the time of the Apocalypse, with its references to "those that say they are Jews but are not" and to "the synagogue of Satan";[159] Justin argues from the prophets that God rejects his own people and accepts the Gentiles in their place; and by the time of Tertullian at the end of the second century it was a commonplace that all Israel's privileges had been transferred to the Church, it was her history that had been described in the Old Testament, it was Christ who had appeared to Moses in the burning bush, and so forth.[160] "Ainsi," concludes M. Simon, "Église et Israel sont synonymes, christianisme et judaisme authentique se confondent . . . L'Ancienne Alliance et la Nouvelle sont, dans leur fond, identiques."[161] Though this Christian reading of Old Testament history was most unfair in the way which became traditional from the end of the first century onwards, nevertheless given charity and temperate expression there was an obvious logic and appeal in it, once granted the premise that the Messiah was Jesus.

Israel's Scriptures are Stolen

A second grievance the Jew felt was closely associated with this: the Christians had stolen his Scriptures. The Septuagint was the

Bible of the early Church. It was here that the oracles of God were contained. If God had revealed any truth, it must be contained in the sacred books. This was axiomatic to Christians, along with the rest of Israel. Very well: they were convinced that Jesus represented God's final and full act of self disclosure. And so it followed that the story of Jesus must all be contained, in prediction, type, or some other form, in the Old Testament, which was accordingly ransacked for anything that might conceivably shed light on this climax of Divine revelation, Jesus the Messiah. So detailed is this procedure that one could almost write a life of Christ from the Old Testament quotations contained in Justin's *Dialogue*! Thus in Isaiah 65:2, "I spread out my hands to a rebellious people," Christ is the speaker, referring of course to his crucifixion. Psalm 3:5 alludes to his death and resurrection, with the words, "I lay down and slept and rose again, because the Lord sustained me."[162] And so it goes on for page after page. The Christian is utterly convinced that the Old Testament is "our book", and he uses even its silences to advantage. This process is of course at work in every stratum of the New Testament. Passages which in the Old Testament refer to Yahweh are unashamedly applied to Jesus in the New.[163] We have sufficiently noticed this pattern of fulfilment in the previous chapter. It must have led many Jews to faith. But what of those who did not believe, but were highly indignant at this handling of their sacred books? Their burning fury comes through even in this Christian reflection of it in Irenaeus, "Had the Jews been cognizant of our future existence, and that we should use these proofs from the Scriptures, they would themselves never have hesitated to burn their own Scriptures, which declare that all other nations will inherit eternal life, but that they who boast themselves as being the house of Jacob are disinherited from the grace of God."[164] They were driven to abandon the LXX to the Christians, and produce a fresh translation altogether under Aquila, about A.D. 130.[165] Especially after the fall of Jerusalem, when their Law was the one consolation left to the poor Jews, it was insufferably galling that the Christians should rob them of that. Some Christians, like Justin, would argue that the Jews had forfeited their right to them by failing to understand them; "your Scriptures, or rather, not yours but ours, for you, though you read them, do not catch the spirit of them."[166] Others like Barnabas, more harshly assert that the Scriptures had never belonged to the Jews at all; they were meant from the outset to be taken spiritually, that is to say, allegorically, and the Jews in taking them literally were both deluded and disobedient: thus "an evil angel deluded them" and "the things which stand thus [i.e. the red heifer being a type of

Christ!] are clear to us, but obscure to them, because they did not hearken to the voice of the Lord."[168] A few took a more lenient view of the Jewish right to their Scriptures, like Aristides;[169] they were prepared to share the inheritance of the Old Testament Israel with the Jews, but these seem to have become increasingly a minority. One can only conclude with Harnack that "such an injustice as that done by the Gentile Church to Judaism is almost unprecedented in the annals of history. The Gentile Church stripped it of everything; she took away its sacred book; herself but a transformation of Judaism, she cut off all connection with the parent religion. The daughter first robbed her mother, and then repudiated her!"[170]

Israel's Law is Broken

This leads us to the third complaint a Jew had against the Christians. They broke his Law—or rather, God's Law. Jesus had done it, in the first instance: he had taken staggering liberties with the Sabbath day; he had set himself up to modify the Torah; he had not been too careful about avoiding ceremonial defilement or relations with Gentile "dogs" and, of course, he had died a death accursed by the Law. Worse still, his followers had repudiated the duly constituted priesthood of Israel, set up rival synagogues, read other contemporary books alongside the Law and the Prophets, enjoyed table-fellowship with Gentiles, and maintained that even so sacred a pledge of Israel as circumcision availed nothing with God. No wonder Trypho begins his discussion with Justin by arraigning the Christians for their breach of the Law.[171]

The Christian attitude to the Jewish Law was varied. But all seem to have agreed that the goal of the Law was Christ. The Law was not against the promises of God,[172] but the "schoolmaster" designed to lead the sensitive pupil to Jesus.[173] This stands out as clearly in a Jewish Gospel like Matthew, or a writing addressed to Jewish Christians like Hebrews, as it does in Paul. But here the agreement ended. Some Christians, like the Judaizers against whom Paul fulminates,[174] argued that the Gentile adherents to Christ ought to conform to the whole Torah; others, that they should at least get themselves circumcised.[175] Pressure in this direction may well have come from a Gentile direction itself, surprising as it may seem. A good case can be made out for supposing that the people who were so keen to get themselves circumcised (*hoi peritemnomenoi*) in Galatia were in fact Gentiles.[176] They saw that the promises were made to the physical Israel; it would be prudent to join them. This would, of course, bring political advantages as well, since the Jews were a recognized religion, while the status of Christianity was at first uncertain and later on decidedly precarious. Though this issue was largely settled, in principle at any rate, by the Council at Jerusalem in A.D. 48, we can imagine that the Judaizers were not satisfied,[177] and Ignatius half a century later can say, "It is better to learn Christianity from a circumcised man [i.e. a Jewish Christian] than Judaism from a Gentile."[178]

A second attitude to the Law was represented by the Jewish Christians. Even allowing for the heterodox element that came into "Ebionism", as it was called, it seems fairly clear that the characteristic attitude of Jewish Christianity both before and after the Great Revolt was to keep the Law themselves, as the earliest Christians had done (at least to the extent of not mixing with Gentiles and being assiduous in temple and synagogue worship), to value circumcision, fasting, sabbaths and so on as valuable ordinances for themselves, the true Israel, but not incumbent upon the Gentile adherents of Christianity any more than circumcision and full keeping of the law was required among the fringe of Godfearers which gathered in every synagogue. James of Jerusalem was a Christian of this sort, and maintained close relations with and earned enormous respect among non-Christian Jews of the capital. The Epistle of James, whether or not it is rightly attributed to the brother of the Lord, is just the kind of document he might have conceived, with little ostensible Christian content but a tremendous amount beneath the surface.

Paul's attitude towards the Law is notoriously difficult to interpret. It is, on the one hand, holy and right and good;[179] it embodies the instruction of the Lord. On the other hand it provides an entry for sin; indeed it even incites sin: "I should not have known what it is to covet if the law had not said, 'You shall not covet'. But sin, finding opportunity in the commandment, wrought in me all manner of covetousness'."[180] As a guide to an understanding of God's will it is splendid; as a means of reunion with God, the God we have sinned against, it is a hopeless failure. And it was never intended to be anything else![181] Paul stresses the historical priority of the promises of God over the giving of the Law; the Law cannot invalidate the promises made 400 years earlier.[182] It is by claiming the promise, not by law keeping, that a Gentile gets incorporated in Abraham, the father of believers;[183] it is precisely the same way that a Jew gets in touch with God.[184] Law keeping cannot put any man in the right with his maker, for two good reasons. The first is that nobody can possibly keep it, for a day, let alone all his life; and no "works of supererogation" tomorrow can make up for my failures of today.[185] But even if they could, this whole approach to a personal, moral God, would be insufferable.[186] God looks for loving trust in his creatures, not a cold, legalistic totting up of merits in the heavenly ledger. Thus it is against the Law as a means of reconciliation with God that Paul contends so strongly. He has no quarrel with Jewish Christians continuing to practise its obligations literally; on occasion he does so himself;[187] but he is not bound by them.[188] They are prudential not categorical enactments as far as he is concerned. For he is dead to the world of Law, Sin, Death;[189] he is in a new world, where God's will is embodied in the person of Jesus, a new and interior covenant, a personal relationship with God, which no legal written prescriptions exterior to him could possibly replace.[190] Not, of course, that he thought he was free to please himself;[191] merely that he saw Christ as the goal of the Law for believers in both moral and intellectual realms;[192] liberated from the system, and the curse imposed by failure to live up to it, through the death of Christ, he was now free to fulfil the Law of Christ, and love his neighbour as himself.[103] Peter's attitude, if we may credit the Acts, was not far different, though his emphasis lay in giving a more positive evaluation of the Law than Paul had done. He spoke with feeling at the Jerusalem Council on the side of Gentile freedom from the Law, a yoke, he declared, which "neither our fathers nor we have been able to bear".[194] He too sees the interior Law of the Holy Spirit, in Gentiles as in Jews, as the fulfilment of what the Old Testament law had stood for; he too stresses *agapē* as the practical working out of the Law.[195] Nevertheless the second century Jewish Christians claimed him, together with James, as their champion so it is probable that he was less free in exercising the privileges of Christian freedom from the Law than Paul was.

But the Church was becoming increasingly Gentile, and increasingly antipathetic to Judaism and its Law and cultus. Barnabas, as we have seen, used the Jewish exegetical method of allegorizing as ruthlessly as Philo. The result was that he transferred the Law entirely into the Christian camp, and maintained that the Jews had no right to it because though it was given to them, they were not worthy to receive it on account of their sins. "Learn now how *we* have received it,"[196] he continues; and proceeds to expound Jesus as the new Law, the new covenant given to a people of his own possession. It was easy enough to turn the Jewish complaint that Christians did not keep the Law, against themselves. One had only to refer to the golden calf, or the murmuring in the wilderness, to be able to claim that the Jews had certainly not kept the Law. A great deal of this sterile argument went on, if we may judge from the reappearance of these themes in the pages of Hippolytus, Eusebius, and Gregory the Great.

Justin's attitude was somewhat similar. He maintained that the ceremonial law was an educational measure on God's part to counteract the stubborness of a people ever apt to apostatize; that it was meant to mark the Jewish people out for a particular divine judgment, and that Jewish worship according to the ceremonial law was both odd and depraved.[197] Most of the seed thoughts for these varying positions can in fact be found in the New Testament itself, but there is one significant difference. Within the first century there is still the hope of winning Israel; though violent at times, the Christian approach was inflamed by love for them and longing to see them acknowledging their Messiah. By the successive turning points of the Great Revolt, the Thirteenth Benediction, and the Bar Cochba Rising, this attitude had changed to one of hatred and antipathy. It was no longer evangelism among the Jews but apologetic against the Jews which interested Christians.

Israel's Cultus is Spiritualized

There was one further exasperation for the Jew. Christians spiritualized his sacred rites.[198] It was a fair complaint. Sabbath, circumcision, sacrifice, priests, temple, all were dispensed with by the early Christians, or at the most regarded as optional extras, of increasingly doubtful orthodoxy. By the time of Jerome it was plain that those who wanted to be both Jews and Christians are in fact neither Jews nor Christians. The seeds of this sad division lay once again in the heart of the New Testament itself, and indeed, in the teaching and practice of Jesus. He lived and died a Jew, and attended temple and synagogue; but he taught that he himself was the New Temple, promised by God long ago to David.[199] While we do not know that he sacrificed, at least he must have been present at them and he did cleanse the temple courts; but he claimed that he would make atonement in person for the sins of the world.[200] Whilst he sent a leper to show himself to the priests in token of his healing,[201] he nevertheless sat very light to the rituals for purity which the Pharisees set such store by, and even hinted at the supersession of the ceremonial law by asserting that what really defiled a man came from within him.[202] Mark's gloss "thus he declared all foods clean" may not have been evident at the time but would inevitably suggest itself after the resurrection when the total significance of Jesus became subject for reflection.

The seeds, then, of this ambivalent attitude to the externals of religion are present in Jesus himself, and according to Acts, they were speedily perceived and applied by the first martyr. Stephen was accused of blaspheming Moses and God, of speaking against the temple and the law, of changing the customs delivered to the Jews by Moses.[203] No doubt these accusations had substance. Stephen's line of argument was the fountainhead of a whole body of apologetic by the Christians which has been well investigated by Professor Moule.[204] Words like "spiritual", "not made with hands" "acceptable to God" were in constant use among Christians. No doubt this was partly in order to parry the jibe of the Jews that "You Christians have no priests, no sacrifices, no altar, no temple, no circumcision". To this the answer would run, "Indeed we have. We have a temple not made with hands, the temple of Christ's body in which we are incorporate. We have a great high priest who has gone into heaven itself there to appear on our behalf and indeed as our forerunner. We have an altar (the cross ?) of which you cannot partake, for you still worship the shadow, not the reality. Your sacrifices are ineffective: they can never bring the worshippers to God. But we are brought near through the eternal sacrifice of the Son of God, and we now offer, as the redeemed, sacrifices of praise thanksgiving, our money and ourselves which are acceptable to God in a way yours can never be, for they spring from a wrong relationship with him. As for circumcision, we have a circumcision made without hands, fulfilling that inner circumcision of the heart praised by the prophets. We have been baptized into the circumcision of Christ, the total putting away of sin which he achieved on the cross; from now on physical circumcision is a secondary matter."

This is how the matter of external ordinances is dealt with in the New Testament, in Paul, Hebrews, Luke and Mark in particular. As for the keeping of the sabbath, we hear little of it, except as a thing deemed essential to the faith by the Jewish-Gnostic heretics at Colossae, and therefore rebutted vigorously by St Paul. In less polemical circumstances, when writing to the Romans, he urges conscientiousness and tolerance in what is after all an *adiapheron*: "One man esteems one day as better than another, while another man esteems all days alike. Let every one be fully convinced in his own mind. He who observes the day, observes it in honour of the Lord . . . he who abstains, abstains in honour of the Lord."[205]

Such an attitude is both moderate and understandable, however hard it must have been for the Jews to stomach. If you believed that fulfilment had come with Christ, it was not unreasonable to regard the Law in its ceremonial regulations a *praeparatio evangelica* which had served its purpose. You might even argue, with the writer to the Hebrews, that what is old is obsolete and ready to vanish away.[206]

But after the disastrous Jewish War and the destruction of the Temple, a tougher attitude prevailed. Most Christians saw the violent cessation of the sacrificial system and disruption of the priesthood in the ruins of the temple as proof positive that God had got no further use for it. This would have been the clinching point of the Epistle to the Hebrews had it been written a few years after rather than a few years before A.D. 70.[207] It is a point which Justin ruthlessly brings home. "Circumcision was given you as a sign that you may be separated off from other nations, and that you alone may suffer that which you now justly suffer, and that your land may be desolate, and your cities burnt with fire."[208] This was a savage way to treat a brave and unfortunate people. Even more shameful is the attitude of the otherwise attractive *Epistle to Diognetus* which mocks the whole Jewish system; sacrifices are "acts of folly rather than divine worship"; their scruples concerning "sabbaths, meats, their boastings about circumcision and their fancies about fasting and the new moons" are dismissed as "utterly ridiculous and unworthy of notice".[209] Ignatius sourly dismisses both Judaism and Jewish Christianity as follows: "both of them, unless they speak of Jesus Christ, are tombstones and dead men's tombs so far as I am concerned, on which only the names of men are inscribed."[210] Barnabas is in his most sparkling form when discussing circumcision. "Abraham, who first enjoined circumcision, looking forward in spirit to Jesus, practised that rite, having received the mystery of the three letters." These, it turns out to be, are his 318 servants, for the Greek numerals for 318, IHT, denote Jesus (IH are the first two letters of his name in Greek, and the T indicates his cross)![211] But Barnabas will have nothing of the more moderate attitude adopted by some of his Christian contemporaries, who are prepared to share the covenant with the Jews, saying, "the covenant is both theirs and ours";[212] he will not allow that circumcision is a special seal on the covenant for the Jew, maintaining that "every Syrian and Arab is circumcised, and all the priests of idols: are these then within the bond of his covenant?"[213] If Justin cast his vote with the minority of orthodox Christians in the early part of the second century, by allowing the Jewish Christians who observed the Law might possibly be saved,[214] Barnabas would assuredly have voted them out with the majority. For all effective purposes, the day of the Jewish mission was ended.

There is a fascinating passage in Origen's *Commentary on the Psalms* which shows how utter and complete was the breakdown in communication between Jews and Christians by the third century. Commenting on the passage in Deuteronomy: "They have stirred me to jealousy with what is no god; they have provoked me with their idols. So I will stir them to jealousy with those who are no people; I will provoke them with a foolish nation," Origen sees its fulfilment in the contemporary scene. "That is why even now the Jews are not roused against the Gentiles, against those who worship idols and blaspheme God. No, they do not hate them, nor does their indignation blaze against them. But it is against the Christians that they are consumed with an insatiable hatred, Christians who have abandoned idols and are converted to God!"[215] Although Origen himself took the unusual step of getting a Jew to teach him Hebrew, this revealing aside in his commentary shows the normal relations between Jews and Christians in his time, and is a pathetic commentary on the failure of the gospel to strike a lasting root in Judaism, its native soil.

FAILURE AND SUCCESS

The story of the attempt to evangelize the Jews in the first 200 years of Christianity was, on the whole, a failure. From the tone of the literature left to us in the New Testament[216] and much more in the Apologists, it is not hard to see why. The destruction of the Temple was seen as divine retribution on the Jews for the slaying of the Messiah; the blame for the crucifixion was increasingly placed on the Jewish nation as a whole, though in the early days it was only the responsible leaders who are arraigned in these terms by the apostles. Such a charge does not figure, for instance, in Paul's approach to the Jews in Pisidian Antioch, who could by no stretch of the imagination be held responsible for the execution of Jesus. The systematic way in which the Christians robbed the Jews of their holy books, their Law, their status and history as Israel has been sketched in the preceding pages, and is in itself explanation enough for the failure of the Jewish mission. If ever any evangelistic enterprise taught the lesson that the gospel cannot be preached without love, this was it. The Christian community failed to make it credible that they were the people of the Messiah.

In the early days, however, before the War of A.D. 66, and even more so, presumably, before the Antiochene church began to preach with such startling results to non-Jews, the gospel did make considerable headway among the Jews of Jerusalem, Syria, Egypt[217] and Rome.[218] Wherein lay its appeal?

First and foremost, no doubt, the person and character of Jesus. If John the Baptist made such an impression on Israel, how much more Jesus? His teaching, his love, his miracles, his whole person must have been a supreme attraction to a spiritual Israelite. If only he could get over the problem of the death of Jesus on a cross, and be convinced of Jesus's resurrection, it would not take a great deal to bring him into the synagogue of the Messiah.

Secondly, the personal witness of the apostles to the resurrection must have been a marvellous attraction. If Jesus had really broken the bands of death and risen to the life of the Age to Come, then he was the leader for them.

The way in which the Christians argued their case so plausibly from Scripture clearly had an enormous impact. They could show by accepted exegetical principles, that almost all the Old Testament speculations about a coming deliverer had been fulfilled in this amazing man Jesus, who, they were convinced, was more than man.

The joyous fellowship of the early community, with its apostolic leadership, its community of food and possessions, its earnest meetings for prayer, its deep and intimate brotherhood—this, too, must have had an appeal all its own. Persecution would only serve to deepen this "love for the brethren".

All these points are very obvious. But there are three, perhaps, which are not so obvious. The first is the political implications of the early preaching. If Jesus was going to return as triumphant Son of Man in the clouds of heaven, and if, as some fragments of tradition about him seemed to indicate, this would be in the lifetime of some of his friends,[219] then clearly here was the final winding-up of history for which they were all waiting; here was the break-in of the theocracy and the defeat of the impious Romans. This *must* have been a factor in the immediate growth of Christianity from its cradle in Jerusalem. We must not, however, overestimate it. For by the time of the Great Revolt the Christian community at Jerusalem realized that armed rebellion was not the way the Son of Man had chosen; and they escaped from the beleaguered city to Pella, refusing to have anything to do with the war, in common with their co-religionists outside Israel. It was the same story, as we have seen, when Bar Cochba tried to persuade Israel that he was the Messiah. Clearly therefore, a sense of proportion soon prevailed; but that does not alter the probability that the fervent Messianic expectation of the day was a great help in attracting members of the Jewish race to Christ in the first two decades after the resurrection.

A second factor which appealed, was the power these Christians had to love each other, to overcome character defects, to endure opposition and death gladly for the sake of Jesus. Stephen did more for his Master in his death than he did in his life. The *dunamis* shown by the Christians appealed tremendously to a magician like Simon Magus or Elymas.[220] We read in the Acts of Jewish exorcists attempting to make capital from the power in the name of Jesus,[221] and later on this continued, despite worsening relations between Christians and Jews. "A man shall have no dealings with the heretics, nor be cured by them, even for the sake of an hour of life. There was the case of Ben Dama, nephew of R. Ishmael, whom a serpent bit. There came Jacob the heretic of the village of Sechanya to cure him ('in the name of Yeshu ben Pandera,' *var. lect.*) but R. Ishmael would not allow him."[222] "Rabbi Akiba said, He who reads in external books and he who whispers over a wound, and says 'None of the diseases which I sent on Egypt will I lay on thee, I am the Lord thy Healer' has any share in the world to come."[223] This is certainly an allusion, like the last more explicit one, to Christian healing in the name of Jesus. The words from Exodus 15:26 "I am the Lord that healeth thee" have the numerical value of the name Jesus, and would be used by Jewish Christians for this purpose when they dared not utter his name openly.[224] There are other examples like this in Jewish sources which not only back up the accounts of apostolic healings in the Acts, but show something of the effect they had on ordinary people who were wondering about the credentials of the new faith.[225] But once again, it is important not to exaggerate. It was not the miracles that brought a man to faith; there were plenty of miracles in the ancient world! But it was these acts of power allied to the preaching of Jesus which had such an impact, as they had in similar circumstances during his life. Stephen, full of grace and power, did great wonders and signs among the people, but it was the force of his proclamation of Jesus as Messiah which they could not resist.[226]

Finally, the offer of pardon struck a very congenial note in Jewish circles. Any religion dominated by the concept of Law and moral responsibility before God must lead either to nomism or despair. How can a man be just before his maker? Judaism had no answer. To fail to keep the Law in one point was to be guilty of all.[227] But Christianity had an answer, a credible answer, a reasonable answer. The followers of Jesus claimed that he, acting on God's behalf, had dealt radically and finally with the problem of human failure on the cross. He had born the curse of the broken Law when he "became a curse for us". He had fulfilled the destiny of the Suffering Servant. Pardon for the man who came to God through Christ was understood to be a present possession, an anticipation here and now of the final judgment. And it brought a release and a dynamic which nothing in Judaism could equal. This must have attracted many a noble Jew as greatly as it did Saul of Tarsus, struggling with the load of his sins. Particularly after the destruction of the sacrificial system Jews would feel the pressure of their sin all the more acutely. Origen records how in his day Jews told him that "as they had no altar, no temple, no priest, and therefore no offerings of sacrifices, they felt that their sins remained with them, and that they had no means of obtaining pardon".[228] Dr Marmorstein has examined the pre-occupation with the question of how forgiveness was to be found which exercised many Jewish minds in the second and third centuries, and produced answers such as the blood of circumcision, the sacrifices of Elijah in heaven, and quite widely, in the sacrifice of Isaac.[229] In *Jubilees*, a pre-Christian book, Isaac's sacrifice was said to have taken place on the 14th Nisan, and to be a type of the paschal lamb; the similarity with Christ's death on that date as "the lamb of God who takes away the sin of the world" is obvious enough. And this cult of Isaac the mediator continued. Rabbi Jochanan in the third century makes Abraham say, "When the descendants of Isaac are guilty of transgressions and evil actions, remember the sacrifice of Isaac and have pity."[230]

The Christians had something more real, more recent, more ethical and far more liberating to offer than the sacrifice of Isaac. As Dr James Parkes well put it, "Judaism proclaimed, indeed, that God forgave sin, but Christianity proclaimed that God redeemed sinners."[231]

5

EVANGELIZING THE GENTILES

THE CHRISTIAN GOSPEL is meant for everybody, Jew and Gentile, educated and barbarian, male and female, bond and free. There was no dispute about that in the earliest Church, even though there was much heartsearching about the extent to which non-Jewish converts should conform to ritual, the Law and the external marks of Israel.[1] Salvation indeed comes from the Jews; its source lies in a man born under the Law.[2] But it is designed for the whole world.[3] How this programme was to be carried out did not immediately concern the first disciples. They had their hands full preaching Jesus and the resurrection to the Jews of the capital. But Luke unfolds the story of the way in which the process was carried out, not only in Jerusalem and Judaea, but Samaria, and to the end of the earth.[4] He leaves us in complete ignorance about what happened to the two main protagonists in his story, Peter and Paul,[5] but in no doubt at all that the good news about Jesus was being proclaimed throughout the civilized world, and was making open and unhindered progress in the hub of the Empire, Rome herself.[6]

In the first part of Acts, he shows us the developing stages in this advance. First, the preaching in Jerusalem (chapters 1:1–6, 7), then its spread throughout Palestine and Samaria (6:8–9:31), then its extension as far as Antioch (9:32—12:24). The second part of his book balances this neatly, with the spread of the gospel through Asia Minor (12:25—16:5), Europe (16:6—19:20) and Rome (19:21 —28:31).[7] Lest we should miss his plan, he concludes each section with a brief summary and an assessment of the success achieved. And in this plan Antioch has a central and most prominent place, for the simple reason that it was in Antioch that the gospel first began to be preached to people who had no connection with Judaism at all.

Antioch, Gateway to the Gentile Mission

We shall not concern ourselves here with the steps towards this momentous climax which Luke traces. The preaching to Samaritans and pious proselytes like the Ethiopian eunuch and Cornelius, though remarkable enough in all conscience, could be regarded as an extension of the bounds of Israel to the "strangers within the gate". Not so the preaching to sheer pagans, which began, we are told, in Antioch.[8] This was a crucial break, and the Jerusalem Church not only accepted it, and sent a one-man commission to approve it, but finally recognized that the Gentile adherents of the faith did not need to keep the Law of Israel nor to have the covenant badge of circumcision: faith and baptism by themselves brought a man into the society of the Messiah, whether he was Jew or Greek.

Why was it in Antioch, we may ask, that the Hellenistic Jews, dispersed because of the opposition at Jerusalem, found that they could contain themselves no longer, but simply had to share with Gentiles the good news of Jesus? There are a variety of reasons. Antioch on the Orontes was the capital of the province of Syria, governed by a proconsul in charge of two legions. It was the third city in the Empire, with its own Games, a tremendous building programme financed jointly by Augustus and Herod,[9] a large and influential but very lax Jewish population,[10] and a reputation for immorality of which even Juvenal disapproved.[11] It was the centre for diplomatic relations with the vassal states of the East, and was, in fact, a meeting point for many nationalities, a place where barriers between Jew and Gentile were very slight, so numerous were the converts to Judaism in the city, and so high the status of the Jews there—they enjoyed full citizen rights.[12] It is not surprising that the earliest preaching of the gospel to Gentiles took place in such a place where, as W. L. Knox acutely noticed, "the appearance of a new version of Judaism which tended to obliterate the distinction between Jew and Gentile was not likely to excite such violent hostility from the Jews as it had in Jerusalem, nor to be overlooked by the Gentiles on account of their contempt for everything of Jewish origin as it was likely to be at Caesarea. Further, in the residence of the legate of Syria there was less to be feared from mob-violence than in the districts subject to the procurators of Judaea, who were drawn from an inferior class, and more open to corruption or intimidation on the part of the leading provincials."[13]

Other factors favoured the rooting of Christianity here, and its rapid spread from such a centre. As one of the largest cities in the Empire, and one of the great commercial centres of antiquity, with business connections all over the world, Antioch saw the coming and going of all sorts of people from every quarter of the globe. Hellenistic city, Roman city, Jewish city, it was the meeting point of the Orient and Greek civilization. It contained not only the Hellenic cults of Zeus and Apollo and the rest of the pantheon, but the Syrian worship of Baal and the Mother Goddess, only partly assimilated to Zeus and Artemis, as well as the mystery religions with their message of death and resurrection, initiation and salvation.

Professor Downey has written two interesting books giving the results and the implications of the excavations at Antioch.[14] Foremost in importance is a series of large mosaics which give us a better impression of daily life in Antioch than we have for anywhere else in antiquity except Pompeii. They emphasize that the moral level was as low as Juvenal and Propertius paint it. Zeus and Ganymede, Zeus's amours with women, Narcissus, Bacchic revels, the Judgment of Paris are all prominent. Religious cults are well attested, too. There is a group of floors depicting the Isis cult, including initiation as described by Apuleius in Book Eleven of *The Golden Ass*. Stoic influence is not lacking; one tomb shows pairs of animals normally hostile, such as lion and ox, tiger and boar, with the legend "friendship"; another extols the Stoic virtue of *amerimnia*, "freedom from care" and another *megalopsychia*, "superiority to fortune". An interesting factor is the increase in abstract philosophical terms like Power, Renewal, Creation, Pleasure, Life, Salvation and Enjoyment. It shows that when Christians spoke of joy, salvation, power, and eternal life, their words would be understood, and the contemporary climate was one which was very interested in such concepts. Evidence of magic is forthcoming, too: the evil eye and the lucky hunchback, together with other apotropaic charms to keep off the influence of evil.[15]

Such was Syrian Antioch, the town where Christianity emerged from its Jewish chrysalis. It is almost a microcosm of Roman antiquity in the first century, a city which encompassed most of the advantages, the problems, and the human interests, with which the new faith would have to grapple.

It was no official policy of the Jerusalem Church to evangelize this great city. On the contrary it was a spontaneous movement arising from Christian men who could not keep quiet about Jesus their Lord,[16] though we may hazard the guess that Nicholas of Antioch, appointed one of the seven at Jerusalem, may have preferred to go back home to share Christ with them than to remain shut up with the apostles in Jerusalem.

It is no part of the purpose of this book to examine the relations between Jewish and Gentile Christians, nor the steps by which the Church became increasingly Gentile in membership. But it will be useful to keep this sketch of Antioch in our mind as we examine three aspects of the early preaching to Gentiles.

It would be a mistake to assume from studies such as those of Dodd[17] that there was a crippling uniformity about the proclamation of Christian truth in antiquity. That there was a basic homogeneity in what was preached we may agree, but there was wide variety in the way it was presented. Nor was this variety always the result of the supposedly rigid and conflicting theologies which were prevalent in different sections of the ancient Church. This will, of course, have had something to do with it: Luke's understanding of the Spirit, the Cross and Eschatology, for instance, is very different from that of Paul or John. But much of the variety will have been necessitated by the needs and understanding of the hearers. Evangelism is never proclamation in a vacuum; but always to people, and the message must be given in terms that make sense to them.

The Process of "Translating" the Gospel

Once Christianity took root in Hellenistic soil, it became necessary to do a tremendous work of translation. Not only words, but ideas had to be put into other dress. Without such a task of translation the message would have been heard, perhaps, but not assimilated.

Kirsopp Lake recognized this clearly in his comment on the preaching of Jesus as "Lord" at Antioch (Acts 11:20).[18] "The good news was the Lordship of Jesus. This distinguishes very clearly the evolution of the preaching. In the first stage, the 'good news' was the coming of the Kingdom of God; this was the message of Jesus himself. In the second stage it was that Jesus was 'the Man' ordained to be judge of the living and the dead:[19] this was the preaching of the disciples to the Jews. The third stage was the announcement that Jesus was the *kyrios*, which doubtless included the Jewish message which Peter delivered to Cornelius, but must also have meant much more to heathen minds, and had connotations quite different from anything contemplated by Jewish-Christian preachers."

Now it is easy to overstress the difference between the three approaches here outlined; and others could easily be added to them. Jesus was the one sent from God in fulfilment of all the promises, the one crucified and risen, in all the strands of preaching which have come down to us. But Lake was right in laying emphasis on the appeal of the Lordship of Jesus to the pagan mind.[20] It would be much more meaningful than "Christ". To be sure, "Christ" was not dropped—the followers of The Way were first called *Christians* in Antioch: but it began to lose its specific Jewish notion of Messiah, and became instead a sort of surname for Jesus: this happened extremely fast in the Gentile Mission—in most of the New Testament references to Christ it already has this formalized ring. "Lord" on the other hand, made particularly good sense in the Hellenistic world where "there are many 'gods' and many 'lords', yet for us there is one God the Father, from whom are all things and for whom we exist, and one Lord Jesus Christ through whom are all things and through whom we exist."[21] Here was the specific confrontation of the Lord Jesus with the Lord Serapis the Lord Osiris and the rest, and somewhat later, increasingly self-consciously, with the Lord Caesar.[22] At the same time it had the advantage of maintaining the primitive baptismal confession "Jesus is Lord"[23] and had the highly significant overtones provided by its application to Yahweh in the Old Testament.[24] In particular this term drew attention to the sovereignty of Jesus over the malign forces of Fate which threatened men on every side, and assured the believer that by reason of the resurrection Jesus was indeed enthroned in the universe at the right hand of God, and "neither death nor life nor angels nor principalities . . . nor powers", *nothing* could henceforth sever the Christian from his Lord.[25]

A similar process of translation is obviously at work with a phrase like "kingdom of God" or "kingdom of the heavens". This is essentially Jewish, and points to the fulfilment of the theocratic hope longed for by prophets and apocalyptists alike in Israel. But in a Gentile milieu it was not a particularly helpful or meaningful idea, and was, moreover, liable to be grossly misinterpreted. Jesus's own proclamation of the kingdom had led to his death; it was easily enough twisted to bear a sinister meaning. The apostles found it equally inconvenient. The Jews of Thessalonica, fired by envy at the success of Paul's preaching, hypocritically professed to be shocked that the missionaries "are all acting against the decrees of Caesar, saying there is another king, Jesus." Something similar seems to have been the charge at Philippi: "these men are Jews and they are disturbing our city. They advocate customs which it is not lawful for us Romans to accept or practise."[26] There were troubles enough for the early missionaries without inviting riots or prosecution by injudicious use of language. Accordingly, we hear less and less about the kingdom of God, though it never entirely drops out, and increasingly synonyms replace it, such as "salvation". The greatest synonym, of course, is Jesus himself. He who proclaimed the kingdom in his lifetime became the content of the proclamation among the early missionaries, and rightly so, because as the gospels make clear, it is through the agency of Jesus that men are brought into the kingdom. Entering the kingdom, receiving the kingdom, being saved, and inheriting eternal life are all taken as synonyms in a fascinating passage in Mark 10, and they are all firmly tied to "following Jesus".[27] The kingdom is inseparable from the King.[28]

Another obvious example of translation for Gentile consumption is Paul's metaphor of *huiothesia*, adoption. This practice was common in Roman society, but it is not a Jewish concept at all; adoption was unknown among them, apart from the special respect in which the king was "adopted" as "son of God". But it was a marvellous word for bringing home to Gentiles the fact that they were once out of relationship with God, with no claim on him, but now, through the divine initiative expressed in Christ the proper Son, they have become members of the family, heirs to its riches, and privileged to call God by the intimate name, *Abba*.

One might greatly multiply examples of the transformation of the gospel into terms readily assimilable by the recipients. We shall examine some of them below. The motive was always that which Paul claimed for himself when discussing what has been called his apostolic opportunism. "I have become all things to all men, that I might by all means save some."[29] In a wise and penetrating article,[30] Professor Henry Chadwick has shown something of the extent to which Paul was prepared to alter the wrappings of his gospel in order to command its contents. He points out that there is a fundamental difference between the defender of orthodoxy, who is anxious to maximize the gap between authentic Christianity and all deviations from it, and the apologist, who is concerned to minimize the gap between himself and his potential converts. "Paul's genius as an apologist is his astonishing ability to reduce to an apparent vanishing point the gulf between himself and his converts, and yet to 'gain' them for the Christian gospel." Other evangelists to the Gentiles may not have been so skilful, but were essentially engaged upon the same operation.

The Variety of its Appeal

Different elements in the good news appealed to different types of Gentile. There were the socially depressed classes, slaves and the poorer freedmen. Clearly the early Christian communities had a large share of such people.[31] Now slaves were commonly (and indeed legally) regarded not as *people* but as *things* in the ancient world,[32] although there are many examples of kind and considerate treatment by generous owners.[33] But when the Christian missionaries not only proclaimed that in Christ the distinctions between slave and free man were done away as surely as those between Jew and Greek,[34] but actually lived in accordance with their principles,[35] then this had an enormous appeal. Not only to be accepted by others of a different class,[36] but to be adopted into the very family of God—this must have been almost too wonderful to be true for the average Hellenistic slave—until he remembered that the founder of this faith was himself a Servant, who knew from personal experience what ignominy and undeserved suffering meant. The whole concept of free grace, unmerited pardon would have been no less powerful an attraction: he never had this from his master! One has only to contrast the temper of the Epistle to Philemon with that of an Egyptian papyrus to take the point. The slave-owner writes: "I commission you by this writ to go to the famous city of Alexandria and search for my slave about thirty-five years of age, whom you know. When you have found him, you shall place him in custody, with authority to shut him up and whip him, and to lay a complaint before the proper authorities against any persons who have harboured him, with a demand for satisfaction."[37] How meaningful the metaphor of *apolutrōsis*, "manumission"[38] must have been when applied to Christ's death, and what a sense of gratitude it must have given such a person to think that the Son of God loved him, and died for him— and was now his true Master in heaven with whom there was no partiality; Christ would reward his faithful slave with the inheritance provided he did his work, with singleness of mind, serving the Lord and not merely his earthly boss.

The universal scope of the gospel appealed greatly to another depressed section of the Graeco-Roman world, the women. It is possible to overemphasize the political disadvantages and social isolation under which women laboured, and H. Kitto[39] and J. P. V. D. Balsdon[40] have brought perspective to the problem of Greek and Roman women respectively. But the fact remains that they were very much the second sex; apart from a few women of the imperial house like Livia and Messalina they had no public rights or influence but were entirely under the *potestas* of their husbands. It was much the same in Judaism.[41] Christianity changed all this. Men and women were of equal value in God's sight; women had followed throughout his ministry, and had remained faithful to him even when the men had run away.[42] Moreover a leading part in the spread of the gospel was undertaken by women; sometimes in public or semi-public, as in the work of a Priscilla, a Lydia, a Phoebe, a Syntyche; and sometimes in the women's quarters of the home or at the laundry.[43] The opportunity of finding a faith where they could be given an equality of status and a real sphere of service must have helped many women to put their trust in Jesus as Lord.

The cultured classes were not in such short supply among the early Christians as a superficial reading of 1 Corinthians 1:26 might suggest. The early Church contained not only "unlearned and ignorant men" but many of the rich priesthood, the wife of Herod's steward and one of his youthful *amici*,[44] leading Pharisees, rich Cypriots like Barnabas and prominent provincials like Paul. In addition, from the earliest days some Romans joined the Church. On the day of Pentecost, we are informed, there was a group of Roman citizens, apparently retaining their own separate identity, who became believers.[45] A Roman proconsul might occasionally be found in their ranks,[46] not to mention less prominent officers like a centurion. Pliny found the whole spectrum of society, including Roman citizens, reflected in the Christian Church in Bithynia.[47] It is almost certain that Flavia Domitilla, a relation of Domitian, was a Christian, together with her husband Flavius Clemens.[48] The same is probably true of first century figures like Pomponia Graecina, wife of the conqueror of Britain,[49] and Acilius Glabrio, another distinguished member of the nobility.[50] Hermas makes it plain that there were rich men in the Roman church of the second century.[51] If we ask what elements in the gospel won these men and women to Christ, the answer is tentative and probably diverse, but would include the following factors. We know from Saul of Tarsus that a sense of guilt, inability to live up even to his own standards, made him long for cleansing. He was not alone in this.[52] The proconsul of Cyprus, it would seem, had already had a strong attraction towards the lofty monotheism and ethics of Judaism, and had gone so far as to have a resident Jewish teacher to instruct him. The superiority of this offshoot of Judaism, Christianity, was demonstrated to him largely because of its power, not only exercised in the blinding of Elymas, but also in the moral dynamic which could make another Roman citizen, Paul, renounce wealth and position in order to go round proclaiming the "teaching of the Lord".[53] We shall have more to say of the place of miracle in the early preaching, but it was very important, not independently in its own right, but as here when related to the Christian message. We are unfortunately not well informed about what elements apart from pardon and power attracted the cultured classes of the Empire to the faith. We shall not be far wrong in supposing that Christianity made its impact primarily by satisfying the moral, the sacramental, the social and the intellectual needs of men in a way which neither paganism nor Judaism could. I have indicated in *The Meaning of Salvation* the quest in both Jewish and pagan thought of the first century for "salvation"; men sought it either through knowledge (ranging from high philosophy to magic) or sacramentalism (including the mystery cults and the Jewish sacrificial system). Here was a religion which combined both, and did so in response to the personal self-giving and challenge of God become man.[54] If the ethics of the Christians were not in theory greatly different from the best of Stoic and Jewish teaching, in practice they were, and they were inspired and en-nobled by a new motivating force, which the Christians claimed was none other than the Spirit of this gracious God active within their lives. They made the grace of God credible by a society of love and mutual care which astonished the pagans and was recognized as something entirely new. It lent persuasiveness to their claim that the New Age had dawned in Christ.[55]

The intellectuals, too, made their way slowly into the Christian movement. They were, the best of them, dominated by a concern for truth, and Christianity offered them One whom they believed was final truth in personal categories. This did not seem very impressive, at first sight, and Paul has to admit it is indeed folly to suppose that the universal wisdom is displayed by the sordid particular of a con-demned criminal dying on a cross.[56] But the resurrection, here again, proved the key. It convinced some men at least that Jesus was what he claimed to be, and could without detracting from the monarchy of God be described in terms of the pre-cosmic Wisdom which was widely thought of in Jewish circles as God's fellow in creation. That is how Paul and John and Hebrews thought of Christ. They gave personal shape, the shape of the man of Nazareth, to the speculations of Philo about the eternal Logos and Sophia. So Chris-tianity was wisdom teaching after all;[57] it did make sense of the world. And what these apostles did for, in the main, the Hellenistic Jewish world, Justin and the other apologists did for Graeco-Roman society. So widespread was the idea of the Logos in the Graeco-Roman world, that it is possible for different scholars to assign three rather different backgrounds for Justin's use of the term (apart from its specifically Christian content)—Middle Platonism,[58] Stoicism,[59] and Philo's writings![60] What he and his successors were concerned to do was to take this term of wide and varied usage, and use it as a vehicle for Christian truth which would enable him to claim as "Christian" all that was good or noble in pagan philosophy, to main-tain that Christianity is as old as creation, and to explain the relation of creation to redemption. Though an operation of this sort was a perilous undertaking which could and did lead to all manner of mis-understanding, it was an absolutely necessary undertaking if the intellectuals could hear in terms which they readily admitted. And Justin, at any rate, does not hesitate to make abundantly clear his main Christian position, which stands out in stark contrast to all other views of the Logos—that "the Logos himself took form, and became man, and was called Christ Jesus".[61] Armed with these convictions, the early Christian intellectuals from Paul and John to Clement and Origen, glow with the confidence of having found the key to understanding the universe, of having arrived while other philosophers were only stumbling along the way. There was, therefore, no need for Justin to remove his philosopher's garb after his conversion. He continued to practise philosophy; but, as he tells us, he "found this philosophy alone to be safe and profitable".[62] One of the tendencies in philosophical schools in the late Hellenistic age was to have a strong religious bent; as Trypho expressed it, "Do not the philosophers turn every discourse upon God ? and do not questions continually arise to them about his unity and providence ? Is not this truly the duty of philosophy, to investigate the Deity ?"[63] Justin agrees that it is . . . though he points out that not all philosophers would accept this. When later he relates how he was led by the old man to Christian belief, he can look back on his philosophical quest as indeed a *praeparatio evangelica*. Pointing out that it prepared him for Christian commitment, he says, "Thus, and for this reason, I am a philosopher. Moreover, I would wish that all, making a resolution similar to my own, should not keep themselves away from the words of the Saviour."[64] Just as Justin had preserved the scandal of the incarnation in his philosophical system, so he makes very clear the need for personal commitment to the Saviour. His last words to Trypho are a call to belief in Christ. The conclusion of his *First Apology* is a plea to the Emperor "to do what is pleasing to God" if he has been convinced by the reasonableness of the Christian case; his *Second Apology* concludes with the prayer that its Roman readers "may, if possible be converted. For this purpose alone we did compose this treatise". The authentic message of Jerusalem was still to be heard, although in the hands of the Christian philosophers it was couched in the language of Athens.

Then there was the religious man in the Hellenistic world. The man who either belonged to or had heard about[65] one of the mystery cults would find a great deal in early Christian ritual, theology, and language which enabled him quickly to understand the Christian message. The apostles used language reminiscent of the mysteries— *mustērion* (mystery), *epoptēs* (initiate), *zōē aiōnios* (eternal life) and the widely used *teleios* root, in connection with which Lucian said that Jesus had introduced a new *teletē* or initiatory rite, into the world.[66] Rebirth through baptism was a common idea, even including a dying and rising with the god;[67] sacred meals in which the worshipper ate the god sacramentally, and thus became temporarily identified with him in apotheosis, were known too.[68] But Christian baptism is differentiated from the first by incorporation into the historical Jesus who rose from death; Christian eucharist does not necessarily make the recipient a *pneumatikos* (spiritual man),[69] nor is he thought of as consuming the God, but rather as having a personal relationship with him. No doubt the exclusive nature of Christianity would intrigue one who had been interested in the mystery cults; here was a cult which brooked no other allegiance (none of the other mystery religions were exclusive) and yet had no costly entry fee— the mystery was an open one to all who would fulfil the command to repent, believe and obey the crucified and risen Author of the cult; and he was no mythical figure of long ago, Osiris or Adonis or the Eniautos Daimōn, but a historical figure who gave every evidence of having been the incarnation of the Divine.[70]

The mystery cults can figure too largely in our understanding of ancient religion. Much more important was the old paganism, the state religion of Greece and Rome, with its pantheon of gods. How the Christians dealt with this situation we shall see below. But there were many disillusioned Romans who had no more time for the state cult[71] (though they still supported it; dire disaster might otherwise ensue)[72] or for the Eastern mystery religions,[73] but honoured the old household and countryside gods[74] and sought to manifest *pietas* in their lives. Juvenal was such a man, and a contemporary of Paul. Cynical about the imperial cult[75] (though himself a priest in it!)[76] cynical about the deifying of abstractions,[77] such as *Pax, Fides, Pudicitia* and the rest ("Why not deify *Pecunia* (money)?" he asks, "for men worship it above anything else"), he had great regard for the simple rustic ceremonies of Ceres and Minerva.[78] Country religion of this sort resisted the gospel to the last, and much of it survived (and still survives) covered with a thin veneer of Christianity. Presumably Christians approached it much as Paul and Barnabas faced a similar bucolic faith at Lystra,[79] by urging the reality of a single Creator God, who, so far from needing to be sustained by offerings, was himself the giver of all. It would not be difficult for the evangelist to move on from the contempt felt by a man like Juvenal for the morals of high society, to convict him of the equal unworthiness of such failures in his own life: Juvenal deprecates sexual licence, for instance, among the rich and important, but is by no means persuaded that it is a bad thing for ordinary people![80] Disgust at the prevailing moral state of society must have been a frequent factor in drawing sensitive people to Christianity, a faith which seemed not only to set high moral standards within a context of love and acceptance, but to possess the power to encourage life of this calibre. It is perhaps worth noting that the Greek equivalent for the old Roman quality of *pietas* so prized by Virgil and Juvenal is *eusebeia*. And this is a word used by the later writers of the New Testament to describe the Christian faith. Could it be that this term was selected by Christians in deliberate contrast to the somewhat dull dutifulness of Roman *pietas*? When "godliness" is mentioned in the Pastorals and 2 Peter, it bears almost exactly the Roman meaning in a few places.[81] but in others is enriched beyond measure. It is the fruit of the divine promises,[82] nourished by the divine power,[83] related to divine truth,[84] and the channel of divine love.[85]

But what about the ordinary man—supposing, for a moment, that such an abstraction existed: what attracted him to Christianity? Undoubtedly the love of the Christians had a lot to do with it,[86] so did the moral qualities they displayed,[87] the warmth of their fellowship,[88] their manifest enthusiasm, the universal applicability of their message. Reconciliation with God had a lot to do with it, the unknown great God who lay behind the idols of ancient polytheism, and from whom men instinctively felt themselves separated. Accordingly, the forgiveness Christianity offered, based as it was on God's own gracious initiative for men and God's effective action in dealing with the problem of human guilt and estrangement on Calvary—all this made an enormous appeal. So did the privilege of knowing and trusting the risen Christ which Christians claimed (and appeared) to enjoy: this added a new dimension to living here and now, without waiting for whatever might befall after death. The assurance and confidence of the Christians, who were quite willing to lose home, comfort, friends, and even life itself in propagating their cause won its share of converts; so did the fear of judgment, which became an increasingly strong emphasis in the second century.[89] But perhaps the greatest single factor which appealed to the man in the street was deliverance, deliverance from demons, from Fate, from magic.

Jesus was represented by the early Christians as in constant conflict with demons.[90] These were very real to ancient man. It is plain from the 'True Doctrine' to which Celsus was urging men to return, that demons were widely regarded as the inferior (but none the less dangerous if affronted) subordinates of the great god.[91] They were active: they caused illness and disaster: they needed to be propitiated.[92] This was the theory that lay behind much ancient sacrifice, as it still does in animist communities. How was one to get free from these *daimonia*? Tatian is a good example of the relief and joy brought by Christ to such a man, whose life had been hemmed in by these dangerous spiritual forces which he did not know how to cope with. He speaks with gratitude of his "rescue from a multiplicity of rulers and 10,000 tyrants"[93] and triumphantly shouts out, "We are above Fate, and instead of the demons which deceive, we have learnt one Master who does not deceive."[94] Justin knew from experience the power of "wicked and deceitful spirits . . . the demons which are hostile to God and whom of old time we served".[95] Since his conversion he knows too "the power of the Helper and Redeemer, whose very name the demons fear; and to this day when they are exorcized in the name of Jesus Christ, crucified under Pontius Pilate, they are overcome. And thus it is manifest to all that his Father has given him so great power, by virtue of which demons are subdued to his name."[96] This is precisely the message of the New Testament itself. Jesus defeated the demons throughout his life, and finally routed them at Calvary; he "disarmed the principalities and powers and made a public example of them, triumphing over them in it (the cross)".[97] The proclamation of Jesus as Lord indicated his sovereignty over the demons, and it made a very great appeal. If Jesus had cast out demons by the finger of God, then indeed God's rule had broken in.

Astrology[98] was a mighty force in the first century; the geocentric cosmology popularized by Hipparchus in the second century B.C. had led to a widespread belief that events on earth were governed by the stars. *Anankē*, "necessity", and *Heimarmenē*, "that which is decreed", must inevitably take their course. This accounts for the courageous resignation of the Stoics. Less noble souls either gave up worship of the gods,[99] thinking it useless if all is predetermined, or else turned to gods which claimed to be superior to Destiny, like Serapis, Isis, Mithras and the others.[100] But Jesus was preached as Lord, Master of the scroll of destiny,[101] the one who breaks the dominance of the astral powers on man. Dr Ralph Martin believes the primitive Christological hymn of Philippians 2:5–11 was directed to precisely such an environment: "It is the open confession that Christ is *Pantocratōr* and sovereign over all rivals; the astral deities prostrate themselves in admission that their regime is ended." The moral implications of this claim that Christ is Lord of destiny could be explained in a way which had no parallel in any of the mystery cults. Martin continues: "It assures us that the character of the God whose will controls the universe is to be spelled out in terms of Jesus Christ. He is no arbitrary power, no capricious force, no pitiless indifferent Fate. His nature is Love . . . His title to lordship can be interpreted only in terms of self-denying service for others."[102] He points out that the Song of the Star[103] in Ignatius is an expression of just this victory over the astral powers. It meant incalculable relief to ordinary Hellenistic man.

This deliverance from Fate was equally deliverance from its capricious opposite, magic. With curious inconsistency, men felt themselves at the mercy not only of blind Destiny but the malignant operation of evil powers by those who had the know-how. Hence the lucky hunchback charms at Antioch and Pompeii; hence the Antiochene mosaic of the evil eye, attacked by all the popular talismans of sword and scorpion, serpent and dog, raven and trident.[104] The power of the risen Christ provided a much more potent weapon.[105] Ignatius, in the passage on Jesus as the Star referred to above, claims joyfully that because of the dawning of this Star "all magic was dissolved and every band of wickedness vanished away, ignorance was removed and the old kingdom was destroyed".[106] Irenaeus goes to some pains to point out the superiority of Christian miracle to magic: it never deceives people as magic frequently does; its effects last, as magic frequently does not; it is exercised for the good, both physical and eternal of the recipients, unlike magic; and its efficacy is firmly based in the supreme miracle, the resurrection of the Lord from the dead on the third day.[107] Here was yet another way in which the immensely popular verse Psalm 110:1 had its fulfilment. Jesus Christ was Lord; and in his joyful faith in Christus Victor the ordinary man of the ancient world found a deliverance through Christianity which he could not find anywhere else.[108]

If, then, these are some of the varying ways in which the emphasis of the gospel was slanted to meet the different needs of the complex Hellenistic society into which Christianity emerged at Antioch and thereafter, we must now examine the fixed elements in the Christian approach to the Gentiles over and above the general message of the kerygma which we examined in chapter 3.

UNITY OF APPROACH

There seems to have been widespread agreement among the early evangelists on three factors which ought always to figure in preaching the gospel to Gentiles, however wide the variety adopted by the missionaries in other respects in order to meet the needs of the particular hearers. These were an attack on idolatry, a proclamation of the one true God, and the moral implications that flow from this.

At Backward Lystra

In the New Testament itself we are provided with two examples of missionary preaching in an entirely Gentile constituency; the

address of Paul at Lystra, and at Athens. The former is a prolego-
menon to the gospel in a backward agricultural area, the latter in the
cultural centre of the world. They do not stand alone. Taken with
passages like I Thessalonians I and Romans I they give us a good
idea of that missionary preaching among the Gentiles which was the
fruit of Jewish apologetic and the forerunner of the onslaughts of the
Apologists in the second century.

At Lystra the scene is primitive. It is concerned with the
Lycaonian-speaking local inhabitants,[109] not the upper classes who
spoke Latin.[110] There are various local touches which suit the vicinity
of Lystra—for instance the temple of Zeus Propolis[111] and the joint
cult of Zeus and Hermes;[112] nevertheless the address is clearly
designed by Luke to be an example of the approach Christians used
in reaching uneducated Gentiles. Paul and Barnabas not only seek
to divert divine honours from themselves—an engaging touch, for
legend had it that Zeus and Hermes had once made a visit to the
peasants of this very area[113]—but pointed out the folly of idolatry.
The idols are literally "nothings" or "futilities", both in Greek and
Hebrew; and so far from idols needing sacrificial offerings from
men, there is but one God, and he gives all things to all men in
common grace. He is the Creator and the Sustainer of the universe,
the provider of all man's needs. This God has not left himself without witness among men; his goodness is denoted by his constancy
and generosity; this good God did indeed allow men to walk in their
own ways in times past; but now (the implication is incscapablc, and
is specifically drawn at Athens) he calls men to repent of their ways
and commit themselves to the Jesus whom he has sent.

Luke has already given us so many examples of the proclamation
to Jews that he does not take up valuable space in showing how the
sermon continued. It would be the normal apostolic kerygma, after
this initial appeal for monotheism, ethical response and the abandon-
ment of idols. Jews were approached via the Old Testament; pagans,
it seems,[114] through the light of natural revelation, leading on to
Christ. Such is St Paul's approach to "the Gentiles who know not
the Law" in Romans 2:12ff., though he uses the argument there for
a different purpose, to show that the Gentiles are guilty for not
having worshipped the God whom they vaguely knew existed behind
the plethora of the pantheon. The Old Testament Scriptures are not
specifically called upon, but they are not far beneath the surface.[115]
The whole approach is reminiscent of great passages in Isaiah and
the Psalms[116] where a stinging indictment of idolatry is delivered.
This tradition was carried on in Wisdom, the *Letter of Aristeas*, the
Sibylline Oracles and Josephus, *Contra Apionem*: it was, in fact, a

basic plank in Jewish apologetic to the heathen. It was simply adopted by the Christians as a necessary foreword to the gospel. It would be pointless to preach Jesus as Lord if he were merely to be thought of as an addition to the already overcrowded pantheon. His whole significance depended on his being the manifestation of the one true God. In this sermon of Paul's at Lystra we see the first part of the process described in 1 Thessalonians 1:9f., "you turned to God from idols, to serve the living and true God"; what that verse goes on to describe, how they were now waiting the return from heaven of Jesus in whom they had put their trust, Jesus who would deliver them from wrath—this we may judge was the invariable sequel in evangelistic preaching to heathen, once the unity of God and the rejection of idols had been established.

At Cultured Athens

In the address at Athens, one of the most discussed areas in the whole New Testament, we find a cultured presentation of very much the same position. It all begins with Paul's spirit being stirred within him at the sight of the idolatry everywhere rife at Athens[117]—and nowhere in the world could idolatry have worn a more attractive guise than among the sculptures of the Acropolis. The forthcoming attack on idolatry is very subtly adumbrated by Luke giving us the Athenian surmise that Paul was in fact adding a couple of new gods to Olympus, in the shape of Jesus and Anastasis, the "Healer" and his wife "Restoration"[118]—incidentally, a splendid testimony to the centrality even in Athens of the apostolic proclamation of the person of Jesus and his resurrection from the dead. The attack is brought to its climax after the altar to the unknown god has provided the launching pad for an exposition of the one true God: "Being then God's offspring, we ought not to think that the Deity is like gold or silver or stone" (to be found in profusion as objects of worship all round Paul and his hearers).

The case for monotheism is sensitively and fully presented. He starts with an inscription which he notices "to an unknown god"[119] and uses it to make a very subtle exposure of the inadequacy of polytheism. Though the precise origin of such an altar is not certain,[120] and there are conflicting accounts in the ancient writers, nevertheless "there seem to have been two main reasons for raising altars to unknown gods; either because an unknown god was considered the author of tribulations or good fortune, or because men feared to pass over some deity and therefore prayed and made sacrifices to an unknown god. And as well as all this, there was always the Greek tendency to see deity in the impersonal and indefinite".[121] Accordingly Paul, having shown them by implication from their own inscription the shallowness and insecurity of polytheism, proceeds from the impersonal and indefinite deity which that inscription presupposed to announce to them the nature of the personal and specific God of the Bible. To be sure he does not quote the Old Testament; that would have betrayed lack of sensitivity and would have been quite meaningless to them: insofar as he makes specific quotations they are from Greek poets—but, as at Lystra, his doctrine of God is entirely biblical, and so indeed is some of his language.[122] This is true apologetic, and also true evangelism, where the content of the gospel is preserved whilst the mode of expression is tuned to the ears of the recipients. God is displayed as the unique Creator of the world and all mankind; he does not inhabit shrines like the Parthenon; so far from needing worship and sacrifice from man he is Giver of all things. As the psalmist had put it long before, "I will accept no bull from your house, nor he-goat from your folds. For every beast of the forest is mine, the cattle on a thousand hills . . . If I were hungry I would not tell you; for the world and all that is in it is mine."[123] But as Professor Bruce acutely observed, "Here are combined the Epicurean doctrine that God needs nothing from men, and cannot be served by them, and the Stoic belief that He is the source of all life. Paul consistently endeavours to have as much common ground as possible with his audience"[124]—even while he is at work undermining their position!

God the Creator is then shown to be the Sustainer of mankind whom he has made of a common stock—an ungratifying thought for the Athenians[125]—for a common goal, that of seeking after him and finding him. Nor is the quest a forlorn one; he is not far from any one of us, for "in him we live and move and have our being", to quote Epimenides, or "we are indeed his offspring" as Aratus expressed it.[126] Paul is using heathen poets to preach biblical doctrine,[127] namely that personal beings owe their origin and significance, their life and everything to a personal Creator God. In times past (cf. the conclusion at Lystra) ignorance of this Creator God, though culpable, was passed over by God: but now the situation is different, since the coming of Jesus Christ has shed blinding light upon the person of God.

This is where the specifically Christian content of the sermon begins—at the point where the hearers have been jolted into awareness of their moral responsibility to the creating, sustaining God. No idol, no abstraction, but the man God has appointed is set before them, together with a challenge to change their attitude to the supreme God who both sent him as Saviour and marked him out as future Judge in virtue of the resurrection. This is not the place to examine the intricacies and the problems of this speech, but the three main points of a polemic against idolatry, a defence of the one true God, and the drawing of strong moral corollaries from man's relationship to him, all stand out clearly. One cannot help being reminded of Romans 1 where Paul makes use of precisely the same material in a different context and for a different purpose. The unity of God, the inanity of idols, and the ethical implications of idolatrous living in wilful estrangement from the true God, are made abundantly plain. "What can be known about God is plain to them, because God has shown it to them. Ever since the creation of the world his invisible nature, namely, his eternal power and deity, has been clearly perceived in the things that have been made. So they are without excuse."[128] Why? Because of idolatry. "Although they knew God they did not honour him as God or give thanks to him . . . They exchanged the truth about God for a lie and worshipped and served the creature rather than the Creator."[129] And the ethical implications? Idolatry led to immorality and to folly, "a base mind and improper conduct". In consequence we read the threefold and terrible "God gave them up"—to the destructive passions they had chosen for themselves.[130] Having chosen to refuse God, they were imprisoned in the walls of their own refusal. This is the appalling backcloth for Paul's magisterial preaching of justification through Christ in the Epistle to the Romans. And though not orientated in the same way, nor expressed with such pungency, this is fundamentally the same position that Paul takes up in the Areopagus Sermon. It was the typical Christian approach to the pagan, be he cultured as at Athens or simple as at Lystra. It served the same purpose as preaching responsibility for breaking the Torah to the Jews.

The Attack on Idolatry

This remained the pattern of Christian preaching to the pagan for centuries. As late as Lactantius early in the fourth century this was the time-honoured approach. "Since there are many steps by which one mounts to the home of truth, it is not easy for anyone to reach the top. For when lights are dazzling one with the brightness of the truth, if one does not keep a firm foothold, down one rolls to the bottom again. Now the first step is to understand religions which are false, and to cast aside the impious worship of gods made with hands. The second step is to perceive with the mind the fact that God is one, most high, whose power and providence made the world from the beginning and direct it towards a future. The third step is to know his Servant and Messenger whom he sent on embassy to earth."[131]

In a sense the Christians were doing nothing new in their attack on polytheism: it had been done by Greek thinkers from Plato onwards,[132] as well as by Jewish apologists.[133] But, leaving aside the Jews, whose exclusive monotheism was without parallel in antiquity and was thought very odd indeed, it is important to realize the extent to which the Christians were striking out an entirely new path. Even granted the tendency towards monotheism which was taking place in the Hellenistic world in the last two centuries B.C., the ancient gods were not simply discarded,[134] though Homer's tales of their loves and wars might no longer find much credit among any with a modicum of education. As we have seen, the world was full of *daimonia*, the forces of nature, which had been clothed in mythological garb by the poets. These were realities: they could not be dismissed. They were, accordingly, commonly regarded as subordinate agents of the one God. "The one doctrine upon which all the world is united," wrote Maximus of Tyre, "is that one God is king of all and Father, and that there are many gods, sons of God, who rule together with God. This is believed by both the Greek and the barbarian."[135] Thus polytheism and monotheism could be reconciled, and worship offered to the subordinate deities was thought of as ultimately reaching the supreme God. That is why it was dangerous to neglect the worship of the customary gods. Although they might not exist in the ways traditionally thought of, if they were slighted, the great God was thereby insulted, and the state accordingly imperilled.[136] That is why the pagans regarded the Christians as atheists,[137] and consequently, as enemies of the state.

It would have been easy to compromise on this issue. A gesture of respect either to the traditional gods or the imperial bust was easy to make and seemed churlish to refuse. But Christians were adamant: the very hint of idolatry produced the strongest reactions in their breasts. The Apologists are full of it. Christians would not go to the theatre, public banquets, gladiatorial shows; employment in the army, the teaching profession, the civil service was highly suspect among many Christians because of the measure of idolatry involved.[138] Public life was riddled with it; and it is hardly surprising that Christians were tempted either to shut themselves away in ghettos away from the world, or to become lax and lose their Christian distinctiveness. The balance was not easy to keep. Paul's own advice about meat offered to idols walked the tight-rope of inconsistency. The lax Nicolaitans of Revelation came into open conflict with the more conservative church members like Antipas who stood firm and refused to compromise in any shape or form. The latter undoubtedly formed the main part of the Church in the first two centuries, and any truck with idolatry was treated as a most heinous sin.

There were two contrasting attitudes an exclusive monotheist could take towards heathen gods; both of them are to be found in the Apologists, and both of them are to be found in the writings of Paul. Either you could say that there were no such things as the deities the heathen worshipped, "an idol has no real existence; there is no God but one"[139]—or else you could regard the idol itself, indeed, as unimportant, but also as the medium through which the evil *daimonia* could reach and harm you. "What do I imply then? That food offered to idols is anything or that an idol is anything? No, I imply that what pagans sacrifice they offer to demons and not to God. I do not want you to be partners with demons."[140]

Paul had, in fact, an inner consistency in this apparently contradictory attitude to idols: but it was highly sophisticated, and though an Origen could combine both strands in a coherent attitude,[141] most second century Christians stressed one strand or the other. Thus the *Epistle to Diognetus* laughs at idolatry, like Isaiah: "Are they not all deaf? Are they not blind? Are they not without life? Are they liable to rot? Are they not all corruptible? These things you call gods; these you serve; these you worship; and you become altogether like them!"[142] But the more common attitude was that of Justin and Tatian, to pour scorn, indeed, on the form idolatry takes, but to take very seriously the demonic forces behind it. The demons were fed by the fat of sacrifices,[143] which was why it was particularly important for Christians to have nothing to do with the sacrificial system. They could, indeed, be overcome; but only by dint of uncompromising opposition and through the name of Jesus. Tertullian summed it up when he said, "Their business is the overthrow of man."[144] The Christian's business, therefore, was to wage total war upon them, relying on the victory of Christ.

A further reason for the whiplash of scorn and execration administered by Christians to idolatry in every shape and form, was their conviction (and a very shrewd one it was) that idolatry and immorality went hand in hand. In practice this was always so: it was one of the unique properties of Judaeo-Christian monotheism to insist that true ethic and true religion were inseparable, that it was impossible to confess allegiance at one and the same time to a good God and live a loose life. In all other religions in antiquity there was no necessary tie between belief and behaviour, although for ceremonial and cultic reasons abstinence from intercourse and stealing and so on might be required by some religions for a limited period.[145] On the whole it remains true that idolatry and immorality were inseparable. And Justin, taking over a long tradition of inter-Testamental Judaism,[146] had a theoretical reason which explained this empirical link between wrong belief and wrong behaviour. The demons had originated through fallen angels having intercourse with human women (Genesis 6:1f.): they then dominated mankind, and "sowed among men murders, wars, adulteries, intemperate deeds and every sort of vice".[147] This view was adopted by his successors, like Athenagoras.[148] It combined the exposure of false creed (idolatry) with wicked conduct (the ethical consequences of idolatry) thus linking together two of the three main charges of the Christians in pre-evangelism of Gentiles, and leading naturally into the third, the establishment of the one true God, the Father of Jesus Christ. But all the same it was a dangerous doctrine; not least because lazy and immoral Christians could easily shrug off responsibility for their vices on to the shoulders of the demons—an antinomian situation with which Origen found he had to deal. "Some of the less intelligent believers think that all human transgressions arise from their [*i.e.* the demons'] antagonistic powers, which constrain the mind of the sinner."[149] Justin, of course, would have been the first to resist any such lawless inferences drawn from his doctrine: almost the first time he mentions the demons in his *First Apology*,[150] he goes on to contrast the immoral and cruel lives which are to be found in those under their sway, with the joy and love, the chastity and humility of the Christians "who stand aloof from the demons and follow the only begotten God through his Son". It was his passionate monotheism that led him into the use of a dangerous weapon in combating what was for all the early Christians (both on ethical and religious grounds) the *fundamental* sin of idolatry: "Idolatry is the principal crime of mankind, the supreme guilt of the world."[151]

LIMITATIONS IN UNDERSTANDING

How far was the Subapostolic Church true to the Gospel?

This note we have just struck of the misunderstanding by common people of what Christian leaders taught is an interesting one. It raises the question of how much authentic Christianity was lost in the translation of the gospel from a Semitic to a Hellenistic milieu. If the general answer of Christian evangelists to the problem crystalized by Tertullian in the famous aphorism, "What has Athens to do with Jerusalem?" was "Much every way", were there areas in which Athens gobbled up Jerusalem, where not only the dress but the body of the gospel became changed?

This question was raised acutely by Adolf von Harnack in his *History of Dogma* and *Mission and Expansion of Christianity*. He believed that the incipient Catholicism of the second century was a corrupt synthesis of Hellenism and the evangelical Christianity of the apostolic age. C. N. Moody in his book *The Mind of the Early Converts* pushed the question further back, and, from the experience of many years of missionary work, reflected on how little of what is taught by the evangelist gets across at any deep level to the convert. This process cannot be relegated to the cleavage between the pristine purity of the apostolic age and the corruption of what followed; the misunderstandings and the limited comprehension were prevalent in the New Testament period itself. Something indeed of St John's theology can be traced through Ignatius and Justin to Irenaeus—but in debased form and impoverished content.[152] There was a conscious attempt by Ignatius and Polycarp, for instance, to imitate Paul, but it is obvious that they did not understand him. His "in Christ" theology, or Christ-mysticism as it has been called, is not to be found in the second century; faith becomes mere belief, grace a commodity, justification a mere formula even on the lips of his most zealous imitators. Harnack's aphorism about Paul has much truth in it, "Marcion was the only Gentile Christian who understood Paul, and even he misunderstood him." Moody reckons, after looking with some care at the leading writers of the second century, that the majority of the Christians had about as much theology in them as the Epistle of James; that a few of the brighter lights may have got as far as the common-or-garden Christianity of St Luke, but that the giants of New Testament theology, Paul and John, were simply not understood; and that the great doctrines they taught were hardly ever assimilated. Grace, justification, sanctification, union with Christ and the other evangelical doctrines that meant much to the apostles Paul, John, Peter and the writer to the Hebrews, had been largely jettisoned and replaced with a religion of a new legalism in ethics and a Christology which lost interest in the humanity of Jesus. A similar attitude is at present very fashionable on the Continent, where whatever is not justification by faith tends, by writers like Käsemann, to be pejoratively labelled *Frühkatholizismus* and dismissed from consideration forthwith. Similar dogmatic presuppositions of a strongly reformed type mar the investigation of Professor Torrance into the doctrine of grace in the apostolic fathers.[153] It seems to be assumed that we know what the gospel is in all its fulness, and that from this enviable position we can judge the Christians of the second century.

The one-sidedness of this procedure has been well displayed by the two books of Professor Maurice Wiles on the interpretation of Paul and John in the early Church.[154] Few, if any, caught the full implications of the lofty theology of these apostolic giants, but they understood enough to make the charges of Harnack and Moody appear less than just. Take the *Epistle to Diognetus* for instance. How about this for an apostolic understanding of the divine plan? "He always was, and still is, and will ever be kind and good and free from anger and true; and he formed in his mind a great and unspeakable plan which he communicated to his Son alone. As long, then, as he held and preserved his own wise counsel in concealment he appeared to neglect us, and to have no concern or care for us. But after he revealed and laid open, through his beloved son, the things which had been prepared from the beginning, he conferred every blessing all at once upon us, so that we should both share in his benefits and see and understand."[155]

How about this for a description of the mission of Christ? "He did not, as one might have imagined, send to men any servant or angel or ruler . . . but the very Creator and Fashioner of all things, by whom he made the heavens, by whom he enclosed the sea . . . This is the messenger he sent to them. Was it then, as one might expect, for the purpose of exercising tyranny or of inspiring fear and terror? By no means, but in gentleness and meekness. As a king sends his son, who is also a king, so he sent him as God, he sent him as a Man to man. As a Saviour he sent him, and as seeking to persuade, not to compel us; for violence has no place in the character of God. When he sent him, God was calling not pursuing us; he sent him in love, not in judgment." But the unknown writer of this letter knew that judgment would come at the parousia. "For he will yet send him to judge us, and who shall endure his appearing?"[156]

How does the atonement stand in the *Epistle to Diognetus*? "He himself took on him the burden of our iniquities, he gave his own son as a ransom for us, the holy one for the transgressors, the incorruptible for the corruptible, the immortal for mortals. For what else could cover our sins but his righteousness? In who else was it possible that we, the wicked and ungodly, could be justified, except in the Son of God alone?"[157] This was no cold theory of substitution, no mere doctrinal tenet, for our author. It was the very mainspring of his Christian love—"how will you love him who so first loved you?"[158] It was the burden of his impassioned appeal to Diognetus to avail himself of the benefits of the Lord's passion. "O sweet exchange," he breaks out, "O work of God beyond all searching out! O benefits surpassing all expectation! that the wickedness of many should be hid in a single righteous one, and that the righteousness of One should justify many transgressors!"[159]

How does a man come to Christianity? It is through faith alone that God can be known, a faith that brings joy, love, and the desire to imitate Christ. "No man has either seen him nor made him known, but he has revealed himself. And he has manifested himself through faith, by which alone it is given to behold God[160] . . . If you also desire this faith and receive first of all the knowledge of the Father[161] [here there is a lacuna in the text, but it continues, evangelically] . . . he will give it to them that love him. And when you have attained this knowledge, with what joy do you think you will be filled? Or, how will you love him who has first so loved you? And if you love him, you will be an imitator of his kindness." Do we wonder how a man *can* imitate Christ (although it is a constant New Testament precept,[162] somewhat soft-pedalled in Protestantism)? Our author meets the objection. "And do not wonder that a man can imitate God. He can if he is willing . . . He who takes upon himself the burden of his neighbour, he who in whatsoever respect he is superior is ready to benefit another . . . he is an imitator of God."[163] Let us not think that this is the barren self-effort with which the second century Christians are often reproached. It is nothing of the kind. Our author knows about the power of the indwelling Christ, making possible this moral transformation. "This is he who was from the beginning, who appeared as if new, and was found old, and yet who is ever born afresh in the hearts of the saints",[164] and again, "God himself has sent from heaven and placed among men the truth, the holy and incomprehensible Word, and has firmly established him in their hearts."[165]

Finally, let us notice the quality of Christian life here recounted just before the famous passage about the Christians being to the world what the soul is to the body. He writes,[166] "Christians are distinguished from other men neither by country nor language nor the customs which they observe. For they neither inhabit cities of their own, nor employ a peculiar form of speech, nor lead a life which is marked out by any singularity . . . But inhabiting Greek as well as barbarian cities . . . and following the customs of the natives in respect of clothing, food, and the rest of their ordinary conduct, they display to us their wonderful and confessedly paradoxical manner of life. They dwell in fatherlands of their own country, but only as aliens. As citizens they share in all things with others, and yet endure all things as foreigners. Every foreign land is their fatherland and every fatherland a foreign land. They marry as do all; they beget children, but they do not destroy their offspring. They have a common table, but not a common bed. They are in the flesh but they do not live after the flesh. They pass their days on earth, but they are citizens of heaven. They obey the prescribed laws, and at the same time surpass the laws by their lives. They love all men, and are persecuted by all," and he goes on to describe the paradox of Christian involvement in the world in terms drawn from St Paul.[167]

It has seemed worthwhile to give these fairly extensive citations from an early second century[168] writing in order to correct the view that the gospel disappeared into Catholic sacramentalism and moralism in the second century, and that nobody understood the warm apostolic religion of the great apostles. Moreover, although the *Epistle to Diognetus* is admittedly one of the noblest Christian writings outside the Canon, and could for that reason be discounted as the exception which proves the rule, I think it is significant for another reason. It is one of the few examples which we have of a genuine piece of evangelistic writing.[169] The Apologies which follow it are more given to that apology which is defence of a given position than the type of apology we find in Luke–Acts which is straining all the time to win converts, the sort of apology which Paul delivered at his trial before both Agrippa and Nero, making his defence into attack, his explanation of the charges against him a weapon for evangelism. And if the Apologists are too preoccupied with the defence of Christians against unjust charges and the attack on paganism to be fair examples of evangelistic method, the remainder of the orthodox writings which date from the first half of the second century, the Apostolic Fathers, are concerned more with the inner workings of the Christian community. So although the *Epistle to Diognetus* may be the showpiece of sub-apostolic Christianity it is no less true that it is of all the second century literature the one most similar in aim and content to the evangelistic writings of the first century. Much of the warmth, the evangelical understanding, the devotion to Christ, which we find here is to be found elsewhere in the literature of the second century. After reading through this literature last summer I have come to the conclusion that the position of Harnack and Torrance was gravely exaggerated, and that much of the true preaching of the apostolic gospel in Gentile surroundings did survive into the next century, and indeed later still. Could anything be more redolent of apostolic doctrine and impassioned warmth than these excerpts from the fourth century monk, Macarius, first as he discusses the atonement and then the need for rebirth?[170]

"If anyone takes his stand upon a righteousness and redemption of his own, not looking for the righteousness of God who is the Lord, as the apostle says, 'who is made unto us righteousness and redemption', he labours in vain and to no purpose. For all the dreams of a righteousness of his own is at the last day manifested as nothing but filthy rags, as the prophet Isaiah says, 'All our righteousness is as filthy rags.' Let us then beg and implore God to 'clothe us with the garment of salvation', Jesus Christ our Lord, the unspeakable light. Souls that have once worn it shall never put it off again, but in the resurrection also their bodies shall be glorified by the glory of that light, with which faithful and noble souls are even now clad, as the apostle says, 'He that raised up Christ from the dead shall also quicken your mortal bodies by his Spirit which dwells within you'."

Preaching on the new birth, he proclaims: "Jesus Christ, taking thought for the salvation of men, employed from the outset all his providential care through the fathers and patriarchs, through the law and the prophets, and in the end came himself, despised the shame of the cross, and endured death. All this toil and care was in order that he might beget children from himself, from his own nature, being pleased that they should be begotten from above. And just as men if they have no children are grieved, so the Lord, who loved mankind as his own image, willed to beget them of the seed of his own Godhead. Accordingly, if any of them refuse to come to such a birth, to be born of the Spirit, Christ is submitted to great grief after suffering for them and enduring so much to save them. He therefore who seeks to believe and to come to the Lord, should entreat that he may receive here on earth the divine Spirit." Macarius has no doubt how that is done. "Let us then welcome the Lord our God, the true healer, who alone is able to come and cure our souls, inasmuch as he has laboured so much for our sake. He is always knocking at the door of our hearts, that we may open to him so that he may come in and rest in our souls. He says, 'Behold, I stand at the door and knock. If any man hear my voice and open the door, I will come in and will sup with him and he with me.' To this end he endured to suffer many things, giving his own body unto death, and purchasing us out of bondage. It was in order that he might come into our soul and make his abode with us . . . That is why he is always knocking, desiring to enter into us. Let us then receive him, and bring him into our lives. For he is our food, our drink, our eternal life. And every soul that has not yet received him within and given him rest, or rather, found rest in him, has no inheritance in the kingdom of heaven with the saints, and cannot enter into the heavenly city. But thou, Lord Jesus, canst bring us thereto, glorifying thy name, with the Father and the Holy Spirit for ever." It would be difficult to say that that man had lost his grip on Christian fundamentals, or that no signs of the New Testament doctrines of faith, grace, the atonement, the new birth and perseverance were to be found in his *Homilies*!

How far did the Subapostolic Church misrepresent the Gospel?

Nevertheless this must not blind us to the perils which transposition into a Gentile idiom had for the content of the Gospel even in the earliest days, and to these we must now turn.

It was in the predominantly pagan soil of cosmopolitan Antioch that the gospel first took root. And it was in Antioch that we see one of the early false turnings taking place as a result of the importation of non-Christian ideas. Ignatius was a man who came to Christianity from paganism. The sacraments are seen in terms which derive from the Mysteries[171] and verge on magic. The Eucharist is the "medicine of immortality, the antidote for death"[172] rather than a corporate encounter with the living Christ. It has become static rather than dynamic, physical rather than sacramental. Similarly the water of baptism becomes important in itself rather than in what it signifies: it has been purified by the suffering (or perhaps the baptism) of Christ.[173] Hermas is another example of this type of thinking; baptism fascinates him, obsesses him. It is the seal, the enlightenment, it brings immortality—so much so that the apostles and teachers are despatched into Hades to baptize and thereby bring to life, those who had died before Christ.[174] Now all this is a far cry from the New Testament—or is it? Did not the Corinthians attach a semi-magical efficacy to baptism? To them it mattered who administered the sacrament;[175] once received it guaranteed salvation;[176] indeed, they engaged in some sort of vicarious baptism for the dead.[177] Paul has to controvert all this: but it is undeniably there even in the fifties of the first century. The same applies to the Eucharist. John 6 could be readily interpreted in an automatic, quasi-magical sense;[178] and 1 Corinthians 10 shows that magical views were attached to the Holy Communion by the Corinthians.[179] When, therefore, Ignatius claims that the coming of Jesus has put an end to magic, one must sorrowfully confess that in some areas of the Church it introduced a new sort of magic, and that the tendencies in this direction can be plainly discerned within the New Testament itself.

Again, we have seen how the preaching to the Gentiles, though it presupposed, and often enough referred to the Old Testament, began with the establishment of monotheism and the opposition to idols. Could this have meant that, despite the fact that the Old Testament was very much the Bible of the Church, it was never really understood ? Once treat it as a quarry for proof texts or passages in which you see Christian meanings, and you are precluded from seeing it in its own right as the history of God's dealings with Israel, of which Christ is indeed the goal and the climax, but not the destroyer. Under these circumstances there must have been a constant tendency to do one of two things, either to neglect the Old Testament altogether, or to misunderstand its relations with the New.

Marcion, of course, is the classic example of the first attitude, and the enormous impression he made on second century Christianity should warn us against supposing that his rejection of the Old Testament was a mere personal quirk. There were many who thought like Marcion. There were others, too, who threw it over— most of the apocryphal gospels for example. To reject the Old Testament and its doctrine of creation led inevitably in a gnostic direction, where the physical was despised and the "spiritual" alone valued. This in its turn led to either licence or ascetisim, according to the predilections of the sect in question.[180] Both were agreed in treating the body as either irrelevant to or a hindrance to spiritual development. Preaching Christianity as a new philosophy (albeit God-given and ultimate) was almost inevitable in the Graeco-Roman world,[181] but it was none the less disastrous. It weakened the roots of the biblical doctrines of creation and of the solidarity of the New Israel with the Old which led to the two greatest dangers of the second century, Gnosticism and Marcionism.

The other direction in which the comparative neglect of the Old Testament by some Christian missionaries led has already been touched on. The trouble in Galatia for example may have been due not so much to the machinations of a counter-mission despatched by James of Jerusalem to make good Judaizers of Paul's converts, but to Paul's own spiritualizing of the Old Testament, replacing circumcision by baptism, and the like. Left to themselves after the scintillating preacher had gone, they read the Septuagint, and found the prime place accorded to the very literal Israel, the very fleshly circumcision. Paul, they may have concluded, had only told them half the story. They would get themselves circumcised and make sure.[182] Granted, they got short shrift from the apostle; granted the political and cultural circumstances of the next eighty years militated against a Judaizing of the Gentile mission. But the influence of this attitude was to be seen in other ways. The eucharist was seen in Old Testament sacrificial terms, the ministry as Levitical priests, and so forth.[183] There was a return to Old Testament categories by men who ought to have been living on New Testament lines. As we have seen, this tendency was prominent in Jewish Christianity: it came in by the back door to those Catholics who took their Old Testament both seriously and literally.

Again, the moralism into which Christianity tended to lapse in the second century has its roots in the New Testament. It is one thing to see Christian behaviour as a new law, the principle of universal love; it is quite another to see it as a revised edition of the old law. Indeed, Hermas in one place equates the gospel with the law of God, as well as with the Son of God.[184] Very soon the Church became obsessed with subjects like what was to be done about post-baptismal sin,[185] and it was a short step from there to reparation, atoning for past misdeeds[186] and the like, which came to its full flower in the Church of the Middle Ages. Christianity becomes a highly regulated ethical system, with the sanction of excommunication. As early as the *Didache* we have a system of ecclesiastical law—and the *Didache* may date from the first century;[187] the ethical document, "The Two Ways", which it enshrines is earlier still. But the seeds of such casuistry are in the New Testament itself, notably in Matthew's gospel which groups the teaching of Jesus into five great blocks to indicate that it is the New Torah, and then proceeds to use it, not as guidelines for the life of love but as legal enactments which must have exceptions[188] in order to cover hard cases. To be sure, this only occurs in one instance in Matthew: but it is the germ of what later grew into a most unhealthy plant from the viewpoint of Christian evangelism.

With the growing emphasis on merit which this attitude bred, went an increasing tendency to regard eschatology as primarily a matter of rewards and punishments. In the New Testament expectation of the end, the person of Jesus is always prominent. It is Jesus, the one who has been this way before as Man and Saviour, who will return as Lord and Judge. The second coming is the complement of the first; it is, in Cullman's famous phrase, the "V" Day to crown the implications of "D" day. But this perspective soon disappears in the subapostolic church. Judgment is frequently held out as a warning and as an incitement to Christian commitment, but we miss the centrality of Christ in eschatology. *The Apocalypse of Peter* is a good example of the collapse of New Testament eschatology. The future is seen entirely in terms of rewards for the virtuous and punishments for the damned (described at length for the gloating solace of Christian readers). The culmination of this sort of thing is Dante's *Inferno*, the origin Virgil's *Aeneid*. It is a different world from the characteristic stance of the New Testament, where rewards and punishments are indeed part of the picture, but not the whole of it; where they are, moreover, seen as consonant with the generosity of God, but not purchased by the merits of men. The subapostolic age thought, no doubt, that they were teaching New Testament Christianity: in fact they lived in another realm altogether. Such are the perils of translating Hebrew-Christian concepts into Greek dress.

These are merely some pointers to the ways in which the gospel was altered by its diffusion in the Graeco-Roman world. They could be multiplied many times. Thus the presentation of Christ in terms of the Cosmic Reason Incarnate which reached its climax in Clement of Alexandria is a long cry from the Saviour from sin of the gospels and epistles. The seed is there, of course, in the Wisdom-Logos thought of Alexandrian Judaism adapted and claimed for Christ in the writings of Paul, John and Hebrews. It was an obvious tool for expressing the good news in terms comprehensible to Greeks. But harm was done when the linguistic illustration became an identification, particularly as the Logos became a veritable storehouse from which thinkers of widely differng schools drew what they wanted!

The Risks and the Gains

The perils of this translation procedure were very real.[189] But the risk was worth taking, even though it was fraught with many disasters. *Of course* it was worthwhile, otherwise Gentile Christianity would have perished as Jewish Christianity did. It is a salutary reflection that the greatest enemy of Jewish Christianity was undue conservatism (in which Jesus was a complement, so to speak, to the Law); whereas the greatest danger to Gentile Christianity lay in undue adaptation to the thought forms of the day (in which Jesus was seen as the key to wisdom and heavenly enlightenment).[190] If conservatism stifles authentic Christianity, liberalism dissipates it. Mercifully there were plenty of Christians in the second century who stuck fairly closely to the apostolic message while adapting its presentation into terms familiar to their contemporaries. There must have been. Their lives and their words made great inroads into paganism; their brave deaths under martyrdom made even greater impact. How moving it is to read of the effect wrought on Justin by the courageous deaths of Christians before him—"I myself, too, when I was delighting in the teachings of Plato, and heard the Christians slandered, and saw them fearless of death and of all things which are counted fearful, I understood."[191] And he himself passed the same way of martyrdom, and it made such an impression that it was recorded and preserved in a second century account. His courage, his quiet refusal to compromise to save his life, or to give the prefect Rusticus any information which would incriminate others, his shrewd taking of the opportunity to give Rusticus an outline of the gospel, all this highlights his deep confidence in Christ, even at the gates of death: "I do not suppose it," he replied, in answer to the prefect's sarcastic enquiry whether he supposed he would ascend into heaven, "I do not suppose it, but I know, and am fully persuaded of it."[192] Yes, the lives, the message, the deaths of Christians showed that the risk of taking the gospel and translating it, as thoroughly as a Justin did, into other thought forms was a very worthwhile procedure. They used the Greek epics; they used the Homeric myths,[193] and also Stoic and Epicurean philosophy when it suited them. We even find Clement of Rome, after arguing for the reasonableness of the resurrection from the fact that seeds die and come to life again in new flowers, laying enormous stress on the phoenix.[194] This Eastern (mythological) bird was said by the poets[195] to die and be reborn from its own ashes every 500 years. Clement really believed this! It is the climax of his argument. He was in this respect as others a child of his age. Even so, it was not the phoenix he was interested in, but Christ. Anything in Greek thought that would help his listeners to lay hold of the wonder and the reality of the resurrection was good enough for Clement. And this is the characteristic aim which the Greek exponents of the gospel set themselves: to embody biblical doctrine in cultural forms which would be acceptable in their society. Not to remove the scandal of the gospel, but so to present their message in terms acceptable to their hearers, that the real scandal of the gospel could be perceived and its challenge faced. That was their aim. Many of them must have succeeded in it much of the time, or there would have been no Church strong enough to face the repeated persecutions from the state in the second and early third centuries. Often the attempt was a failure; something of the content of the message was lost with its Jewish wrappings which had been discarded. That was regrettable, but inevitable—assuming that the attempt to reach the Gentiles was worth making. And to question that is to question the universality of Christianity itself. If Christ is for all men, then evangelists must run the risk of being misunderstood, of misunderstanding elements in the gospel themselves, of losing out on the transposition of parts of the message so long as they bear witness to him.[196] Christians are called to live dangerously.[197] The principle of the incarnation must be carried into Christian preaching. It was, in the preaching of the early missionaries to the Gentiles, and the same would hold good (with reservations) for many of their second century successors. At all events they took the risk, and insofar as they were centred in Jesus Christ, his incarnation, death and resurrection, God honoured their witness. It is all too easy for us with hindsight to fault their ethics and their Christology, their failure to preserve the balance between adaptability and conservation, but it would be good to be able to feel confident that the Churches of our own day were succeeding half as well, and were displaying anything like the same courage, singleness of aim, Christcentredness and adaptability as those men and women of the first Christian century.

6

CONVERSION

"THE IDEA OF conversion in the sense we give it today, remained for a long time, perhaps until the arrival of Christianity, utterly foreign to the mentality of the Graeco-Roman world." With these words Gustave Bardy began his important book on the subject.[1] It is a conclusion which for example A. D. Nock would consider somewhat exaggerated in detail but correct enough in general outline,[2] and it is a healthy reminder of how strange the Judaeo-Christian insistence on conversion must have seemed to first century Gentiles.

CHRISTIAN CONVERSION

But first of all, what is "the idea of conversion in the sense we give it today?" We normally use the word, in a religious context, in one of two ways, either to indicate that a man has left one religious position (or, indeed, none) for exclusive attachment to another; alternatively, we speak of conversion in a man who up till a certain period had been a merely nominal adherent of his faith, but had then awoken to its significance and importance with enthusiasm and insight. Why should conversion of this nature have seemed foreign to the ancient world?

There are, I think, three reasons. In the first place, Hellenistic man did not regard belief as necessary for the cult. So long as the traditional sacrifices were offered, so long as the show went on, all would be well.[3] You were not required to believe in the deities you worshipped: many intelligent men like Lucretius and Juvenal scoffed at the stories of the traditional gods, but were careful to continue the sacrifices, on which the safety of the state and the well-being of society were held to depend.

Secondly, Hellenistic man did not regard ethics as a part of religion. It made little necessary difference to your behaviour whether you were a devotee of Mithras or a worshipper of Isis. Some cults demanded ritual purity for a period of initiation or during the performance of the cult, it is true; but none insisted a total break with the past, a renunciation of all that is wrong, and made this demand spring from the very nature of the deity worshipped. This point is widely admitted with regard to ancient religions,[4] but contested with regard to philosophy. The Cynics and Stoics in particular, we are told, introduced so high a conception of virtue, and made its performance depend so utterly on following the philosophical school in question, that here we have a good parallel to Christian conversion. A. D. Nock advocates this position in his famous book *Conversion*, but he overstates the similarities and underestimates the differences between Christianity and the philosophical schools. It is true that philosophy became a popular and important cultural factor in the first centuries B.C. and A.D. as a corrective to the licence of the times, as an intelligible explanation of phenomena, and as a disciplined, noble way of life which produced some of the finest characters of paganism—Marcus Aurelius, Epictetus and Seneca. It is also true that Stoic ethics and Cynic missionary zeal have a lot in common with the early Church, and even that the philosophers thought of a conversion experience in some ways parallel to the Christian, in which the seeker is like a man plunged into deep water who gradually nears the surface and then suddenly breaks surface and is able to breathe.[5] But this is only part of the story: John Baillie[6] follows Nock blindly in assuming that these conversions are strictly comparable to Christian conversion, including the assurance of salvation and the guarantee that the recipient can never fall away. How far that is from the truth is shown from the deep uncertainty and indeed moral inconsistency of even the best of them. Marcus Aurelius,[7] like Cicero before him,[8] has to end in agnosticism, and confess that he has no compelling reason for belief that the gods exist: is this the confident language of one who has found? Seneca has to confess that as he comes to die he is profoundly uncertain about the soul's nature, its future, its destiny and constitution.[9] "Do we know how to live? Do we know how to die?"[10] So far from assurance, a deep question mark filled the inmost beings of these noble pagans. One has only to compare the grim resignation of their deaths with the radiant confidence of the early Christian martyrs to see the difference between search and discovery. What is more, the glaring gap between precept and practice in a man like Seneca,[11] for example, makes nonsense of the idea that here we have something very like a Christian conversion. Nock[12] quotes *Epistle* 6:1 where Seneca writes, "I understand, Lucilius, that I am not merely being improved but that I am being transformed . . ." Would that there were more signs of it in his life! He could claim that he was entirely disinterested in the pursuit of wealth, that he did not mind whether he was rich or poor[13]—but in

practice he acquired enormous wealth, some of it by most question-
able means, and did not show himself in the least anxious to get rid
of it.[14] "A great fortune is great servitude,"[15] he proclaimed—and
clung on to it. His toughness on his creditors was one of the economic
causes behind the Boadicea Revolt in Britain, which cost the Empire
one of its best legions. Again, he could speak admirably about his
slaves as fellow-men, not slaves but lodgers under his roof, his
friends in the basement, and so forth.[16] But for all the fellow-feeling
he professed, he neither allowed them to share in his way of life, nor
did he think of freeing a single one of them.[17] As Bardy justly
points out, the philosopher was expected to preach, not to practise
what he preached. Men came to him for advice, not for example.
This separation of belief from behaviour was one of the fundamental
differences between the best of pagan philosophical religion and
Christian conversion.

The third reason why the idea of Christian conversion was so surprising to Hellenistic man was the exclusive claims that it made on
its devotees. Christians were expected to belong, body and soul, to
Jesus, who was called their master, *despotēs*, and was said to have
redeemed them from alien ownership into his own. Henceforward
they were to acknowledge no other "Lord", be he emperor or pagan
deity. This all seemed very strange, for ancient religion was never
exclusive. To be sure, the Mysteries were not open to those who
were not initiated; in this sense they were exclusive. But they were
not exclusive in principle: they did not demand a man's total
allegiance, nor did they prevent him from belonging to any other
mystery religion, from performing his ancestral worship, or doing
obeisance to the imperial statue. Whether a man turned to philosophy or magic, to astrology or gnosis, to the rites of Osiris or of
Mithras was immaterial in one important respect, that every one of
them was deemed to supplement not to supplant a man's ancestral
religion.

Conversion, then, in our sense of an exclusive change of faith, of
ethic and of cult, was indeed utterly foreign to the mentality of the
Graeco-Roman world. That is why the Jews excited such interest,
amazement, hatred and fascination. At this period of intensive
religious syncretism, here was a faith which stood out like a sore
thumb. Passionate monotheists, dedicated to the overthrow of
idolatry, equipped with the noblest of ethic, an ancient history, a
holy book, they exercised both attraction and repugnance as they
spread all over the Mediterranean basin. Hardly a writer between
A.D. 50 and 150 fails to mention them. Their influence was enormous. Augustus's wife Livia had a Jewish slave whom she held in

such high regard that she actually sent offerings to the temple at Jerusalem.[18] Claudius had the prominent Jew, Alexander, as his friend and financial adviser.[19] Nero's concubine, Poppaea Sabina was a "Godfearer".[20] Josephus was an intimate of the Flavian Emperors, and, of course, the whole Herod family had been educated at Rome and were on close and friendly terms with the imperial family. Judaism, therefore, was exceedingly well known, and respected while it was disliked. It introduced into the ancient world the idea of conversion in this total, life-changing sense we are considering. But it had very limited success. Despite the advantages they possessed in protective legislation afforded to no other faith, in widespread dissemination, in synagogues which welcomed Gentile adherents, in a Holy Book and an ethic which were manifestly superior to anything else in the contemporary world, they nevertheless failed to convert the Roman Empire; indeed, they never looked like doing so. But where Judaism failed, Christianity succeeded. It made, as we have seen, great and rapid gains both from Jews and Gentiles, and welded them into what was soon to be called a *tertium genus*, a third race.

It is at this point that the uniqueness of Christian conversion stands out. They called on Jews as well as Gentiles to put their faith in God's Messiah and join the company of his people. For the Gentile this would be conversion *to* a new faith; for the Jew it would be, in an important sense, conversion *within* the faith in which he had been nourished, and of which Christ was the summit and goal. But the shock would be as great for the Jew, or even greater, than for the Gentile. Both would have to be baptized into the Church of the Messiah. And whereas for the Gentile that would be much preferable to circumcision, to the Jew it was a great stumbling-block. It meant renouncing all claim to be God's elect simply on the grounds of birth and circumcision. It meant becoming like a new-born child, and washing away all impurities in the bath of baptism—and that was what they were accustomed to thinking took place when a proselyte was baptized into Israel.[22] A more humbling renunciation of all privilege, all acquired and inherited merit and standing before God, could not be imagined. The *skandalon* of conversion to Christianity was absolute.

This is a salutary reminder in days like our own when Christians tend to be rather shy about the uniqueness of their religion. "Dialogue" replaces "mission" in the vocabulary, and "conversion" is an unacceptable concept. Recently Professor J. G. Davies has launched an assault on both the word and the idea of conversion.[23] He criticizes the Church for attempting to extend its own numbers by proselytism and individual conversion. The true aim of Christians, he thinks, should be to enter into dialogue with the world, not subject it to monologue; to send men into the world with God's reconciling message in their lives, rather than to try by lip to exert an influence on the social and economic life of their generation. That is to say, Dr Davies is coming down firmly on one side of the old divide, social gospel or spiritual gospel. But the New Testament firmly rejects the dichotomy.[24] The early preachers did not enter into dialogue with the world, except to understand it and to present their life-changing message in terms comprehensible to their contemporaries. They believed they had got good news for their friends, and they knew that good news was embodied in Jesus Christ. Him they proclaimed. And as men came to trust him, their lives began to be transformed, their social and cultural pursuits changed, and the love of God which they had freely received drove them out to the social involvement which Professor Davies rightly advocates. Once sever the fundamental root of conversion to Christ from the Christian message, and it becomes a broken and a lifeless plant, however beautiful the flowers of Christian concern and social involvement it displays. Christian conversion was a new and unique thing in the ancient world; humbling, dynamic, stark. What did it offer, and what did it involve? In short, how was a man converted?

CONVERSION THROUGH THE SPIRIT AND THE WORD

We have already considered in chapter 1 some of the attractions which Christianity presented to the ancient world, but if we are to believe the Christians themselves it was not merely for these reasons that the gospel spread so fast and so widely. The man who, more than anyone in the early Church, has given us his assessment of the factors in evangelism is St Luke. And for him the two main ones are the very factors which men do not provide, namely the Spirit of God and the Word of God.

It is a commonplace that the main theme of Acts is the work of the Holy Spirit, and that he is the supreme agent in the Christian mission. Yet this is the very factor which is most often forgotten in assessing conversion in the early Church. The Christians were convinced that the Spirit of Jesus had come into their midst and indwelt their very personalities in order to equip them for evangelism, for making him known to others. Acts is the story, seen from one apostolic man's perspective, of how this was worked out. J. H. E. Hull has recently drawn attention to this in *The Holy Spirit in the Acts of the Apostles*. He says, "The evangelization of the world was

Luke's outstanding interest and concern . . . The Church received the Spirit not for its selfish secret enjoyment but to enable it to bear witness for Christ."[25] Every initiative in evangelism recorded in Acts is the initiative of the Spirit of God. From 1:8 where the world mission is adumbrated, up to the Roman imprisonment of Paul at the end of the book which enables the gospel to be heard freely in the capital, each new advance is inaugurated by the Lord the Spirit.[26] It is the Spirit, the gift of the ascended Jesus, who fills and so signally uses the disciples on the day of Pentecost, likewise Peter before the Sanhedrin, Stephen at Jerusalem, Philip with the eunuch.[27] It is the Spirit who drives Paul out on his mission, and prompts him in where best to exercise it;[28] it is the Spirit who leads Peter to evangelize Cornelius, and the Antioch Church to evangelize the heathen on the first missionary journey.[29] So far from the Spirit being the possession of the Church, as Käsemann would have it with his astonishing reading of primitive Catholicism into the Acts,[30] the Spirit is what creates, validates and energizes the Church. "The greatness of Luke's view," as E. Schweizer rightly sees, "lies in his showing more impressively than anyone else that the Church can live only by evangelizing, and by following whatever new paths the Spirit indicates."[31] Of course, Luke was not the only one who stressed the primacy of the Spirit in mission. The same point is made in St John's Gospel[32] and frequently in Paul. The Spirit is linked with the proclamation of the gospel time and again in his writings; passages like Philippians 1:19, 1 Thessalonians 1:5, Ephesians 6:18f. are typical. The initiative lies with God: just as it did in creation and redemption, so it does in mission.[33]

The second great medium for evangelism is the Word of God.[34] This is frequently linked with the Spirit in the New Testament writings, as if to stress that it is through the Word of God that the Spirit of God is accustomed to act. In each of these passages just quoted, the two are integrally connected. The Word of God is the very sword which the Spirit uses.[35] One of the great merits of C. K. Barrett's *Luke the Historian* is the way he highlights this truth. "The prime agency by which the Spirit extends the sovereignty of Christ is the Word of God"[36] and with that he would include phrases like "the word of the Lord", "the word of salvation", "the word of the gospel", and "the word" *tout simple*. Wherever the early Christians went, it was the Word they carried (8:4). For eighteen months and more at Corinth it was the Word which gripped Paul (18:5). It was the same at Ephesus during the two years of his mission: "All the residents of Asia heard the Word of the Lord." When Luke wants to indicate the success of the mission, he says that the Word of the Lord grew and prevailed.[37] The Word makes its own impact on Theophilus (Luke 1:1, Acts 1:1), the centurion Cornelius (10:44), the proconsul of Cyprus (13:7), the citizens of Antioch (13:44). No wonder the Twelve made it their priority (6:4). No wonder they committed their converts to it (20:28). No wonder the nameless amateur missionaries of 8:4 took it as their great weapon. Does a man believe? Then it is because the Word brings faith (4:4). Does a man receive the Spirit? It comes from hearing the Word (10:44). Does a man become a Christian? It is due to God's illuminating the heart of the hearers of the apostolic message. Is a man a counterfeit Christian? Then it is because he has no part in the Word (8:21). It is no exaggeration to say that the Word is the prime agency under the Spirit of God for the mission of the Church in evangelism.

In emphasizing this "Word", they almost certainly used a basic pattern. We have already examined several attempts to reconstruct it, of which the most celebrated is C. H. Dodd's. The difficulties experienced in assessing the precise limits of this "Word" will never be surmounted, for the simple reason that there was as great flexibility in approach among the early Christians as there was unity in aim and similarity in content. But we shall not be far wrong in taking these three points as basic to the Word which they announced.

First, *they preached a person*. Their message was frankly Christocentric. Indeed, often enough the gospel is referred to simply as Jesus or Christ: "He preached Jesus to him."[38] To the Jews Jesus was the fulfilment of God's work in history:[39] to the Gentiles Jesus marked the end of God's apparent disinterest.[40] Jesus the man, Jesus crucified, Jesus risen, Jesus exalted to the place of power in the universe from which he would return in judgment at the end of the age, Jesus who meantime was present among his people in the Spirit, and demonstrated this through signs and wonders as well as through the meteoric rise of the Church. This, it seems, was the main burden of what they taught about Jesus. There was little about his life, if we may judge from the Pauline epistles and the speeches in Acts; little about his teaching and his miracles.[41] The stress all fell on his cross and resurrection and his present power and significance. The risen Christ was unambiguously central in their message.

Second, *they proclaimed a gift*. The gift of forgiveness, the gift of the Spirit, the gift of adoption, of reconciliation. The gift that made "no people" part of the "people of God", the gift that brought those who were far off near.[42] The Jews had done nothing to merit it,[43] any more than the Gentiles had: it proceeded entirely from the grace of God. The gospel is "the word of his grace"; it is only "through the grace of the Lord Jesus" that men can be saved, or find life, or be justified.[44] Because the author of this salvation is none other than God himself, the offer is directed to all men without distinction—except the distinction of being in themselves unacceptable. Particular stress is laid in Acts on two elements in the gift of God, elements which were foreshadowed in Jeremiah and Ezekiel as the marks of the New Covenant,[45] namely forgiveness of sins and the internal possession of the Holy Spirit. The combination is found as early as the Pentecost sermon: "the forgiveness of your sins and the gift of the Holy Spirit" are the two aspects of Peter's offer. It was the same at Paul's conversion. Ananias told him to be baptized and wash away his sins, and then he could be filled with the Holy Spirit.[46] Pardon for the past and power for the future were two prominent aspects of the gift of God which the apostles proclaimed.

Third, *they looked for a response.*[47] The apostles were not shy about asking men to decide for or against the God who had decided for them. They expected results.[48] They challenged men to do something about the message they had heard. "What shall we do?" was the response of the crowd on the day of Pentecost. The answer is clear enough in the pages of the New Testament. Men must do three things. They must first and foremost repent, change their attitude to their old way of life, be willing to let go their sins. It involved a radical break with the past. It could not be real in the absence of "deeds which demonstrated repentance".[49] It meant burning their books for the Ephesian magicians, and washing Paul's stripes for the Philippian jailer. It was God's indispensable condition of acceptance. All men everywhere must repent: the challenge came to "every one of you".[50] There was no escaping it. It did not necessarily mean the soulful bewailing of past sins: essentially it was a changed attitude towards *God*, God whom they had offended and in practice deposed from his rightful place of sovereignty in their lives. Together with repentance goes faith; "repentance towards God" is matched by "faith towards the Lord Jesus Christ" in the brief summary of Paul's gospel for Jew and Greek alike in Acts 20:21. In order to receive the gift of forgiveness and the Spirit, a man must believe on Jesus (10:43, 11:17, 16:31, etc.).[51] The content of the faith is often not specified: men heard the preaching and believed.[52] But it is the message about Jesus that formed the content of their faith. It is interesting to notice how often the Christocentric character of this faith is stressed in the New Testament by the use of the Greek proposition *eis* with the accusative.[53] In saving faith a man commits himself "onto Christ", and thenceforth exercises

151

Christian faith by remaining *en Christō*, "in Christ". He cannot live in Christ before he has entrusted himself to Christ. The leap of faith is inevitably prior to the life of faith.

The third condition incumbent upon all who wanted to begin the Christian life was, of course, baptism. We shall be considering this below. It was the seal both on God's offer of forgiveness and the Spirit and on man's response to that offer in repentance and faith. But while we are considering conversion, repentance and faith, it is worth noting this comment of J. R. W. Stott, to whose essay *The Meaning of Evangelism* I am much indebted: "Now both repentance and faith are described in Acts in terms of 'turning'. Repentance is a turning from wickedness (3:26) whereas faith is a turning 'to God' (15:19, 26:20) or 'to the Lord' (9:35, 11:21). This, then, is the meaning of conversion (15:3). 'To turn', intransitive (3:19, AV 'be converted') is to turn from the vanity of idols to the living God (14:15) 'from darkness to light, and from the power of Satan to God' (26:18), or from sin and self to Jesus Christ."[54] This is a fact worth pondering when it is remarked how rarely the Greek word for conversion is met with in the New Testament. Conversion is nothing other than turning to Christ in repentance and faith, and there is no shortage of emphasis on that subject in the apostolic writings.

CONVERSION, BAPTISM AND THE NEW LIFE

The decisive turning to Christ in repentance and faith was given a physical sign and seal, baptism.[55] Sacramentally this marked the beginning of Christian experience. Just as circumcision had marked the transaction between God's gracious initiative in Old Testament days and man's trusting and obedient response,[56] so baptism signified entry into the Christian society.[57] This is not the place to examine the doctrine of baptism in the New Testament: it has received a great deal of careful examination in recent years. But the main point as far as we are concerned is the universal and quite unselfconscious link in the early Church between the invisible encounter of man's faith with God's grace, and its outward expression in baptism. So far from being in some way antithetical to grace and faith, as much Protestant thought has in the past imagined, baptism is the sacrament of justification by faith. To say "In Christ Jesus you are all sons of God, through faith" is tantamount to saying "As many of you as were baptized into Christ have put on Christ".[58] It is not by accident that Romans chapter 6 with its teaching on union with Christ in death and resurrection through baptism comes immediately after Romans chapter 5 with its high doctrine of justification. They belong together. Those who repented and believed the Word were baptized. That was the invariable pattern, so far as we know.[59]

Baptism was understood and expressed in a variety of ways in apostolic days. It was the mark of incorporation within the Body of Christ—"by one Spirit we were all baptized into one Body".[60] It was the mark of purification, of cleansing from the old sins.[61] It was the mark of justification—"you were washed, you were sanctified, you were justified in the name of the Lord Jesus."[62] It was the bath of rebirth, or the water of regeneration.[63] It was the mark of the New Covenant which the prophets looked for with longing, when God's law would be interiorized in the believer.[64] It was initiation into the realm of the Spirit, himself the first instalment of God's eschatological blessings for men and the pledge of ultimate redemption.[65] It meant such a close union with Christ that the believer was participant in his death and resurrection.[66] These are only a few of the New Testament ways of understanding baptism. The important thing is that they all make it abundantly clear that baptism and conversion belong together; it is the sacrament of the once-for-allness of incorporation into Christ.

In subapostolic times its uniqueness was recognized even when it was thought of in unscriptural categories. For instance, Ignatius regards it as a weapon against the evil powers, almost as an amulet,[67] while at the same time clinging so strongly to its unrepeatable nature as entry into the Church that he forbids its administration without the Church's local leader, the bishop.[68] Hermas preserves many of the New Testament insights though he does not fully understand them. Baptism for him is the seal of the Spirit, "because men go down into the water dead and they come up alive",[69] a view which hovers between magic and Romans 6. In the *Mandates* he declares that repentance is the necessary precondition of baptism, and a holy life is its result.[70] The really agonizing question with which he wrestles is what happens when a holy life does not result? What is to be done about post-baptismal sins? Had he really understood Paul's doctrine of union with Christ in death and resurrection through faith and baptism, had he really seen that baptism seals upon the believer the effects of the atonement, he would not have produced the doctrine of penance to which he was inexorably led by a high doctrine of baptism and a moralistic conception of sin. But at all events he shows the relation of baptism to conversion in an ordinary man's view of the second century. Of course there are fuller and more biblical accounts of baptism in writers like Barnabas[71] and Justin,[72] leading up to the more serious discussions in

Hippolytus and Tertullian at the end of the century.[73] Water baptism and Spirit baptism are one; they constitute the "illumination" whereby "the children of ignorance and necessity" become "the children of knowledge and free choice". Baptism is the laver of regeneration, the water of life, spiritual circumcision. It is the entry into Christian life.[74]

In the early days of the Church, baptism was administered straight away on profession of faith and repentance. The Philippian jailer was baptized without delay or catechesis; so was Paul himself; so were the Corinthians; so was the Ethiopian eunuch.[75] The latter's case is particularly interesting, for Acts 8:37 (in which Philip says the eunuch may be baptized if he believes with all his heart, whereupon the Ethiopian replies "I believe that Jesus Christ is the Son of God") is missing in all but the Western text of Acts. Though the origin of this Western text is still shrouded in obscurity, it must have been in the first or very beginning of the second century. And if Cullmann is right in supposing that this verse enshrines the earliest baptismal ritual of which we have any sure knowledge,[76] it is a fair inference that baptism followed immediately upon profession of faith in Christ throughout the first century, at least in some areas. However, the *Didache* suggests that very soon a period of instruction in the Christian faith, particularly its ethical side, preceded baptism.[77] For no sooner has the author finished his teaching about the Two Ways with its instruction in the life a catechumen must live than he proceeds at once to baptism.[78] It may be that Carrington and Selwyn are right in finding traces of a primitive baptismal catechism in the New Testament itself.[79] It would not be surprising if the early missionaries did soon evolve a stylized form of Christian instruction just as they seem to have done, at least to some extent, with their gospel preaching. The fourfold ethical instruction which Selwyn characterizes by its Latin terminology of *deponentes* (the putting off of the old evil nature), *subjecti* (proper Christian submission in various areas of political and social life), *vigilate* (the charge to watch and pray) and *resistite* (the need for standing firm in the faith and resisting the assaults of the devil) does seem to be well attested in the writings of Paul, Peter and James, though whether it preceded baptism or followed it is more problematical.[80] In any case, procedure during the second century is likely to have been far from homogeneous. In Justin, for instance, whilst the baptismal fast is prominent (as it was in the *Didache*) there is no indication of much organized preparation for baptism: "As many as are persuaded and believe that these things which we teach and describe are true and undertake to live accordingly, are taught to pray and ask God, while fasting, for the forgiveness of their sins. Then they are led by us to a place where there is water, and they are reborn after the manner of the rebirth by which we too were reborn: for they are then washed in the water in the name of the Father and Lord God of all things, and of our Saviour Jesus Christ, and of the Holy Spirit."[81] It is possible, but not probable, that the *disciplina arcani* or reserve about explaining the Christian mysteries prohibited Justin from saying more about the catechetical methods employed; but it is difficult to see why, if that were the case, he should have given so much information about the actual rite of baptism, and even more about the eucharist. It is much more likely that the Church was not yet uniformly rigid in its preparation of postulants for baptism. Commitment to Jesus as Lord, belief in the Christian teaching, willingness to live the Christian life, and baptism into the triune Name—these were the main points from which the later catechesis, such as we meet in the *Apostolic Tradition* of Hippolytus, developed with its full blown Apostles' Creed, its detailed ethical regulations and its three year period of instruction. We have certainly travelled a long way from the New Testament by the time of Hippolytus at the end of the second century. But baptism has not, *pace* Harnack,[82] been turned into a magical means of entry into the community of the saved, by assimilation to the Mystery Religions. In these the initiate was, as we have seen, normally subjected to no moral or ethical demands (that is why these religions were so popular). In Christianity these demands were essential. Moreover, in the Mysteries the postulant was granted "knowledge" only after initiation. In Christianity, however, the initiation itself was the climax of a long period of learning about God, the Creator, Redeemer and Judge, and after three years or so[83] of mixing with the Christian congregation in their worship, particularly in hearing the Word of God read and preached. It was only after the sermon and before the eucharist proper that the catechumens were dismissed with a special prayer and blessing, the *missa catechumenorum*. The Christians made no secret of their faith, its offers and its demands: Irenaeus gives a full outline of Christian ethic and doctrine and maintains that this is taught and preached throughout the world: "the preaching of the truth shines everywhere and enlightens all men that are willing to come to a knowledge of the truth." It is the same gospel that is proclaimed, the same teaching that is given, in the churches of Germany, Spain, Gaul, the East, Egypt or anywhere else. The Church believes these things "as if she had one soul . . . and proclaims them as if she had but one mouth".[84] There was no hiding of doctrine from Christian enquirers; there was no withholding of fellowship. It was the sacraments which were hedged around so carefully. Granted that pagan influences contributed to the growth in some quarters of an almost magical conception of grace in the sacraments, nevertheless the main features of New Testament baptism were carefully maintained. The very intensity of the ethical requirements, the very insistence on understanding the faith, the probationary period in the fellowship of the Church but not fully of it, the great build-up for the once-for-all unrepeatable rite of baptism, all in their various ways emphasized an aspect of baptism in the New Testament days; even though the Church's postponement of baptism, sometimes until the death-bed, and her hesitation in admitting forgiveness for post-baptismal sin revealed an imperfect understanding of what baptism had meant to the first Christians.

In view of its development in the succeeding century, it is instructive to have another look at the Acts of the Apostles, and see how much of the later practice is foreshadowed there. Baptism was administered on profession of repentance and faith in Jesus. It brought forgiveness and the indwelling of the Holy Spirit, as we have seen. But it also brought a man into a new community, in which he shared a common life with his Christian brethren.[85] This was a *moral* life. It was known as "The Way"[86] the implications of which are plain enough from the *Didache*.[87] He lived his life in the presence of God and tried to please him in everything.[88] He was intimately related to his brother Christians in bonds of obligation and love; he shared his goods with them, he cared for the poor, the widows, the famine-stricken.[89] And the baptismal life not only involved holy living and Christian love, but also worship and fellowship, witness and instruction.[90] The first converts continued in the apostles' doctrine and fellowship, the breaking of bread and the prayers: and with one accord they bore their testimony to Jesus. Baptism, in short, set the seal on conversion in every way, individual, corporate, ethical, educational, and theological. Conversion, baptism and the new life at least as far as adults were concerned,[91] were inseparable.

CONVERSION AND THE MODERN MIND

A study of conversion as it was understood and practised in the earliest Church raises certain problems for us today, of which the following three are perhaps the most common.

First, then, one may ask, was this preaching for decision strictly necessary? After all, Jesus had seen Abraham as a Christian before his time; Paul had seen David in a similar light.[92] Justin claimed

Socrates for the Christians. Tertullian later on spoke of the *anima naturaliter Christiana*, and he was thinking not of the "once born" product of a Christian home, but of pagan Greeks.[93] Ought we not to follow in their footsteps capitalizing on the good that is in every man rather than take our cue from the aggressive missionary activity of much Christianity both ancient and modern ?

That position is often heard these days, and it is a reasonable enough reaction to the overemphasis on the spoken word and the underemphasis on the quality of life and community which has marked a good deal of Western Protestantism. But granted the biblical doctrine both of man and of God it will not stand critical investigation. If there is one God, Creator, Redeemer, Judge, as the early Church passionately asserted, then those who have been brought back from their rebellion against him into fellowship with him cannot but pass on the knowledge of that rescue to others; the new life cries out to be shared. We shall examine the motives behind the mission of the Church in a later chapter. Here it is sufficient to say that in obedience to Jesus Christ's express command they could not do less than go and preach the gospel to all who would hear. And once preached it could not but be divisive because it would not fit in with the comfortable contemporary synthesis of religions, but made absolute claims on man's loyalty and allegiance in the name of an Absolute God.

To be sure, Jesus and Paul saw the saints of the Old Testament as "Christians before Christ" because here were men who trusted entirely in God's mercy to themselves and did not try to establish themselves or acquire merit in his sight. Their faith rested on his grace—precisely as it does with a Christian. The only difference is that the Christian has a clearer understanding of the alchemy of grace in the light of Calvary. Undoubtedly a man like Justin was on dangerous ground when he claimed that Socrates was partaker in the divine Logos;[94] he was deliberately laying hold of anything that was good in paganism in the conviction that all that is good comes from God. But he did not make the mistake of thinking that the "good" pagan did not need converting—or he might have spared himself the trouble of writing his Apologies and suffering martyrdom. No, insofar as Socrates opposed the polytheism of his day, he was acting reasonably (*meta logou*—Justin is using Stoic thought forms here to his Christian advantage). But he knew well that Socrates had only a small part of the Logos, who later embodied himself completely in human form and was called Christ Jesus. "Whatever philosophers uttered well," he maintained elsewhere, "they elaborated by finding and contemplating some part of the

Word. But since they did not know the whole of the Word, which is Christ, they often contradicted themselves."[95] So far from thinking that Socrates and other good men of the pagan past were Christians, the apologists did not hesitate to point out their failings in sincerity, trustworthiness and sexual morality.[96]

Tertullian is wildly represented when his *anima naturaliter Christiana* is taken to mean that the natural man is a decent Christian at heart.[97] "The human race," he tells us roundly, "has always deserved ill at God's hand", on account of men's culpable disobedience to God, their wilful neglect of him, and their vices and crimes which affront the Judge and Avenger of sin.[98] Tertullian is no Broad Churchman. When he speaks of the soul that is by nature Christian he is not denying the need of that soul to be converted to Christ. Far from it; in the very next chapter of his *Apology* he makes it abundantly plain that "men are made, not born Christians".[99] All he was doing in the previous chapter was to follow the line adopted by Paul in Romans 2:15 and draw attention to the conscience within every pagan's breast which despite the way men maltreat it with depraved customs and slavery to false gods, still bears some sort of testimony to the God who implanted it there. Their very oaths and swear words, "God will repay me" and the like, bear witness to God the Judge. It is in this context that he cries out, "O noble testimony of the soul by nature Christian!" There is, in fact, no support to be derived from the writings of the early Church for the current attempt to effect a synthesis between Christianity and other religions or atheism. They had every inducement to syncretize in the first two centuries, when death was often the penalty for refusing to do so, and they withstood the temptation.

A second modern reflection on the realist language so often used by the early Christians about baptism would be the very opposite of the objection we have just been considering. How is it possible that they should have spoken in terms verging on the magical of the sacrament of baptism? Those who make this criticism usually come from a strong Protestant background, and perhaps need to take more seriously than they have been accustomed the possibility that the sacraments may normally *effect* what they symbolize. As circumcision effected and did not merely point to incorporation into the Old Covenant, so baptism incorporates a man into Christ. This is a strand of teaching found in Paul, Peter and John,[100] and its strident emphasis in Ignatius need not necessarily be due to his pagan background! Part of our difficulty in divided Christendom is that we find it impossible to keep together the different aspects of truth which the apostolic age apparently combined. Bishop Lesslie Newbigin pointed out in his celebrated book *The Household of God* that there are at least three understandings of the Church in the New Testament, each with its appropriate means of entry. The apostles thought of the Church as the extension of Israel, and consequently baptism was the appropriate mode of entry, as circumcision had been in the Old Testament. The Church was equally the fellowship of believers, for which repentance and faith are the conditions of acceptance. It is no less true that the Church is the community of the Spirit, and the only way to join this community is to allow the Spirit of Jesus access to one's life. It goes without saying that the Catholics have tended to stress the first of these concepts, the Protestants the second, and the Pentecostals the third. All are equally valid; but each one becomes falsified if taken in isolation and to its logical extreme. When we examine the subapostolic Church it is remarkable to see the extent to which they did retain the New Testament genius of holding all three of these insights in fruitful tension. For all their insistence on the real efficacy of baptism, the second century Christians were well aware of the difference between promise and performance, between authentic and nominal Christians, just as the first century writers were. St John, for instance, speaks of counterfeit Christians who "went out from us but they were not of us"[101] and Paul knows Corinthian churchmen who though duly baptized and participants at the eucharist,[102] are nevertheless as much under God's displeasure as was Simon Magus, described as "in the gall of bitterness and the bond of iniquity" even after his profession of faith and baptism.[103] In view of their duller spiritual perception in many ways, it is surprising that the Apostolic Fathers are so clear about this distinction between membership of the empirical Church and the universal Church. Ignatius prays that he may not merely be called a Christian but found one;[104] Polycarp looks for a joyful resurrection with Christ if he does His will;[105] *2 Clement* argues that "if we do the will of our Father we shall belong to the spiritual Church, but if not, we shall fall under the Scripture which says, 'My house became a den of brigands'. Let us therefore choose to belong to the Church of life (or living Church) so that we may win salvation."[106]

The third modern objection which is always brought against any definite, challenging preaching for conversion is that it is too emotional, too hasty and naïve, and appeals only to a certain type of person. We must not be misled by the truncated account of gospel preaching given in Acts into supposing that the apostles made hasty and ill-conceived appeals for decision on every occasion. It would be hard to see how the Christian movement would have spread so rapidly had they been so foolish. On the contrary they really gave themselves to this proclamation of the Word. They spent a great deal of time at it, day in day out, year in year out. Paul might spend only a few weeks in Thessalonica, but whole years in Corinth and Ephesus. He could argue all day long with Jewish theologians;[107] he could talk all night till Eutychus fell out of the window, and when that little problem was sorted out, he could go on talking till day-break![108] He could preach with all his heart in Pisidian Antioch and then defer the matter for another week.[109] He argued with passers-by in the market place at Athens, he held discussions in the lecture hall of Tyrannus, he entered into extended dialogue with Felix and Agrippa.[110] It is interesting to note[111] the nuance of words like *diamarturesthai*[112] "to testify strenuously", *kataggellein*[113] "to proclaim forcefully", *dialegesthai*[114] "to argue", *diakatelenchein*[115] "to confute powerfully" when applied to the apostolic evangelistic preaching. Sometimes we read of joyful proclamation of good news (*euaggelizein*),[116] at other times of patient comparison of scriptures as enquirer and evangelist examined the Old Testament (*suzētein*,[117] *paratithesthai*,[118] *sumbibazein*[119]), sometimes of the utter defeat of the objector in argument (*sunchunein*).[120] Primitive evangelism was by no means mere proclamation and exhortation; it included able intellectual argument, skilful study of the scriptures, careful, closely reasoned teaching and patient argument. It was no doubt because of the careful teaching instruction they were giving that the authorities were worried about this new movement: "You have filled Jerusalem with your teaching."[121] If it had had an inadequate intellectual basis it would not have lasted long. The fashionable separation, derived from Professor Dodd, of separating *kērugma* from *didachē*, preaching from teaching, in primitive evangelism is misleading, and unconsciously perhaps supports this suspicion that the Apostles appealed primarily to the emotions. In fact evangelism is called *teaching* in several places in Acts.[122] The hearers would inevitably want to know a good deal about Jesus before putting their faith in him. Indeed, the separation of preaching from teaching has combined with other factors to enable Bultmann to maintain at the same time a high degree of scepticism about the historical Jesus and a reverent, almost infallibilist attitude to the preached word, which a man must not question or argue with, but respond to. But this is not what the apostles asked for. They looked for faith which was self-commitment *on evidence*, not a leap into the dark. They were tied to history by the very fact of the incarnation and they did not seek to escape from it. The gospel docs indeed challenge men to decision, but not an emotional or ill-considered commitment.

Mediated to us as it is through human beings, it always engages every aspect of our humanity.

Take the conversion of St Paul. So far from its being exceptional, I believe it is meant by St Luke to be normative for all Christians everywhere. That is why he gives us three accounts of it. Not, of course, that the shattering heavenly vision, the blindness, the prostration on the ground and the voice like thunder are to be expected again. They are the mere external trappings of Paul's conversion. But the principles lie deeper. This encounter with Christ touched Paul at every level of his being. *His mind* was informed and illuminated: Jesus was not, as he had thought, accursed, but was the Lord. *His conscience* was reached: he faced up to the fact that he had been kicking against the pricks. *His emotions* were stirred as he saw the implications of his rebellion against Christ. But this was a mere incidental on the way to his will, Christ's real goal. *His will* was bent in trusting surrender to Jesus who had called him, and who was from henceforth to be Lord of his life. And in consequence *his life* was transformed: in direction, immediately, and in achievement as time went on. His supreme aim henceforth was to live for his Redeemer: "I was not disobedient to the heavenly vision, but declared first to those at Damascus then at Jerusalem . . . that they should repent and turn to God." (Acts 26:19).

This conversion of St Paul is rightly called in 1 Timothy 1:16 a pattern for subsequent believers. Despite the enormous variety of temperaments, backgrounds and capacities of the men reached by the gospel in the early Church, an illuminated mind, a quickened conscience, a humbled grateful heart, a yielded will and a changed life were the common factors in the conversion of them all. Let us glance at some of these men and women who have left us a record of their initial encounter with Christ, and see as far as we can what led them to take the momentous step of repentance, faith and baptism.

CONVERSION: SOME EXAMPLES

One would give a lot to know how the man in the street was won to Christ in antiquity. We can speculate, as Harnack does, that "one person would be brought over by means of the Old Testament, another by the exorcizing of demons, a third by the purity of Christian life; others by the monotheism of Christianity above all by the prospect of complete expiation, or by the prospect it held out of immortality, or . . . by example".[123] This is highly probable: but we do not *know*, because the ordinary man in the street has not left us his recollections.

For these we must turn to the more educated and wealthy, whose writings have come down to us. It is not always possible to be sure how much is personal testimony in such writers, and how much literary or evangelistic commonplace. But it is possible to discern two main types among them. They overlap, to be sure, but the search for truth and the search for deliverance seem to have been the two main paths by which those who have left literary records speak of their conversion.

One of the main factors which led thinking people to Christianity was the discovery within it of the true philosophy, an intelligible and credible account of God, the world and man. The intellectual questing and insecurity of that era was very great. Writers like Festugière, Cumont and Nock have illustrated this graphically from the primary sources. A doctor, Thessalus, travelled all the way from Asia to Egypt in search of a god who could reveal to him the secrets of herbal medicine.[124] Lucius, in Apuleius's romance, has to travel the world before finding release and truth in Isis and her mysteries. The astrologer, Vettius Valens, crossed land and sea in order to find out, if he could, the mysteries of the elements. This was the itch which gnosticism, magic, and the mystery religions set out to cater for. But it was in Christianity that men like Justin, Tatian and Theophilus found rest. Justin tells us of his search for truth: he sat under a Stoic but learnt nothing about God from him—for he did not know himself, and said such instruction was unnecessary! He went to a Peripatetic, but was put off by his obsession with his fees. The Pythagorean and the Platonist did not satisfy him either, and it was not until he came across to an old man in the open country one day, that he discovered, in conversation with him, the true wisdom and knowledge he had been seeking. The help of this wise Christian, prayer to God for light, and musing over the writings of the prophets "and of the friends of Christ" led him to faith. He came to this decision on his own. The old man did not demand any instant reponse from him. But having spoken, he left the truth of his words to make their own impact on Justin's understanding, and they did. The sweetness and power of the words of the Saviour brought Justin to his knees.[125]

Tatian travelled much the same path. It was the Old Testament Scriptures, in particular, which satisfied his quest for truth. "I sought how I might be able to discover the truth," he tells us, "and while I was giving my most earnest attention to the matter, I happened to meet with certain barbaric writings, too old to be compared with the opinions of the Greeks, and too divine to be compared with their errors; and I was led to put faith in these by the unpretentious cast of the language, the genuine character of the writers, their intelligible account of creation, the foreknowledge they displayed of future events, the excellent quality of the precepts, and their declaration that the government of the universe is centred in one Being."[126] Athenagoras the Athenian was another cultured opponent of Christianity who was converted through reading the Scriptures.[127] It is a curious fact, remarked on by B. P. Pratten in his translation of Athenagoras, that his two surviving works correspond precisely with the two parts of Paul's Areopagus address: his *Plea for Christians* is an attack on polytheism, and his *Resurrection of the Dead* is a defence of that doctrine which once caused the Athenians such mirth. Theophilus of Antioch is another intellectual who was won over by the superiority of the Scriptures over anything else he had ever come across: the fulfilment of prophecy, the warning of judgment and the offer of immortality were three elements in the biblical message which met his longing for reality.[128] Clement of Alexandria was another who came to Christ primarily along the path of the intellect. In the first book of the *Stromateis* he tells us of his quest for truth as a pagan philosopher. He found it through intercourse with some remarkable Christians from Greece, Syria, Italy and Egypt. Of these the greatest was Pantaenus, a missionary in India who had come to work in Egypt. This man, he tells us, gathered honey from the flowers in the prophetic and apostolic meadow to such effect that he instilled in his hearers a deathless element of knowledge. The Scriptures, he found, kindle the living spark of the soul.[129]

It would be a mistake to suppose that these men had a merely intellectual conversion. Far from it. Tatian, and probably Clement, had been initiated into the mysteries and had been repelled by their obscenities and emptiness.[130] And as Tatian had longed for deliverance from the power of sin in his life, the 10,000 tyrants, as he graphically puts it, who hold men's will in bondage;[131] so Clement was deeply aware of the transformation he had undergone from being a child of wrath into a child of God. Quoting Ephesians 2:3 he writes, "Those who are unbelievers are called children of wrath, reared in wrath. But we are no more nurselings of wrath; we have been rescued from error and restored to the truth. In this way, then, we who were once sons of lawlessness, through the kindness of the Word have now become sons of God."[132]

There is a second group of Christians who show from their writings that it was primarily through the longing for deliverance that they came to faith in Christ. Barnabas knew the liberation from the yoke of *Ananke*, Necessity, which the new Law of Jesus

Christ, written in his heart, had brought him.[133] Similarly Ignatius seems to be speaking from personal experience when he rejoices in the sheer newness of eternal life, and the deliverance from the forces of magic, ignorance, sin and death which Christ had brought to men. Through his baptism into Christ he had been delivered not only from evil habits and ignorance but also from Necessity.[134] The *Clementine Recognitions* reflect much the same atmosphere. The unknown author tells us that he was much troubled when he was a pagan by the problem of whether or not there was any life after death. Reflecting on these things got him down, but he could not escape from such thoughts, for he had within him "that most excellent companion, who would not suffer me to rest—the desire for immortality". Unimpressed by the speculations of the philosophers on the subject, for they were "accounted true or false not in accordance with their nature and the truth of the arguments, but in proportion to the talents of those who supported them" he was fortunate enough to fall in with a Christian preacher, and eventually was converted. He found in Christ the answer to his doubts, his lust, his hunger for immortality, and his longing for a coherent, simple, convincing explanation of the world.[135] So while the quest for deliverance predominated, the hunger for truth was a significant factor for him as it was for the other group.

Deliverance from the guilt and power of evil has always been a major impetus to conversion. It was so with St Paul; it was so with St Augustine. So it was with the following two examples, taken from very different strata of society. Justin tells us[136] of the dissolute wife of a dissolute husband, who was converted in Rome about A.D. 150. Apparently it was through the lives and words of her Christian friends, for it was to them that she repaired when her husband rejected all her efforts to win him, too, for Christianity. The change in her life so enraged him that he set out to annoy her by his excesses, sexual and alcoholic, and eventually publicly denounced her for her Christian allegiance and thereby triggered off repressive measures against the Church to which Justin alludes in his *Second Apology*. Who can doubt that the temperate lives of her Christian friends, contrasting so sharply with her own, made her feel guilty, and was the main factor in leading her to the One who could both cleanse and empower?

The other example comes from high society. Cyprian was an aristocratic orator from Carthage; rich, cultured, but beneath it all he was very much aware of his sin and wondered if there could be any chance of a fresh start for one like himself. He described the situation in his letter to Donatus. "I used to wander blindly in the darkness of night, buffeted this way and that in the stormy sea of the world; hither and thither I floated, ignorant of my own life, and a stranger to the truth and the light. Given the manner of life I lived in those days, I used to think that what God in his tenderness promised me for my salvation was difficult, indeed distasteful. How could a man be reborn and quickened for a new life in the water of baptism? How could one be regenerated and have done with all the past, and, without physical changes, be altered in heart and soul? How, I asked myself, was such a conversion possible? For I was captured and held prisoner by the countless sins of my past life; I did not believe it was possible to be rid of them. So I became slave to my vices. I despaired of better things. I learned to make excuses for my faults which had become my familiar friends." What an honest admission of the truth to which Paul gave classic expression in Romans 7! And like the apostle, Cyprian found the enormous relief of baptism into Christ, forgiveness, and the moral transformation wrought by the Holy Spirit. "The water of regeneration washed away the stains of my past life. A light from above entered and permeated my heart, now cleansed from its defilement. The Spirit came from heaven, and changed me into a new man by the second birth. Almost at once in a marvellous way doubt gave way to assurance, what had been shut tight, opened; light shone in dark places; and I found what had previously seemed difficult had become easy, and what I had thought impossible could be done. You know it all well enough; you understand as I do what it is that brought me this death to sin and this resurrection to godly living. You know it full well: I am not boasting."[137]

Such were the ways in which the moral and the intellectual challenges of Christianity combined to win converts throughout the whole social scale in the early Church. Sometimes one side would predominate, sometimes the other. But all the cases we have considered follow in some important respects the pattern of conversion which we saw in the New Testament and particularly clearly in the case of St Paul. For all their differences, the profound change which came over these men and women when they entrusted themselves to Christ affected their intellect, their conscience, their will and their subsequent life. Henceforth it was their intention, and progressively their achievement, to say with the apostle, "I have been crucified with Christ; it is no longer I who live but Christ lives in me. And the life I now live, I live by faith in the Son of God, who loved me and gave himself for me."[138]

7

THE EVANGELISTS

WE HAVE SEEN in the previous chapter the unique character of Christian conversion. This naturally prompts the question, who were the men who brought about these conversions, and what were they like? In this chapter we shall examine first the identity of the early preachers and then the quality of their lives and deaths.

THE EVANGELISTS: WHO WERE THEY?

The Professional Ministry—Apostles and "Ordained" Men

The obvious and immediate answer is, the apostles. The essential qualifications of the twelve apostles of Jesus were that they should be with him, and that he should send them forth to preach.[1] They were apparently given a "trial run" during the ministry itself,[2] but after the death and resurrection of their Master preaching the gospel became their main concern. Acts tells us how they found themselves becoming chocked by administration, and deliberately delegated this work so that they could give themselves to prayer and the ministry of the Word.[3] How they discharged this ministry we simply do not know. Very likely the roving nature of their work hindered them from leaving any written records behind them. At all events Eusebius, at the beginning of the fourth century, can give us very little more than broad generalizations about their work, though it is obvious that he gathered together every scrap of information about them that he could. He is reduced, as far as most of them are concerned, to asserting vaguely that "by the power and assistance of heaven the saving Word began to flood the whole world with light like the rays of the sun. At once, in accordance with the divine Scriptures, the voice of its inspired evangelists and Apostles 'went forth to the whole earth and their words to the end of the world'. In every city and village arose churches crowded with thousands of men, like a teeming threshing floor."[4] Eusebius, it is clear, was as much in the dark about it all as we are. He records the rumour, preserved in the *Acts of Thomas*, that the apostles drew lots in order to decide their destinations in different parts of the world, and "Thomas

166

obtained by lot Parthia, Andrew Scythia, John Asia . . . but Peter seems to have preached to the Jews of the dispersion in Pontus and Galatia, Bithynia Cappadocia and Asia, and at the end he came to Rome."[5] These same *Acts of Thomas* maintain that Judas Thomas went to India. Although the evidence is late,[6] it may well be true. Pantaenus also is reputed to have gone to India and to have found Christians there before him, who were rejoicing in the original Hebrew of St Matthew's Gospel left them by another apostolic figure, St Bartholomew![7] Despite the fact that "India" could be applied to almost anywhere east of Suez, and that precision is not to be looked for, it is by no means improbable that some of the earliest Christians, perhaps even apostles, followed the trade route to India. It is interesting that the *Acts of Thomas* has been shown to contain accurate information about the route to the Far East and the conditions prevailing there in the first century A.D.[8]

There is a small amount of information, of very doubtful value, to be gleaned from the second and third century apocryphal gospels, romances, and acts about the activities of different apostles in various parts of the world. This suggests that they did scatter with the intention of preaching the gospel to the whole known world, in accordance with their Lord's command.[9] Justin summarizes in a sentence their courage, dedication and achievement: "From Jerusalem there went out twelve men into the world; they were unlearned and had no ability in speaking; yet by the power of God they proclaimed to every race of men that they were sent by Christ to teach to all the Word of God."[10]

The situation is complicated not only by our ignorance of what the Twelve did in their mission (with the exception of Peter and John, of whose movements we are given slightly more information both in the New Testament and the second century literature) but by the ambiguity of the term "apostle".[11] It was applied both to the apostles of Jesus Christ (that is to say the original twelve and Paul,[12] and possibly one or two others who had known the incarnate Jesus and received a commission from him after the resurrection),[13] and also to roving missionaries sent out by the churches and supported by the gifts of the faithful. Paul is aware of this wider category of apostles, "apostles of the churches" as he calls them,[14] and aware, too, of the dangers they represent. Quite unsupervised in their teaching, they could go seriously astray doctrinally or ethically, and could involve whole churches in their weaknesses. These are the men he has in mind when in 2 Corinthians he arraigns them as Satan's messengers, false apostles and the like.[15] Other people said just the same about him![16] The Book of Revelation knows this wider circle of apostles,[17] so does Hermas,[18] but it is the *Didache* which though professing to be the teaching of the twelve apostles (in the restricted sense) tells us most about the apostles who were wandering missionaries.

They are grouped with prophets and teachers, and Harnack[19] has made out a good case for supposing that this was a threefold division of peripatetic Christian leaders which was extremely ancient, and probably modelled on Jewish precedent; they stand out in sharp contrast to the settled ministry of bishops, presbyters and deacons which are to be found almost universally in the second century.[20] Both types of ministry are found side by side in the *Didache* and Hermas. The main characteristics of the roving ministry were that they did not stay long in any one place, that they were dedicated to poverty (and accordingly supported by the gifts of the congregations they visited, for they would accept nothing from the pagans),[21] and that they were not elected by the churches, like the settled ministry, but felt themselves called to this work directly by God: their lives, their message, and their Christian effectiveness were their credentials. Men like this were very highly honoured. As those who spoke the word of the Lord they were, the *Didache* tells us, to be honoured as the Lord himself.[22] Genuine ones among them were to be honoured with the first fruits of winepress and threshing floor, of oxen and sheep "for they are your high priests".[23] But the extent of the respect paid to such travelling teachers invited abuses. They could easily sponge on the community; they could outstay their welcome; they could wheedle food or money from the unsuspecting under the plea of inspiration. So the *Didache*, while honouring the apostle as the Lord, says roundly, "but let him not stay more than one day, or if need be a second as well; if he stay three days, he is a false prophet." Again, "no prophet who orders a meal in the spirit shall eat of it; otherwise he is a false prophet" and "whosoever shall say in a spirit, 'Give me money or something else' you shall not listen to him, but if he tell you to give on behalf of others in need, let no man judge him."[24]

This, then, was one type of Christian minister, a full-time wandering missionary, sometimes with and sometimes without the *charisma* of prophecy (this, presumably, is the difference between teachers and prophets).[25] Origen refers to men of this sort when he replies to Celsus: "Christians do all in their power to spread the faith all over the world. Some of them accordingly make it the business of their life to wander not only from city to city but from town to town and village to village in order to win fresh converts for the Lord." So far from being motivated by selfish considerations, "they often refuse to accept the bare necessities of life; even if necessity drives them to accept a gift on occasion, they are content with getting their most pressing needs satisfied, although many people are willing to give them much more than that. And if at the present day, owing to the large number of people who are converted, some rich men of good position and delicate high-born women give hospitality to the messengers of the faith, will anyone venture to assert that some of the latter preach the Christian faith merely for the sake of being honoured? In the early days when great peril threatened the preachers of the faith in particular, such a suspicion could not easily have been entertained; and even at the present day the discredit with which Christians are assailed by unbelievers outweighs any honour that some of their fellow-believers show them."[26] Eusebius gives us much the same picture. Writing of the second century he says, "There were still many evangelists of the Word eager to use their inspired zeal after the example of the apostles for the increase and building up of the divine Word",[27] and again, "very many of the disciples of that age whose hearts had been ravished by the divine Word with a burning love for philosophy (i.e. Christianity) first fulfilled the command of the Saviour and divided their goods among the needy. Then they set out on long journeys, doing the work of evangelists, eagerly striving to preach Christ to those who had never heard the word of faith, and to deliver to them the holy gospels. In foreign lands they simply laid the foundations of the faith. That done, they appointed others as shepherds, entrusting them with the care of the new growth, while they themselves proceeded with the grace and co-operation of God to other countries and other peoples."[28] One notices various New Testament overtones here. They must have been influenced by the example of Jesus who had so impelling a sense of mission that he left Capernaum early one morning saying, "Let us go on to the next towns, that I may preach there also; for that is why I came out."[29] They were undoubtedly moved by the voluntary poverty of the disciples on their mission, and of the first Christian community at Jerusalem which shared out all its goods. The example of Paul, always pressing on to find new fields to conquer, leaving the new converts to fend for themselves after the minimum of instruction; the urge, which Paul shared, to preach Christ where he had not been named; and the call to Timothy to do the work of an evangelist[30] (even if, as the context suggests, this was not his natural gift), all combined to fire the zeal and emulation of many a second century Christian. The evidence indicates that there were many of them who became full time wandering evangelists, devoting their whole lives to the forwarding of the Christian faith, and trusting God and the Christian communities to supply their daily needs.

But the regular ministry, too, engaged in the work of evangelism. Undoubtedly the main task of the presbyterate was to build up the Christian community in such a way that every member of it discovered and exercised his own particular ministry; the presbyters or bishops were God's gift to the Church whose task was "to build up the saints for their work of ministry",[31] and to this extent their function was internal rather than external, church-orientated rather than world-orientated. But evangelism was not neglected. In his farewell address to the Ephesian presbyters, Paul sets his own evangelistic example before them as a model.[32] In the Pastoral Epistles, it is made clear that any aspirant for the office of presbyter must both be a good teacher and held in respect by those outside the Church.[33] Why should this be if part of his work was not to reach those outside the Church with the gospel? This is precisely what we see the second century bishops doing. For all his preoccupation with doctrinal soundness, eucharistic regularity and episcopal pre-eminence within the Church, Ignatius writes to his fellow bishop Polycarp, "I exhort you, press on in your course, and exhort all men that they may be saved."[34] That Polycarp followed this advice is made supremely clear from the manner of his death. When the old man was brought into the stadium at Smyrna, "the whole multitude both of the heathen and Jews who lived at Smyrna, cried out in uncontrollable fury 'This is the teacher of Asia, the father of the Christians, the overthrower of our gods, he who has been teaching many not to sacrifice or to worship the gods'."[35] Irenaeus, too, for all his theological and church-building activities, was most at home as an evangelist. He made a practice of preaching in the villages as well as the towns of Gaul where he was bishop, and did so not only in Greek, the language which many of the educated inhabitants would understand, but also in the vernacular. Such was his concern to fulfil the evangelistic role of the bishop that he took the trouble to learn and become fluent in the language of the despised barbarians, of whom even the best of pagan philanthropists took no account. At the beginning of his *Adversus Haereses* he charmingly apologizes for his rusty Greek.[36] So assiduous were his preaching labours in a foreign language that he had forgotten a good deal of his native tongue! That such a point could ever be made speaks volumes for the evangelistic zeal of the best of the regular clergy;[37] no doubt many never approached it. But this outward look remained deeply embedded in the concept of ministerial responsibility. It was no innovation when the *Apostolic Constitutions* laid down in the third century this requirement for bishops, "Warn and reprove the uninstructed with boldness, teach the ignorant, confirm those that do understand, and bring back those that stray."[38]

There is one other class of "full-time" Christian which must be reckoned among the evangelists, along with the apostles and wandering evangelists, and the more settled bishops and presbyters of the early Church. This is the small but influential group of theologians and philosophers. Pantaenus, the founder of the famous catechetical school at Alexandria, was first and foremost a missionary to "India". Trained as a Stoic philosopher, he was converted to Christianity and then "showed such zeal in his enthusiasm for the divine Word that he was even appointed as a herald of the Gospel of Christ to the heathen in the East, and was sent as far as India . . . After many achievements he was head of the school in Alexandria until his death."[39] If missionary bishops were no rarity in the early Church, neither were missionary theologians. In the first instance men like Pantaenus wandered around, like the Cynic philosophers, gathering crowds of hearers in the public places of the towns they visited. Celsus complained of the spread of the faith by these means, "We see that those who display their trickery in the market places and go about begging would never enter a gathering of intelligent men, nor would they dare to reveal their noble beliefs in their presence: but whenever they see adolescent boys and a crowd of slaves and a company of fools, they push themselves in and show off." This was an accusation that hurt Origen very much. How could anyone call "readings of the Bible, and explanations of the readings" together with "exhortation to goodness" *trickery*? Did the Cynics not adopt precisely the same method? And as for the claim that only the ignorant were attracted by Christianity presented in this guise, Origen indignantly and lengthily denies it.[40] Christianity is the true philosophy, and market place evangelism is one perfectly proper way for an educated Christian to disseminate it.

Sometimes these philosopher-evangelists engaged in public discussions with able pagans, and we have reflections of this type of spreading of the doctrines of the gospel in the setting of Justin's *Second Apology*, where Crescens the Cynic is assailed for his calumnies against the Christians in order to win the favour of the audience, or the *Octavius* of Minucius Felix, where Caecilius is given a public trouncing. But no doubt there were many occasions where it was the Christian philosopher who was vanquished in the discussion; this may have led to the growing preference for the catechetical "school". In any case there was value in the extended treatment and the careful follow-up which could be undertaken in a settled "school" as opposed to the random outdoor meeting. The first of these schools which we hear of (apart from Paul's activities in the school of Tyrannus, which must have been very similar) is that of Justin. He operated in Rome[41] and interested enquirers came to his addresses there. Tatian, once his pupil,[42] set up his own school, and so did Rhodon and other intellectually able Christians.[43] These schools were certainly not exclusively devoted to the cultivation of Christian learning within the Church; they were intentionally set up as evangelistic agencies, by godly intellectuals who recognized their debt both to Greek and barbarian, to intellectual and ignorant. All were welcome: when the simple predominated the more profound truths of Christianity were passed over, and the teachers concentrated on giving "milk". When able enquirers formed the main part of the gathering, the deeper mysteries of the faith were expounded.[44] Their aim was throughout pastoral and evangelistic; that is why they adapted their message to the capabilities of the hearers. "We confess that we do want to educate all men with the Word of God, even if Celsus does not wish to believe it"[45] was Origen's proud boast, and he carried it out. In addition to his Christian pupils in the school at Alexandria, he had pagan hearers to whom he gave instruction in the faith.[46] Indeed, Julia Mamaea, the queen-mother, heard him lecture.[47] It would be a mistake to think that the apologists and theologians were anything less than evangelists. The objective of their lives was to bring men of all sorts and intellectual abilities to the truth about God, man and the universe as it was revealed in Jesus Christ.

The Informal Missionaries—Men and Women

So far we have been considering the evangelistic outreach of what one might loosely call "professional Christian propagandists". But this must not lead us to suppose that the "professional" played an unduly large part in the spread of Christianity. The very fact that we are so imperfectly aware of how evangelism was carried out and by whom, should make us sensitive to the possibility that the little man, the unknown ordinary man, the man who left no literary remains was the prime agent in mission. Harnack was absolutely right when he declared, "It is impossible to see in any one class of people inside the Church chief agents of the Christian propaganda." On the contrary, "we cannot hesitate to believe that the great mission of Christianity was in reality accomplished by means of informal missionaries."[48]

It had always been so. The very disciples themselves were, significantly, laymen, devoid of formal theological or rhetorical training. Christianity was from its inception a lay movement, and so it continued for a remarkably long time. In a sense, the apostles inevitably became "professionals". But as early as Acts 8 we find that it is not the apostles but the "amateur" missionaries, the men evicted from Jerusalem as a result of the persecution which followed Stephen's martyrdom, who took the gospel with them wherever they went.[49] It was they who travelled along the coastal plain to Phoenicia, over the sea to Cyprus, or struck up north to Antioch.[50] They were evangelists, just as much as any apostle was. Indeed it was they who took the two revolutionary steps of preaching to Greeks who had no connection with Judaism, and then of launching the Gentile mission from Antioch. It was an unselfconscious effort. They were scattered from their base in Jerusalem and they went everywhere spreading the good news which had brought joy, release and a new life to themselves. This must often have been not formal preaching, but the informal chattering to friends and chance acquaintances, in homes and wine shops, on walks, and around market stalls. They went everywhere gossiping the gospel; they did it naturally, enthusiastically, and with the conviction of those who are not paid to say that sort of thing. Consequently, they were taken seriously, and the movement spread, notably among the lower classes.

We get a graphic picture of this informal evangelism in Origen's reply to Celsus. "We see in private houses workers in wool and leather, laundry workers and the most illiterate and bucolic yokels, who would not dare to say anything at all in front of their elders and more intelligent masters. But they get hold of the children privately, and any women who are as ignorant as themselves. Then they pour out wonderful statements: 'You ought not to heed your father or your teachers. Obey us. They are foolish and stupid. They neither know nor can do anything that is really good, but are taken up with mere empty chatter. We alone know how men ought to live. If you children do as we say, you will be happy yourselves and make your home happy too.' And if just as they are speaking they see one of the school teachers coming, or one of the more educated class, or even the father himself, the more cautious of them flee in all directions, but the more reckless urge the children on to rebel. They whisper, 'With father and teacher here we can't explain. We don't want to have anything to do with silly obtuse teachers. They are corrupt and immoral themselves, and what is more, they inflict punishment on you! So, if you like, leave father and teacher, and come along with the women and your playmates to the women's quarters, or the leather shop or the laundry, and you will get the full story.' With words like this they win them over." Such is Celsus's sarcastic

173

complaint.[51] In fact, of course, it pays the highest compliment to the zeal and dedication of the most ordinary Christians in the sub-apostolic age. Having found treasure, they meant to share it with others, to the limits of their ability. There is a touching example of this determination in the quarters of the imperial page boys on the Palatine Hill in Rome.[52] Here there is a third century picture, drawn

This crude drawing of a youth worshipping a crucified man with an ass's head bears the mocking inscription 'Alexamenos worships his God'. It was found in the quarters of the Imperial Pages on the Palatine: third century.

in a youthful hand, of a boy standing in the attitude of worship, with one hand upraised. The object of his devotion is a figure on a cross, a figure of a man with an ass's head. Underneath is scrawled, "Alexamenos worships his God." Clearly one of the pages was a Christian, and unashamed of it. His schoolfellows were spitefully mocking him for his stand. But he was not abashed, if we may judge by another inscription written in a different hand: "Alexamenos is faithful!" Perhaps this was his own response to the cruel cartoon. Perhaps it was that of one of his classmates who had come to recognize the truth of what Alexamenos proclaimed.

All of this makes it abundantly clear that in contrast to the present day, when Christianity is highly intellectualized and dispensed by a professional clergy to a constituency increasingly confined to the middle class, in the early days the faith was spontaneously spread by informal evangelists, and had its greatest appeal among the working classes.

If there was no distinction in the early Church between full-time ministers and laymen in this responsibility to spread the gospel by every means possible, there was equally no distinction between the sexes in the matter. It was axiomatic that every Christian was called to be a witness to Christ, not only by life but by lip. Everyone was to be an apologist, at least to the extent of being ready to give a good account of the hope that was within them.[53] And this emphatically included women. They had a very large part to play in the advance of Christianity.

We can trace this prominence of women back to the ministry of Jesus. He attracted many women into his movement, and they were dedicated and persevering in their allegiance. His women disciples were present at the crucifixion; their hands helped Joseph of Arimathea lay Jesus in the tomb. They were there on the first Easter Day, and in the subsequent weeks of waiting in Jerusalem. They were there on the day of Pentecost, and it was a woman's house that formed the headquarters of the Jerusalem Church. A glance through the Acts confirmed this impression of the significant part played by women in the spread of the gospel: Dorcas, Lydia, Priscilla, the four prophesying daughters of Philip whose fame was widespread in the second century, the upper-class women of Beroea and Thessalonica, and the rest. The Epistles confront us with a deaconess, possibly even a female apostle![54] Eight of the twenty-six people mentioned in the greetings in Romans 16 are women, and the rivalries of women workers in evangelism are rebuked in Philippians 4.[55] The part played by women is all the more remarkable in view of the fact that in Jewish circles and in paganism alike it was very much a man's world. It was easy enough to sneer at the "stupid women" who gossiped Christianity at the laundry;[56] yet these same women were among the most successful evangelists. Whether we look as early as 1 Peter[57] or as late as the *Apostolic Constitutions*[58] the words and example of the Christian wife are taken for granted as the major influence through which the husband's conversion may be looked for. This was no easy matter, as we have seen in chapter 2. Tertullian gives us a graphic picture of the problem at the end of the second century, and it will not have changed much from a hundred years earlier.[59] Is the husband opposed to his wife's Christianity? Then he will hinder her from going to worship, preclude her from offering hospitality to Christian visitors, object to her evenings out at Christian meetings, make sexual and social demands which are offensive to her Christian standards. Is he a tolerant type of man? Even so, he must wonder if the wife's early rising to pray is not magic, if her visits to church do not give foreboding of poison that she will administer him! In any case, what of the social proprieties? She will be expected to accord with pagan standards in matters of personal attractiveness and public religion. She will have to endure laurel wreaths on her front door in commemoration of pagan deities. She will have to sit and listen to dirty songs in the public house with her husband. Yet, difficult though it was,[60] many women must have succeeded in winning their husbands for Christ. Tertullian grudgingly admits as much, anxious though he is to discourage any mixed or second marriages. The very fact of her Christian commitment and life gives some proof of the numinous to her pagan husband, strikes awe into him, and makes him think twice before annoying her, laying traps for her, and spying over her. "He has felt mighty works. He has seen experimental evidences. He knows her changed for the better. Thus even he himself is, by his awe of her, a candidate for God."[61]

The New Testament tells us of women labouring in evangelism, acting as hostess to the Church in their houses, prophesying and speaking in tongues, and acting as deaconesses. This prominence of women continued, as we have seen, in the second century. Sometimes it would be exercised through public speaking, sometimes through martyrdom. The preaching of a Maximilla, a Thecla, or the four daughters of Philip the evangelist had a power which was not to be denied. Whilst the doctrines of the Montanists were repugnant in the Great Church, its fascination was real enough, and constituted as real a threat as Marcionism had done a generation earlier. *The Acts of Paul and Thecla* are sheer romance as they stand, but the picture of a woman preaching, baptizing, martyred for the faith was no figment of the imagination. Tertullian remarks, with distaste, about some women in heterodox churches "they venture to teach, to debate, to exorcize, to promise cures, probably even to baptize."[62]

Courage under persecution made an equally strong impression on Hellenistic society. There is probably some very ancient tradition

Christos Pantokrator from the fourth century mosaic found at Hinton St Mary is equated with Bellerophon conquering the Chimaera. Pagan mythology is made to subserve Christian conviction. See p. 142 and notes.

Christian teachers, Good Shepherd and *Orante* from a third century sarcophagus in the Lateran collection, found in a Christian catacomb on the Via Salaria, Rome.

A leaf of an ivory triptych of the fourth century, preserved in Florence, showing St Paul preaching to the Maltese.

From the Cemetery of Domitilla: the beheading of one Acilius for his faith. Date uncertain. See p. 307f.

A late (?fourth century) mosaic of a chalice and fish in a Christian house at Ostia. See p. 216.

The inscription to Domitilla, niece of Vespasian, who was almost certainly a Christian. It was found in the Cemetery of Domitilla, Rome. Date uncertain.

Fresco of Shadrach, Meshach and Abednego in the fiery furnace: an indication of early Christians' confidence in the face of persecution. From the Cemetery of Priscilla, Rome: third or fourth century.

behind a part of the Thecla story as she faced the probability of martyrdom, and was rescued by the good offices of Queen Tryphaena, who was so impressed by her cool courage. This queen was a real person who lived at the end of the first century.[63] It is by no means impossible that a dedicated Christian woman like Thecla could win over a queen to the faith. We have seen reason to believe that one of the most important women in the empire, niece of Domitian and mother of two sons designated to succeed him as Emperor, was a Christian. Flavia Domitilla was a lady who was prepared to face anything for her faith. She and her husband, Flavius Clemens, "were charged with atheism, an accusation for which many others who affected Jewish ways suffered, some with death and others with the confiscation of goods."[64] For Clemens, as we have seen, this meant death; for Domitilla exile. Nevertheless their witness was not in vain. The Christian faith struck deeply in this family, and it was on their property on the Via Ardeatina that one of the earliest Christian burial grounds was situated.

The almost superhuman dedication of which early Christian women were capable is illustrated by the accouns of some of the martyrdoms. *The Passion of Perpetua* is one of the gems among early Christian literature. Aged twenty-two, married a year previously, and with a baby at her breast, Perpetua was martyred for her faith in the year A.D. 203 in Carthage. Before her death, she managed to record her impressions of her imprisonment. Her father tried everything to make her recant. First, he was rough with her, but found that he distressed her to no effect. Then he turned to appeals; his grey hairs, her mother, and supremely her own tiny son who would not be able to survive her, were all thrown into the scales to induce her to change her mind. But she remained firm, and went with dignity and courage to her death. The effect of such devotion to Christ can well be imagined.

Quarter of a century earlier, the Gallic slave girl, Blandina, died with just as much courage and fidelity to Christ as Perpetua, the aristocratic African lady. The moving story is told by eye-witnesses in Vienne in A.D. 177, and their letter was reproduced almost in full by Eusebius.[65] She was a recent convert, and her mistress was fearful not for their lives, but lest Blandina should draw back in the face of death. She need not have worried. Tortured with fiendish ingenuity, she quietly maintained, "I am a Christian woman, and nothing wicked happens among us." Put on the gridiron, thrown to wild beasts in the arena, forced to watch the murder of her Christian companions, impaled upon a stake, this remarkable girl, "weak and despised though she was, had put on the great and invincible athlete,

Christ, and through many contests gained the crown of immortality". She was finally despatched by being put in a net and tossed by a bull; but not before she had nerved a fifteen-year-old boy, Ponticus, to martyrdom by her example, and had prayed lovingly and persistently for her persecutors. If women like this were at all typical throughout the varied social strata of the Church, it is hardly surprising that the gospel overcame the enormous obstacles in its way, and began to capture the Roman Empire.

THE EVANGELISTS: WHAT OF THEIR LIVES

Their Example

Christians claimed that one God, good, loving and upright, was the creator of the whole world; that he had disclosed himself personally in Jesus of Nazareth, through whose death and resurrection a new relationship with God was available for all men who wished to have it; and that his Spirit was available to enter human lives and morally transform them from within, while at the same time binding the Christians together in a loving fellowship to which there was no parallel in antiquity. Moreover, it was seen to be the task of every member of this fellowship to do all in his power to spread the gospel to others. Naturally, therefore, the lives of the Christians came under close scrutiny. The truth of their claims must have been assessed to a very large degree by the consistency of their lives with what they professed. That is why the emphasis on the link between mission and holiness of life is given such prominence both in the New Testament and the second century literature. Peter holds both together when he in one and the same breath urges holiness of life springing from "reverence for Christ as Lord in your hearts", and outreach to others, "be ready always to give an account of your faith to anyone who asks you a reason for the hope you cherish". Inevitably Christians will get abused, but when they do they must keep their conscience clear so that those who revile their good behaviour in Christ may be put to shame.[66] Similarly Paul makes the link between a holy life and effective evangelism inescapably plain. It was the quality of his life, his self-sacrifice, his caring, that convinced the Thessalonians that what he proclaimed was not the word of men but the word of God.[67] They themselves believed in their turn. They began to imitate the lives of the Christians they knew,[68] and from their midst the gospel spread throughout Macedonia and Achaea: but Paul only says this after noting in the previous verse that they became an *example* to all the believers in Macedonia and Achaea.[69] Life and lip went together in commending the Christian cause.

Similarly, when reflecting on the power of the gospel to open eyes that were once blind to its truth and to bring men into the light which the God who created and redeemed them intended them to enjoy, Paul emphasizes two conditions. There must be a clear proclamation of Jesus as Messiah and Lord; and it must be backed up by the lives of men who are not self-centred in their approach, but are willing to be entirely at the service of the Corinthians, with their lives open to inspection at every point. "We have renounced disgraceful, underhand ways; we refuse to practise cunning or to tamper with God's word, but by manifesting the truth (i.e. both in behaviour and proclamation) we would commend ourselves to every man's conscience in the sight of God."[70]

This connection between belief and behaviour runs right through Christian literature. The two cannot be separated without disastrous results, among them the end of effective evangelism. That is why the New Testament writers are so intolerant both of doctrinal and moral defections among their converts. The false philosophies with which Colossians, 1 John and the Corinthian letters deal all had appalling moral consequences. Similarly the whole anti-heretical literature of the second century is as concerned with right conduct as it is with orthodox creed. The two were inextricably intertwined in the mission and appeal of Christianity. When slandered about atheistic opinions, Thyestian banquets and Oedipoean morals[71] the Apologists pointed to the lives of the Christians which gave the lie to this popular libel. And then they pointed out that the pagans who raised these objections were guilty of the very same crimes themselves. Theophilus, for example, repudiates the charge of atheism by pointing out that the Christians believe in one moral God, author of the universe.[72] He refutes the charge of incest and promiscuity by showing that evil thoughts are utterly offensive to the Christian conscience; how much more licentious deeds.[73] He refutes the charge of murderous cruelty by pointing out that believers were forbidden even to go to gladiatorial shows lest they become hardened to cruelty and condone murder. "Be it far from Christians to conceive any such deeds; for with them temperance dwells, self-restraint is practised, monogamy observed, chastity guarded, righteousness exercised, worship performed, God acknowledged; truth governs them, grace guards, peace screens them, and the holy Word guides . . ."[74] Having defended the Christians, he turns to reproach the pagans for these very same things. "Why then do Epicurus and the Stoics teach incest and sodomy? With these teachings they have filled libraries, so that from boyhood this lawless intercourse is learned."[75] The poets have inculcated cannibalism by their teaching.[76] The pagans have imputed wickedness to their gods, and have, moreover, tolerated plenty of genuine atheists—why then should they persecute the Christians for their supposed atheism?[77] And underriding it all is a subtle contrast between the gratuitous opposition if not active persecution inflicted on the Christians, and their response in loving their enemies, as the gospel enjoins.[78]

This was standard treatment in the Apologists. Some of it may well be idealized; judging from the faults Hermas and Clement find with the Church, writing as they do from within its fellowship, the picture undoubtedly was touched up. But it could never have been painted if it did not pretty nearly reflect the truth. Unless the Christian ethic really did mark out its practitioners as a new race, it would have been no good claiming as much. Athenagoras has a moving passage in which he is contrasting the moral lives of Christians with the charges brought against them. "Among us you will find uneducated persons and artisans, and old women who, if they are unable in words to prove the benefit of our doctrine, yet by their deeds exhibit the benefit arising from their persuasion of its truth. They do not practise speeches, but exhibit good works; when struck they do not strike again; when robbed they do not go to law; they give to those that ask of them, and they love their neighbours as themselves."[79]

What, then, were the particular elements in this different life led by the Christians, which made such an impression on the ancient world?

Their Fellowship

The fellowship which the Church offered, transcending barriers of race, sex, class and education, was an enormous attraction. One thinks of the sequel to the Pentecost sermon: the converts "devoted themselves to the apostles' teaching and fellowship, to the breaking of bread and the prayers."[80] The Antioch church[81] must have been a place of remarkable fellowship not only between Jews and Gentiles who had put their faith in Christ, but also among other sectors of the Christian community. Quite apart from their generosity in supporting the Jerusalem church in its need, and their vision in sending Paul and Barnabas out on the first Missionary Journey (for whose success they cared sufficiently to second to the enterprise their two most prominent teachers), there are other indications of the quality of their church life. It was a church where worship was central, and where fasting was an indication of their earnest determination to seek God's will. It was a church which cared so much about fellowship that Jews and Gentiles converted to the faith broke down centuries-old barriers and ate at the same table. It was a church where an aristocrat like Manaen, an ex-Pharisee of the most rigid type like Saul, Barnabas, an erstwhile Levitical landowner in Cyprus, Lucius, a Hellenistic Jew from Cyrene, and "Simeon the Swarthy", almost certainly an African, could all work together in harmonious leadership of the believers. Such loving fellowship was not peculiar to Antioch. Paul thanks God for the love of the Thessalonians;[82] but he prays that that love may abound more and more towards all men as well as towards one another.[83] This internal cohesion of love was implanted by God himself, so in a sense Paul had no need to mention it;[84] but he did so in order to draw attention to one area in which their love was deficient, the aggressive independence towards leaders which was a national characteristic of the Macedonians.[85] Despite this blemish the Thessalonian correspondence leaves no room to doubt the reality of the fellowship which marked the infant church there. Greed and arrogance about spiritual gifts threatened this fellowship at Corinth;[86] disunity at Philippi and Rome,[87] immorality in the churches to which 2 Peter and Jude were directed,[88] snobbery among the recipients of James.[89] But the speed and earnestness with which these failures in fellowship were unmasked and reproved by the Christian leaders is eloquent proof of the universal conviction that the extent and power of the Christian outreach depended on the unity and fellowship of the brotherhood. This unity was no dull uniformity. From the outset there was variety in doctrinal emphases, forms of church government, and attitudes to food and the observance of sacred days; but these were not allowed to interfere with the mutual respect and trust of children of the same heavenly Father who knew they would have to give an account to him of the conscientious decisions they had come to in these matters. Romans 14:1–3 is as good an example as any of the proper display of Christian tolerance, not allowing secondary differences of practice to disturb primary unity of fellowship. The quality of this fellowship was very striking. Within the original group of his own disciples Jesus had forged a unity which comprised irreconcilable opposites of the temperament of John and Peter, and of the political views of Simon the Zealot and Matthew the tax collector. This he continued to do subsequently in his Church. Allegiance to Jesus brought harmony to conflicting attitudes (even if, as at Corinth, it was achieved only after the greatest difficulty). A striking example of this is the change in Mary and the brothers of Jesus after the resurrection. Previously they had not believed in the claims of Jesus, and remained, in Mark's graphic phrase, "on the outside".[90] But Acts 1:14 shows them after the resurrection united with the disciples in a common fellowship, a common table, and common prayer. It could not have been easy for them to admit they had been mistaken, nor to play second fiddle (for a time, at any rate[91]) to those who were related much less intimately to the risen Christ than themselves. But the divine alchemy of *koinōnia*,[92] joint participation in the unifying Holy Spirit, brought about this remarkable change. It is interesting that the Christians should have so readily adopted this word for their fellowship. It was in common secular use to denote unofficial associations designed to foster some communal activity—dining clubs, burial clubs, trade guilds. These were well-known aspects of Roman life, and were usually tolerated by the government unless they infringed the law in some respect. Formally, then, there was little to distinguish Christian associations for fellowship from any other: the initiation, the equal partnership, the cult meal, the mutual benefits were all standard procedure. But materially there was a difference— in the quality of the fellowship. Here were societies in which aristocrats and slaves, Roman citizens and provincials, rich and poor, mixed on equal terms and without distinction: societies which possessed a quality of caring and love which was unique. Herein lay its attraction. Here was something that must be guarded at all costs if the Christian mission was to go ahead. It is for this reason, among others, that we find Christian unity such a crucial matter not only to the New Testament writers, but to Ignatius, Clement, and the second century authors in general. It was, as Paul told the Corinthians, only a church which was manifestly united, where each member could and did speak as the Holy Spirit possessed him, that would convince the visiting outsider that God was among them.[93] There is no doubt that many were convinced this way. Pagan fraternities were often extremely immoral: Justin refers to idol factories where the sculptors "are practised in every vice, as you very well know; even their own girls who work alongside them they debauch".[94] In contrast the Christian fellowship, and particularly the *Agapē*, was notable both for its real concern and for its purity. Tertullian describes the affection which marks the Christian brethren assembled together—fittingly called "brethren" because of their common relationship to the heavenly Father.[95] He explains that the meeting is opened and closed with prayer. Worship, fellowship and feasting are all carried out under the Father's eye. The lowly, the needy, the sick are shown particular consideration. Contributions are voluntary and proportionate to each one's income: they are used "to support and bury poor people, to supply the wants of boys and girls who are destitute of means and parents, and of old people now confined to the house, and such as have suffered shipwreck . . . or any who happen to be in the mines or banished to the islands or shut up in prison for their fidelity to God's Church". "One in mind and soul, we do not hesitate to share our earthly good with one another. All things are common among us except our wives"—the very area where the pagans most inclined to sharing, as Tertullian unkindly pointed out. The religious nature of the Christian gatherings "permits no vileness or immodesty". "As much is eaten as satisfies the cravings of hunger; as much is drunk as befits the chaste . . . They talk as those who know the Lord is listening to them. Each is asked to stand up and sing a hymn to God, either of his own composing or from the holy Scriptures—a proof of the measure of our drinking! We go forth from the feast," concludes Tertullian, "not like troops of mischief-doers nor bands of vagabonds nor to break out into licentious acts, but to have as much care of our modesty and chastity as if we had been at a school of virtue rather than a banquet." As we have seen, Pliny the Younger came to much the same conclusion after investigating these Christian meetings for himself.[96]

This testimony from Tertullian is all the more interesting because there had been a mass turning to Christ in North Africa shortly before he wrote. The quality of Christian fellowship to which he draws attention had had large-scale effects in his native land. As in the earliest days of Christianity this fellowship was absolutely crucial to the advance of the Church. Men had to be attracted in from the existing—if shallow—fellowship of their pagan clubs (*collegia*) and taverns (*thermopolia*) by another fellowship which was richer and more rewarding. Those who themselves were animated by mutual hatred saw how the Christians loved one another, Tertullian tells us, and this must have been a powerful adjunct to the preaching of "the sacred words with which we nourish faith, animate hope, make confidence assured, confirm good habits, and administer rebukes and censures".

The Transformed Characters

If the loving fellowship of the Christian community was one prerequisite for effective evangelism, another was a transformed character. The New Testament records lay great emphasis on this. The transformation of John, that Son of Thunder, into the Apostle of love, or of Peter, that mercurial hothead, into a man of rock is an essential part of the logic of the gospel. This is what contact with Christ does for a man. He becomes changed into likeness to Christ from one degree of glory to another by the Lord the Spirit.[97] Sometimes they expressed it in terms of imitation of Christ: the qualities of his character had to be seen in the life of any man who had undergone a genuine conversion; sometimes they used the language of mystical union with Christ or the indwelling of the Holy Spirit to get across the idea of this growing metamorphosis. The faithful pastor "travailed in birth-pangs until Christ be formed" in his converts.[98] And unless that process had progressed to a considerable degree in his own life there would have been no converts to shepherd. Luke makes it very clear from the careful parallels he draws between the life and witness of Stephen and Jesus, of Peter and Paul. Christlikeness of life is a *sine qua non* of evangelism. The contrast between the old life and the new was part of early baptismal catechesis: the "putting off" of the old life with its pagan habits and lusts was the complement of "putting on" Christ and the type of life he lived. The sort of contrast Paul makes between the "works of the flesh" and the "fruit of the Spirit" in Galatians 5 must have been a commonplace, and it was very obvious to pagan eyes. The Apologists are full of such contrasts. We have noticed the famous passage in Justin where he claims "we who formerly delighted in fornication now embrace chastity alone; we who formerly used magic arts dedicate ourselves to the good and unbegotten God; we who valued above all things the acquisition of wealth and possessions now bring all we have into a common stock and share it out to all according to their need; we who hated and destroyed one another and on account of their different manner of life would not live with men of another tribe, now, since the coming of Christ, live happily with them, and pray for our enemies and endeavour to persuade those who hate us unjustly to live conformably to the good precepts of Christ, so that they may become partakers with us of the same joyful hope of a reward from God the ruler of all."[99] The link between holy living and effective evangelism could hardly be made more effectively. In particular, Christians stood out for their chastity, their hatred of cruelty, their civil obedience, good citizenship and payment of taxes (despite the severe suspicion they incurred on this count because they refused to pay the customary civil formality of praying to the emperor and the state gods). They did not expose infants: they did not swear. They refused to have anything to do with idolatry and its by-products. Such lives made a great impact. Even the heathen opponents of Christianity often admitted as much. Both Pliny and Lucian recognized the pure life, devoted love, and amazing courage of the Christians;[100] so did Marcus Aurelius and Galen.[101] And Christian writers, aware of how crucial this holiness of life was to the advance of the mission, are always stressing its importance. Hermas and Ignatius, 1 and 2 *Clement*, the *Didache* and the *Epistle of Barnabus* are all full of exhortations to holy living and, if need be, dying. Ignatius writes to the Ephesians, in an evangelistic context, "Allow them to learn a lesson at least from your works. Be meek when they break out in anger, be humble against their arrogant words, set your prayers against their blasphemies; do not try to copy them in requital. Let us show ourselves their brethren by our forbearance, and let us be zealous to be imitators of the Lord."[102] The dangers of an inconsistent Christian witness are brought out in 2 *Clement*.[103] Talking of the desire to "save those that are without" the writer warns against careless, unloving behaviour which will cause God's name to be blasphemed among the heathen. "For when the heathen hear from our mouth the oracles of God they wonder at their beauty and greatness; then, discovering that our deeds are not worthy of the words we utter, they turn from their wonder to blasphemy, saying that it is all a myth and delusion." It is difficult to overestimate this moral emphasis in second century Christianity.[104] And although there is some justification for the widely held view that the faith had degenerated into a moralism[105] enforced by fear of judgment in the future and exclusion from the Christian community for the present, nevertheless we know that the lives of Christians weighed heavily in bringing men like Minucius Felix and Tertullian to Christ:[106] moreover they seem to have had a decisive effect in bringing about the great swing to Christianity in North Africa towards the end of the second century, even if, as Dr Frend suggests, Carthaginian nationalism had something to do with it as well.[107]

Their Joy

Again, the sheer joyous enthusiasm of the early evangelists enhanced their absolute claims for Jesus Christ. If he really was the only way to God, if there was salvation in no other,[108] then it is not surprising that they should commend him with such enthusiasm to others. Jesus had promised his joy as a permanent possession of his Church, a joy which no man could take from them.[109] And they demonstrated that this was so. They might be thrown into prison for their views: but they were still singing hymns to God at midnight![110] It was from a prison that Paul wrote Philippians, that epistle of joy and confidence.[111] Conversion and joy are closely related in the Acts of the Apostles,[112] and it remained a characteristic thing about the early Christians which attracted others into their company. Their new faith did not make them miserable. Often outward circumstances were unpleasant enough, but that could not rob them of the joy which was their Christian birthright. The Thessalonians received the word in much affliction . . . but equally, in joy inspired by the Holy Spirit.[113] The disciples had an infectious joy that they were allowed to suffer for their Master's sake.[114] They rejoiced in the hope of sharing a future with God;[115] they rejoiced in the sufferings which came to them along the Christian path;[116] they rejoiced in God himself,[117] and the companionship with him that nothing could deprive them of. "Be content with such things as you have: for He has said, 'I will never leave you nor forsake you.' "[118] The joy that Jesus had displayed even in the face of death[119] was shared by his followers. Paul rejoiced to finish his course with joy, even though he knew that would probably mean martyrdom.[120] This joy came from the confidence that nothing could ultimately harm the man whose Creator, Redeemer, Sustainer and Friend was none other than God himself.[121] "We are not ashamed of Christ," cries Tertullian, "for we rejoice to be his disciples and in his name to suffer."[122] Sometimes this joy even in persecution led to an unhealthy lust for martyrdom: Ignatius immediately comes to mind. But there was a very right and proper side to even this somewhat macabre delight. He was in haste, so the *Martyrdom of Ignatius* informs us, "to leave this world as soon as possible so that he might meet the Lord whom he loved".[123] Alongside the unbalanced belief that martyrdom was the *summum bonum* for the Christian, was the thoroughly biblical belief that "in Thy presence there is fulness of joy", and that "to depart and to be with Christ is far better".[124] A joy which took a man cheerfully to his death for the sake of One he could not see made a profound impression on the ancient world. Joyful Christian lives, and even more, joyful Christian deaths were major factors which attracted non-Christians to Christ. If the gospel filled an evangelist like Philip with such enthusiasm and joy that he was prepared to leave a flourishing work in Samaria in quest of a single coloured man, and a eunuch at that (one of the untouchables according to the Old Testament); if he was prepared actually to *run* in the desert where the heat would be around 120°F. in order to reach this man and be of service to him—then it is not surprising that his message carried conviction and the Ethiopian believed.[125] Similarly, if men could, for the love of one they had never seen, "rejoice with joy unspeakable and full of glory" even when faced by a brutal death as human torches in Nero's gardens[126]—then it is not surprising that the Christian gospel carried conviction, and many believed.[127] If it could inspire men with such enthusiasm and joy, Christianity was assured of a very serious hearing indeed.

Their Endurance

This joy of the Christians both in life and death is closely linked with their patient endurance of scourging, insults and martyrdom which had an incalculable effect in bringing observers to faith. "The oftener we are mowed down by you, the more in number we grow. The blood of Christians is seed," said Tertullian; and he spoke from much personal experience.[128] It was not merely the fact that these men and women, drawn from all ranks in society and none, were prepared to hazard their lives for the Lord Jesus, but the manner in which they carried their witness through until death which caused such admiration. As Tertullian pointed out in that same passage, "Many of your writers exhort to courageous bearing of pain and death . . . and yet their words do not find so many disciples as Christians do, teachers not by words but by their deeds." A Seneca or a Helvidius Priscus might meet death with courageous resignation: Christians faced it with joyful exultation. It was the same with minor annoyances. The spirit of non-retaliation for evil, inculcated by Jesus, had so taken root even in the earliest days of the Church, that when Peter and John were imprisoned and threatened by an imposing meeting of the Sanhedrin for their Christian activities, they did not bluster or complain, much less give up. They did not hold a committee meeting to decide what should be done next. They simply joined their friends, and gave themselves to prayer, and then continued preaching the risen Christ.[129] Paul regarded the physical brutalities he suffered in the cause of the gospel as the marks which branded him as Jesus's bondslave;[130] he was given the privilege of not only believing on Christ but also of suffering for his sake.[131] In a very poignant sense he filled up in his own person the complement of the Messianic sufferings on Christ's behalf.[132] Peter's own peace of mind as he faced death on the morrow was such that he was peacefully sleeping between his guards.[133] Clement records how both Peter and Paul endured with equal equanimity stonings, trials from enemies without the Church and strife and jealousy from some within, and showed the way to the prize of endurance as they passed from the world and were taken up into the Holy Place.[134] And we have seen how many in the second century were fired by their example—Justin at Rome, the martyrs of Scilii, of Vienne and elsewhere. *The Acts of Martyrs* record that their deaths sometimes resulted in their executioners becoming Christians, and even when this did not occur, the way they died certainly convinced men of the innocence of their creed. Wicked men would not cheerfully sacrifice themselves like that. There is a moving story recorded by Clement of Alexandria which tells that the man whose denunciation of the apostle James had led to his arrest by Herod Agrippa, was so impressed by his testimony to Christ in court that he himself became a Christian, and was led away to execution along with James. "On the way he asked James for forgiveness. And James looked at him for a moment and said, 'Peace be to you', and kissed him. So both were beheaded at the same time."[135]

Their Power

There was one other notable characteristic about the early evangelists, though it is one which reads strangely to modern Western eyes: the sheer power that went with the proclamation of the Christian message. It was not merely the conviction with which they spoke, though this, too, was noted by the pagans: St Paul uses an interesting word for this assurance in preaching, *plērophoriā*, which appears to suggest that the preachers were so full of the Spirit of God, so persuaded of the truth and relevance of their message, that it overflowed from them and men received what they had to say, "not only in word but also in power and in the Holy Spirit and with full conviction" (*plērophoriā*).[136] That was in itself impressive enough in a society bored with the endless chatter of philosophers who had little conviction about the value or truth of their various positions.

But there was another dimension to this power. It involved healings and exorcisms, and this was a factor of incalculable importance for the advance of the gospel in a world which had inadequate medical services and was oppressed with belief in demon forces of every kind. Harnack summarizes the situation well: "The whole world and its enveloping atmosphere were filled with devils; not merely idolatry, but every phase and form of life was ruled by them. They sat on thrones, they hovered round cradles. The earth was literally a hell, though it was and continued to be a creation of God. To encounter this hell and all its devils Christians had command of weapons which were invincible."[137] This was indeed the impression which the Christian Church gave. The Gospels, particularly St Mark's, show beyond doubt that Jesus shared the contemporary belief in demons and their Satanic head. Some modern writers like G. B. Caird and H. Schlier[138] take this fact as decisive for Christian belief; others, like Trevor Ling and Edward Langton[139] believe that we are not bound by beliefs which Jesus shared in common with a very different age, and which he had to share if there was to be a real incarnation. But all agree that Jesus did believe in these forces of evil, and that he sent forth his apostles not only to preach repentance

188

but to cast out demons.[140] According to Luke's account they came
back radiant with joy at finding these demonic forces subject to them
through the name of Christ.[141] This continued throughout not only
the apostolic Church but into the second and third centuries, to look
no further. Christians went out into the world as exorcizers and
healers as well as preachers. The Acts is full of the "signs and wonders" of exorcism and healing which backed up the Christian claim
that Jesus had conquered the demonic forces on the cross, that he
had come to bring salvation or health to the whole man, not merely
his "soul". The early, though unauthentic, conclusion of St Mark
links the preaching of the gospel with these exorcizing signs which
would follow.[142] Hebrews, too, speaks of the confirmation of the
apostolic message which was provided by God bearing witness "by
signs and wonders and various miracles and gifts of the Holy
Spirit".[143] Peter and John do not merely proclaim good news to the
crippled man at the temple gate: they give him the power to walk,
in the name of Jesus Christ of Nazareth.[144] It was the apostolic
healings and exorcisms as well as the apostolic preaching which
resulted in "more than ever believers" being "added to the Lord".[145]
It was the sheer power of the name of Jesus to heal when uttered in
faith that convinced Simon Magus that he was a mere amateur in
magic and made him ask for baptism:[146] once again, healing and
exorcism were the twin factors which produced this conviction of
divine power. "The multitudes gave heed to what was said by Philip
(who, we are told in the preceding verse, proclaimed to them the
Christ) when they heard him, and saw the signs which he did. For
unclean spirits came out of many who were possessed . . . and many
who were lame were healed."[147] When Paul spent two years at
Ephesus, he was not solely concerned with debating daily in
Tyrannus's lecture hall, "so that all the residents of Asia heard the
word of the Lord".[148] No, as the very next verse tells us, "God did
extraordinary miracles by the hand of Paul"; the sick were healed
and the demons cast out. This continuation of the healing and
exorcizing work of Jesus can be traced through the Epistles,[149] and
continued after the end of the apostolic age. The Apologists are full
of it. Justin, for instance, explains that Jesus was made man "according to the will of God the Father for the sake of believing men and
for the destruction of demons".[150] The evidence for this claim? He
continues, "And now you may learn this from what goes on under
your own eyes. Many of our Christian men have exorcized in the
name of Jesus Christ who was crucified under Pontius Pilate number-
less demoniacs throughout the whole world, and in your city. When
all other exorcists and specialists in incantations and drugs have

failed, they have healed them and still do heal, rendering the demons impotent and driving them out." The power of the name of Jesus was more effective than any charm, and the Christians were careful to distinguish its effect from magic. There was nothing secretive about it, nothing of mystic gestures, special potions and closely guarded formulae. Irenaeus, in the course of a long discussion on this subject, says, "Those who are in truth Christ's disciples, receiving grace from him, do in his name perform miracles . . . Some do really and truly cast out demons, with the result that those who have thus been cleansed from evil spirits frequently believe in Christ and join themselves to the Church. Others still, heal the sick by laying their hands upon them, and they are made whole . . . It is not possible to name the number of the gifts which the Church throughout the world has received from God, in the name of Jesus Christ, who was crucified under Pontius Pilate, and which she exercises day by day for the benefit of the Gentiles . . . Nor does she perform anything by means of angelic invocations, or by incantations, or by any other wicked or curious art; but by directing her prayers to the Lord, who made all things, in a pure, sincere and straightforward spirit, and calling on the name of our Lord Jesus Christ, she has been accustomed to work miracles for the advantage of mankind."[151] In contrast to the partial or temporary cures effected by Gnostics and pagan magicians, the cures effected by this reliance on the name of the Lord Jesus Christ are, he claims, both permanent and complete.[152]

What a lot we would give to have accurate documentation of these cures! There is undoubtedly a lot of exaggeration in the Apologists. It was a credulous age. We are unimpressed by Irenaeus's repeated and earnest claim that he knows of an instance where a man was actually brought back from the dead "on account of some particular necessity" and in answer to the believing prayer of the community.[153] Some mistake in diagnosing death had surely been made in this instance: could not the same be said of all the healings and exorcisms of which we read? It is hard to accept this. The effectiveness of the name of Jesus in healing and driving out demons is too widely attested, in modern as in ancient times, for incredulity on this point. Both Origen and Celsus believed in demons and exorcism: Celsus, though muttering constantly about magic, cannot deny the reality either of Christian exorcism or the miracles of Jesus. Origen points out that unlike magic Christian miracles are always wrought for the benefit of men, that they are done by men whose lives are examplary, not wicked, and by faith in the power of God, not of evil.[154] No magical lore and sophisticated training was necessary: indeed "it is generally speaking uneducated people who do this kind of work" by means of prayer, reliance on the name of Jesus, and some brief allusion to his story.[155] For it was not the power of men, or their knowledge of the right formulae which produced these cures, but "the power in the word of Christ".[156]

It is an interesting fact arising from all this evidence that exorcisms were done in an evangelistic context. They were so clearly designed to back up the claims of the preached word that a primitive creed was a normal feature of the process. It was no mere utterance of the name of Jesus, but a recital of the saving events of the gospel which accompanied these healings. The emphasis, accordingly, was thrown not on the exorcizer but on Jesus in whose name it was done, and the gospel he had brought to light. Justin is explicit on this point. Though they will not yield to exorcism in the name of other men, "every demon when exorcized in the name of this true Son of God —who is the Firstborn of every creature, who became man by the Virgin, who suffered, and was crucified under Pontius Pilate . . . who rose again from the dead and ascended into heaven—is overcome and subdued."[157]

Tertullian is another writer who has a great deal to say on this subject. He claims that the Christian power of exorcism is undeniable and well known. In the course of an argument to show that demonic forces lie behind the pagan gods, he challenges his readers: "Hitherto it has been merely a question of words. Now for a test case, now for a proof that 'gods' and 'demons' are simply different names for the same thing. Let someone be brought before your judgment seats who is plainly demon-possessed. Bidden to speak by any Christian whatsoever, that spirit will confess he is a demon, just as frankly as elsewhere he has falsely asserted he is a god." This is all *à propos* of Tertullian's impassioned plea that they should believe in the one true God and "worship him after the manner of our Christian faith and teaching". If his pagan audience is disposed to mock at Christ, "Who is this Christ with his fables? Is he an ordinary man? a sorcerer? was his body stolen from the tomb by the disciples?", then "mock as you will, but get the demons to mock with you! Let *them* deny that Christ is coming to judge every human soul . . . Let *them* deny that, condemned for their wickedness, they are kept for that judgment day. Why, all the power and authority we have over them is from our naming the name of Christ, and recalling to their memory the woes with which God threatens them at the hands of Christ as Judge . . . Fearing Christ in God and God in Christ, they become subject to the servants of God and Christ. At our command they leave, distressed and unwillingly, the bodies they have entered.

Before your very eyes they are put to an open shame."[158] In his *To Scapula* Tertullian makes just the same appeal to empirical verification of this power of the Christians. "We do more than repudiate the demons. We overcome them. We expose them daily to contempt, and exorcize them from their victims. This is well known to many people."[159] Such claims would be pointless and injurious were they not true. The same story is repeated in Minucius Felix[160] and Tatian,[161] and continues in the third century in Origen,[162] Cyprian[163] and the *Apostolic Constitutions*.[164] It was one of the undeniable marks of the power of the Christian message; so much so that, as we have seen, Jews and pagans tried to use the name of Jesus as a magic charm.[165] Always the emphasis was not on the miracle itself but on its supporting role attesting the truths of the gospel message proclaimed by the evangelists. A passage in the *Apostolic Constitutions* crystalizes the point well. "These gifts were first bestowed upon us, the apostles, when we were about to preach the gospel to every creature, and afterwards were necessarily provided to those who had come to faith through our agency, not for the advantage of those who perform them, but for the conviction of the unbelievers, that those whom the word did not persuade the power of signs might put to shame."[165] The *charismata* given in the apostolic age had not been revoked: they continued in the Church of the third century.

As signs to validate the Christian evangel, these exorcisms were no more invariably successful than was the preaching of the word. Some put them down to magic, others remained quite unmoved by them.[167] But it is evident that, allied to the proclamation of the gospel, they had a great converting effect in an age which was hagridden with the fear of demonic forces dominating every aspect of life and death. The greatest intellectual of the third century can soberly claim, "The Christian, the real Christian who has submitted himself to God alone and his Logos, will not suffer anything at the hand of demons: for he is superior to them."[168] Christus Victor indeed!

Such was the power wielded by the early Christians. It greatly influenced the spread of the gospel. Are we to put it all down to delusion? Such is the general attitude in Western Christendom. But it is interesting to find on the one hand scholars of the calibre of Professors T. K. Oesterreich of Tübingen[169] and John Foster of Glasgow[170] taking it very seriously, and on the other hand missionaries and ministers in the younger churches of Africa and Asia equally convinced of the reality of exorcism and the power of healing in the name of Jesus.[171] There seem to be quite well authenticated cases of both in this country.[172] But the conclusion I reached in

The Meaning of Salvation still seems to me to be on the whole true. "Where medical knowledge is so advanced as it is in the West, where 2,000 years of Christian evidences, not to mention the sacred Scriptures, abound to authenticated Jesus's Messiahship, the conditions would appear to be lacking in which we might have a right to expect miracles in the New Testament sense, though we cannot exclude the possibility. However, in missionary areas, where there is only a tiny church in a vast pagan stronghold, where there is a shortage of medical means, where there may be no translations of the Scriptures available or where the people are as yet illiterate, where, furthermore, there are definite spiritual lessons to be reinforced by it—there, on the fringes of the gospel outreach, we have a situation in which we may expect to see God at work in miraculous ways today. That he does so is attested by all the missionary societies working in primitive areas."[173]

Whether or not this be a fair assessment of the contemporary scene, there can be no doubt that in the early days of the Church the power of the Christian evangelists was a factor to reckon with in addition to their love, the quality of their fellowship, the character of their lives, the courage of their deaths, and the joy and enthusiasm with which they bore testimony to their Lord.

8

EVANGELISTIC METHODS

CHRISTIANITY IS ENSHRINED in the life: but it is proclaimed by the lips. If there is a failure in either respect the gospel cannot be communicated. We saw in the last chapter the quality of Christian living which backed up the proclamation the evangelists made. In this chapter we shall look at some of the methods they employed in explaining the difference which Christ had made to their lives.

When we think of evangelistic methods today, preaching in a church building or perhaps a great arena comes readily to mind. We must, of course, rid ourselves of all such preconceptions when thinking of evangelism by the early Christians. They knew nothing of set addresses following certain homiletical patterns within the four walls of a church. Indeed, for more than 150 years they possessed no church buildings, and there was the greatest variety in the type and content of Christian evangelistic preaching.

PUBLIC EVANGELISM

Synagogue Preaching

The synagogue provided the seedbed for evangelism among the Jews. Wherever there were Jews, there were synagogues, and all loyal Israelites were expected to attend weekly; furthermore, they attracted a number of "godfearers" among thoughtful Gentiles. Here was a ready-made congregation for Christian missionaries to address. It is unfortunate that in his book *The Influence of the Synagogue upon the Divine Office* C. W. Dugmore should pay so little attention to the superb opportunity which the synagogue system provided for Christian evangelists to exploit: for undoubtedly it was one of the most important factors in the early spread of the faith. Synagogues were intended to foster devotion, discipline and learning. Of these learning is not the least important. Recently Professor Rowley has reminded us that the synagogue was above all the place of the Torah, where the Law was read and the commandments inculcated.[1] The service consisted of the *Shemah*, prayer, the reading of the Law and the Prophets, usually followed by an exposition, and the Blessing. Any member of the congregation might be called upon to read the Scriptures; anyone might be asked to give the exposition. This belonged to no privileged or priestly class. Indeed, the only priestly element in the whole service was the Blessing, which was dispensed with when no priest was present. This elasticity in ministry accounts for the fact that Jesus was invited to read the Prophets in his home synagogue at Nazareth, and that Paul was so often invited, as a distinguished Pharisee visitor, to read and address the congregation during the course of his missionary journeys. Such opportunities were gratefully accepted by the Christian missionaries to Israel in the decisive three decades or so before the door into the synagogue was slammed in their faces.

The sermon in the synagogue at Antioch in Pisidia is as much a model of missionary approach to the Jews as the addresses at Lystra and Athens are of two varieties of Gentile missionary preaching. Luke intends us, without doubt, to see it as typical of evangelism within the context of the synagogue. The address has three parts, each marked by an appeal to the attention of the listeners.[2] In the first he shows how the history of God's people leads up to the coming of the Messiah. The second is devoted to an exposition of the good news of Jesus, in whom the ancient prophecies have been fulfilled, the Davidic blessings concentrated, the divine sonship realized. It lays stress on his death and burial and resurrection. It honestly faces the difficulty of his rejection by Israel and his death on a cross: this was all in fulfilment of the scriptures. The third part of the sermon stresses the forgiveness of sins which is available through the risen Jesus, the freedom he offers which was never available under the Law of Moses, and the need for response in faith to him. A solemn warning concludes the sermon: God's mercy is not to be trifled with.

Here was preaching eminently suited to the situation of the hearers. The Christian missionary began where they were, rooted in the history of Israel, stressing the common origin and the common belief which united both preacher and hearers. He showed the relevance and the fulfilment of the ancient Scriptures: this religion is not something new, but the climax of God's self-disclosure, the fruition of the history of Israel. The main facts about Jesus are clearly presented: he is central in the kerygma, and there is no attempt to evade the problems which belief in his Messiahship inevitably involves for the Jew. This realistic facing of problems must have led time and again to the searching of the Scriptures which we have seen to have been one of the major factors in the mission to the Jews.[3] The preaching is intensely relevant, alike to the circumstances, concerns and consciences of the hearers. The evangelist makes use of personal testimony, of appeal and of warning in bringing home the thrust of his message. He is aiming to convince them that the Messiah is Jesus, and also to bring them to the newness of life which he himself has found in Jesus.

Roland Allen has pointed out four characteristics in this approach to the Jew in synagogue preaching.[4] First, we note Paul's conciliatoriness and sympathy with the susceptibilities of the hearers: clarity in presentation, readiness to welcome what is good in their position, and sympathy with their difficulties, all mark this wise and tactful approach. Second, he shows courage in openly recognizing difficulties, proclaiming unpalatable truth, and in his uncompromising refusal to make difficult things seem easy. Third, comes respect for his hearers, their intellectual powers and spiritual needs; and finally there is an unhesitating confidence in the truth and power of the gospel message. We shall not go far wrong in supposing these were typical characteristics of synagogue preaching in the early days of the mission while the opportunities were still open.

Open Air Preaching

Apart from working in and through the synagogues, the disciples followed their Master in preaching in the open air. The Acts give us plenty of examples of this, e.g. in Jerusalem, Samaria, Lystra and Athens. Such impromptu meetings can only be effective in places where numbers of people naturally pass or foregather—the temple area was a favourite site for this very reason. All such efforts must be lively and challenging. And if there is some "visual aid" to emphasize the power of the gospel, so much the better. The tongues at Pentecost and the cure at the Beautiful Gate of the Temple served two main purposes apart from their benefit to the recipients: they drew the crowds so that they could be reached by the preaching, and they demonstrated in unmistakeable terms the fundamental doctrines of the gospel—God's love for the unlovely, and his power to break the forces of sin and suffering in human life.[5] If the meeting attracted the unfavourable attention of the authorities, be they Jewish or Roman, this was no disaster. It gave an added significance to the preaching, and facilitated the subsequent break-up into small groups for discussion and further instruction.

Open air preaching was no innovation in Judaism. It had long been carried on both in Palestine and elsewhere, in courtyards, open fields, river banks and market places. When a celebrated preacher (*darshan*) came to a town or village, "then all the Jews would gather about him, raise a platform for him, and would listen to him and learn from him."[6] Indeed, some synagogues went so far as to sponsor preaching and teaching tours by gifted interpreters of Torah.[7] So there was nothing particularly novel in the open air work of Christian missionaries. The ancient world was used to it, both in its Jewish form, and as practised by the wandering Cynic missionaries. The evidence is not as full as we should like, but there can be no doubt that this open air evangelism continued throughout the first two centuries. As we have already seen, Irenaeus was accustomed to preaching in the market places not only of the city of Lugdunum but also of the market towns and villages round about.[8] Cyprian even dared the authorities to arrest him as he preached in the market place during a period of persecution.[9] We may glean some idea of the content and method of this preaching from the following examples.

Eusebius at the start of his *Ecclesiastical History* records the remarkable correspondence between Jesus and Abgar of Edessa. Whatever their source, Eusebius mistakenly took them for genuine letters; at all events they were, he tells us, to be found in the public archives of Edessa, written in Syriac. They can scarcely be later than the second century. Their content does not concern us except for the promise of Jesus to send one of his disciples to Edessa, and this was, so the story goes, fulfilled when Thaddaeus came there after the resurrection. Finding Abgar in a receptive mood, and indeed already believing what he had heard about Jesus, Thaddaeus healed him of his disease and "preached the word of God".[10] When asked to say more "about the coming of Jesus, how it happened, and about his power, how he did these things", Thaddaeus replied, "I will be silent at the moment, but since I was sent to preach the word, summon for me tomorrow an assembly of all your citizens, and I will preach before them, and sow in them the word of life, both concerning the coming of Jesus, how it happened, and concerning his mission, and for what reason he was sent by the Father, and concerning his power . . . and his lowliness and humiliation, and how he humbled himself and put aside and made little of his divinity, and was crucified, and descended into Hades, and rent the partition which had not been rent since the foundation of the world, and raised the dead, and whereas he went down alone, it was with a great multitude that he went up to his Father."[11] Though this is quite incredible as a record of Thaddaeus and Abgar, it is instructive enough about open air preaching in the early days of Christianity. There is considerable restraint in the account. Miracle is severely subordinated to preaching, to which it serves as an illustration and pointer, just as it did in the Acts of the Apostles. The preaching itself is centred on the person, mission, passion, resurrection and power of Jesus of Nazareth, just as it was in the earliest Church.

A second example comes from Rome. The author of the pseudo-Clementine *Recognitions* explains how he heard an open air preacher one autumn in Rome. He stood up in a public place and said, "Men of Rome, hearken. The Son of God is come in Judaea, proclaiming eternal life to all who will, if they shall live according to the will of the Father who has sent him. So change your manner of life from the worse to the better, from things temporal to things eternal For you know that there is one God who is in heaven, in whose world you live unrighteous lives before his holy eyes. But if you repent, and live according to his counsel, then, being born into the other world, and becoming eternal, you will enjoy unspeakable blessings. But if you refuse to believe, your souls will, after the dissolution of the body, be thrown into the place of fire, where, suffering eternally, they will repent of their unprofitable deeds. For every man the opportunity of repentance is confined to this present life."[12] Once again the straight, direct proclamation: nor would it have seemed improbable to Romans who took their astrology seriously that "the Son of God" had been born in Judaea.[13] The challenge to repentance and faith, coupled with the promises of joy and the warnings of hell are characteristic of second as much as of first century Christian preaching.

The response must also have been not uncommon. The writer regrets that nobody took the preacher seriously enough to go into Judaea and establish the truth of what was being preached. The total effect appeared to be nil. But that was not quite true. The writer himself began to reflect, "Why do I blame others, being guilty myself of the very same crime of heedlessness ? Right, I shall hasten into Judaea, having first settled my affairs." This took longer than expected. But at length he embarked, and found himself at Alexandria, rather than Judaea, on account of adverse winds. On making enquiries he was told of "one acquainted with Jesus, a Hebrew, by name Barnabas, who says that he is one of his disciples. He is staying around here, and readily proclaims to all who wish to hear the terms of his (i.e. Christ's) promise". "Then I went with them," continues the writer, "and when I came I stood listening to his words with the crowd that stood around him. I could see that he was speaking the truth, not with any dialectic skill, but was setting forth simply and without preparation what he had heard and seen the manifested Son of God do and say. And even from the crowd which stood around him, he produced many witnesses of the miracles and teaching (*sc.* of Jesus) which he was narrating."[14] The simple directness of this wandering preacher, accepting no fees, and content to get temporary accommodation where he could, a man utterly convinced of the truth of his message, must have been usual among the open air preachers. The same artlessness, the same spontaneity, the same appeal to the witness of those who, like the preacher, had found the truth, were characteristic of this type of evangelism. Even more instructive, perhaps, is the author's account of the sequel. The mockery, the joking, the heckling, even the physical danger to the preacher, which he describes must have happened on countless open air platforms. "But while the crowds welcomed the things he so artlessly spoke, the philosophers, impelled by their worldly learning, set about laughing and scoffing at him, making jokes and pulling him to pieces with excessive presumption as they brought to bear the great armoury of their syllogisms. But he set aside their trifling, and refused to try conclusions with their subtle questioning, but without embarrassment went on with what he was saying.

"And then one of them asks, 'Why is it that the mosquito, although it is so small, should be equipped not only with six feet, but with wings as well—while the elephant, the largest of animals, is wingless and has only four feet?' " The preacher is unabashed. "There is no point in telling you the reason for the different structure of mosquito and elephant, for you are completely ignorant of the God who made both!" He could, he says, answer their frivolous questions if they asked them sincerely, but he refuses to get sidetracked by bogus issues like these, impelled as he is by the concern to fulfil his commission. "We have a commission only to tell you the words of him who sent us. Instead of logical proof we bring before you many witnesses from among yourselves . . . It is, of course, open to you either to accept or to disbelieve adequate testimony of this sort. But I shall not cease to declare unto you what is for your profit: for to be silent would mean loss for me, just as to disbelieve would mean ruin for you." Laughter, disagreement, and violence followed this exchange, and "Clement" had difficulty in getting the preacher away unharmed to his lodging in order to enquire of him further about the Christian faith.

Although the pseudo-Clementines are an imaginative historical novel, they must have had verisimilitude in order to have gained and held a wide readership. We may take it that this picture of open air evangelism is a realistic enough sketch of what was happening up and down the Middle East in the early centuries of the Church's life.

Prophetic Preaching

So far we have been examining "orthodox" Christian preaching, either in the synagogue or the open air, such as we might expect to find today. But in the early days of the Church we have the prophets to consider, men who spoke directly in the name of Christ. The phenomenon is well attested in the New Testament. There were prophets in Jerusalem and Caesarea, in Antioch, Rome, Corinth, Thessalonica and the churches of Asia Minor.[15] Prophecy was a gift some possessed and others did not:[16] it was very highly prized, next to the apostolic office itself, because in both Jesus was directly communicating with his people.[17] Prophets join apostles in having a foundational character for the Church[18] simply for this reason that both are agents of revelation. Frequently referred to in modern literature on the subject as "ecstatic", prophecy cannot properly be so described. The prophet was not filled with a compulsive urge: and he was in control of his mind (*nous*) in contrast to the speaker in "tongues", whose mind remained uninformed.[19] Prophecy, accordingly, was coherent speech, under the direct domination of the Holy Spirit. It was exercised by men and women alike, and appears to have been very varied in content. It could vary from the predictions of Agabus,[20] the mysteries of the Apocalypse, the indication of a certain Christian for office,[21] testimony to Jesus,[22] to use in evangelism[23] and edification, consolation, teaching.[24] This direct word from God must, if it be genuine, be in accord with the content of the apostolic faith. Paul stresses that the genuineness of prophecy is to be judged by the recipients,[25] and judged in accordance with whether or not it enshrines apostolic doctrine.[26] The *Didache* stresses the importance of godly behaviour in those who lay genuine claim to this gift.[27] Prophecy continued in the Church, and the Montanist movement was no isolated eruption. Tertullian justly points out that the bishop of Rome had acknowledged the prophetic gifts of Montanus, Prisca and Maximilla before being brought to a different mind through the false accusations of Praxeas against the prophets themselves and their churches.[28] Granted that prophecy declined as episcopacy grew in power (so much so that the bishop eventually claimed to absorb the prophetic function!), and as the canon of the New Testament increasingly made it less necessary, it continued well into the third century and made a great impression on ordinary people.

There is a famous passage in Origen's *Contra Celsum*[29] which has a bearing on this type of preaching. He deals with Celsus's complaint that "there are many who are nameless, who prophesy at the slightest excuse for some trivial cause both inside and outside temples. And there are some who wander about begging and roaming around cities and military camps, and they pretend to be moved as if giving some oracular response. It is an ordinary and common custom for each one to say, 'I am God (or a son of God, or a divine Spirit). And I have come. Already the world is being destroyed. And you, O men, are to perish because of your iniquities. But I wish to save you. And you shall see me returning again with heavenly power. Blessed is he who has worshipped me now. But I will cast everlasting fire upon all the rest, both on cities and on country places. And men who fail to realize the penalties in store for them will in vain repent and groan. But I will preserve for ever those who have been convinced by me.' " So much for the prophecies. The preachers then seem to have continued in tongues, if we may judge by Celsus's next remark. "Having brandished these threats they then go on to add incomprehensible, incoherent and utterly obscure utterances, the meaning of which no intelligent person could discover; for they are meaningless and nonsensical, and give a chance for any fool or sorcerer to take the words in whatever sense he likes."

It has sometimes been argued that this accusation of Celsus's, with which Origen is manifestly ill at ease, betokens pagan prophecy[30] or else Montanism.[31] Both suggestions are unlikely. These men belonged to the Great Church, and as W. L. Knox pointed out, the content of their proclamation is Celsus's parody of "a perfectly good ante-Nicene preaching of a rather enthusiastic type".[32] Knox's contention has been remarkably vindicated very recently, by the discovery of Melito's *Homily on the Pascha*.[33] Now Melito, bishop of Sardis towards the end of the second century, was a prophet as well. Eusebius tells us that "he lived in all things in the Holy Spirit."[34] Much the same could be said of Ignatius, who on occasion spoke under direct inspiration as a Christian prophet: "When I was among you I spoke with a great voice, the voice of God," he reminds the Philadelphians.[35] At the end of his *Homily* Melito suddenly turns to Christian prophecy: Christ speaks through him in the first person. The change is startling. Melito is preaching: "The Lord, having put on human nature, and having suffered for him who suffered, having been bound for him who was bound, and having been buried for him who was buried (*sc.* in sin), is risen from the dead, and loudly proclaims this message (*phōnēn*)." Now comes the prophecy.

"Who will contend against me? Let him stand before me.
It is I who delivered the condemned. It is I who gave life to the
    dead.

It is I who raised up the buried. Who will argue with me?
It is I, says Christ who destroyed death. It is I who triumphed
over the enemy,
And trod down Hades, and bound the Strong Man
And have snatched mankind up to the heights of heaven. It is I,
says Christ.

"So then, come here all you families of men, weighed down by
your sins
And receive pardon for your misdeeds. For I am your pardon.
I am the Passover which brings salvation. I am the Lamb slain
for you.
I am your lustral bath. I am your life. I am your resurrection.
I am your light, I am your salvation, I am your King.
It is I who bring you up to the heights of heaven.
It is I who will give you the resurrection there.
I will show you the Eternal Father. I will raise you up with my
own right hand."[36]

Such direct inspiration of a prophet did not obliterate his own
stylistic characteristics. The Melito of this prophetical conclusion to
his sermon is manifestly the same man who wrote the more sober
beginning. Compare the following extract, for example. "Jesus is
all. When he judges, he is Law, when he teaches, he is Word, when
he saves, he is Grace, when he begets, he is Father, when begotten
he is Son, when he suffers he is Lamb, when buried he is Man, when
risen he is God. Such is Jesus Christ. To him be glory for ever,
Amen."[37] The man's rather florid Asiatic style[38] is taken over and
heightened in rhythm, in assonance, and in sheer power and
directness when he is inspired to prophesy as the representative of
Jesus. It is not difficult to see how preaching of this dynamic
excitable type could merit the scorn of a Celsus: it is not difficult,
either, to imagine the appeal it exercised over the emotional Oriental
mind of the ordinary hearer. At all events, prophecy of this nature
was undoubtedly used in evangelistic preaching as early as I
Corinthians,[39] and was still found to be flourishing at the end of the
second century.

The Value of Preaching

Preaching, then, whether in synagogue, Christian assembly, or
open air, whether normal or under direct inspiration, was a not
unimportant factor in the methods of the mission. Nevertheless
the break with the synagogue, the rise of persecution and the absence
of Christian buildings for worship all hindered formal proclamation

of the gospel. It was not easy to gather a large assembly without inviting police action, and Latourette is undoubtedly right in his judgment that "the chief agents in the expansion of Christianity appear not to have been those who made it a profession or made it a major part of their occupation, but men and women who carried on their livelihood in some purely secular manner and spoke of their faith to those they met in this natural fashion."[40] However, despite the hazards and the difficulties, great numbers of Christians must have really given themselves to preaching all over the ancient world. St Paul was not the only man who made it the main purpose of his life to tell others about Christ, nor who felt constrained to cry, "Woe unto me if I preach not the gospel." A lovely example of the attitude to preaching adopted by one of the great intellectuals at the end of the second century, Origen, is found in his *Commentary* on Psalm 36. One might expect that the head of the Catechetical School in Alexandria, the man who outgunned the philosophers on their own ground, was somewhat dull in his preaching and academic in his approach to it; in fact, the very reverse was the case.

In this commentary on Psalm 36 Origen is talking of Christian preachers under the metaphor of arrows of God. "All in whom Christ speaks, that is to say every upright man and preacher who speaks the word of God to bring men to salvation—and not merely the apostles and prophets—can be called an arrow of God. But, what is rather sad," he continues, "I see very few arrows of God. There are few who so speak that they inflame the heart of the hearer, drag him away from his sin, and convert him to repentance. Few so speak that the heart of their hearers is deeply convicted and his eyes weep for contrition. There are few who unveil the light of the future hope, the wonder of heaven and the glory of God's kingdom to such effect that by their earnest preaching they succeed in persuading men to despise the visible and seek the invisible, to spurn the temporal and seek the eternal. There are all too few preachers of this calibre." He fears that professional jealousy and rivalry often render what few good preachers there are useless in reaching those they try to win. And continuing in a very humble and sensitive vein Origen shares with the reader his dread that he should himself ever turn into the devil's arrow by causing anyone to stumble through what he did or said. "Sometimes we think we are confuting someone, and we speak ill-advisedly, and become aggressive and argumentative as we endeavour to win our case no matter what expressions we use. Then the devil takes our mouth and uses it like a bow from which he can shoot his arrows."[41] Such was the inner fear of a man of whom Eusebius could say, "As his doctrine, so was his life; and as his life, so also was his doctrine. That is how, through God's grace, he induced many to imitate him."[42] It is hardly surprising that with such a character many pagans flocked to him to hear the word of God even in a time of active persecution. As he himself put it, there are all too few preachers of that calibre.

Teaching Evangelism

One of the less felicitous aspects of Dodd's great book *The Apostolic Preaching and its Development* is the arbitrary separation it makes between preaching and teaching, between *kērugma* and *didachē*. This has been noticed by a number of scholars, but has recently been exposed in a full-scale treatment by R. C. Worley, *Preaching and Teaching in the Earliest Church*. He shows that both in rabbinic Judaism and in early Christianity there was no such clear-cut distinction between the work of the evangelist and the teacher. This is, in fact, apparent throughout the period from St Paul to Origen. Both of them evangelized through teaching the Christian faith. Origen's school at Alexandria was originally intended to inculcate basic Christian teaching. At the age of eighteen he was already leading this school "for elementary instruction in the faith".[43] But it was an evangelistic agency as well as a didactic one. "Some of the Gentiles came to him to hear the word of God", and became strong, courageous Christians who sealed their testimony with their blood, men like Plutarch, Severus, Heron and Heraclides, as well as women like Herais: all were martyred.[44] The preaching and teaching went together, and there was much practical work as well, the visiting of prisoners, the encouragement of those condemned to death for their faith, as well as working for a living and the exercise of great abstinence in food, drink, sleep, money and clothing. We have already made some mention of schools of Christian teaching or philosophy like this: the first we know of was started by Justin in Rome. It was well known that he would give instruction in the faith to any who wished, while maintaining himself by lecturing in philosophy, as he had done in his pre-Christian days. He gives a guarded account of his activities in his defence before the city prefect of Rome, Rusticus, which issued in his execution. In reply to Rusticus's query, "What kind of doctrines do you profess?" Justin replied, "I have endeavoured to learn all doctrines; but I have come to rest at last in the true doctrines, that is to say the Christian, even though they do not please those who hold false opinions." His search for truth had led him to Christ. When Rusticus asked him, "Where do you assemble and where do you bring your followers to?" Justin replied, "I live above one Martin, at the Timotinian Bath. And during the whole time (and this is the second time I am living in Rome) I am unaware of any other meeting than his. And if anyone wished to come to me, I passed on to him the doctrines of the truth."[45] Here, then, was a Christian intellectual, settling for a while in Rome, staying at the home of another Christian, next door to a Bath where everyone gathered daily for social intercourse—an ideal situation—and with his own attic above Martin's apartments to which he could invite the interested enquirers. Justin's explanation of Christian philosophy and his appeal for Christian commitment went hand in hand. This mixture of teaching and evangelism seems to have been taken up by a number of second century converts from the ranks of the intellectuals: Quadratus and Aristides, Athenagoras and Tatian, Pantaenus and Clement. We must remember that these men were no dons, writing their Apologies in safety and at leisure. They were missionaries, preachers, evangelists, and in many instances, martyrs.

It may well be that the whole inspiration for this teaching evangelism came from St Paul who took over the lecture hall of Tyrannus when he was staying for his three years in Ephesus. This was a most impressive piece of Christian opportunism, where the chance for wider ministry was cheerfully accepted. Paul reached through this method a clientele he would otherwise not have touched. We even read that the Asiarchs were so well disposed towards him that they urged him not to risk his life by going into the theatre and facing the tumult which was brewing up there.[46] This is perfectly astonishing in view of the fact that the Asiarchs were the officials charged with the supervision of the imperial cult, and we can be very certain that Paul would have had nothing to do with this. Nevertheless he had so won the respect and perhaps the friendship of these officials that they went out of their way to restrain him from entering on a dangerous situation. Had they been impressed, if not convinced, by what they heard in the lecture hall of Tyrannus?

Two points emerge clearly from this account of Paul in Ephesus In the first place, the intellectual content of his addresses must have been very stimulating. Here was a man who could hold his own, and presumably make converts, in the course of public debate, *dialegomenos*.[47] He had done it in the synagogue when he first arrived at Ephesus (the same word, *dialegomenos* is used, together with *peithōn*, persuading), and he had won men to Christ: he did it subsequently in this daily encounter with pagans in the lecture hall of Tyrannus. Indeed, so characteristic of Paul was this *arguing* the gospel that he has to deny that he was at it in the temple before his arrest: "They did not find me disputing with anybody or stirring up a crowd in the temple or the synagogues or in the city."[48] The full range of intellectual equipment would have been necessary for such front line work. Not, of course, that Paul or anyone else in the early Christian mission thought that argument alone could bring anyone into the kingdom of God. But they knew that it could break down barriers which obstructed men's vision of the moral and existential choice which faced them, of whether to respond to Christ or not.

The second quality which went with this intellectual liveliness was enthusiasm. This is obvious enough from the whole account— for instance, the first reaction of Paul on hearing of a tumult in the theatre is the urge to go and get involved! Now the Western Text of Acts 19:9 gives a most interesting reading, which may be, if not original, at least based on good local knowledge, as many of the Western readings in Acts appear to be. After recording that "Paul argued daily in the hall of Tyrannus" it adds "from the fifth to the tenth hour", i.e. from eleven a.m. to four p.m. Presumably Paul worked at his tentmaking in the cool of the morning, while Tyrannus was lecturing. Then, when public life stopped at eleven, and with it Tyrannus's lectures, Paul took over the school and disputed with all comers. He must have been enthusiastic in order to embark on such a project at so unpropitious a time. He must have been enthusiastic in order to succeed: as Lake and Cadbury point out, more people would be asleep in Ephesus at one p.m. than at one a.m.[49] F. F. Bruce aptly comments, "He must have infected his hearers with his own energy and zeal, so that they were willing to sacrifice their siesta for the sake of listening to Paul."[50]

Testimony

This note of enthusiasm pervaded the early Christians in every aspect of their evangelism. Even the most academic of them were convinced that they had found the truth in Christ, and were not embarrassed to add their personal testimony to the message they delivered. "Myself being one of them," says Justin as he begins his *First Apology* for the Christians. This personal testimony to the truth of the message was an integral part of Christian *marturia*, witness. It is to be found everywhere in the literature of our period.

The frequency of this note of personal testimony in the New Testament needs no emphasis: the writers are full of the difference which being in Christ has made to their lives, and actively commend him to others. They break out joyfully, "Thanks be to God for his inexpressible gift!",[51] or speak sorrowfully of "sinners of whom I am chief"[52] or joyfully of Christ's wonderful deliverance from the "law of sin which dwells in my members."[53] They did not obtrude themselves, but neither did they shrink from bearing personal testimony out of their own experience to the truth of what they proclaimed to others.

This remained an important factor in second century evangelism. Listen to one of Justin's colleagues, Euelpistus, as he faces execution for his Christianity. "And what are you?" asks the prefect. "I too am a Christian," he replies, "having been set at liberty by Christ."[54] Or turn to the last chapter of Clement of Alexandria's *Exhortation to the Heathen* which is an extended and enthusiastic appeal to them to commit themselves to Christ, intermingled with the joyous consciousness of what Christ has done for him—adopted him, made him right with God, given him wisdom and Christlikeness. "Such, then, is our position who are the attendants of Christ . . . God is the whole life of those who have known Christ."[55] At the end of his *Address to the Greeks* Tatian expresses his readiness to have his doctrine and his life examined, utterly confident that he "knows who God is and what is his work".[56] Elsewhere he utters a paean of praise to Christ for having rescued him from bondage to evil, condemnation and error, and the "ten thousand tyrants" that had dominated his life.[57] A number of other instances of this enthusiastic testimony to the truth of the gospel in their own experience have been mentioned in chapter 6. Wherever one looks in the literature of these two centuries it is the same story. Doctrinal imprecision, even imbalance abounds; heresy is common; antinomianism an ever-present danger; but there is no denying the zeal and the sense of discovery which marked the witness of the early Church both in their public and their private testimony, both in their written and their spoken word. It was this utter assurance of the Christians that they were right about God and Christ and salvation, which in the end succeeded in convincing the pagan world that it was in error.

HOUSEHOLD EVANGELISM

The Value of Home Evangelism

One of the most important methods of spreading the gospel in antiquity was by the use of homes. It had positive advantages: the comparatively small numbers involved made real interchange of views and informed discussion among the participants possible; there was no artificial isolation of a preacher from his hearers; there was no temptation for either the speaker or the heckler to "play to the gallery" as there was in a public place or open-air meeting. The sheer informality and relaxed atmosphere of the home, not to mention the hospitality which must often have gone with it, all helped to make this form of evangelism particularly successful. We have already noticed how Celsus complained of it: it was in private houses that the wool workers and cobblers, the laundry workers and the yokels whom he so profoundly despised did their proselytizing. Even the children were taught that if they believed "they would become happy and make their home happy as well".[58] The *Clementine Recognitions* give us a sample of the house meetings which must have been common in the second century when Clement is made to arrive at Peter's residence in Caesarea. Having heard through chatter in an inn that a certain Peter was in the town and was going to hold a discussion the next day with one Simon, a Samaritan, Clement asks to be shown to his lodging. He found it, knocked, was welcomed in, and before long was listening to extended instruction from the apostle.[59] Again, we find in another part of the same literature an account of how Peter and his company came to a house, previously agreed on: "The master of the house welcomed us, and led us to a certain apartment, arranged like a theatre, and beautifully built. There we found considerable crowds waiting for us, who had come during the night . . ." and before long the discussion was in full swing.[60]

But we are not dependent on statements from opponents like Celsus or novelists like the author of the pseudo-Clementines for information about household evangelism. It is a significant feature in the New Testament itself. Jason's house at Thessalonica was used for this purpose,[61] so was that of Titius Justus, situated provocatively opposite the synagogue (with which Paul had broken) at Corinth.[62] Philip's house at Caesarea seems to have been a most hospitable place, where not only visiting seafarers like Paul and his company but wandering charismatics like Agabus were made welcome.[63] Both Lydia's house and the jailer's at Philippi were used as evangelistic centres,[64] and Stephanas apparently used his home at Corinth in the same way. His household was baptized by St Paul in person, no doubt after some instruction in basic Christianity and a profession of faith,[65] and we subsequently learn that he used his home "for the service of the saints".[66] The very earliest Christian community met in the upper room of a particular house, owned by the mother of John Mark in Jerusalem.[67] It is hardly surprising that the "church in the house" became a crucial factor in the spread of the Christian faith.

The Sociological Significance of the Home

This emphasis on the house as the fundamental unit of society had a long history both in Israelite and Roman culture. Sociologically

Pagan praying figure (Orante) from Pompeii, now in the Museo
Nazionale at Naples: first century A.D.

Fresco of a Christian praying figure from a house on the Caelian Hill,
Rome, similar yet distinct: ?fourth century A.D. See p. 216 and notes.

The first century Cross on the wall of the House of the Bicentenary at Herculaneum together with the wooden cabinet found beneath it. See p. 214ff. and notes.

Lawrence's cabinet containing the four gospels from the fifth century Mausoleum of Galla Placidia at Ravenna. See p. 215 and notes.

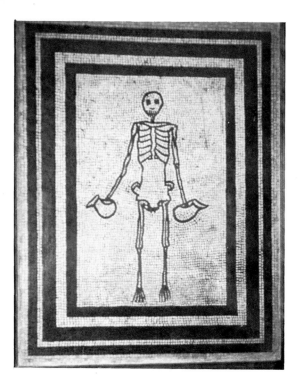

A first century mosaic from Pompeii, now in the Museo Nazionale, Naples, showing how this prosperous society was haunted with the thought of death. See p. 22.

A first century Pompeian fresco of the Phoenix, the mythical bird that rose from death, with the envious inscription, "O Phoenix, you lucky thing!" Clement of Rome used this bird as an illustration of the resurrection of Christ. See p. 142 and notes.

PHOENIX FELIX ETTV

speaking, the early Christians could not have hit on a sounder basis. The work of Jeremias[68] and Stauffer[69] among others has shown how fundamental to God's economy of salvation in Israel was the house. It is Noah and his house who are brought into the ark, Abraham and his house who are brought into the covenant, David and his house to whom the kingdom is promised, and so forth. Such is the solidarity of the house that David goes out of his way to do kindness to the lame Mephibosheth simply because he is the sole surviving member of the house of Jonathan. It was not only the wife and children who were included in this household of Israel: so were the servants and resident aliens. Thus the command in Deuteronomy 14:26: "You shall eat there before the Lord your God and rejoice, you and your household" is synonymous with 12:12, "You shall rejoice before the Lord your God, you and your sons and your daughters, your menservants and your maidservants."

The family is no less basic in Graeco-Roman society and thought. There was controversial discussion over the relative claims of the household and the state. Part of the strains at the end of the Roman Republic were due to the clashes of rival *familiae*: part of the success of the Caesars was due to the concept of the supremacy of the *domus Augusta*, the household of the Emperor which was dispersed in various parts of the world.[70]

The household, even under the Empire, was a complex institution. Its undisputed head was the father, and he enjoyed sweeping powers over the members of his family whom he could try at a family court if he felt so disposed, and in particular over the womenfolk and slaves in his household who remained under his unquestioned *manus* and *potestas*. Apart from his own kith and kin, the "household" would include the slaves, who were dependent on it for their very livelihood and place (such as it was) in society; also the freedmen, who frequently took the family name and remained in the looser connection with it known as *clientela*. This involved them in loyalty to the head of the household, and him in acting on their behalf in terms of financial or alimentary protection, and if necessary legal intervention. A further group often reckoned with the *familia* were the *amici*, the trusted friends to whom intimacy was granted and from whom reliable support and devotion was expected. This was the position within the household of Herod the tetrarch enjoyed by Manaen,[71] who subsequently became a Christian. This was the relationship with Tiberius enjoyed by Pontius Pilate, a relationship which could be destroyed if malicious reports reached the Emperor suggesting that Pilate showed favour to an Imperial pretender: "If you release this man you are not Caesar's friend."[72]

The family understood in this broad way, as consisting of blood relations, slaves, clients and friends, was one of the bastions of Graeco-Roman society. Christian missionaries made a deliberate point of gaining whatever households they could as lighthouses, so to speak, from which the gospel could illuminate the surrounding darkness. Stauffer may have gone too far when he claimed that there is an almost ritual *oikos*-formula to be found in the New Testament, but he is quite right in stressing the centrality of the household to Christian advance.

Conversion of the Husband

Whether or not the baptism of whole "houses" in this inclusive sense of the term indicates the baptism of children is beyond the purview of this study. To my mind the probabilities are that Jeremias rather than Aland[73] is right in this matter, and that infants were sometimes (to put it no higher) baptized along with the rest of the *familia* of which they formed part, particularly in view of the solidarity of the Jewish family in circumcision and proselyte baptism,[74] which were administered to infants and adults alike; and in view of the fact that Roman households were united in a common religious cult (the *Lares*) irrespective of age or personal beliefs. However that may be, the household proved the crucial medium for evangelism within natural groupings, whatever member of the family was first won to the faith. It was preferable, of course, if the father was converted first, for then he would bring over the whole family with him. This is what happened in the case of Cornelius, when he contemplated a change of *superstitio*. He gathered together his blood relatives, his slaves and his friends, and together they heard the preaching of Peter.[75] When Cornelius professed faith, his whole *familia* (and it was a large one. When Peter entered the house "he found many persons gathered")[76] was baptized with him.[77] The action of the head of the family committed the rest of his dependent group. The same happened in the case of Lydia, a textile sales-woman from Thyatira operating for the time being in Philippi. Her whole household (no doubt largely slaves, together with some freed-men, but without spouse and children in this case, as she seems to have been unmarried), was baptized.[78] So was that of the Philippian jailer when he professed faith.[79] It was the natural thing.

Conversion of the Wife

It was not so easy when Christianity entered the home through the agency of a member of the household other than its head. Jesus had foretold that allegiance to him might well split the family, and so it proved time and again. There is a heart-rending account in Tertullian of the plight of a Christian woman in a pagan household,[80] and of the eventual divorce and persecution arising from a mixed marriage in Rome in his day;[81] this makes it easy to see the wisdom of Paul's apparently narrow advice to the unmarried to ensure that they only married a Christian. "Do not be mismated with unbelievers"[82] was not only sound theology based on a profound conception of marital unity, but wise practical advice arising from having witnessed the miseries of mixed marriages. When the wife was won to faith subsequent to marriage, however, there was every reason, Paul declared, to believe that God intended to reach the whole family through her: if she was set apart for God, she should reckon that her husband and children came within the same saving purposes of God, and so far from leaving them or shrinking away from them, she should strive by her godly behaviour to win them.[83]

This was no easy matter. If, as seems quite possible, Pomponia Graecina, the wife of Britain's conqueror, Aulus Plautius, was a Christian, she found it an impossibly demanding challenge in the high position in society which she occupied. Devoted, as Tacitus tells us, to her "foreign superstition", she used the murder of Julia her cousin by marriage as an excuse to retire from public life, and under cover of protracted mourning for her (it went on for forty years!) she attracted less attention by her new way of life. However she did not escape the accusations of society, and "was handed over to her husband's judicial decision. Following ancient precedent, he heard his wife's case publicly in the presence of kinsfolk (*propinquis*) involving as it did her character and, indeed, life itself—and he pronounced her innocent."[84] That story illustrates clearly enough the perils a Christian wife could run for her faith at the hands of her own husband, and is a reminder of how difficult it was to break into the structure of the *familia* from beneath. Perhaps she had some success after all: in the oldest part of the Catacomb of Callistus in Rome is a second century inscription recording the burial of a Christian, Pomponius Graecinus—the identical *cognomen* as well as *nomen gentile* suggests that he enjoyed blood relationship with this Pomponia Graecina, but we cannot be sure.[85]

Conversion of the Slaves and Freedmen

We do not know of any impression made on the household through the conversion of children, though this is in itself not improbable. Whether an Ignatius, a Justin, a Hermas or a Clement was able to make any headway with his own parents we simply cannot say. But the slaves and freedmen certainly did provide a way of penetrating even into the great families of the Roman aristocracy. There were members of Caesar's household who were Christians by the time Paul wrote to the Philippians:[86] it seems that Paul had made a great impression, if not actual converts, among the members of the praetorian guard appointed in rotas of four to guard him during his imprisonment. "It has become known," he could write, "throughout the whole praetorian guard and to all the rest that my imprisonment is for Christ."[87] If we are to assume, as on balance seems probable, that the last chapter of Romans was in fact directed to Rome and not to Ephesus,[88] several further inferences may be drawn about the spread of the gospel through freedmen, though perhaps not so many as J. B. Lightfoot supposed.[89] Lightfoot assembled first century Roman parallels for most of the names in Romans 16, but this amounts to very little because of the frequency with which most of the names occur in funerary inscriptions elsewhere in the Empire. However with "those who belong to the family of Aristobulus"[90] and "those in the Lord who belong to the family of Narcissus"[91] it is rather different. Aristobulus was a grandson of Herod the Great, and was educated and lived his life in Rome. He was a great friend of the Emperor Claudius, and it looks as though he left his *familia* of slaves to the Emperor at his death,[92] in which case they would continue to be known as *Aristobuliani*. It would seem probable that some of this Jewish entourage of this member of the Herod family had come to Christian faith, particularly as the next person Paul mentions is his fellow-countryman, Herodion; this is a characteristic slave name which we might expect to find among the retainers of one of the Herods.

The *Narcissiani* passed into imperial hands by a less savoury route. The powerful freedman Narcissus exercised tremendous influence over the Emperor Claudius, whose private secretary (*a libellis*) he was. He possessed enormous wealth as well as power, and had a very large *familia*. This passed into the hands of Nero when, after the murder of Claudius in A.D. 54, Narcissus was driven to suicide at the instigation of Agrippina. It was apparently some of this household who were among the Christian recipients of the Epistle to the Romans. Certainty is unattainable in tracing the influence of the slaves and freedmen of these large households upon their masters. But it is probable that it was largely through their agency that the aristocratic families were eventually reached with the gospel.[93] Take the *gens Acilius*, for instance, whose eldest sons regularly carried the cognomen *Glabrio*. This was an illustrious old senatorial family, one of whose members, Acilius Glabrio, was consul with Trajan in A.D. 91 and was forced to fight with a lion by the Emperor Domitian. There must have been some strong reason to induce even so unprincipled a tyrant as Domitian to take such unprecedented action against the highest office bearer in the state! Dio[94] makes it clear that his "atheism and Jewish ways" were the primary cause of Domitian's resentment, though Suetonius adds that the Emperor suspected him of revolutionary tendencies.[95] This suggests strongly that he was a Christian, whose loyalty to Christ forbade him to call the Emperor by the blasphemous titles which he imposed even upon the senatorial families of addressing him as "Our Lord and God".[96] Such refusal must have looked like political disaffection to Domitian's morbid mind. Indeed, according to Hegesippus, he went to the trouble of arresting the grandsons of Jude, the Lord's brother, on the same suspicion that they were potential revolutionaries, but was reassured as to their peaceful intentions and bucolic pursuits on seeing their horny hands![97] At all events, Glabrio killed the lion, was accordingly released, but wisely went into voluntary exile. This did him no good however: the Emperor had him executed, colouring the story to make it appear that Glabrio had voluntarily demeaned his consular station in order to become a gladiator and fight the lion. He was buried in the family vault which not long afterwards became a Christian catacomb. Was he a Christian? This is how Hertling and Kirschbaum assess the probabilities. "We have the lion slaying consul of the year 91, who may have been a Christian. His descendants are buried above or near a crypt which later formed part of a Christian cemetery. Some of these descendants were themselves Christians. The cemetery was named after a Priscilla. And, as we have seen, there were in the second century a number of Priscillas in the family of the Glabriones. These various details do not add up to a categorical proof, but it would be foolish to attribute them all to pure chance."[98]

It is perhaps fruitless to pursue this matter further, but I cannot help wondering if the family was not reached through a couple who appear in the New Testament, Aquila and Priscilla. Aquila is presented to us as a Jew, born in Pontus, who was expelled from Italy almost certainly through Claudius's legislation in A.D. 49[99] following the riots in the synagogues at Rome over "Chrestus". It is a singular factor that his wife is mentioned before him in four of the six New Testament references to the pair. Is it possible that Priscilla was a free-born[100] member of the *gens* who married this Jewish freedman who had, naturally, taken the *nomen gentile* of his patron, Acilius? Was it through this dedicated Christian couple that the Christian faith entered the family of the Acilii to such effect that the head of the family himself was a Christian by the nineties? This is pure conjecture,[101] but it is not impossible, and it is just the sort of thing that unquestionably did take place in the first two centuries, as the gospel spread through the great households of the Empire.

The progress of Christianity among the upper classes through the activities of slaves and freedmen may well be illustrated by a house in Herculaneum, where the House of the Bicentenary at once fascinates and tantalizes. It belonged to Gaius Petronius Stephanus, and is one of the finest private houses in the town. The owner was emphatically not a Christian: the frescoes of Cupids at play, Daedalus and Pasiphaë, and a nude Mars and thinly draped Venus make that tolerably certain. It so happens that a number of papyrus records were found in this house, which reveal the tortuous progress of a Roman lawsuit in which Caltoria, the widow of Stephanus, seeks to establish her legal claims over a girl, Justa, of uncertain paternity, who had been born within the household. The girl claimed to be a freedwoman. No supporting documentation on either side seems to have been forthcoming, but the decisive evidence in the case was then afforded by the bailiff of the deceased Stephanus. This man, Telesphorus, had the courage to testify against Caltoria, whom he still served as a freedman. He showed that Justa had been born after the manumission of her mother, and he referred to her in his evidence, quite precisely, as *co-liberta mea*. Legal delays, curiously modern, persisted. Depositions were made in A.D. 75–76. Judgment had still not been given in A.D. 79.

What could have induced Telesphorus to take this action, so prejudicial to his personal interests in the household of Caltoria? Was it simply his sense of fair play? Was it the fact that he had originally, it appears, been brought into the family by Stephanus as Justa's tutor? Or was there a deeper reason?

The house, though splendid in design and décor, had fallen on hard times. That it why, no doubt, Caltoria was so keen to get her hands on Justa's person and possessions. The first floor of the building had been turned into two flats, and let. In a room which could have belonged to either flat a most interesting find has been made. The room appears to have been a small chapel. A patch of white plaster had been let into the wall at some time subsequent to the construction of the room. Plainly marked in the centre of this plaster is a sizeable cross. It is not absolutely certain that this affords proof of Christian ownership. Some experts doubt whether the cross became a Christian symbol so early, but the recent discoveries of the cross, the fish, the star and the plough, all well known from the second century, on ossuaries of the Judaeo-Christian community in Judaea put the *possibility* beyond reasonable cavil.[102] Moreover, a wooden cross was found in another house in Herculaneum, and there are one or two probable examples at Pompeii, notably that from the House of Pansa, so there is no good reason why this mark in the wall at Herculaneum should not be a Christian emblem.[103]

The alternative explanation, that the cruciform mark was caused by the rapid pulling away of a small shelf from the wall, is rendered improbable by the fact that the nail marks, fixing it to the wall, are top and bottom, not at the sides which would be normal for a shelf. The conclusion suggests itself that here we have a Christian chapel, and the cross on the wall was snatched away as a prized possession when the Christian occupant fled before the rising mud and lava which engulfed the stricken town on August 24th, A.D. 79.

This conclusion is strengthened by a consideration of the other piece of furniture which the room held. It was a small wooden cupboard, a yard or so high and half as wide, found directly beneath the cross on the wall. It looks as if it was used for worship. Indeed, it bears a striking resemblance to the *lararia* so common in Pompeii and Herculaneum, the wooden chests in which the household gods were housed.[104] I suggest that this Christian prayer desk, if such it is, was directly developed from the pagan *lararium*, and furnishes us, therefore, with yet another example of pagan customs, cult-objects, words and symbols "baptized" by the growing Christian movement.

But what is all this doing in the middle of a pagan house? Clearly, Caltoria was not a believer—or she would not have engaged in a protracted, sordid and selfish lawsuit. But it is not improbable that Telesphorus and Justa were believers, that they formed a tiny Christian cell in that room, that they were the ones who ripped the cross from the wall in their flight. This hypothesis would give a very adequate explanation of Telesphorus's courage in withstanding Caltoria on Justa's behalf.

But is it credible that the patrician owners of such a house would permit their freedman to turn one room into a chapel for a cult believed to be subversive, a cult which had induced Nero to take such drastic action against it fifteen years earlier? It certainly does not seem at first sight at all probable. Perhaps the chapel was in fact used by another freedman, Marcus Helvius Eros by name, who seems to have been the tenant of the other flat. His personal seal was discovered in one of the rooms adjoining the chapel. Nevertheless the most likely candidate remains, I think, Telesphorus. A man who had proved his worth as family bailiff to such an extent that he was awarded his freedom and was put in charge of the whole household is just the sort of person in whom an indulgent master, Stephanus, or the widow, Caltoria, who depended on his expertise, might well tolerate the introduction of an *externa superstitio*. After all, as we have seen, Roman religion was syncretistic, not exclusive.

If this admittedly very speculative reconstruction is anywhere near the truth, it gives concrete attestation of the process which we know must have been going on at the time, the gradual infiltration of the middle and upper classes of Roman society by Christianity through the lives and words of slaves and freedmen in their emment. This is how that unique institution, the Christian home, began to make an impression on surrounding paganism.

Indirect Evangelism in the Home

The earliest Christian meetings took place in homes. It is only to be expected, therefore, that Christians should have borne witness to their faith through the decoration of these homes.

The evidence suggests that they did so in a tentative and allusive way. They affected decorations which would mean much to a fellow Christian, but would either seem unremarkable to the non-Christian or might excite mild comment, which in turn, could give the Christian householder an opportunity to bear witness to his faith.

Second and third century mosaics at Ostia and Rome show this process at a reasonably advanced stage. In Ostia, for instance, there are mosaics showing the eucharistic loaves, a chalice, and the fish motif. There is, moreover, a fascinating complex of three houses on the Caelian Hill in Rome. The use of *opus reticulatum* together with herring-bone tiling in the construction, points to the first century as the date of building at all events for the nymphaeum of the first house. This is confirmed by the frescoes found there, very similar in design and execution to the fourth style at Pompeii. At a time which it is impossible to specify, but before the mid-second century, this house was modified so as to take over the adjoining house. And that house contained in its triclinium a remarkable picture of an *orante* (a figure with arms outstretched in prayer), very similar to those found in the Catacombs. Such a figure betrays the Christian ownership of the house. But it does so in a very subtle way. The National Museum at Naples has two good examples of *oranti* of pagan origin, dating from before A.D. 79, for they were found at Pompeii. For all their similarity, there is a striking difference between the pagan *orante* and the Christian one, which was evidently modelled on it. The former keeps the upper arms to the side of the body, while extending the forearms in supplication. The Christian figures regularly stretch out the whole arms in supplication.[105] The similarity to the pagan type would allow the Christian *orante* to go unchallenged by most visitors to the home. But the churchman would recognize it at once: and the pagan acquaintance interested enough to enquire about its peculiarities would provide his host with an ideal opportunity of explaining the faith to him.

This house evidently remained in Christian hands. For the tradition that John and Paul, two Romans of the days of Constantine, were martyred there under Julian the Apostate for their refusal to join the army and become implicated in its idolatry, has been vindicated by the discovery of a tomb (almost certainly theirs) in this house, together with those of various others buried near them for the benefit of proximity to the martyrs. This is very remarkable, for the site lies within the walls: the tradition that they were murdered on emerging from the house, and forthwith buried clandestinely beneath the stairs, seemed highly improbable because burial within the walls was illegal. The graves, however, have been found, and a tiny oratory over the central grave provides possibly the oldest pictorial representation of any Christian martyrdom—not only of John and Paul themselves, but of Priscus, Priscillian and Benedicta, themselves martyred for seeking out the remains of their Christian friends and paying homage at their tomb. This house, in fact, changed in the course of 200 years, from a pagan abode, to a Christian home and then to a martyr shrine. The middle stage of this progression illustrates the point we are making: a room decorated quietly and unobtrusively but quite definitely with a Christian *orante* and the accompanying ambivalent emblems of vine and shepherd both of which could be merely a pastoral motif, or could betray a Christian meaning.

I suggest that this method of declaring allegiance to Christ goes back a long way before the martyrs Paul and John. We see occasional signs of it at Pompeii. One of the murals discovered there was a painting of the Judgment of Solomon.[106] It is, of course, possible that this was Jewish, but in view of the predilection for Old Testament scenes in Christian iconography it is perhaps more probably a Christian work, and this is widely agreed. If so, it is admirably suited for stressing the importance of right decision, and the need for complete honesty and openness before a greater than Solomon. An admirable text—set in an interesting and arresting fresco.

An even more obvious example is the mosaic atrium of the House of Paquius Proculus in the Via dell' Abondanza at Pompeii. This was an upper-middle-class home, decorated with rich mosaics in the vestibule, atrium and peristyle. When disaster hit this house in A.D. 79, seven children were trapped in one of the rooms off the central atrium, and their skeletons have been recovered. It seems almost certain that this was a Christian home. Not only was a graffito of the famous *Rotas-Sator* square[107] found here (sadly destroyed by an Allied shell in the Second World War), but the impluvium of the atrium bears silent but eloquent testimony to the Christian faith of its owners. The inner band of mosaic was fairly new when the city was destroyed by Vesuvius. It carries decorative designs of birds, animals and so forth. The most striking is a group on the left of the impluvium. The central plaque of this group depicts a face: taken on its own it might indicate anyone. But taken in connection with the adjoining plaques it evidently signifies Jesus. For on the left are two crossed fishes, and on the right a lamb. It is difficult to doubt that many an evangelistic conversation began in the atrium of that house as Paquius Proculus explained the meaning of his mosaic redecorations.[108] (See Endsheets.)

Varieties of House Meetings

Where there was a Christian home, the uses to which it was put were very various. The Acts of the Apostles alone shows us such homes being used for prayer meetings,[109] for an evening of Christian fellowship,[110] for Holy Communion services,[111] for a whole night of prayer, worship and instruction,[112] for impromptu evangelistic gatherings,[113] for planned meetings in order to hear the Christian gospel,[114] for following up enquirers,[115] for organized instruction.[116] We find Paul making a most interesting use of his "hired house" in Rome: he was no longer able to go out to preach the gospel, so he invited leading Jews to come to his residence for a full day of talk and discussion.[117] His approach was superb. He took the initiative, and explained the reason for his presence in Rome, before they could produce any garbled accounts that may have reached them from Judaea. He was brief, factual, conciliatory and to the point. He offered them hospitality: he showed his understanding of the Scriptures, his loyalty to the hope of Israel, and his deep conviction that in Jesus salvation was to be found. When Paul claimed in his farewell address to the Ephesian elders that he had taught them "in public and from house to house, testifying both to Jews and to Greeks of repentance to God and of faith in our Lord Jesus Christ"[118] it was no idle boast. Like Baxter many centuries later, he had discovered that this house-evangelism was more fruitful than any. After years of faithful preaching, Richard Baxter turned to house meetings, giving Monday and Tuesday entirely to this work, from morning to night "taking about fifteen or sixteen families in a week, that we may go through the parish, in which there are upwards of 800 families, in the year. I cannot say yet that one family hath refused to come to me . . . And I find more outward signs of success with most that do come than from all my public preaching to them."[119] I suspect the Apostle would have said the same.

The Children in the Home

We know all too little of the effect of this sort of home on the children. But there is at any rate some evidence that Christian homes were making their mark very early upon the children brought up in them. Bishop Polycarp was brought up in a Christian home,[120] so was Marcion.[121] Two of the Christians martyred with Justin *c.* A.D. 165 were Paeon and Euelpistus. The former, replying to the prefect's enquiry as to where he learnt his Christianity, replied, "From our parents we received this good confession." And Euelpistus answered, "I willingly heard the words of Justin. But from my parents too I learned to be a Christian."[122] Justin Martyr himself, though born of pagan stock, informs us that "many men and women of the age of sixty and seventy years have been disciples of Christ from childhood",[123] and this agrees with the statement of Pliny that in Bithynia in A.D. 112 he had found among the Christians not only adults but little children (*teneri*): the new faith had ensnared "many of every age".[124] This is not surprising when we recall the solidarity of the family in both Jewish and Graeco-Roman society, and the care with which Jews trained their children in the faith, and pagans educated their young. It would be odd if Christians did not bestow equal pains on their children and if this did not, at least frequently, bear fruit. The Pauline epistles speak of Christian children and their obligation to "obey your parents in the Lord, for this is right. 'Honour your father and mother (this is the first commandment with a promise) that it may be well with you and that you may live long on the earth'."[125] This injunction had its correlative for the parent in the Christian home, of course, "Fathers, do not provoke your children to anger but bring them up in the discipline and instruction of the Lord."[126] The New Testament has little enough to say about the teaching and training of a child: but it is clear that children can partake in the kingdom of heaven, that their attitude of trusting obedience is in fact a model for adults to follow if they are to gain eternal life.[127] The duty of the parents to train up their children is paramount: it is through the witness and example of the Christian home that children are brought into and nourished within the fellowship. There is a delightful glimpse of children and wives appearing at Tyre to wave Paul and his company goodbye: together they all knelt down on the beach and prayed, and then bade each other farewell.[128]

The responsibility of the parents to lead their children to trust the Lord is stressed in the subapostolic writings. The *Epistle of Barnabas* enjoins, "Thou shalt not slay the child by procuring abortion; nor, again, shalt thou destroy it after it is born. Thou shalt not withdraw thy hand from thy son, or from thy daughter, but from their infancy thou shalt teach them the fear of the Lord."[129] This passage in *Barnabas* comes from the document "The Two Ways" which, probably based on a Jewish original, had great influence on the ethical side in the earliest Church. Polycarp writes in similar vein, "Let us teach, first of all, ourselves to walk in the commandments of the Lord. Next, teach your wives to walk in the faith given to them, and in love and in purity tenderly to love their own husbands in all truth, and to love others equally in all chastity: and to train up their children in the knowledge of God."[130] Clement of Rome lays equal stress on the example, the training, the discipline of the house where Christian faith is the guiding principle. "Let us reverence them that have the rule over us, let us honour our elders, let us train our young in the fear of God, let us direct our women in the good way . . . Let our children partake of the training that is in Christ. Let them learn how humility avails with God, what pure love can do with him, how the fear of him is good and great and saves those who live therein in holiness and a pure mind."[131]

In none of these instances is there any suggestion that direct evangelizing is necessary or fitting in the Christian home. Indeed, the children of believers are already treated as being in the Christian fellowship unless they contract out; like the child of a proselyte to Judaism they are regarded as within the covenant unless they determine to cut themselves off from it. And even then they do not need to be converted in the sense which we examined in chapter 6; rather, they need to be corrected by their parents and brought back to the Christian way from which they had strayed: it appears that the early Christians took very seriously indeed the words of Jesus asserting that the kingdom of God belonged to children.[132]

Three Christian Homes

An example of the offspring of a Christian home going astray is given in the writings of Hermas. Hermas is a Christian who has been very remiss in his duties towards his own household, which includes his wife, children and servants.[133] It is repeatedly stressed that he is responsible for all his children,[134] all his household.[135] He has not taken pains to help his wife overcome her uncontrolled tongue[136]— which may refer either to gossip or grumbling. He has not been instructing his family but has allowed them to become corrupt.[137]

"Your seed, Hermas, have set God at nought, have blasphemed the Lord, and have betrayed their parents by great wickedness."[138] But, although Hermas has narrow views about the possibility of a second repentance, he is convinced that both the wife and children will find mercy if he bestirs himself in their behalf.[139] The family is not to be regarded as pagan, in need of becoming Christian, but lapsed from their Christian profession and in need of discipline, help and teaching about living the Christian life. It is in this sense that Hermas is charged with the conversion of his family. "You are indulgent, and do not correct your family" is the charge against him: the remedy is "that you should convert your family which has sinned against the Lord and against you, their parents". "But the great mercy of the Lord has had pity on you and your family, and will make you strong and will establish you in his glory; only do not be slothful, but have courage and strengthen your family. For as the smith, by hammering his work, overcomes the task which he desires, so also the daily righteous word overcomes all wickedness. Do not cease, then, correcting your children, for I know that if they repent with all their hearts, they will be inscribed in the book of life with the saints."[140]

Another passage in Hermas shows the crucial importance of the united Christian family if it is to have any impact on the surrounding world; and this unity is easily marred not only when the young are disobedient, but when the parents bear grudges and take no interest in the children. "But, Hermas, no longer bear a grudge against your children, nor neglect your sister (i.e. wife), that they may be cleansed from their former sins. For they will be corrected with righteous correction if you bear no grudge against them. The bearing of grudges works death. But you, Hermas, had great troubles of your own because of the transgressions of your family, because you did not pay attention to them; but you neglected them and became entangled in their evil deeds."[141]

Origen came from a very different Christian family, a family whose light must have shone out brightly in the dark days of the Severan persecution in A.D. 202. His father Leonides was arrested for his faith and, in due course, martyred. Origen wrote to his father encouraging him to stand firm in the hour of his trial, and not to weaken out of consideration for them: after the father's death Origen undertook to keep his mother and the other six children by teaching, young as he was (a mere seventeen at the time). The quality of the Christian instruction in this home is shown by Eusebius: "Origen had even then (A.D. 202) made no little progress in the doctrine of faith as he had been conversant with the Holy

Scriptures from a child. He had been considerably trained in them by his father, who, besides the study of the liberal sciences, had also carefully stored his mind with these. First of all, therefore, before he studied Greek literature, he led him to frequent exercise in the study of sacred things, appointing him to commit and repeat some passages every day; and these things were not unwillingly done by the child, but studies most cheerfully performed with great diligence." So zealous was the lad that he could not remain satisfied with the main points in the passages of Scripture which he read, but "gave his father trouble by his questions of what the passage of the inspired Scripture really meant". The father—characteristically—"rebuked him to his face, telling him not to enquire into things beyond his age, nor to search beyond the obvious meaning of Scripture. But inwardly in his own heart he was delighted and gave most hearty thanks to Almighty God, the author of all good, for the privilege of being the father of such a child." The mother, too, seems to have been a delightful character, not too serious to have a sense of fun even in the most dangerous situation. When young Origen was longing to go and join his father and get arrested and martyred, she prevented him by hiding his clothes![142]

If this was a good example of a Christian home at the end of the second century, spreading the gospel among its children by precepts and example, by worship and sharing in holy things together as a family, no less attractive a picture can be read between the lines of the story of a first century pair, Aquila and Priscilla. Whether or not they were Christians before they met Paul at Corinth is disputed, but thereafter there could be no doubt about the matter. Theirs was a busy home: leatherworkers[143] by trade they plied their skills and made time for Christian evangelism as well. It was, obviously enough, a worshipping home. As Jews they would have prayed daily in the home together; as Christians they would have done no less. They were regular attenders at the synagogue, and it was here they discovered Apollos,[144] and seeing that they could be of help to this most promising and talented man, they invited him round to their home and instructed him further in the faith. Though Luke's description is not completely clear, it would seem probable that Apollos had no knowledge of the risen Lord until they informed him: he had merely been impressed with the preaching of John the Baptist who foretold the coming of one mightier than himself.[145] Theirs was a generous home, too. They were prepared to have lodgers, like Paul and Apollos: they were prepared to open their home up to the Christian community, with all the inconvenience that must have sometimes involved. A church met in their home in

Corinth, Ephesus and Rome.[146] Clearly these people kept open
house, and went to the trouble of writing commendatory letters for
their visitors upon departure, putting them in touch with Christians
elsewhere.[147] They did not forget absent friends either, but were
assiduous in sending greetings.[148] There must have been something
infectious about their relationship with one another which impressed
visitors to the home. Apollos learnt "the way" from his stay in their
home;[149] and although already an able expositor of Scripture, we
read that he learnt to show from the Scriptures that Jesus was the
Messiah. Much the same thing happened to Paul. When he met
them he appears to have been somewhat depressed after his comparative lack of success at Athens.[160] Companionship with them
revived him: he argued in the synagogue weekly and began to convince both Jews and Greeks.[161] Moreover we read that he became
gripped by the Word while he was staying with them;[162] in this an
indication of the family study of the Scriptures in which they
engaged? Though much is guesswork as we try to look at the lives
of these folk, it is clear enough that they had a warmth of faith in
Jesus and love for him that led them to sacrifice privacy, security,
finance, and even personal safety (on one occasion they risked their
lives for Paul)[153] in order to promulgate the Christian gospel. Homes
like this must have been exceedingly effective in the evangelistic
outreach of the Church.

PERSONAL EVANGELISM

Personal Encounters

If public proclamation of various types and the private use of the
home were crucial factors in the spread of the gospel, no less important was personal evangelism, as one individual shared his faith with
another. The first chapter of St John gives us the pattern. From the
moment each man finds the truth about Jesus he is constrained to
pass it on. It was through the personal witness of John the Baptist
that the two disciples found Jesus.[154] No sooner had one of them,
Andrew, made the discovery, than he found his brother Simon
Peter, and brought him to Jesus.[155] Next, Jesus himself takes the
initiative and encounters Philip of Bethsaida,[156] we are not told how.
But Philip carries on the good work and finds Nathanael,[157] and he
in his turn is brought to confess that Jesus is the Son of God. This
is more than the individualism[158] of the author of the Gospel asserting itself. It is a reflection of the importance of personal evangelism
in the outreach of the Church.

It was in this way that many of the most impressive converts were made. Pantaenus, as we have seen, led Clement of Alexandria to Christ. Justin seems to have done the same for Tatian, after himself being won to Christianity through his encounter with the old man in the fields.[159]

There is a charming passage at the beginning of the *Octavius* of Minucius Felix which shows the attractive power of friendship to introduce another to Christian faith. The author is reviewing his recollections of his friend Octavius after his death. "The sweetness and charm of the man so clings to me that I appear to myself in some sort as if I were returning to past times, and not merely recalling in my recollection things that have long since happened . . . You would think that one mind had been shared between us two. Thus he alone was the confidant of my loves, the companion with me in my mistakes; and when, after the gloom had been dispersed, I emerged from the abyss of darkness into the light of wisdom and truth, he did not cast off his associate but—what is more glorious still—he outstripped him."[160]

But it was by no means only among similar temperaments and like-minded people that this method of personal evangelism proved effective. One of the most striking examples in the New Testament is that of Philip and the Ethiopian eunuch.[161] Philip was one of the Seven who relieved the apostles of administering the funds and the food in the communal life of the earliest Jerusalem Church. But he had evangelistic gifts as well, and these seem to have occupied his time more than the administrative task to which he was appointed! At all events we find him exercising a most successful ministry in Samaria. But he was so closely attuned to God that he recognized the still small voice calling him to go away from the limelight into a most improbable place,[162] the Gaza strip of desert, where he would be unlikely to find anyone to minister to. Being a man accustomed, it seems, to obey God,[163] Philip went. He saw a high ranking Ethiopian eunuch returning home in his chariot from Jerusalem, and so enthusiastic was he, so willing to be of service to this coloured man, that he actually ran towards him. To see a man running in the desert would, in itself, have fascinated the eunuch as he read the Scriptures aloud to himself, but when he found Philip coming alongside and politely asking in effect if he could be of any service, he invited him to mount the chariot. And there in a carriage bound for Ethiopia down the desert road sat this unlikely couple, poring over Isaiah 53, which the eunuch happened to be reading. Philip knew his Scriptures and how to apply them to the gospel of Jesus. This he proceeded to do so effectively and with such directness that the man believed. His heart had obviously been prepared beforehand by his searching for the truth within Judaism; his seriousness is clear from the fact that he was reading the Scriptures on his journey. Nevertheless it was the personal intervention of God's man for the occasion, Philip, which brought him to faith and baptism and sent him on his way rejoicing. There was, on the face of it, little enough in common between these two men, yet the one was used to bring the gospel to the other through this apparently chance encounter. If it be objected that this account in Acts is highly stylized, the answer must be that this sort of thing did happen, and was known to happen, or there would have been no point in Luke inventing so astonishing a situation. I have no doubt that Luke intended the story of Philip to illustrate the value of this personal evangelism, and the need that those who practise it have for humility and obedient trust in God, for tact and knowledge of the Scriptures, for directness in pointing to Jesus and for bringing the man to the point of decision. It is not only Luke's sermons in Acts which suggest guidelines for future generations.

Visiting

In a similar way, the story of Ananias[164] points to another form of personal confrontation which proved effective in evangelism: visiting. Ananias proved in many ways the epitome of the reluctant visitor, and yet he became a very useful one. The story could hardly have failed to encourage the bashful reader of Acts, as he considered his friends or acquaintances whom he might visit as a messenger of Christ. Here was a task for which God needed Ananias, and called him. He was to visit a certain house. So far so good. But then it was made clear to Ananias that the man he was to seek out there was Saul of Tarsus, who was in need of what he, Ananias, could give him. That changed the picture at once. God could never mean that. Why, it was well known that Saul was far too tough, too prejudiced, too antagonistic to be interested in the Christian gospel. Ananias is reluctant to go, and understandably so. But it dawns on Ananias that God has in fact prepared the way for this visit. Saul is not the opponent he was: he is in fact a man in great need; and, moreover, God has a great plan for his life. Accordingly, Ananias thought better of his refusal, and went. No doubt his feet dragged as he got nearer the house. No doubt his hand trembled as it knocked at the door. But he obeyed. His approach was simple, friendly, direct. He addressed him as "Brother Saul", in what was an amazing act of faith. His message was clear and relevant to Saul's situation. He spoke of the Lord Jesus who could open blind eyes and fill an empty life. And his obedience was rewarded with the accession to the Church of a notable convert. Now as every parish visitor knows, Sauls are not won at every visit: but a story like this must have stimulated many a Christian reader to knock on doors for the furtherance of the gospel. This is what the ordinary Christians of whom Celsus disapproved so strongly kept doing: this is how the message spread.

Evangelism of this direct personal nature was a feature of early Christian expansion. The apostles were always at it—Peter and John with a beggar near the Temple, Peter with a Roman officer in his house, Paul as a shipwrecked mariner talks to the chief man of the island about his Lord. It is interesting to notice how in 1 Thessalonians Paul calls himself both the father and the nurse of many of the recipients.[165] It was he who had brought them to faith, and so had begotten them in the new birth: he enjoyed the same relationship with Onesimus,[166] and with some of the Corinthian Christians.[167] This indicates the personal counselling which Paul had given to them, which resulted in their becoming his "children" in Christ.

The Conversion of Gregory by Origen

As a final example of this sort of evangelism coming from the end of our period, it would be difficult to better the account of Gregory's conversion through Origen. We are fortunate in being able to reconstruct a good deal of the story from their own writings, Origen's *Letter to Gregory*, and Gregory's *Panegyric on Origen*.

Gregory was the son of an affluent pagan home in Pontus. His father, he tells us, died when he was fourteen, and looking back later he could see that this sudden loss was "the beginning of the knowledge of the truth to me".[168] He finds it difficult to be explicit about what this bereavement meant to him. He knows it was not his conversion, "for what power of decision had I then, who was but fourteen years of age? Yet from this very time this sacred Word began somehow to visit me . . . And though I thought but little of this in that olden time, yet now, at least, as I ponder it, I consider it no small mark of the holy and marvellous providence" exercised over him that God's visitation of him should begin with this experience or orphanhood which burned itself into his youthful memory. As he recalled God's prevenient grace later on in life, he wrote, "And when I reflect on this, I am filled at once with gladness and with terror, while I rejoice indeed in the leading of providence, and yet am also awed by the fear lest, after being privileged with such blessings, I should still in any way fall short of the end."

However, at the time, his career was all he was thinking about. He studied rhetoric and law with a view to taking the place in public life for which his wealth and parentage had given him a good start. The suggestion came that he should go abroad for further studies. But where? Beirut was "not far distant from this territory, somewhat Latinized, and credited with being a school for these legal studies". Rome was another possibility. But circumstances arose which pointed to Palestine. The Roman governor of Palestine had Gregory's brother-in-law on his staff; the latter sent for his wife, Gregory's sister, and provided her with a military escort, "a larger supply of public vehicles than the case warranted, and more cheques than could be required for our sister alone". So Gregory and his brother Athendorus went with the convoy, intending to go on to Beirut and there prosecute their legal and linguistic studies. But once again, as he looked back in after-life, he saw the hand of God in the events which led him to the place where he was converted and nourished in the faith at the hands of Origen. "These were the apparent reasons for our journey," he continues. "But the secret and yet the truer reasons were these—our opportunity of fellowship with this man, our instruction through that man's means in the truth concerning the Word, and the profit of our soul for its salvation. These were the real reasons that brought us here, blind and ignorant as we were of the way of securing our salvation. Wherefore it was not that soldier [*sc.* provided as escort] but a certain divine companion and . . . guardian, who always leads us in safety through the whole of this present life, as through a long journey, that carried us past other places, and Beirut in particular, (which city we were especially bent on reaching) and brought us here, disposing and directing all things until by any means he might bring us into connection with this man who was to be the author of the greater part of our blessings."[169]

So much for the secret hand of God in the operation. How did Origen react to the unexpected arrival of these complete strangers? It is clear that he really put himself out on their behalf. They were anxious "like some wild creatures, or fish, or birds that had got caught in the nets, to slip out again and escape, and leaving him to make for Beirut",[170] but they had met their match in Origen. He "studied by all means to keep us in close association with him, contriving all kinds of arguments . . . and bringing all his powers to bear on that object." How did he do it? Seeing that philosophy was their goal, he began there, and told them if they were to be philosophers worthy of the name, they must "seek first of all to know themselves, what manner of persons they are, and then the things that are truly good such as a man ought to strive after, and then the

227

things that are really evil, from which a man ought to flee." Gregory could not recall all the arguments used by Origen to persuade them to stay and study "philosophy" with him, but he remembers that the great man persisted in his attempts day after day, and he recounts the impression Origen made on him: "He possessed a rare combination of a certain sweet grace and persuasiveness, along with a strange power and constraint." Moreover the genuine warmth and friendship of the man had its own mute attraction: "the stimulus of friendship was also brought to bear on us—a stimulus not easily withstood, but keen and most effective—the argument of a kind and affectionate disposition, which showed itself beneficently in his words when he spoke to us and associated with us." These were the factors that persuaded the youths to stay, almost against their will, until "he at last carried us off fairly, somehow or other, by a kind of divine power". Gregory described what it felt like. It felt like having the warmth of the true Sun begin to rise upon him. It felt like being pierced by Origen's words, as by an arrow:[171] how fascinating that Origen's own prayer that he should be one of God's arrows was so signally granted in the case of this young convert! Using a different simile, Gregory says that his conversion through the agency of Origen was like a spark to tinder. "And thus, like some spark lighting upon our inmost soul, love was kindled and burst into flame within us—a love at once to the Holy Word, the most lovely object of all, who attracts all irresistibly towards himself by his unutterable beauty, and to this man, his friend and advocate. And being most mightily smitten by this love, I was persuaded to give up all those objects or pursuits which seem to us befitting, and among them even my boasted jurisprudence—yea my very fatherland and friends, both those who were present with me then, and those from whom I had parted. And in my estimation there arose but one object dear and worth desire—philosophy [*sc.* Christian truth] and that master of philosophy, this inspired man." And he goes on to tell of the intimacy of relationship he began to enjoy with his teacher, who took Gregory and his brother in hand like a gardener a wild plant, or a farmer an uncultivated field, and set to work on them.[172] The fruit of that work was seen in years to come, when Gregory became a celebrated missionary bishop, and was instrumental in a widespread turning to Christianity among his own people in Pontus.

The zeal and opportunism of Origen stand out in this account. So does his tact, his persistence, his friendship, and his singleness of purpose: "He did not aim merely at getting us round by any kind of reasoning; but his desire was, with a benignant, affectionate and most generous mind, to save us." The pains he took to build them up in the faith are admirably portrayed in Gregory's *Panegyric*, which gives us the first detailed curriculum of Christian higher education. But what is not so apparent from this account is the earnest prayer and confident use of the Scriptures in evangelism which Origen employed. Something of his priorities in this matter may be gleaned from his letter to Gregory. "Do you then, my son, diligently apply yourself to the reading of the sacred Scriptures. Apply yourself, I say.[173] For we who read the things of God need much application, lest we should say or think anything too rashly about them. And applying yourself thus to the study of the things of God, . . . knock at its locked door, and it will be opened to you . . . And applying yourself thus to the divine study, seek aright, and with unwavering trust in God, the meaning of the Holy Scriptures, which so many have missed. Be not satisfied with knocking and seeking; for prayer is of all things indispensable to the knowledge of the things of God. For to this the Saviour exhorted, and said not only 'Knock and it shall be opened to you; and seek and you shall find' but also, 'Ask, and it shall be given unto you'."[174]

It was through the wise, dedicated, individual evangelism of Christians like Origen that some of the most notable converts were brought into the Christian Church. Hand-picked fruit was the best.

LITERARY EVANGELISM

First Century Apologetic

In addition to speaking to people about Christ. whether in public, in small house groups, or as individuals, one further method was open to the early carriers of the gospel. Those with the talent could write. And they did. In fact, they invented an entirely new literary form, the Gospel, to carry their evangelistic message. So far as we know, Mark was the first to have this brilliant idea of constructing from the floating stories about Jesus and catechetical fragments used in preaching and teaching the pagan hearers of the good news a written account of Jesus which was different from anything that had appeared in the world of letters before. It was not history: no historian would be content to give no account of the first thirty years of his hero's short life, nor to concentrate half his account on the death of the subject. It was not biography, for the same reason. It was a written *confessio fidei*, a testimony from the lips of many witnesses collected together by the author and arranged in order to show what sort of a person Jesus was, to give the evidence on which the disciples had followed him and had adjudged him the Messiah and Son of God, and by the strongest possible implication, challenge the readers to make the same act of faith in Christ as they themselves had done.

This purpose is explicitly stated in the Fourth Gospel. No doubt it had many contributory aims, and they have been widely discussed in modern times. But the primary aim is unambiguously (or almost unambiguously)[175] stated in 20:30f. "Now Jesus did many other signs in the presence of his disciples which are not written in this book; but these are written that you may believe that Jesus is the Christ, the Son of God, and that believing you may have life in his name." He wants to so highlight Jesus, his person and significance, by the "signs" he selects, that he can bring his readers, be they Jewish or Greek,[176] to the place where they are convinced that he is indeed the long-awaited Jewish Messiah, the veritable Son of God. Such intellectual assent should lead the reader, as it had the writer, to commitment to this Christ, commitment which opens the door to a new dimension of living, life shared with God.

Although John is the only evangelist who so specifically explains his purpose in writing, two others, Mark and Luke, seem to have had a similarly evangelistic aim. The absence of much *didachē* in Mark, the short pericopae, each producing a question, a mighty work, a controversy about Jesus's person or claims, combine to give the impression of being designed to inform the reader about Jesus, and to challenge him to decide for or against him. The book is kerygmatic through and through. This has been clearly perceived by Professor Moule. He regards Mark's Gospel as "the result of a conscious desire to preserve the sporadic traditions of incidents and to set them on permanent record for evangelistic purposes". He goes on to point out that "since the outline of the Good News (which we know as the 'kerygma') was already necessarily in use in Christian preaching (as it had been from the beginning) it was natural to attach these floating units to this already existing framework. Once this was done, it becomes easier to imagine Matthew as compiled for the same purpose but with much more material and with particular apologetic requirements in view."[177] I should be inclined to qualify this last suggestion somewhat; the orderly arrangement, the emphasis on teaching, on church officers, and the beginning of casuistry make it more probable that Matthew's gospel was primarily designed for the *insider*, and in particular for the preachers and teachers of the Christian mission. This view is shared by F. V. Filson, who in his commentary on Matthew writes, "His aim is not directly and primarily evangelistic. He seeks chiefly to support the work of faithful teaching rather than stirring appeal for initial repentance and faith."[178]

But there can be little doubt that St Luke's twofold work had a very definite evangelistic purpose. Whatever we make of the shadowy Theophilus to whom the volumes are dedicated, whether he was an interested enquirer, a magistrate wondering whether or not to take cognizance of this new religion, or even perhaps a new and shaky convert whom Luke sets out to establish in the faith, is not of prime importance. The books were clearly designed for publication, through the good offices of Theophilus; it was wise, in antiquity, to dedicate your book to some great man through whose influence, and often at whose expense, it would be published.[179] Luke meant his writings to be widely read in the Graeco-Roman world of which he wrote with such insight and skill in the Acts. He wanted men to read it in order not merely to defend Christianity against the slanders to which it was exposed, but supremely to make Christians of them. In his hands the defensive weapon of apologetic is used for attack. From first to last he concentrates on a single subject, salvation.[180] Many modern writers, such as Barrett,[181] Moule,[182] O'Neill[183] recognize this, but none has seen it more acutely than van Unnik.[184] The theme of salvation is, he rightly discerns, the key to the purpose of Luke-Acts. The horn of salvation has arisen in David's House (1:69), so that salvation may come to men (1:71). This is achieved through the advent of the Saviour, Jesus Christ the Lord (2:11), who brings light to the Gentiles and salvation to God's ancient people Israel (1:77f.). Unlike Matthew and Mark, Luke continues the Isaiah quotation of the Baptist to include the words, "and all the world shall see the salvation of God" (3:6). In his two volume work he shows how all the world did come to see the salvation of God.

The Gospel of Luke explains what this salvation means. It includes healing (7:3), forgiveness (7:50), wholeness (8:36), new life (8:50), and is brought to men uniquely through Jesus (19:10). When Jesus enters a man's house, he brings salvation with him (19:9).

The Acts explains how this Messianic salvation was spread throughout the ancient world. To Jews (e.g. 13:26) and Gentiles alike (e.g. 13:47f.) the offer of salvation is made. It resounds through the chapters of the book. Evangelism is the supreme concern of the writer. That is why he repeats the kerygma so often in his sermons, proclaimed to the Jews in the first part of the book and to the Gentiles, intelligent and backward alike, in the later part. He wants to make sure that Theophilus and the other readers on the fringe of Christianity get the essence of the gospel message into them by dint of constant repetition. That is why he is at pains to explain the headway made by the gospel throughout the Roman world: it is to stress the universality and the spread of this message of salvation. The tiny mustard seed grows into a tree which takes root even in Rome herself, and all the forces of chaos and Antichrist cannot stop its victorious march—hence the concentration on the shipwreck. The gospel is designed for every type of man, be he centurion or barbarian, Cypriot landowner or Ethiopian eunuch, magician or proconsul, jailer or female business executive. The wide variety of those who respond to the preaching of the gospel by the apostolic Church in Acts is parallel to the equally wide variety of those who respond to the preaching of the Kingdom by Jesus in the gospel. Both are the fruit of Luke's deep concern that all men should come to share in the salvation of Christ. The thrice repeated story of the conversion of Paul serves the same end; so does the very last picture we get in the Acts, of Paul preaching the good news with complete freedom of speech in his own hired house in the very centre of the Empire. All the force of Nero's Rome cannot quench the evangelistic zeal and optimism of that final word of the two volume composition, the triumphant *akōlutōs* ("unhindered"). I believe, in fact, that there is scarcely any exaggeration in Professor Moule's conclusion that "all four Gospels alike are to be interpreted as more than anything else evangelistic and apologetic".[185]

Second Century Apologetic

This writing of evangelistic literature designed to be read by the uncommitted did not end with the four Evangelists. It continued strongly in the apologetic writing of the second century.[186] But unfortunately tendencies which were already beginning to make themselves felt in the New Testament documents became heightened in the Apologists. It has long been recognized that there is a strong anti-Jewish element in parts of St Matthew's Gospel, and in St John too, where "the Jews" are always mentioned in contradistinction, if not open opposition, to Christian believers. It is hard to believe that the acrimony between the Church and the Synagogue which was building up during the first century, has not influenced the presentation of the Christian message in these gospels, and perhaps also in Luke-Acts if T. W. Manson is right in supposing that an important theme in these books is to make it abundantly clear to the secular power that Christians are to be sharply differentiated from Jews.[187] At all events, in most of the second century pieces of apologetic that we possess there is a hardness of approach which could hardly have been calculated to win the friendship and goodwill of the non-Christian readers. There is an acrimony about Justin's *Dialogue* with the Jew, Tyrpho, a biting scorn for the pagan gods among Apologists like Tatian and Tertullian, which almost certainly frustrated the genuine evangelistic concern which these men undoubtedly possessed. To launch a full-scale and at times bitter assault on a man's cherished beliefs is not the best way of inducing him to change them. For all the discernible bias in the New Testament Gospel writers,[188] they never made a mistake. A warmth, a Christ-centredness, a deep and obvious concern for people marks every page of the gospels and Acts, with the possible exception of a chapter like Matthew 23; but in the second century this too often gives way to a rather cold, almost arrogant battering of the opposition. The love must have been there, as is clear from the way in which these Apologists lived and died; but it is to a large extent masked in their writings, and to that extent one may well imagine that not many pagans or Jews were won to the faith through these documents, if in fact they read them. It is interesting that Celsus, who reckoned to be well up in Christian literature,[189] never appears to have read any of the words of the Apologists. Were they written more perhaps in the interests of Christian readership than for external consumption? There is, to my knowledge, no example of an outsider being converted to Christianity by reading an Apologetic writing. For all the concern expressed in the concluding paragraphs of most of the Apologies for the conversions of the readers, it seems probable that the tone in which the writing had been couched would have effectively stood in the way of such an outcome. There are exceptions to this generalization. The *Octavius* of Minucius Felix, the latter part of the *Protrepticus* of Clement and the *Epistle to Diognetus* have a real warmth about them. The short *Second Apology* of Justin has its own charm, too: it was specifically written, he tells us, for an evangelistic purpose. He invites the emperor and senate, to whom it is addressed, to give this book of his publicity. "And if you give this book your authority, we will expose him [*i.e.* Simon Magus] before all men, so that, if possible, they may be converted. For this end alone we did compose this treatise."[190] But in general, the Apologists marked a sad declension from the loving, tactful, subtle teaching evangelism of St Luke who tried to make defence of the faith against slander an occasion for propagating the faith among the unconverted.

The Place of the Scriptures

On the whole, it seems, the written word did not play such a big part in the evangelistic outreach of the Church as we should have expected. The writings that really evoked an abiding interest were the Scriptures. There is abundant evidence, some of which we have already considered, to show that Christians, unlike Jews, did use the Scriptures evangelistically. From the Acts of the Apostles down to Gregory and Origen we find the same story repeated time and again. Discussion with Christians, arguments with them, annoyance at them, leads the enquirer to read these "barbaric writings" for himself. And once men began to read, the Scriptures exercised their own fascination and power. Many an interested enquirer like Justin and Tatian, Athengoras and Theophilus,[191] came to Christian belief through finding, as he read, that "the Word of God is living and active and sharper than any two-edged sword",[192] and that "the sacred Scriptures are able to instruct you for salvation through faith in Jesus Christ".[193] The author of pseudo-Justin's *Hortatory Address to the Greeks* urges the Greeks to read those passages in the Sibylline Books and Virgil which are patient of a Christian interpretation "for the knowledge of these will constitute your necessary preliminary training for the study of the prophecies of the sacred writers." It was here that truth resided: it was these that the enquirer must study. "From every point of view, therefore, it must be seen that in no other way than only from the prophets who teach us by divine inspiration, is it possible to learn anything concerning God and true religion."[194] Similarly, the author of pseudo-Justin's *Discourse to the Greeks* indicates the impact made on him by the study of these same Scriptures, after coming to them for the first time from the "madness and intemperance" of Homeric poetry,[195] and the "drivelling theogony" of Hesiod.[196] "O trumpet of peace to the soul that is at war! O weapon that puttest to flight terrible passions! O instruction that quenches the innate fire of the soul! The Word exercises an influence which does not make poets: it does not equip philosophers or skilled orators, but by its instruction it makes mortals immortal, mortals gods: and from earth transports them to the realms above Olympus. Come, be taught. Become as I am, for I too, was as you are. These have conquered me—the divinity of the instruction, and the power of the Word: for as a skilled serpent charmer lures the terrible reptile from its den and causes it to flee, so the Word drives the fearful passions of our sensual nature from the very recesses of the soul."[197]

This stress on Scripture as a potent factor in bringing men to faith continued. Jerome tells us that in the third century Pamphilus of Caesarea "readily provided Bibles not only to read but to keep, not only for men but for any women whom he saw addicted to reading. He would prepare a large number of volumes, so that, when any demand was made upon him, he might be in a position to gratify those who applied to him."[198] And Ulfilas, the famous fourth century evangelist of the Goths, actually translated the Bible into Gothic to be the spearhead of his work. The importance which he attached to it is shown by the fact that until his feat of translation, the Gothic language had never been reduced to writing. He produced an alphabet and put the Scriptures down in it, only omitting the Books of Kings because of their warlike character: the Goths, he thought, needed no encouragement in that direction![199] His pupil, Auxentius, not only celebrated the forty years of Ulfilas's episcopacy when "he flourished gloriously and with apostolic grace preached in Latin, Greek and Gothic without intermission", but recorded his personal indebtedness to the loving training in the Scriptures which the evangelist gave him. "To him I of all men am most debtor, inasmuch as he bestowed on me more labour than on any other, and received me from my earliest days at the hands of my parents as his disciple, and taught me the Holy Scriptures and declared to me the truth, and by the mercy of God brought me up both physically and spiritually as his own son in the faith."[200]

To the use of the Scriptures the early Christians added prayer as a prime necessity in all evangelistic enterprise. When the Twelve poured out their hearts to God in prayer they were filled with the Holy Spirit, they spoke the Word of God with boldness, and multitudes believed.[201] Paul knew that prayer was one of the great ways of binding Satan and preparing the hearts of hearers for the gospel. He asks the Ephesians to pray for him that utterance may be given him in opening his mouth boldly to proclaim the mystery of the gospel.[202] He asks the Corinthians to give "underground assistance" to his gospel assault on the strongholds of evil by means of prayer.[203] Similarly, Justin knows that it is only through prayer, not mere intellectual argument, that "the gates of light may be opened to you: for these things cannot be perceived by all, or understood, but only by the man to whom God and his Christ have imparted wisdom."[204] "Pray without ceasing," urges Ignatius, "on behalf of other men. For then there is hope of repentance that they may attain to God."[205] Evangelism was God's work, through men. They knew that he would not reveal himself to pagans in saving power unless they displayed their utter dependence on him through prayer.

It was then, with the Scriptures and prayer as their main weapons, backed up by their love, their burning zeal to share their faith with others, and the sheer quality of their living and dying that the early Christians set out to evangelize the world.

9

EVANGELISTIC MOTIVES

THE ENTHUSIASM TO evangelize which marked the early Christians is one of the most remarkable things in the history of religions. Here were men and women of every rank and station in life, of every country in the known world, so convinced that they had discovered the riddle of the universe, so sure of the one true God whom they had come to know, that nothing must stand in the way of their passing on this good news to others. As we have seen, they did it by preaching and personal conversation, by formal discourse and informal testimony, by arguing in the synagogue and by chattering in the laundry. They might be slighted, laughed at, disenfranchised, robbed of their possessions, their homes, even their families, but this would not stop them. They might be reported to the authorities as dangerous atheists, and required to sacrifice to the imperial gods; but they refused to comply. In Christianity they had found something utterly new, authentic and satisfying. They were not prepared to deny Christ even in order to preserve their own lives; and in the manner of their dying they made converts to their faith.

What was the secret of such zeal? What motivated the Christians to such tireless and unsefish evangelism? There seem to have been three main motives common to the Christian evangelists of these first two centuries, and we shall look at them in turn.

A SENSE OF GRATITUDE

There can be little doubt that the main motive for evangelism was a theological one. These men did not spread their message because it was advisable for them to do so, nor because it was the socially responsible thing to do. They did not do it primarily for humanitarian or agathistic utilitarian reasons. They did it because of the overwhelming experience of the love of God which they had received through Jesus Christ. The discovery that the ultimate force in the universe was Love, and that this Love had stooped to the very nadir of self-abasement for human good, had an effect on those who believed it which nothing could remove. "The Son of God loved me

and gave himself for me,"[1] cried Paul in amazement, and his subsequent life of self-sacrifice in the cause of the gospel showed the
extent to which he had been gripped by love of this quality. It was no
exaggeration when he claimed that "God's love has been poured
into our hearts by the Holy Spirit who has been given to us".[2] John's
attitude was much the same. When treating the subject of love, he
realistically pointed out that man as such has none worthy of the
name. "In this is love, not that we loved God, but that he loved us
and sent his Son to be the expiation for our sins." And then comes
the corollary, "Beloved, if God so loved us, we ought also to love one
another." And how is this love expressed? By the Christian presence? Yes indeed. "No man has ever seen God; if we love one
another God abides in us and his love is perfected in us." But not
only by the Christian presence; the Christian witness is no less
indispensable. So John continues, "And we have seen and do testify
that the Father sent the Son to be the Saviour of the world." In a
word, Christian evangelism has its motivation rooted in what God is
and what he has done for man through the coming and the death
and the resurrection of Jesus. "We love because he first loved us."[3]
This is what Paul meant when he wrote that "the love of Christ
grips us, because we are convinced that one has died for all; therefore all have died. And he died for all, that those who live might live
no longer for themselves but for him who for their sake died and
was raised."[4]

This loving gratitude to the God who had saved them played a
notable part in evangelism in the second century no less than the
first. It is well brought out in the apocryphal *Quo Vadis* legend,
which gives us some idea of popular motivation at the end of the
second century.[5] Opposition had made Rome unsafe for Peter.
Common-sense counsels advised him to withdraw from the city.
"But Peter said to them, 'Shall we act like deserters, brethren?' But
they said to him, 'No, it is so that you can go on serving the Lord',"
a prudential piece of worldly wisdom which has often subsequently
dulled the keen edge of Christian dedication! Peter reluctantly
acquiesced, but "as he went out of the gate he saw the Lord entering
Rome; and when he saw him he said, 'Lord, whither goest thou
here?' And the Lord said to him, 'I am coming to Rome to be
crucified.' And Peter said to him, 'Lord, art thou being crucified
again?' He said to him, 'Yes, Peter, I am being crucified again.' And
Peter came to himself; and he saw the Lord ascending into heaven.
And he returned to Rome rejoicing and giving praise to the
Lord . . ."[6] Although this story is specifically concerned with
martyrdom rather than evangelism, the two cannot easily be sep-

arated. Peter was tempted to save his life at the cost of disloyalty to his commission from Christ; and a vision of the Lord suffering crucifixion for him was the compelling factor which drove him back onto the path of complete and utter dedication, even to death itself. That reflection upon the cross as the supreme impulse to costly service for others in the name of the gospel was unquestionably the greatest single element in keeping the zeal of Christians at fever pitch.

One finds this same love as the mainspring for Christian service throughout the writings of the second century, sometimes in unexpected places. Thus pseudo-Justin remarks at the very outset of his *De Monarchia*, "It is the part of a lover of man, or rather of a lover of God, to remind men who have neglected it of that which they ought to know."[7] His love for men which shows itself in seeking to reach them with the truth, is the offspring of his love for God. One can almost hear the warmth of love and gratitude inflaming Clement of Alexandria as he exhorts the heathen, "Man, that had been free by reason of simplicity, was found fettered to sins. The Lord then wished to release him from his bonds, and clothing himself with flesh—O divine mystery!—vanquished the serpent and enslaved the tyrant death; and, most marvellous of all, man that had been deceived by pleasure, and bound fast by corruption, had his hands unloosed, and was set free. O mystic wonder! The Lord was laid low, and man rose up." This was the ground of his appeal, "Receive Christ, receive sight, receive thy light". In the same chapter he writes, "Let us become acquainted with him, that he may be gracious. And though God needs nothing, let us render to him the grateful recompense of a thankful heart and piety, as a kind of house-rent for our dwelling here below." And again, "It has been God's fixed and constant purpose to save the flock of men: for to this end God sent the Good Shepherd. And the Word, having unfolded the truth, showed to men the height of salvation, that either repenting they might be saved or refusing to obey, they might be judged." He calls on his readers to "return grateful thanks for the benefits we have received, and honour God through the divine Word . . . What then is the exhortation I give you? I urge you to be saved. This Christ desires. In one word, he freely bestows life on you . . . Cleanse the temple; abandon pleasures and amusements to the winds and fire, as a fading flower . . . and present thyself to God as an offering of first fruits."[8] Changing to a nautical metaphor he continues, "Exert your will only, and you have overcome ruin; bound to the wood of the cross, you will be freed from destruction; the Word of God will be your pilot, and the Holy Spirit will bring you to anchor in the haven of heaven."[9] Gratitude to God for creation, protection, but supremely for the person and the passion of Christ was manifestly one of the driving forces of Clement's life, and this is the more interesting in the ancient equivalent of a professional theologian; his studies had not dulled the warmth of his love for his Lord.

We have already seen how the author of the *Epistle to Diognetus* makes great play with the same motive. Having spoken of the amazing self-sacrifice of the Son, he asks, "How will you love him who has first so loved you?" Professor John Foster has made an interesting observation in this respect. Noting the use of *Logos* to describe Christ in the seventh chapter of the *Epistle*, he comments, "Here was a man who had begun, as it were, to preach on the Prologue to St John's Gospel, choosing his text because the heathen (the tutor of Marcus Aurelius?) would be at home with the idea of *Logos*, and through *Logos* might come to 'only begotten Son'. And then as the preacher gets to 'only begotten Son' (it is there in the last verse, 18, of the Prologue) he finds himself preaching on John 3:16, not because of what the heathen will be at home with, but because the gospel is just that." He goes on to describe his discovery. "The impression that from the Prologue the preacher had moved on to John 3:16 was not wrong. For here in the last stage of his discourse the actual words of John 3:16 will no longer be kept back. Word for word the same in the Greek, and occurring in the same order, can there be any doubt that this passage was here uppermost in his mind?

For God loved men, for whom he made *the world* . . .
to whom *he gave* reason (logos)
to whom he sent *his only begotten son*
to whom he promised the kingdom which is
in heaven (= eternal life).

If he began by preaching to the philosopher, he ends by just preaching the gospel."[10]

It is important to stress this prime motive of loving gratitude to God because it is not infrequently assumed that the direct command of Christ to evangelize was the main driving force behind the Christian mission. A great deal is made in some missionary writings[11] of "The Great Commission" in Matthew 28:18–20. No doubt this was important. Obedience to the Lord was the great new commandment Jesus had left to those who loved him: "If you love me, keep my commandments." But in point of fact it is quoted very little in the writings of the second century. Among the Apostolic Fathers it comes only in the spurious longer recension of Ignatius.[12] Irenaeus quotes it once, in a context where he is speaking about the descent of the Spirit on the Church.[13] This is interesting, for it shows that the command was not seen as a new legalism, the duty incumbent upon all Christians, but rather what Roland Allen called a "spiritual" as opposed to a "legal" command.[14] No sanctions are attached to it. It is rather associated with the promised presence of Christ on the mission, which "is not a reward offered to those who obey; it is rather the assurance that those who are commanded will be able to obey".[15]

As he points out, it would be only a minor loss if the textual doubts surrounding those verses were proved justified, and if it could be clearly demonstrated that Jesus never spoke those words. "The obligation to preach the gospel to all nations would not have been diminished by a single iota. For the obligation depends not upon the letter but upon the Spirit of Christ, not upon what he orders but upon what he is, and the Spirit of Christ is the Spirit of Divine love and compassion and desire for souls astray from God."[16]

Whereas, however, the precise terms of the Great Commission do not appear to have played a great part in sending the early Christians out in evangelism, the example of Christ and the sense of responsibility to him were very important. Mission, they saw, was grounded in the very nature of a God who gave: it must be no less evident in those who claimed to have relationship with such a God. Paul was not alone in taking very seriously his position as a servant of God, an ambassador for Christ, a fellow-workman with God, like a trusted steward in a great household.[17] Peter saw Christian responsibility in similar terms: the oracle through which God spoke, the undershepherd in the Lord's employment,[18] whose privilege and responsibility it was to give a reason for the hope within to anyone who enquired about it.[19] Privilege and responsibility are words which well describe St Paul's understanding of his evangelistic call. He did not lose heart in the often discouraging task of proclaiming the gospel, because he has "received this ministry through the mercy of God".[20] It is to him a matter of surpassing wonder that God should have had mercy on a persecutor like him. Three times in his letters[21] he refers to his humble wonder at the trust placed in him by God, each time in the context of a deeper sense of his own unworthiness. In 1 Corinthians 15:8f. he wrote, "Last of all, as one untimely born, he appeared also to me. For I am the least of the apostles, unfit to be called an apostle, because I persecuted the Church of God. But by the grace of God I am what I am, and his grace toward me was not in vain. On the contrary, I worked harder than any of them, though it was not I but the grace of God which is with me." In Ephesians he coins a word in order to emphasize his humble status in contrast with the amazing privilege of being called to preach the good news: "Of this gospel I was made a minister according to the gift of God's grace which was given to me by the working of his power. To me, though I am the very least (*elachistoterō*) of all the saints, this grace was given, to preach to the Gentiles the unsearchable riches of Christ."[22] In a later letter, 1 Timothy, he refers to "the glorious gospel of the blessed God with which I have been entrusted" and continues, "I thank him who has given me the strength for this, Jesus Christ our Lord, who appointed me to his service, though I formerly blasphemed and persecuted and insulted him: but I received mercy because I had acted ignorantly in unbelief." He goes on to reflect on the "faithful saying" that "Christ Jesus came into the world to save sinners" and adds the heartfelt comment, "and I am the foremost of sinners."[23] This is not pious exaggeration. The privilege of representing God, the challenge of the responsibility of doing it adequately, made a growing impression on him throughout his life, of his own unworthiness coupled with the abundant love and patience and strength of the Lord who had commissioned him.

It was not only a sense of privilege and responsibility in representing Christ and inviting men in Christ's stead to be reconciled to God which thrilled these evangelists; they were moved by the very example of Jesus himself. "Have this mind among yourselves which you have in Christ Jesus," writes Paul, "who though he was in the form of God, did not count equality with God a thing to be grasped, but emptied himself, taking the form of a servant, being born in the likeness of men . . . He became obedient unto death, even death on a cross."[24] Such is the pattern of the one they are to emulate. It is interesting that in a speech attributed to him in Acts, St Paul makes use of the same allusion to the Servant as he does in Philippians, but applies it not to Jesus, but to those who are carrying on Jesus's work. "Behold, we turn to the Gentiles. For so the Lord commanded us, saying, 'I have set you to be a light for the Gentiles, that you may bring salvation to the uttermost parts of the earth'."[25] Whether they thought of themselves primarily as imitating the work of Jesus in ministering to the Gentiles as well as to Israel, or rather as so integrated with him as a body with its head or as branches in a vine, is for the present purpose unimportant. The significant thing is that they saw that the evangelistic work of the Servant, which was supremely embodied in the activity and death of Jesus, had now been entrusted to themselves. Origen took this point strongly when in answer to Celsus's jibe that Jesus appeared in a squalid little province like Judaea, he replied, "There was no need for many bodies to be in several places and to have many spirits like Jesus, so that the whole world of men might be enlightened by the Word of God. For the one Word was enough, who rose up as a 'sun of righteousness' to send forth from Judaea his rays which reach the souls of those who are willing to accept him." He continues by pointing out that many have, in imitation of Christ, carried out the message from Judaea into the rest of the world. "If anyone should want to see many bodies filled with a divine spirit, ministering to the salvation of men everywhere after the pattern of the one Christ, let him realize that those who in many places teach the doctrine of Jesus rightly and live an upright life, are themselves also called Christs by the divine Scriptures in the words, 'Touch not my Christs, and do my prophets no harm'."[26]

There is another passage in Origen which sheds light on how seriously he took the responsibility of being the visible representative of his Master. In his *Commentary* on Romans 9:1 he considers Paul's professed willingness to be cut off from Christ if that would benefit his Jewish brethren and bring them to faith. Origen asks the reader if *he* has sorrow and grief for the lost, like that. Does he care so much that he would be willing to be separated from Christ for their sake? Of course that could not happen. Nothing will be able to separate the Christian from the love of Christ, as Paul has made clear at the end of the previous chapter. Nor would it be possible to save others if one were about to perish oneself. But even though it could not happen, Origen persists in his challenging enquiry, would the reader be willing for such a fate in order to rescue others? "Have you learned the lesson of dying to live from your Lord and Master? Have you learned from him who though by nature immortal and inseparable from the Father nevertheless died and descended into Hades? In the same way Paul imitated his Master, and was willing to be accursed from Christ for his brethren's sake, although nothing could separate him from the love of Christ! Is it so wonderful that the Apostle should be willing to be accursed for his brethren's sake, when he knew that the one who was in the form of God emptied himself of that form, and took on himself the form of the Servant and was made a curse for us? Is it so wonderful if, when the Lord was made a curse for slaves, the slave should be willing to be a curse for his brethren?"[27]

This gratitude, devotion, dedication to the Lord who had rescued them and given them a new life, this sense of being commissioned by him and empowered by his Spirit to do the work of heralds, messengers and ambassadors, was the main motive in

evangelism in the early Church. These men had been gripped by
the love of God which had taken concrete form in the person of
Jesus and had stooped to unbelievable depths in the agonies of
Calvary. Magnetized by this love, their lives could not but show it,
their lips could not help telling it; "we cannot but speak of the
things which we have seen and heard"[28] well sums up the attitude
of spontaneous loving devotion to God which acted as the mainspring of their evangelistic efforts. They were convinced that the
salvation promised long ago in the Scriptures had actually become a
reality through what Jesus had done. How could they keep quiet?
In such a day of good tidings they could not hold their peace.

A SENSE OF RESPONSIBILITY

A second factor which weighed heavily with the Christians was
their responsibility before God to live lives consistent with their
profession. They lived their lives under the eye of God, and they
were determined to please him in all they did. Their Master's aim
and achievement with regard to his heavenly Father had been "I do
always what is pleasing to him",[29] and this was their goal. Thus Paul
prayed that the Colossians might "lead a life worthy of the Lord,
fully pleasing to him, bearing fruit in every good work",[30] and what
he prayed for others he was concerned with himself. He knew the
possibility of making spiritual shipwreck, like Hymenaeus and
Alexander.[31] He dreaded the possibility that "after preaching to
others I myself should be disqualified". So he disciplined himself
in the race of the Christian life, like an athlete. "Every athlete
exercises self-control in all things. They do it to receive a perishable
wreath, but we an imperishable."[32] That is why he bent all his ener-
gies to win people for Jesus Christ, and so be faithful to his commission to be an apostle of his Lord: "To the Jews I became as a Jew
in order to win Jews . . . To those outside the Law I became as one
outside the Law—that I might win those outside the Law . . . I have
become all things to all men that I might by all means save some. I
do it all for the sake of the gospel, that I may share in its blessings."[33] To some, as we know, his different postures to Jews and
Gentiles savoured of compromise and men-pleasing: he refutes this
indignantly in the Letter to the Galatians and the Corinthian
Correspondence, but in the end it is not human assessment that
matters to him. "With me it is a very small thing that I should be
judged by you or by any human court," he wrote to arrogant Corinthians who presumed to run a popularity poll of their visiting
teachers. "I do not even judge myself. I am not aware of anything

against myself, but I am not thereby acquitted. It is the Lord who judges me. Therefore do not pronounce judgment before the time, before the Lord comes, who will bring to light the things now hidden in darkness and will disclose the purposes of the heart. Then every man will receive his commendation from God."[34]

The question of final judgment before God at the Great Assize featured prominently in Paul's thought, as it must have done in that of every sincere and earnest Jew. But a great revolution had taken place in his mind since he became a Christian. Hitherto he had been working in order, by the mercy of God and by strict keeping of the Law, to acquire a verdict of "acquitted" at the Last Day. On the Damascus Road he discovered that this was an impossibility. However conscientiously he lived, his best was not good enough for a holy God. He came to see the truth which Jesus had proclaimed so shatteringly in parables like the Wedding Garment and the Great Supper that God accepts the unacceptable if they trust in him alone.[35] He saw that men had always been accepted on these terms with God—Abraham, David and the heroes of his nation's history— all were in themselves sinful men who cast themselves on the mercy of God and found in him their security, not in their own fancied goodness.[36] This truth Paul made peculiarly his own, and clothed it in the quasi-juridical language of the law court, or perhaps of the throne room (for it goes beyond any conception of human justice).[37] He saw that on the cross Jesus, the God-man, accepted the judgment which rested on all men, exhausted it of its curse, and rose triumphant to demonstrate this. "He was delivered for our offences, and raised again because of our acquittal,"[38] he joyously proclaims. The verdict of the Last Day need no longer be awaited in awful suspense; it is anticipated here and now. "Since we are justified by faith—" here and now already in this present age—"we have peace with God through our Lord Jesus Christ".[39] United with Christ a man could face the judgment unafraid, released from the paralysing terror of wondering all through his life if he would be accepted or rejected at the last.

This confident assurance of salvation anticipated here and now, albeit to be consummated in the future, did not, however, alter the fact that the Christian would have to stand before the judgment seat of Christ to give an account of how his life had been spent in the Master's service. This was one of the several safeguards against antinomianism that went with Paul's doctrine of justification through grace alone. Secure in the knowledge that God would accept him (that was guaranteed by the cross and resurrection, and sealed upon the believer in baptism),[40] he nevertheless determined so to live that he would not be ashamed before his Lord on that great day. He determined, according to the address to the Ephesian elders, to be true to his call "testifying both to Jews and to Greeks of repentance towards God and faith in our Lord Jesus Christ" whatever obstacles should lie in his path. "But I do not account my life of any value nor as precious to myself, if only I may accomplish my course and the ministry which I received from the Lord Jesus, to testify to the gospel of the grace of God."[41]

Perhaps his clearest explanation of the force this consideration had with him is to be found in 2 Corinthians 5. He is considering the probability that his own death will precede the Parousia, and he envisages it without relish. But in any case his aim is single: "Whether we are at home or away [*i.e.* whether we live or die[42]] we make it our aim to please him. For we must all appear before the judgment seat of Christ, so that each one may receive good or evil, according to what he has done in the body. Therefore, knowing the fear of the Lord, we persuade men."[43] This fear of which he speaks is not the craven fear óf the underdog, but the loving fear of the friend and trusted servant who dreads disappointing his beloved Master. This fear was a contributory factor in the ceaseless evangelistic activity of the apostle Paul. He was not afraid, in handling this difficult subject, to speak of a reward for faithful service as well as disappointment and loss for unfaithfulness. After all, Jesus had constantly done so, particularly in parables like the Talents. Paul spoke joyfully of the "crown of righteousness which the Lord, the righteous judge, will award to me on that day, and not to me only, but also to all who have loved his appearing".[44] No doubt it was this thought which, as he puts it a few verses further on, "gave me strength to proclaim the Word fully, that all the Gentiles might hear it."[45] On the other hand, he is well aware that the unfaithful Christian evangelist who builds self-centred superstructures upon the foundation of Christ in his church-building will indeed be saved, but like a man who has escaped from a fire which has consumed all his possessions. The Day will disclose the nature of every man's work, he tells the Corinthians. It will be revealed, so to speak, in fire which will burn up the wood, hay and stubble but merely serve to emphasize the value and validity of the gold, silver and precious stones of Christ—centred work. "The fire will test what sort of work each one has done. If the work which any man has built on the foundation [*sc.* the one foundation of Christ, which is the starting point for the whole enterprise of Christian living and service] survives, he will receive a reward. If any man's work is burned up, he will suffer loss, though he himself will be saved, but only as through fire."[46]

It should be plain from the sensitive treatment which Paul gives to this question of future judgment as a motive for Christian service that here is no crude doctrine of punishment and reward. The Christian knows from the outset that through the grace of God he will be saved, provided he does not apostatize from the Saviour. The question of his security, so to speak, does not arise. But the enjoyment of that destiny with God is very much dependent on the character he takes out of this life with him. And that character is formed by the extent of his obedience to Christ in loving self-sacrifice for others. God does indeed reward the faithful servant, but the reward is a closer conformity to the character of Christ, which is itself the height of happiness. God's rewards are still the products of his grace: they are awarded *de congruo* not *pro meritis*. Indeed, if we may judge from the Parable of the Talents, the reward for faithfulness is increased responsibility, increased intimacy with God and capacity to enjoy him. This is very different from treating rewards and punishments as a sanction on holy living. On the other hand, it is a mistake to suppose, with Amos Wilder,[47] that the concept of reward and punishment in Christian ethics is merely a "fictional sanction" because to do right for any other reason than that it *is* right is to act non-morally. He fails to distinguish between motive and intention. It is true that a morally good action must spring from a good intention, but it is no less true that the New Testament envisages several motivating forces which lead men to that intention to do the good action. Christian self-respect,[48] consideration of the general good,[49] or appeal to reason,[50] to what befits the Christian profession[51] or to well grounded social convention[52] are all adduced, together with rewards and punishment, as motivating forces to induce the Christian man to choose the good out of deliberate intention.

When we come to the second century writings, however, the emphasis on rewards and punishments grows, and there is a strong tendency to see Christian obedience in terms of merit. Thus Justin points out that whereas it would be quite possible for Christians to deny their loyalty to Christ and thus escape the unpleasant consequences of police action and execution, "we would not live by telling a lie. For impelled by the desire of the eternal and pure life, we seek the abode that is with God . . ." The desire for eternal life seems to occupy a more central place in his theology than it did in the New Testament, particularly as he goes on to contrast it with the punishment to be meted out "at the hand of Christ upon the wicked in the same bodies united again to their spirits which are now to undergo everlasting punishment". But all the same, Justin has not deserted the New Testament perspective entirely. He "hastens to confess his faith" as one who has demonstrated to God by his works that he follows him, and that he loves to abide with him where there is no sin to cause disturbance".[53] Here is a genuine love for God, which is the hallmark of authentic Christian witness and service.

The extent to which the day of judgment figured in the personal responsibility of Christians is illustrated by the place it assumes in the very ancient catechism on The Two Ways, incorporated in the *Epistle of Barnabas.* "Thou shalt remember the day of judgment night and day. And thou shalt seek each day the society of the saints, either labouring by speech, and going out to exhort, and striving to save souls by the Word, or else working with thine hands for the ransom of thy sins."[54] He returns to the subject in his final exhortation, begging his readers to remember "the day when all things shall perish with the Evil One; 'the Lord and his reward is at hand'," and to be "taught of God, seeking out what the Lord asks from you; and do it that you may be safe in the day of judgment".[55]

Polycarp is quick to stress that " 'by grace ye are saved, not of works'," but refers almost immediately to him who "comes as the Judge of the living and the dead. His blood will God require of those who do not believe in him. But he who raised up Christ from the dead will raise us up also if we do his will."[56] And again, "If we please him in this present world we shall receive also the future world, according as he has promised to us that he will raise us up again from the dead, and that if we live worthily of him, we 'shall also reign with him' provided only we believe."[57] The personal relationship with God is still to the fore, the understanding of salvation through grace is still clear, but the stress on personal responsibility in the light of the judgment is increased. The philosopher-Christian Athenagoras, after speaking of the moral virtues of the Christians, asks, "Should we, then, unless we believed that a God presides over the human race, thus purge ourselves from evil? Most certainly not. But because we are persuaded that we shall give an account of everything in the present life to God, who made us and the world, we adopt a temperate, and benevolent and generally despised manner of life, believing that we shall suffer no such great evil here, even should our lives be taken from us, compared with what we shall there receive . . . from the great Judge."[58] Much the same consciousness of God ever present, ever watchful, is to be found throughout the writings of Justin. Heaven and God were living realities for these men, who gambled with death by their Christian allegiance and evangelism. He points out the curious inconsistency of persecuting Christians, whose moral standards are impeccable, and in a moving passage explains that it does not unduly worry him, because he knows God is in control of the situation. "Because we persuade men to avoid such instruction [*sc.* the 'sodomy and shameless intercourse with women in imitation of Jupiter and the other gods' which he has mentioned above] we are assailed in every kind of way. But we are not concerned, since we know that God is a just observer of all. But would that even now someone would mount a lofty rostrum and shout with a loud voice 'Be ashamed, be ashamed, ye who charge the innocent with those deeds which you openly commit . . . Be ye converted: become wise!'" '59

Enough has been said to show how seriously the Christians in the early days of the Church took their responsibility to live every day in the light of eternity, conscious that their every action was subject to the scrutiny of the one God, their Saviour, who would judge the quick and the dead.[60] Though they tended as the years went by to get the narrow idea of reward and punishment too central in their thinking,[61] it was a genuine New Testament emphasis that they were distorting. Had not St Paul written, "If I preach the gospel, that gives me no ground for boasting. For necessity is laid upon me. Woe to me if I do not preach the gospel! For if I do this of my own will, I have a reward: but if not of my own will, I am entrusted with a commission."[62] The note of personal responsibility and accountability before God the sovereign Judge was a prominent spur to evangelism in the early Church.

A SENSE OF CONCERN

Jesus came to seek and to save the lost.[63] That was the supreme purpose of his incarnation and atonement. He did not believe that man was able to put himself in the right with God or with his fellows. It was with sober realism that he said to his contemporaries, "If you, who are evil, know how to give good gifts to your children . . ."[64] Advisedly "Jesus did not trust himself to them, for he knew all men".[65] He knew that evil was not external to man, but intrinsic: "For from within, out of the heart of man, come evil thoughts, fornication, theft, murder, adultery, coveting, wickedness, deceit, licentiousness, envy, slander, pride, foolishness. All these evil things come from within, and they defile a man."[66]

With such a forthright and radical evaluation of human nature, it is not surprising that Jesus refused to regard anyone as "good" without qualification; indeed, he declined the attribution for himself.[67] No one can lay claim to goodness before God. All alike are in need of rescue from the predicament which wrongdoing has involved them in. And Jesus came to bring this salvation to mankind. Naturally, therefore, a clear dualism runs through every strand of the gospel record of Jesus's teaching. Mankind is divided into those who accept him as the way to God and those who do not.[68] There are two ways a man may tread—the broad way which leads to destruction or the narrow way which leads to life: no third option.[69] There are two rulers which may hold sway in a man's life, God or Mammon.[70] There are two possibilities open to a man: he may have a share in God's own life through relationship with Jesus, or remain spiritually dead.[71] Men are divided in his parables into sheep and goats, wheat and tares, wise virgins and foolish, those who accept the invitation to the Wedding Feast and those who determine to remain outside: "there shall be weeping and gnashing of teeth."[72] On whether men declare themselves for him or against him depends their eternal destiny.[73] Entry into the kingdom of God depends upon relationship with him.[74] Always we meet this religious dualism. It is one of the most objectionable elements in the gospel to modern man. No doubt it was to men of the first century. The scandal of Christ's particularity has always been the supreme obstacle to Christian commitment. But these early Christians believed implicitly that Jesus was the only hope for the world, the only way to God for the human race. Now if you believe that outside of Christ there is no hope, it is impossible to possess an atom of human love and kindness without being gripped with a great desire to bring men to this one way of salvation. We are not surprised, therefore, to find that concern for the state of the unevangelized was one of the great driving forces behind Christian preaching of the gospel in the early Church.

Nowhere is this better documented than in the writings of St Paul. He shared the same radical dualism as his Master. He saw mankind, Jew and Gentile alike, as lost, guilty, spiritually dead, out of touch with God, and without hope in the world.[75] And he, through the mercy of God, had been rescued from a similar predicament.[76] Why, then, he had a positive duty to give himself to the task of proclaiming to men far and wide their danger and need, and the wonderful steps God had taken to meet it. The picture we get of Paul from the address accredited to him by Luke before the Ephesian elders rings very true at this point to the contents of his own letters. With tears of earnestness he preached both publicly and from house to house, urging his hearers to repent and put their faith in Christ. He was prepared to sacrifice his own life in the cause of prosecuting the advance of this gospel.[77] For he saw himself, as Ezekiel had done long ago, as God's watchman, charged to give the people warning of the danger they stood in, so long as they refused to heed the proffered mercy of God. That is what he is alluding to when he cries out, "Therefore I testify to you this day that I am innocent of the blood of all of you, for I did not shrink from declaring to you the whole counsel of God."[78] If the watchman gave warning and men still refused to hear, then their blood would be on their own head: and that is what Paul is saying was the case. But if he had demurred at his commission to be watchman, if he had declined to dedicate himself to evangelism, then he would have been responsible for their fate. Had not God said to the prophet Ezekiel, "Son of man, I have made you a watchman for the house of Israel; whenever you hear a word from my mouth, you shall give them warning from me. If I say to the wicked, 'You shall surely die', and you give him no warning, nor speak to warn the wicked from his wicked way, in order to save his life, that wicked man shall die in his iniquity; but his blood will I require at your hand?"[79]

That is why Paul has to say to the Romans, "I am under obligation, both to Greeks and to barbarians, both to the wise and to the foolish: so I am eager to preach the gospel to you also who are in Rome."[80] He was in debt to Christ, and in debt to those who had never heard of Christ. He was Christ's ambassador, God's watchman. The need of those who were strangers to Christ impelled him onwards in the cause of evangelism. He believed that behind the indifference and opposition to the gospel which he encountered there was Satanic activity. "The god of this world has blinded the minds of the unbelievers, to keep them from seeing the light of the gospel of the glory of Christ, who is the image of God."[81] That was the situation, as he saw it. He was confronted by no less than the god of this age, the Satanic power of evil, whom Jesus himself had recognized as the usurper-king of this world, the one who had ousted God from his rightful place in the hearts of his subjects.[82] The supreme aim of the Enemy was to keep people away from the gospel: his method was to blind their eyes both to their need of it and to its power to make new men of them. But Paul was not downhearted at even so daunting a prospect. He knows that "it is the God who said 'Let light shine out of darkness' who has shone in our hearts to give the light of the knowledge of the glory of God in the face of Christ."[83] Between those two cosmic forces of the god who blinds man's mind, and the God who causes his light to break into man's heart, there is an apparently insignificant verse, yet it is the crucial link between them. "What we preach is not ourselves but Jesus Christ as Lord with ourselves your servants for Jesus's sake," writes the apostle.[84] It is through the preaching of the gospel by

humble folk who do not advertise themselves but confidently proclaim the Lordship of Jesus, that God's light breaks into blinded
hearts. How ridiculous to suppose that mere talking could bring
light to a darkened soul. But such is God's paradoxical way of
working, and Paul had seen too much of its practical outworking to
doubt its truth. He knew that, ridiculous as it may have seemed, "it
pleased God through the folly of what we preach to save those who
believe."[85] Accordingly, he could write, "I am not ashamed of the
gospel: it is the power of God for salvation to every one who has
faith."[86]

This lively awareness of the peril of those without Christ persisted as a major evangelistic motive in the second century. The
stress on judgment in the subapostolic writers is so great that it was
the subject of ridicule among some pagans. "We get outselves
laughed at," writes Tertullian, "for proclaiming that God will one
day judge the world", and proceeds with the dubious expedient of
arguing that the philosophers and poets of the Greeks teach the
same, and that they got the idea from Jewish and Christian writings!
Justin faces the same merriment from opponents who maintain that
"our assertions that the wicked are punished in eternal fire are big
words and bugbears, and that we wish men to live virtuously
through fear, and not because such a life is good and pleasant."[87]
Justin does not have much difficulty in answering that charge, but
the very fact that it could be made is indirect evidence of the extent
to which the fear of judgment was used in evangelistic preaching.
Sometimes it was employed in tones of great asperity, as if Christians gloated over the fate of the ungodly.[88] This is particularly
noticeable in the apocryphal material, but is also to be found among
Apologists, who lived under the enormous stress of knowing they
could be subjected to martyrdom at any time. It is not surprising if
at times they grew strident, as when Tertullian employs the volcano
as an illustration of the fate of the ungodly. "A notable proof this is
of the fire eternal! a notable example of the endless judgment which
still supplies punishment with fuel! The mountains burn, and last.
How will it be with the wicked and the enemies of God?"[89] Justin
remarks somewhat acidly, "Hell is a place where those are to be
punished who have lived wickedly, and who do not believe that
those things which God has taught us by Christ will come to
pass."[90]

A similar attitude may perhaps be discerned in the reply of Polycarp, before his martyrdom, to the proconsul who had threatened
him with the fire if he would not recant. "You threaten me with the
fire which burns for an hour," replied Polycarp, "and after a little is

extinguished. But you are ignorant of the fire of the coming judgment and of eternal punishment, reserved for the ungodly."[91]

But on the whole this note of gloating is uncommon. Much more frequent is the clear statement of the peril of the unconverted and the consequent desire of the Christians to help them to the knowledge of the truth. We have already seen that Justin published his *Second Apology* for the express purpose that if possible, the readers might be converted.[92] His motivation of concern for their plight comes out clearly in this statement. "We therefore pray you to publish this little book, appending what you think right, that our opinions may be known to others, and that they may have a fair chance of being freed from erroneous notions and ignorance of the good, who by their own fault are become subject to punishment."[93] Now Justin takes a very positive view of the *praeparatio evangelica* among the Greeks afforded by philosophy, and is clear that men like Socrates and Plato "spoke well in proportion to the share He had of the spermatic word" but "since they did not know the whole of the Word, which is Christ, they often contradicted themselves";[94] nevertheless it is highly significant that he has such clear notions about hell and punishment for those who turn their backs on the fulness of truth which is contained in the Christian gospel. Puzzled, no doubt, as to why so many of his intelligent contemporaries could not see their way to faith, he came to the same conclusion which we have seen Paul wrestling with above: it was the work of the forces of evil, blinding men's eyes to the truth of God. "For I myself, when I discovered the wicked disguise which the evil spirits had thrown around the divine doctrines of the Christians, to turn aside others from joining them . . . now confess that I boast and with all my strength strive to be found a Christian."[95] Presumably that was why Justin laid such stress on urging the enquirer to pray to God for light: only divine illumination could pierce the demonic darkness which kept men from the truth.[96]

Tertullian, often so fiery, knows how to plead with men to repent in view of the coming judgment. "Do not forget the future," he writes to Scapula, the proconsul of Carthage. "We who are without fear ourselves are not seeking to frighten you, but we would save all men if possible by warning them not to fight with God."[97] A little earlier he had written, "We have sent this tract to you in no alarm about ourselves, but in much concern for you and for all our enemies, to say nothing of our friends. Fot our religion commands us to love even our enemies, and to pray for those who persecute us . . . All men love those who love them: it is peculiar to Christians alone to love those that hate them. Therefore, mourning over your ignorance, and having compassion on your human error, and looking on that future of which every day shows threatening signs, necessity is laid upon us to come forward in this way [*i.e.* by writing] that we may set before you the truths you will not listen to openly."[98]

But it seems to have been Clement and Origen who were most sensitive about the need of those without Christ, and adept at pleading with them. We have already sampled the calibre of Origen's preaching, his inner concern to be an arrow in the Lord's hand, and his comments on Romans 9:1 where he asks the reader, "Do you have sorrow and grief for the lost? Do you care enough to be separated from Christ for them?" His predecessor in the Catechetical School at Alexandria, Clement, had equal warmth, as his *Protrepticus* makes clear. This is no mere Apology. It is a missionary tract, full of love and concern for those whom he is seeking to win. It may not be amiss to close this chapter with some excerpts from this treatise, as a reminder that the warmth of Christian love for the unevangelized and genuine concern for their well being did not end with the apostolic age.

"Do you not fear, and hasten to learn of him—that is, hasten to salvation—dreading wrath, loving grace, eagerly striving after the hope set before us, that you may shun the judgment threatened? Come, come, O my young people! For if you become not again as little children, and be born again, as saith the Scripture, you shall not receive the truly existent Father, nor shall you enter the kingdom of heaven. For in what way is a stranger permitted to enter? Well, I take it, when he is enrolled and made a citizen, and receives one to stand to him in the relation of Father: then he will be occupied with the Father's concerns, then he shall be deemed worthy to be made his heir, then he will share the kingdom of the Father with his own dear Son."[99] Sometimes he warns: "O the prodigious folly of being ashamed of the Lord! He offers freedom, you flee into bondage. He bestows salvation, you sink down into destruction. He confers everlasting life, you wait for punishment and prefer the fire which the Lord 'has prepared for the devil and his angels'."[100] Sometimes he reproaches: "But you, maimed as regards the truth, blind in mind, deaf in understanding, are not grieved, are not pained, have had no desire to see heaven and the Maker of heaven, nor, by fixing your choice on salvation, have sought to hear the Creator of the universe, and to learn of him: for there is no hindrance to stop the man who is bent on coming to know God."[101] Sometimes he gives his testimony to the truth of what he is preaching: "Hear me, and do not stop up your ears; do not block up the avenues of hearing, but lay to heart what is said. Excellent is the medicine of immortality! . . . Had we not known the Word, and been illuminated by him, we should have been in no way different from the fowls that are being fed and fattened in darkness, and nourished ready for death."[102] Sometimes he argues the benefits of Christian living: "And let not any shame of this name preoccupy you. This does great harm to men, and seduces them from salvation. Let us then strip for the contest, and nobly strive in the arena of truth, the Holy Word being the judge, and the Lord of the universe prescribing the contest. For it is no insignificant prize, the goal of immortality that is set before us."[103] Is it the cost of renouncing sinful ways that deters them? Clement has his argument ready: "But ye are not able to endure the austerity of salvation. Nevertheless although we delight in sweet things, and prize them higher for the pleasurable sensation they give us, yet, on the other hand, it is the bitter things which are distasteful to the palate which are curative and healing, and the harshness of the medicines strengthens people of weak stomach . . . Yes, it is harsh at first, but that is a good discipline for youth!"[104] He is entirely Christ-centred in his preaching: "The Lord is the way, a strait way, but leading from heaven; strait in truth but leading back to heaven; strait, despised on earth, but broad, adored in heaven."[105] Indeed, so taken up with his Lord is he, that in one remarkable passage he speaks directly in his Master's name, which, as we have seen, was a characteristic of early Christian prophecy. "Hear me, both barbarians and Greeks. I call on the whole race of men, whose Creator I am, by the will of the Father. Come to me that you may be put in your due rank under the one God and the one Word of God . . . For I want, I want to impart to you this grace, bestowing on you the perfect boon of immortality; and I confer on you both the Word and the knowledge of God, my complete self . . . I desire to restore you according to the original model, that ye may become also like me . . . Come to me, all ye that labour and are heavy laden, and I will give you rest."[106]

Perhaps most remarkable of all, Clement has learnt the art of pleading with men. "Believe him who is man and God; believe, O man. Believe, O man, the living God, who suffered and is adored. Believe, you slaves, him who died; believe, all races of men him who alone is God of all men. Believe, and receive salvation as your reward. Seek God and your soul shall live. He who seeks God is concerned with his own salvation. Have you found God? Then you have life. Let us then seek, in order that we may live. The reward of seeking is life with God."[107]

Again, " 'Become righteous', says the Lord. 'Ye that thirst, come to the water; and ye that have no money, come, and buy and drink without money'. He invites to the laver, to salvation, to illumination. He almost cries out, saying, 'The land I give thee, and the sea, my child, and heaven too. All the living creatures in them I freely bestow on thee. Only, O child, thirst for thy Father . . .' You have, O men, the divine promise of grace; you have heard, on the other hand, the threatening of punishment: by these the Lord saves, teaching men by fear and grace. Why do we delay? Why do we not shun punishment? Why do we not receive the free gift? Why, in short, do we not choose the better part, God instead of the evil one, and prefer wisdom to idolatry, and take life in exchange for death? 'Behold', he says, 'I have set before your face death and life'. The Lord tries you, that you may 'choose life'."[108]

There is a great deal more in these closing chapters of the *Protrepticus* which shows us the love and the skill of this remarkable preacher: his change of tone from entreaty to argument, from argument to warning, from warning to expostulation, is sensitive and shrewd. His adaptability in using the figures of speech that would be most likely to strike a responsive chord in his various readers, with metaphors from culture, the mysteries, the sea, the games, the human body, and so forth, cannot fail to arouse the admiration. One wonders why he took all this trouble. The answer is clear: he gives it us himself. His concluding paragraph begins, "Enough, methinks, of words, though, impelled by love to man, I might have gone on to pour out what I had from God, that I might exhort to what is the greatest of blessings—salvation."[109] That was it. He was so concerned for the welfare of those to whom he wrote that no effort was to be spared in the effort to interest them, captivate them, convince them, and finally win them to Christ. Concern for the unevangelized was one of the great driving forces in this cultured Christian scholar. No doubt the same was true of many an uncultured and unscholarly follower of Christ who has left no memorial, but was as keen as Clement to introduce other people to his Lord.

10

EVANGELISTIC STRATEGY

THE CHRISTIAN GOSPEL was intended for all men everywhere. The early Christians had no hesitations on that point: it was the agreed starting point for mission. The very nature of God demands a universal mission: if there is but one God, whose will for all men is that they should be saved, then the preaching must be worldwide. If this supreme God has revealed himself uniquely in Jesus of Nazareth, and in him has acted decisively for man's redemption, then the news of this greatest of all events must be spread far and wide. The nature of the gospel no less than the nature of God involves the Church in a mission to all mankind. The first generations of the Christian Church recognized this clearly.

But the questions still arose: where should they begin from? what portion of their enormous task should they tackle first? what plan of advance, if any, should they adopt? It would be a gross mistake to suppose that the apostles sat down and worked out a plan of campaign: the spread of Christianity was, as we have seen, largely accomplished by informal missionaries, and must have been to a large extent haphazard and spontaneous. Nevertheless there are several factors which seem to have determined the direction the Christian gospel eventually took, and we shall see reason to believe that they influenced the minds of at least some of the early evangelists.

GEOGRAPHY

Geography in Strategy

As we saw in chapter 1, the first century A.D. provided remarkable facilities for the spread of a faith through the fact that the whole civilized world adjacent to the Mediterranean basin was under the control (and the very effective control) of a single power, Rome. This power had adopted a single language, Greek, as the *lingua franca* of the Empire: even in so barbaric a spot as Lystra, some half of the inscriptions which have been recovered were written in Greek. Communications both by land and sea were excellent, and the Roman attitude towards private faiths was lenient so long as they did not impinge adversely upon public order. The way was, accordingly, wide open for the rapid dissemination of opinions whose advocates were sufficiently courageous, persistent, and self-sacrificial. Christians proved that they possessed these qualities, and they reaped corresponding rewards in terms of converts.

One has only to glance at the pattern of expansion in early Christianity to appreciate the significance of geographical factors in its overall strategy. Before the missionary journeys of St Paul there were Christians in Palestine and coastal Syria, in Tarsus and in Rome. Twenty years later these Palestinian, Cilician, Syrian and Roman bridgeheads had all been exploited and the gospel carried into the surrounding country. In Italy, for instance, there were Christians to be found at Tres Tabernae, Apii Forum, Herculaneum, Pompeii[1] and Puteoli as well as in the capital itself. In addition to these expanding areas Christianity had now been planted in extensive areas of Asia Minor reaching up to the Black Sea, in Macedonia and Greece, in Cyprus and Crete, and in Cyrene and Alexandria. Sea and land routes within the compass of the Roman Empire had clearly played a significant part in the direction of the advance of the new faith. A century later the picture is even clearer. The Western part of the Empire, where we have no knowledge of a Christian presence in the first century, had now got flourishing churches in Spain, France and Germany: once again the geographical factors are paramount. The evangelization of Germany ran down the Rhine to Cologne and the Moselle to Augusta Trevorum: that of Gaul proceeded up the great Arar River west of Marseilles to Vienna and Lugdunum, while the spread of the gospel in the important western province of Africa Proconsularis was initiated from Carthage, a cultural and trading centre of distinction. In Egypt the gospel has spread from Alexandria up the Nile, which was of course the great means of communication in that country.[2] There were, indeed, some exceptions to this general rule of evangelizing along the natural means of communication within the Roman empire.[3] Two obvious ones are the case of India and Armenia.[4] There is, as we have seen, some evidence to suggest that the gospel was carried to India in the first and second centuries A.D. But if so, does this constitute so great an exception to the generalization? Hardly, for the trade links between the Empire and India were very strong and the sea route was easy. Armenia is not really an exception either for it constituted a sort of no man's land between the Empire and the East. Roman policy was to foster friendly relations with Armenia but not to exercise direct control. And though Trajan temporarily reversed this policy by annexing the country, it soon reverted to its independent status, and was in fact the first kingdom (apart from Osroëne) officially to adopt Christianity. The closeness of the ties both of physical contiguity and of trade and friendship between the Empire and Armenia accounts for this spilling over of the missionaries from their normal beat within the bounds of the Roman world.

Of course the Christians were not the first to use the roads and the trade routes of the Empire as their main avenues of advance. The Jews had done so before them. It is significant in the highest degree that in every major area where the Christians penetrated in the first two centuries the Jews had been there before them: as Jesus had said to the disciples in a similar context, "Here the saying holds true 'One sows and another reaps'. I sent you to reap that for which you did not labour. Others have laboured, and you have entered into their labours."[5]

Geography in Tactics

Apart from these general strategic considerations, geographical factors played a part in the local tactics of Christian mission. A good deal of attention has been paid to the grouping of five provinces in the address of the First Epistle of St Peter. F. J. A. Hort, after careful study, concluded that the order of mention—Pontus, Galatia, Cappadocia, Asia and Bithynia—indicated the sweep of an actual intended journey which would naturally be followed by one landing at a seaport in Pontus. "The contemplated journey is doubtless that of Silvanus, by whom the Epistle was to be conveyed."[6] Although such a journey was for the purposes of edification, not evangelism, it is not unlikely that the original missionaries to the area followed much the same route, establishing small groups of believers at towns and villages on the way, before moving on.

There are indications that a similar procedure may have been adopted in Central Asia Minor. One of the strongest arguments for the South Galatian destination of St Paul's Epistle to the Galatians is the geographical. North Galatia, the area inhabited by the ethnic group of Galatae, is one of the most mountainous, inhospitable and trackless areas of the Anatolian plateau. Those who best know the geography of Asia Minor follow Ramsay almost to a man in believing that the recipients of Paul's Epistle were the Galatians of the Roman Province of that name in the south of Asia Minor including Pisidian Antioch, Iconium, Lystra and Derbe where Paul planted churches during his first missionary journey. These towns were either on or contiguous to the southern fork of the trade route from Ephesus to the East. The gospel spread along the lines of natural communication. The same seems to have been the case in coastal Asia Minor. The testimony of St Luke is that during the two years and more of Paul's ministry in Ephesus "all the residents of Asia heard the word of the Lord",[7] and the Book of Revelation suggests how it may have taken place. Personal investigation of the area, coupled with the order of mention of Ephesus, Smyrna, Pergamum, Thyatira, Sardis, Philadelphia and Laodicea convinced Ramsay that the author was thinking of the great circular road which joined these cities up. "All the seven cities stand on the great circular road that bound together the most populous, wealthy and influential part of the Province, the west-central region."[8] Along that road a messenger would have had to travel if he had started from Ephesus, the most important town in the whole of Asia. Along that same road, years before the messenger who carried the Apocalypse of John, had gone informal and dedicated messengers of the Christian Church who carried with them the good news of the risen Christ. Ramsay makes the further well-founded conjecture that each of the seven cities was the head of a postal district, and that they were addressed, therefore, not only as individual but as representative towns. From them John's message would be transmitted to the more outlying areas of proconsular Asia. No doubt the gospel itself spread in much the same way, along the lines of geographical contiguity and road networks.

There seems to be some evidence that geography functioned in yet another way in determining the shape of the early Christian mission. Eusebius[9] gives the story to which we have already alluded that the apostles drew lots in order to decide to which part of the world each one should go and evangelize. This receives slight support from the statement in the *Acts of Thomas* to the same effect,[10] and the possibility of such a procedure is clear from the fact that it was by no means of drawing lots that the Eleven set about finding a successor to Judas in the apostolic college. Nevertheless one must remain sceptical of any such share-out. Eusebius has clearly very little to go on. His statement that John got Asia is based on the fact that there is good evidence for Johannine activity there; that Peter got north-eastern Asia Minor is based on the address of 1 Peter; his acquaintance with Paul's journeys betrays no knowledge apart from what might be gained from his letters: accordingly his other two items of information, that Andrew took Scythia and Thomas Parthia can scarcely evoke much confidence, especially as there are other traditional destinations for Thomas! That there was some sort of division of labour by provinces, however, is not only probable *a priori*, but is supported by various pointers. Thus in general terms Paul and his associates preach to the Gentiles, while the "pillar

apostles" stick to the men of Israel.[11] Paul, moreover, is unwilling
to build on another man's foundation.[12] He is the pioneer missionary
par excellence. Hence his hesitations about visiting Rome—were it
not for overwhelming reasons which drove him in that direction, as
we shall see below. Hence, too, his absence from Cyprus and Egypt
and from the Bosphorus: they had been evangelized by others.
Geographical factors, then, played an important part in forming the
strategy and tactics of the Christian mission.

INFLUENCE

The Aims of St Paul

There can be no doubt that the early missionaries were influenced
by the strategic importance of certain towns and areas, and made
these their first goal in the wider context of preaching the gospel to
the whole world. The most obvious example of this is the work of
St Paul, though we must beware of extrapolating too readily from
the example of this astonishing man. But the relative profusion of
the material dealing with his plan of mission does enable us to see
how one of the ablest minds in the early Church saw his vocation
and sought to implement it, and we shall hardly be wrong in supposing that at least some of his ideals were shared by his brother Christians.

In his remarkable book, *Missionary Methods*, Roland Allen has
pointed out that St Paul, in his evangelistic strategy, seems to have
selected places which were centres of Roman administration, of
Greek civilization, of Jewish influence, and of commercial importance. He gives good reasons for each of these propositions, but
wisely concludes by pointing out the other side of the picture. Some
of the places where Paul preached were obvious centres—Corinth,
Thessalonica, Ephesus, Rome. But others were not. Beroea, for
instance, was not as important a place in Macedonia as Pella: yet he
preached in the one but not in the other. The same could be said of
other provinces. Allen reminds us that "St Paul plainly did not
select where he would preach simply on grounds like these: he was
led of the Spirit, and when we speak of his strategic centres we must
recognize that they were natural centres; but we must also recognize
that for missionary work they were strategic centres because he
made them such. They were not centres at which he must stop, but
centres from which he might begin; not centres into which life
drained, but from which it spread abroad."[13] He continues, "The
seizing of strategic points implied a strategy. It is part of the plan of
attack upon the whole country. Concentrated missions at strategic

centres, if they are to win the province, must be centres of evangelistic life." It was centres like these that the early Christians set out to found, centres which, in Allen's graphic phrase, were railway stations rather than prisons.

The strategy of a man like St Paul was basically simple: he had one life, and he was determined to use it to the greatest extent and at the best advantage possible in the service of Jesus Christ. His vision was at once personal, urban, provincial and global.

Personal and Urban

In personal terms, he was anxious to use every opportunity to speak of Christ. These might or might not be premeditated. When he invited the leaders of the Jews in Rome to come to his house for discussions on Christianity from the Scriptures, we may assume he gave some thought and planning to the venture beforehand. When he was nearly lynched in the temple area in Jerusalem and addressed the crowd from the steps of the Roman barracks of Antonia, we may be sure that he had no chance to prepare what he was to say! But on both occasions he proclaimed Christ. On both occasions he furthered the supreme strategy of his life. When he found himself explaining his mission before a pagan crowd of limited understanding in the market place at Lystra, when he did the same before a very different audience on the Areopagus, when he selected the lecture hall of Tyrannus or made friends among the Asiarchs of Ephesus, or when he took advantage of an illness to preach to the Galatians, we see a basic consistency. Here is a man whose life is consumed by a single desire, to which every eventuality and circumstance is made subservient.

But precisely because this was his overmastering passion, he had to be selective. He had only one life. And in order to make the most of it, he seems to have made a deliberate policy of going for leaders in a community, through whom, if he were successful in bringing them to Christian commitment, the message might be widely disseminated. "You heard my teaching in the presence of many witnesses," he wrote to Timothy. "Put that teaching into the charge of men you can trust, such men as will be competent to teach others."[14] It goes without saying that natural leaders are not always spiritual leaders; probably Timothy was no natural leader himself. Nevertheless they sometimes are: and Paul would appear to have laid particular store by his opportunities to preach the gospel to men like the proconsul of Cyprus, the chief man of Malta, the procurators Felix and Festus, King Agrippa and Bernice, and, supremely, the Emperor himself. These men were of no more intrinsic value to God than any beggar in the streets; but their influence, if converted, was infinitely greater.

For all the pride which the subsequent Church took in the presence within its ranks of all kinds of people, with a preponderance of the poor, the outcast, the slaves and the women, nevertheless this lesson was never forgotten. Before long men of the calibre of Justin and Clement, Origen and Tertullian were members of the Church, and they were not blind to the importance of reaching influential people with the gospel. Origen's lectures were attended by no less a person than the queen-mother, Julia Mammaea. The legends of Abgar, King of Edessa, and of King Gundaphorus in India, not only have a substratum of truth behind them, but show the direction of Christian strategy in the second century. The conversion of Armenia's king, Tiridates, under Gregory the Illuminator, is another case in point. It led to the adoption of Christianity by the whole country. It was the same story in Pontus in the mid-third century: Gregory Thaumaturgus, one of the aristocracy, led a mass movement in the province to the Christian faith. Here were two classic cases of the value of taking potential influence into account in evangelistic strategy.

Secondly, Paul's strategy was urban. He made for the centres from which his gospel could sound out into the surrounding area, as it did from Thessalonica and Ephesus. The Acts of the Apostles records his visit to city after city of importance: Antioch, the third city in the Empire, Philippi; the Roman *colonia*; Thessalonica, the principal metropolis of Macedonia; Corinth, the capital of Greece under Roman administration; Paphos, the centre of Roman rule in Cyprus; Ephesus, the principal city of the province of Asia. It is hard to escape the conclusion that this succession of important cities which Paul made the centres, sometimes of prolonged missionary activity, was not hit on by accident. It was part of a definite plan for planting the good news in key positions throughout the Empire. The climax of his urban policy is seen in the determination he long cherished, and eventually achieved in a very different way from his expectations, of visiting Rome. The significance of this desire and its accomplishment has been brilliantly illuminated by Professor Henry Chadwick in his *The Circle and the Ellipse*. In this he argues that Paul found Christianity a circle, centred on one city, Jerusalem, and left it an ellipse, with two foci, Jerusalem the mother city and Rome the seat of Empire. It was Paul who, by his insistence on making for Rome unwittingly put in motion the process which eventually gave rise to the papacy: then the ellipse shrank to a circle once more, but a circle where the centre of Christian influence and imperial power coincided. After Constantine this had incalculable effects both for good and ill on the Christian Church. It certainly illustrates the extent to which an urban policy dominated the strategy of the Christian mission.

Provincial and Global

Paul's strategy was, thirdly, provincial. It is well known that Paul is accustomed to refer to the provincial rather than, as St Luke so often does in Acts, the ethnic names of those to whom he writes. Macedonia, Achaea, Asia: these are the names of provinces. This was natural for a Roman citizen such as Paul. He seems to have made a point of setting up two or three centres of the faith in a province, and then passing on, and allowing the native enthusiasm and initiative of the converts to lead them to others whom they could win for Christ. Thus, in Macedonia, he preached in Thessalonica, Beroea and Philippi; in Achaea he won converts in Athens and Corinth; in Cyprus, Salamis and Paphos. The central importance of Ephesus attracted him so much that he spent a full two years there, and the word of God spread throughout the province of Asia.[15] It was no doubt during this period that Colossae and Laodicea were evangelized, through the agency of those whom Paul had brought to faith.[16] This provincial strategy proved extremely effective. Paul seems to have taken very seriously the doctrine of each church as *pars pro toto*. He did not work intensively for long years in a single place, but set up light-bearing communities of men who had found salvation in Christ, who could thereafter be "the sign, earnest and instrument of God's total plan of salvation" in that province.[17] That is how he can dare to say, "I have completed the preaching of the gospel of Christ from Jerusalem as far round as Illyricum . . . But now I have no further scope in these parts, and I have been longing for many years to visit you on my way to Spain."[18] His preaching had been representative; each province had heard something of the gospel, and little Christian communities were planted there to continue the work.

This leads naturally to Paul's greatest vision, the gospel for the whole world. That is why he moved restlessly on throughout the Mediterranean, from East to West. That is why he had to see Rome. That is why he planned to make Rome his base for yet more evangelism in the furthest Western boundaries of the known world. "It is my ambition to preach the gospel to places where the very name of Christ has not been heard."[19] The world was Paul's parish: how could it be less since it was the world which God loved and redeemed, the world over which the Christ who authorized the mission was exalted as *kyrios*? Hahn has shown how "Paul did not entertain a moment's doubt that the gospel must be preached in the whole world."[20] The world mission was inseparable from his call to be an apostle to the Gentiles: it was a divine necessity laid upon him, debtor as he was both to Greeks and Jews, to share with them the richness of Christ: it was, as Hahn puts it, "based on the gospel itself and its world-wide horizon . . . It is the light in the darkness of a world that has been usurped by 'the god of this world'. The word of the cross is the divine wisdom as opposed to all worldly wisdom. Therefore the powers of this world are overcome by the preaching and spreading of the gospel, and Paul is led in a triumphal march through the countries, propagating the savour of Christ."[21]

This global vision did not die after St Paul. It radiates from the writings of the second and third centuries. Justin sees in this hope the fulfilment of Scripture, when he says of the apostles, "They depend on Christ the eternal Priest; and through their voice it is that all the earth has been filled with the grace and glory of God and of his Christ. Wherefore David also says: 'Their sound has gone forth into all the earth, and their words to the end of the world'."[22] Much Christian writing from the Acts of the Apostles to the *Ecclesiastical History* of Eusebius is deeply imbued with this hope, and it comes to its climax in some remarkable words of Origen, all the more impressive because he wrote at a time when Christianity was still suffering persecution. In the eighth book of his *Contra Celsum* he rebuts the *reductio ad absurdum* that if everyone were converted the Empire would be left uneducated and defenceless: "Yet on such a basis as this neither would the emperor be left alone, nor would he be deserted, nor would earthly things be in the power of the most lawless and savage barbarians. For if, as Celsus has it, everyone were to do the same as I, obviously the barbarians would also be converted to the Word of God, and would be most law-abiding and mild. And all other worship would be done away and only that of the Christians would prevail. *One day it will be the only one to prevail*, since the Word is continually gaining possession of more souls."[23] It is true that pagans are still in the majority: but God will answer prayer, and the day will come when the whole Empire turns to God.[24] Meanwhile, persecution may well be the Christian's lot. To this Origen replies, "We are only persecuted when God allows the tempter and gives him authority to persecute us . . . If it is his will that we should again wrestle and strive for our religion . . . we will say, 'I can do all things through Christ Jesus our Lord who strengthens me'."[25] He is not dismayed whoever may be the emperor for the time being: "God knows what he is doing in the matter of the appointment of kings."[26] The Christian takes with the utmost seriousness the claim of Jesus, " 'Be of good cheer: I have overcome the world'. And he really has overcome the world, so that the world prevails only in so far as he who overcame it wills, for he received from his Father the victory over the world. And by his victory we are encouraged."[27] What a superb world vision for any man to hold in an age of persecution! Origen himself wavers. He wonders, is Celsus right in thinking that "it is impossible for the inhabitants of Asia, Europe, and Libya, both Greeks and barbarians to be agreed"? He concludes, "It probably is true that such a condition is impossible for those who are still in the body; but it certainly is not impossible after they have been delivered from it."[28] And in those words of Origen's we see with the utmost clarity the tension between faith and realism as the early Christians wrestled with the global implications of their faith with its universal message and the resurrection as its pledge of triumph after trial.

It would be a great mistake to suppose that this outline of a strategy in terms of personal influence, urban and provincial boundaries culminating in a world goal, was consciously adopted by the majority of Christians. It clearly was not. We have already seen how ordinary believers in the second and third centuries, like their forbears in Acts 8, wandered to tiny villages and hamlets with their good news—no doubt entirely innocent of any urban strategy. Men went outside the Empire to Arabia and India both as traders and as Christians with no self-conscious thoughts about any provincial strategy; was not the gospel intended for barbarian as well as Greek? No doubt it never crossed the mind of the majority of the faithful that Caesars might one day become Christians[29] and that the Church might spread throughout the inhabited world. But certainly *some* Christians thought of these things, and a perhaps largely unconscious strategy of this nature emerged from the interplay of the Holy Spirit, the words and example of Jesus, the opportunities that presented themselves for witness, and the conviction common to the early Christians that they had found the very elixir of life, the secret to the riddle of the universe; how could they keep silent about it?

ESCHATOLOGY

The Hope of the End

There can be no doubt that the expectation of the imminent return of Christ gave a most powerful impetus to evangelism in the earliest days of the Church. One has only to turn to 1 Thessalonians 1:5–10 to see how the preaching of the gospel both by Paul to the

Thessalonians and subsequently by them as "the word of the Lord sounded forth" into the surrounding regions, was set in the context of an urgent eschatological hope, as they awaited the return of God's Son from heaven. The primitive preaching, as we have seen, frequently came to its climax in a proclamation of the imminent return of Christ and a challenge to repentance and faith in the light of the culmination of all things. Christians lived in the last days, and must, accordingly, redeem the time by taking every opportunity of evangelism: "Convince some who doubt; save some by snatching them out of the fire."[30] In the event, Christ did not return speedily and in glory. Accordingly, the question arises how far the evangelistic energy of the first century Christians was the outcome of a mistaken eschatology.

On this there are several things to be said. There can be no doubt that eschatological expectation played a notable part in galvanizing the Church into mission in the second and third centuries, long after the hope of any early return had been shown to be groundless. If evangelism had depended on such an expectation, it would have declined rather than expanded as the delay grew longer. To be sure, the eschatological expectation of these centuries was both various and at variance with many emphases in the earliest Christian hope. It took on an increasing tendency to eudaemonism, to viewing the end of history in solely personalist terms, in concentrating to an unhealthy degree on rewards and punishments. But it never seems to have lost the assurance of God's ultimate victory. And this exercised a most powerful simulus towards co-operating in the work of the Lord here and now, while opportunity still offered. Thus in the early subapostolic period, we find the *Epistle of Clement* has a strong expectation of the parousia, associated with judgment, the resurrection, and a life of loving obedience to the Lord in the meantime. "Far be from us that which is written, 'Wretched are they who are of a double mind and of a doubting heart'; who say, 'These things we have heard even in the times of our fathers; but, behold, we have grown old and none of them has happened unto us'."[31] Clement then produces the analogy of the vine and its coming to maturity: "The Lord shall suddenly come to his temple, even the holy one, for whom you look."

The same saying, probably derived from an early Christian prophecy, is to be found in *2 Clement*, and is used to urge men to repentance, obedience, and eventual inheritance of the promises of God.[32] The *Epistle of Barnabas* sees the saving a soul by the Word as a result of remembering the day of judgment night and day.[33] The hope of the End continues to be important throughout the period:

Theophilus is impressed mainly by the thought of punishment,[34] Clement of Alexandria by the hope of immortality,[35] Ignatius equally by the thought of judgment and grace,[36] Justin by reflecting on hell.[37] Tatian most interestingly sets his eschatology where it belongs, in relation to his doctrine of creation, and he subordinates both the sovereignty of God.[38] Irenaeus gives the parousia full treatment.[39] Christ will indeed come again, and this will mean ruin for the impenitent and resurrection for those who believe and obey: he carefully defends this doctrine against the charge of vindictiveness, and shows that a man is damned not because God will not forgive him but because he wilfully shuts his eyes to the light and refuses to be forgiven. Each man, in fact, goes to the place of his choice.

Eschatological expectation, then, continued to play a great part in the conscious thinking of a Church bent on mission, long after it was very clear that the hopes of a speedy return of Christ had been abortive.

It is assumed almost without discussion in contemporary New Testament scholarship that the earliest Christians not only supposed (which, no doubt, they did) but also taught that the parousia and the culmination of all things would be within their lifetime.[40]

The evidence on which the widespread assumption is based has always appeared to me to be frail. To be sure, some of the hastily-instructed Thessalonian converts had stopped work and were sitting round awaiting the Second Coming, but Paul takes pains to explain that they were mistaken:[41] in 2 Thessalonians, moreover, he warns them that there is to be a historical interval before the climax of history.[42] Certainly he classes himself with those who are alive and remain until the coming of the Lord when writing to the Thessalonians. It is likely, however, that he is making a polemical point rather than a definite declaration that he would survive.[43] Indeed, if he were in fact making such an assertion, it would have been impossible for him to continue, "But as to the times and the seasons, brethren, you have no need to have anything written to you. For you yourself know well that the day of the Lord will come like a thief in the night."[44] This thief metaphor is found in four different strands of New Testament tradition.[45] Would it have been so widely retained if there had been dogmatic teaching by the earliest Christians of a parousia during their lifetime? Moreover, how then could we explain not only the parables such as the householder making his unexpected return after long delay, the lightening saying,[46] and, most striking of all, the repeated refusal of Jesus to assert the time of his return; indeed, his denial that he knew?[47] Are we so sure that the disciples assumed they knew better than their Lord? Is it not much more likely that there was no such sudden traumatic change in parousia teaching as much modern New Testament scholarship assumes, but that there was always a sense of the imminence of the Return which was not however associated with temporal proximity? "Sudden" the parousia would be: "soon" it might not.[48] Kurt Deissner is on the right track when he writes, "But when we remember that certain inconsistencies can be found in all apocalyptic descriptions, and that both sets of ideas can be found in the same passage (*e.g.* Mark 13), we have to explain the differences not as contradictions but as variations upon a single eschatological idea which is adapted to the eternal circumstances of a particular audience. In this way, for example, the eschatological picture presented by Paul in 2 Thessalonians 2:1ff. can be entirely reconciled with 1 Thessalonians 4:13–17 . . . It is essential to be ready, for the end will come when it is not expected (1 Thessalonians). But this is no reason to become fanatical, or to let oneself be "troubled"; for much has still to take place before the day of the Lord dawns (2 Thessalonians). He goes on to point out that there is never any question of the possibility of calculating a date for these events, according to the New Testament, even when they are described as being "near". They lie beneath the sovereign hand of God, and the proper human response is simply this: "Watch and pray".[49]

This is not to deny that there was plenty of variety in eschatological expectation among the Christians of the first generation, as later. But within this variety there was a deep unity of conviction that God would complete by personal intervention on the last day what he had begun at the creation and redeemed by the cross and resurrection. Whether it was the assurance of the Lord's presence with them in power until the consummation of the age, as in Matthew; or the emphasis on the coming Messianic banquet in the heavenly city, as in the Apocalypse; the stress on the Holy Spirit as the partial fulfilment of the eschatological promises of Jesus, as in John; the ever extending world mission or the progressive heading up of all things in Christ, as in Acts and Ephesians—the personal return of Christ was central to their eschatology just as the personal achievement of Christ was central to their gospel. For all the realized eschatology of the Fourth Gospel, chapters five and twenty-one show that the writer still cherishes the primitive hope; the return of Christ is a prominent feature in the Acts despite the emphasis there given to the role of the Church and the Spirit in the time before the end. The Epistle to the Ephesians, often said to have dispensed with the apocalypticism of the earlier preaching, knows there is to be a day of redemption in the future of which the Spirit in our hearts is the pledge and first instalment.[50] For all its variety of emphasis, the New Testament picture of the goal of human existence is remarkably homogeneous. It will be personal encounter with the God who has created and redeemed; it will involve a world where the run caused by human sin will be finally righted by the act of the Redeemer. Such a hope imposed an inevitable challenge. Christians must so live that they would not be ashamed to meet their Lord at his return, or at the "anticipated parousia" of death if this should come first. And Christians must be involved in the work of the Creator-Redeemer God in spreading the message of what he has done for sinners and what he will do to the obstinately rebellious who reject his salvation. With such a motive, such a strategy, it did not very much matter if a Christian's eschatology was crudely apocalyptic or enshrined the Christian gnosticism of the Alexandrians; whether chiliasm or the ascent of the soul to God was the main emphasis. The supreme spur to holy living and dedicated missionary work was this consciousness of the imminence of the end, of the limitations on the opportunities for evangelism, of the ultimate accountability we all have to God.

Indeed, it sheds an interesting light on the seriousness with which the early Church took their eschatology when we recall that from the days of the Apocalypse until Irenaeus chiliasm, the belief in the literal reign of Christ for 1,000 years on earth at the climax of history, was held by most of the writers of whom we have any knowledge, before it was replaced by the spiritualized other-worldliness of Clement and Origen. Paul Althaus has some interesting things to say on the value of this chiliastic view, despite its obvious crudities. "The decline and retreat of chiliasm was of great significance: it meant the watering down of the living hope of the imminence of God's kingdom, and the disappearance of the eschatological outlook of primitive Christianity."[51] As an objective vision of a sort of Utopia for lazy saints, chiliasm is repulsive; "but as an expression of the relationship between concrete historical service and the world to come, or of the responsibility of orientating everything here and now upon earth towards the kingdom that is to come, it has real and obvious value as a parable." In short, "chiliasm means to be true to this world, even in the certainty of death, for the sake of the resurrection."[52] It is hardly surprising, therefore, that not only in the first and second centuries, but in later periods of the Church, missionary zeal has often flowered most notably in circles which held a strongly realistic hope and a likely expectation of the coming kingdom.

The Gift of the Spirit

It is difficult to overestimate the importance of eschatology on the mission of the early Christians. They believed that the long-awaited kingdom of God belonging to the day of salvation, the kingdom of which the prophets had spoken, was already ushered in through the person and work of Jesus of Nazareth. They saw his death and resurrection as decisive in inaugurating the last days, and they were conscious thereafter of living in the last chapter, so to speak, of the book of human history, however long or short that chapter might be. But the death and resurrection of Jesus had not finalized the promises, or fully realized the kingdom. God's will was not yet done on earth as it is in heaven. However, the Church had two great and interconnected possessions during the interim period before the end. It had the Spirit, and it had the world mission.

The Holy Spirit was seen as the eschatological gift *par excellence.* Pentecost was rightly interpreted by Peter as the proof that the last times had arrived.[53] The Spirit is the foretaste of God's future: we have "the first fruits of the Spirit" as the pledge of the new creation which God has in store for his people.[54] Indeed, the Spirit is more than the first instalment. He is part of the fulfilment. When the puzzled disciples asked their departing Master when he would usher in the Kingdom, he declined to give them any date, but instead promised them the Holy Spirit to equip them for world mission.[55] The period before the end is no barren period of waiting; it is the time of the Spirit, the time of evangelism. This is no merely Lucan perspective.[56] It is to be found in many strands of the New Testament. In the Little Apocalypse, Jesus says that before the end shall come, his followers must face hardship and ill treatment in the cause of world mission, "in synagogues and before governors and kings for my sake, to bear testimony before them. And the gospel must first be preached to all nations."[57] The same point is made in John, where the Spirit, the personal embodiment of the end, is sent to bear witness to Christ alongside the testimony of the disciples.[58] 2 Peter speaks of "hastening" the coming of the Lord; this would have been readily understood.[59] The rabbis used to say that if only the whole of Israel would repent for a single day the Messiah would appear.[60] The Christians were clear that their task was to call both Israel and the nations to repentance, and that it was only the gracious forbearance of the Lord, awaiting the spread of the good news to the whole of his creation, which delayed the longed-for goal: "The Lord is not slow about his promise as some count slowness, but is forbearing toward you, not wishing that any should perish, but that all should reach repentance. But the day of the Lord will come, like a thief . . ."[61] The very old stratum of tradition recorded in Acts 3:19f. makes the same point, that the return of Christ to establish the kingdom is in some way dependent on the repentance of man. Hence the need for evangelism.

The Place of the Gentiles

But what about the place of the Gentiles? Jewish eschatology at its best knew that there must be a place for the Gentiles in the purposes of God. Jeremias has succinctly set out the evidence in his book, *Jesus' Promise to the Nations*. Moreover, Jesus himself, although he restricted his own activity, at least for the most part, to Israel, clearly taught the possibility of the incorporation of believing Gentiles in the kingdom of God.[62] How, then, was this to be brought about? There was a major difference of opinion on this subject among the early Christians, which had the greatest possible effect upon the strategy of their missionary activity.

The Jerusalem Church seems to have taken what we might call the majority view of Old Testament indications about the fate of the nations, which was broadly this. Insofar as the nations were opposed to Yahweh and his people they would be utterly defeated in the final day.[63] But on the other hand, they were creatures of God, just as Israel was. He was the God of the whole earth, and therefore would not exclude from his mercy the believing Gentiles who made the journey to Mount Zion and joined themselves to the people of Israel. Indeed, so strongly marked is this emphasis in the Psalms and the prophets, that Jeremias can say with little exaggeration, "In all the passages of the Old Testament, without exception, in which reference is made to the eschatological pilgrimage of the Gentiles, the goal of the pilgrimage is the scene of God's revelation of himself, Zion, the holy Mountain of God. From this it is to be inferred that the movement is always thought of as 'centripetal'; the Gentiles will not be evangelized where they dwell, but will be summoned to the holy Mount by the divine epiphany."[64] It was this branch of Old Testament teaching which lay behind the mission of Jewish Christianity. This is why they sought to circumcise their converts: not on account of mere legalistic or ritualistic prejudices, but in order to bring them fully within the people of God, where alone they would be safe in the day of judgment and would share in the fruition of God's kingdom to be realized in Jerusalem. This is why the opposition of the "Judaizers" to Paul was so vehement and persistent. For in their eyes Paul, by his mission to the Gentiles, was reversing the priorities in God's plan of salvation as recorded in the Scriptures; whilst by his rejection of circumcision for his converts he was guilty of plain disobedience towards the ordinance of God. The strategy of the Jewish mission was clear enough. They must do their utmost to bring Israel to accept the Messiah; when Israel had done so, the way would be clear for the final drama, the coming of the Gentiles to the Mount Zion, and the culmination of God's plan for his redeemed creation. "To the Jew first" was the divine strategy both of mission and of eschatology.

Paul, and after him the majority of Christian thinkers, understood matters in the reverse order, and, following indications in the teaching of Jesus himself, inclined to what one might call the minority view in the Old Testament. Paul took seriously the many passages about the invincible ignorance of Israel, their culpable blindness of heart and the sovereignty of God in salvation.[65] He saw that the history of salvation had so often seen a remnant used to raise up a believing community. Was not the slowness of Israel to recognize its Messiah proof of that hardness of heart which she had so often displayed towards the bearers of God's revelation in the past ? Clearly, God's purposes are not thereby thwarted; the success of the Gentile mission proved that.[66] Yet it was impossible that the covenant-making God could have forsaken Israel. No, their blindness was only partial; some Jews believed. And their rejection was only temporary: God would make them jealous by means of the conversion of the Gentiles. The branches of the wild olive grafted into the stock of Israel would make the natural branches, dispossessed through unbelief, realize what they were missing, and turn to the Lord. "I want you to understand this mystery," he writes. "A hardening has come upon part of Israel until the full number of the Gentiles come in. And so all Israel shall be saved."[67] These are the mighty themes of election, mission and eschatology with which Paul wrestles in Romans 9–11. There is growing support for the view that he saw his collection for the impoverished Christians of Jerusalem as a symbolic fulfilment of the Old Testament prophecies foretelling the pilgrimage of the Gentiles to Jerusalem.[68] No doubt this is why Paul did not only take the money collected from the Gentile churches with him; in itself not only a relief measure proper to those who had received the good news in the first place from Jewish hands, nor merely an ecumenical gesture of deep significance in the growing split between Jewish and Gentile Christianity. Paul saw it as something much deeper, alive with eschatological significance. The collection, and the varied delegation of delegates who brought it, were representatives of the gospel's fruit among the Gentiles, bringing their offerings and themselves to Mount Zion in fulfilment of the ancient prophecies and in expectation of the parousia. This, Paul no doubt hoped, would provoke impenitent Israel to jealousy and lead to its conversion.[69]

Neither of these two eschatologies in fact turned out to be correct. The Jewish Christians were mistaken in their hope that Israel would turn to Christ *en masse*, that the Gentiles would be attracted to Zion, and that God's kingdom would be established that way. Paul and Gentile Christianity was mistaken in their hope that the conversion of Israel would follow such concrete evidence of God's saving work among the heathen as was afforded by the collection and the delegation of converts who accompanied the apostle. Nevertheless, as both programmes knew very well, God was sovereign in salvation. Men had been mistaken in their interpretation of the Scriptures relating to Christ's first coming, although they studied them earnestly. It was not unlikely that men would prove equally fallible in interpreting the Scriptures relating to his second advent. But that did not absolve them from attempting an interpretation of history. They may have been mistaken in their estimate of the unfolding of God's plan before the parousia, but they were not mistaken in the three basic convictions that they cherished. First, God was sovereign, and would bring in his kingdom in his way at his time. Second, God was the Creator and Redeemer of the whole world, and the Gentiles had as much place as the Jews in his purposes. Third, the role of the Church in the interval before the end was evangelism "to the Jew first and also to the Greek" in the power of the Holy Spirit given to them both as the guarantee of the coming kingdom and as a constituent part of it. Eschatology and mission were irrevocably united in the person of the Spirit.[70] As William Manson put it, "The parousia lay right over the path of the world mission, and its coming would be conditioned by the fulfilment of the missionary task."[71]

EPILOGUE

IT IS NOT possible to assess realistically the extent to which the evangelism conducted by the early Church was successful. For one thing, we have no means of comparing their "successes" with their "failures". For another, God's assessment of success may differ greatly from our own: and, as we have seen throughout this book, evangelism is supremely God's work in the lives of men, in which he enlists human co-operation. Nor is it possible to read off from a study of evangelism in antiquity the answers to our contemporary problems in communicating the gospel. However, some aspects of their approach stand out significantly, and are important for the Church to take heed of in any age, and not least in our own when we are not notably successful at sharing the Christian faith with those who do not believe.

One of the most striking features in evangelism in the early days was the people who engaged in it. Communicating the faith was not regarded as the preserve of the very zealous or of the officially designated evangelist. Evangelism was the prerogative and the duty of every Church member. We have seen apostles and wandering prophets, nobles and paupers, intellectuals and fishermen all taking part enthusiastically in this the primary task committed by Christ to his Church. The ordinary people of the Church saw it as their job: Christianity was supremely a lay movement, spread by informal missionaries. The clergy of the Church saw it as their responsibility, too: bishops and presbyters, together with doctors of the Church like Origen and Clement, and philosophers like Justin and Tatian, saw the propagation of the gospel as their prime concern. They seem not to have allowed the tasks of teaching, caring and administering to make them too busy to bring individuals and groups from unbelief to faith. The spontaneous outreach of the total Christian community gave immense impetus to the movement from the very outset.

What is more, this infectious enthusiasm on the part of such diverse people of differing ages, backgrounds, sex, and cultures was backed up by the quality of their lives. Their love, their joy, their changed habits and progressively transformed characters gave great weight to what they had to say. Their community life, though far from perfect, as Christian writers were constantly complaining, was nevertheless sufficiently different and impressive to attract notice, to invite curiosity, and to inspire discipleship in an age that was as pleasure-conscious, as materialistic and as devoid of serious purpose as our own. Paganism saw in early Christianity a quality of living, and supremely of dying, which could not be found elsewhere.

Unless there is a transformation of contemporary church life so that once again the task of evangelism is something which is seen as incumbent on every baptized Christian, and is backed up by a quality of living which outshines the best that unbelief can muster, we are unlikely to make much headway through techniques of evangelism. Men will not believe that Christians have good news to share until they find that bishops and bakers, university professors and house-wives, bus drivers and street corner preachers are all alike keen to pass it on, however different their methods may be. And men will continue to believe that the Church is an introverted society com-posed of "respectable" people and bent on its own preservation until they see in Church groupings and individual Christians the caring, the joy, the fellowship, the self-sacrifice and the openness which marked the early Church at its best.

Together with this enthusiasm on the part of the ordinary lay members of the Church as well as its ordained ministers to share the good tidings with those who had never heard them, went a deep sense of the seriousness of the issues involved. These men really believed that men without Christ might suffer eternal and irrepar-able loss, and this thought drove them to unremitting labours to reach them with the gospel. There was no hint of universalism in the early Church, and when something very like it appeared in the later writings of Origen,[1] he was forthwith reckoned to be heretical and, despite his saintly life and herculean labours for the faith, was never canonized. The thought that their gospel was veiled to un-believers, who were blinded in mind by the devil, impelled other Christian missionaries besides Paul to "proclaim not ourselves, but Christ Jesus as Lord, and ourselves your servants for Jesus's sake",[2] in the hope that God, in his goodness, would illuminate their hearts and reveal Jesus Christ to them. These early missionaries were very conscious of their responsibility to seek the Lord's approval in all they did. They were accountable to him, and he had bidden them proclaim the good news to all the world. How could they face him unashamed if they had flouted his last command ?

A further significant factor was the eschatology of the early evangelists. It was strong and clear. The God who had created, who had intervened to reconcile all men with himself, would one day put the seal on his redemptive work through the parousia. In chapter 10 we examined the place that eschatology played in their evangelistic outreach. It is not too much to say that without a coherent eschatology it is not possible to do effective evangelism. The message of salvation must not only be related to the individual, the Church and the Lord, but also to the whole purposes of God in his world. It is strange that in a century when New Testament scholarship has recognized as never before the centrality of eschatology in the primitive kerygma, a century moreover which is deeply concerned with the meaning of history, contemporary evangelism should either be completely silent or raucously literalistic on the subject. Communism and humanism both have clearly defined eschatological goals; Christians have one which makes much more sense than either,[3] but are mute about it. This could certainly not be said of the early Church. In Jesus Christ they had, and they fearlessly proclaimed, a firm point of reference for the evaluation of all history and a sure pledge of a realistic eschatology. Their message was related to these great issues, and did not burke them. The modern decline of belief in heaven and hell, or even in any life after the grave among many professing Christians is an insuperable barrier to dynamic evangelism. When we no longer see ourselves as dying men preaching to dying men, the absoluteness of the command to evangelize becomes muted, and we draw back before a task which at the best of times is difficult, delicate and very demanding.

We have seen that the early Christians possessed a clear understanding of the good news they proclaimed. Their kerygma was no dull monochrome, but rather a many-splendoured thing. Its precise contents and the way in which it was presented depended to a large extent upon the skill of the evangelist in translating words and ideas into terms readily understood by those to whom he spoke, and upon the background and conditions of his hearers. We have seen the great variety in the gospel as preached to Greek and to Jew, to intellectual and to savage, a variety which was enhanced by the varying insights into different aspects of Christian truth to be found in different sectors of the Church. But one thing was constant: their message was Christocentric through and through. The content of their proclamation was none other than the person of Christ. They made use of all the cultural and intellectual pathways which would facilitate the reception of this message. Intensely sensitive to the felt needs of the listeners, the thought world in which they moved, the very language which would strike the clearest note in their minds, their aim nevertheless remained both simple and direct, to introduce others to Jesus Christ. It is the same whether we listen to the apostle Paul on Mars Hill or the monk Macarius in the

Egyptian deserts. All are clear on the need for a decisive turning to Christ in repentance, faith and baptism; for continuing in the apostolic teaching through faithful study of and obedience to the Scriptures; and for joining in the apostolic fellowship through participation in the common life of the Church, by prayer, service, and regular reception of the Eucharist. Believing as they did in the finality of Christ they lived their lives accordingly; and in urging other people towards conversion they saw themselves participating in and forwarding God's purpose for his whole creation.

This Christ to whom they bore witness was no theological abstraction, no redeemer figure similar to Gnostic patterns: the early Christians did not make a radical disjunction between the Jesus of history and the Christ of faith. As we have seen, they regarded the words and deeds of the historical Jesus as so crucial to their proclamation of the exalted Lord that they used *pericopae* from the gospels evangelistically. Moreover, their Christ was no ecclesiastical figure, interested only in men's souls. He was the cosmic Christ, the author, sustainer, and final goal of the universe. Accordingly, many of the early evangelists were bold enough to claim all truth everywhere as Christian truth; whatever Plato and the poets had said that was true, stemmed ultimately from the Lord the Christians worshipped. Whatever insight into the world of human affairs these Christians gained served to deepen their understanding and appreciation of their Lord. The charge of obscurantism, which has sometimes been levelled against evangelists of a subsequent age, could never have been sustained against them. Truth was a unity, and it derived from the ultimate reality made personal in him who was Way, Truth and Life. It was this conviction which nerved them to proclaim the Absolute in a world which was dominated by the Relative in its morals, religions and concept of history; and for the most part they did it without fear and without censoriousness. Their gospel was big enough to embrace earth and heaven, this life and the next. They were concerned with labour relations, slavery, marriage and the family, the exposure of children, cruelty in the amphitheatre and obscenity on the stage: increasingly they came to see that the gospel carried political implications as well. But this never seems to have prevented them from holding a strongly transcendental perspective. There was no dichotomy between a social and a spiritual gospel to these men who held a unitive concept of truth. So far from being so heavenly-minded that they were no earthly good, they demonstrated that those who are genuinely heavenly-minded are the very people who are deeply committed to doing God's will on earth. Needless to say, the delicate balance between social and spiritual, this world and the next, was not always preserved. At times the Church swayed towards such syncretism as Paul found in the Colossian church, or the rigorism of a Tertullian: their understanding of the all-inclusive nature of their gospel was often imperfect. Yet on the whole the early Church seems to have done rather better than Christians of later ages in holding together the "this worldly" and the "other worldly" aspects of their faith. This meant that they were concerned about this life without feeling that to leave it was the greatest of all evils: and such an attitude is sufficiently rare in any age to excite notice.

The very strength of the grasp which many of the early Christians had on the essentials of their faith brought two dangers with it. On the one hand it played into the hands of Gnosticism, as if men were saved by the knowledge they had of the true God and the correct propositions they made concerning his nature and activity. On the other it encouraged a codifying of Christian truth in credal formulae which came to be used more as a test of orthodoxy or as arguments in apologetic, than as pointers to what God in Christ had done for men. As we saw in chapter 4, this was particularly the case with the confrontation between Christianity and Judaism, where churchmen soon ceased to be messengers charged with glad tidings, and unfortunately became both arrogant and argumentative. They seem to have given up all hope of winning the Jewish people for their Messiah, and concentrated instead on trying to establish the Christian claims in opposition to those of Israel. There is a world of difference between apologetics of this sort and evangelism.

Turning to the methods used in evangelism, we met with no very great surprises. Granted their presuppositions that the ultimate truth about God and man had been revealed in Jesus, and that the basic alienation between God and man had been resolved through Jesus, it is natural enough that they used every means in their power to share this discovery with others. We have seen that house meetings of various sorts and personal conversations between individuals played a very prominent part in the progress of the gospel in ancient times. The hospitality and even the decoration of their homes, their chance conversations indoors or in the open air, visiting, open-air preaching, addresses in church and synagogue, arguments in the market place and the philosophical school, personal testimony, letter writing and the explanation of Scripture were all used to further the supreme aim which these early Christians cherished, of making Christ known to others. When men have the will to speak of their Lord, they find no shortage of ways in which to do it. Indeed, it is the motivation of these men and women which impresses us more than their methods. Their moving allegiance to God, their profound sense of discovery, their deep concern for their Christless fellows drove them out into unremitting service in the cause of the gospel.

Evangelism today is often associated with the great public meeting. It is a remarkable fact that the early Church seems to have made very little use of this method of commending the gospel. The reason lay, partly at any rate, in the historical situation in which Christianity was born. Large-scale public associations were banned by imperial edict during the majority of the period under review. Apart from the large meetings in Jerusalem (and that city was always regarded as a special case by Roman governors, sensitive as they were to intense nationalistic feeling) recorded in the early chapters of the Acts, we hear of nothing comparable until the widespread turning to Christianity in North Africa towards the end of the second century, before Tertullian wrote. It was always impolitic, and potentially dangerous, to organize a large public meeting: this was to invite police action. Naturally, therefore, the emphasis lay on home and personal evangelism, and these methods have a permanent importance for any church which is concerned to grow.

But there may have been a further reason which led the early Christians to eschew mass evangelism for the most part. Did they, perhaps, realize the dangers which a shallow, widespread scattering of the seed could bring in its wake? No sooner do we hear of mass movements than we hear of the baptism of heathen ideas and customs into Christianity. Tertullian complained of it in Africa; Anne Ross has recently shown how it took place in Britain.[4] Indeed, it happened all over the Empire as soon as Christianity was adopted as the official religion under Constantine. But a century earlier Gregory Thaumaturgus had run into this very problem in Pontus where he was prominent in widespread and large-scale evangelism.[5] "After the persecution [*i.e.* of Decius in the mid-third century] was over, when it was possible to address oneself to Christian worship with unrestricted zeal, Gregory returned again to the city and, by travelling over all the surrounding country, increased the people's ardour for worship in all the churches by holding a solemn commemoration in honour of those who had contended for the faith. Here one brought bodies of martyrs, there another. So much so that the assemblies went on for the space of a year, the people rejoicing in the celebration of festivals in honour of the martyrs. This also was one proof of his great wisdom, that while he completely altered the direction of everyone's life in his own day, turning them into an entirely new course, and harnessing them firmly to the faith and to the knowledge of God, he slightly lessened the strain upon those who had accepted the yoke of the faith, in order to let them enjoy good cheer in life. For as he saw that the raw and ignorant multitude adhered to idols on account of bodily pleasures, he permitted the people—so as to secure the most vital matters, i.e. the direction of their hearts to God instead of to a vain worship—he permitted them to enjoy themselves at the commemoration of the holy martyrs, since life would become more serious and earnest naturally in process of time, as the Christian faith came to assume more control of it." That was the theory of the thing. In practice it did not always work out like that; instead paganism continued to flourish, decked out in Christian dress. This ever-present danger was accentuated in mass evangelism. Perhaps this helps to account for the sparing use made of it in the advance of early Christianity.

In these first two centuries or so of the Church's existence we find many faults, much that dishonours the name they professed. But we also find an evangelistic zeal and effort, exerted by the whole broad spectrum of the Christian community to bring other people to the feet of their ascended Lord and into the fellowship of his willing servants. This is a permanent reminder of the Church's first priority. Evangelism was the very life blood of the early Christians: and so we find that "day by day the Lord added to their number those whom he was saving". It could happen again, if the Church were prepared to pay the price.

NOTES

¹ Matthew 28:19.
² Melito of Sardis wrote, "Our philosophy first grew up among the barbarians but its full flower came among your nation [sc. Rome] in the great reign of your ancestor Augustus, and became an omen of good to your Empire, for from that time the power of the Romans became great and splendid." He went on to argue that the fates of Rome and the Church were so intertwined for good that the Church should not be persecuted by Marcus Aurelius, to whom he addressed his Apology (Eusebius, *Historia Ecclesiastica* 4.26. 5–11).
The argument that God prepared the world situation specially for the birth of Christianity is found more clearly stated in Origen. "For 'righteousness arose in his days and abundance of peace' began with his birth; God was preparing the nations for his teaching, that they might be under one Roman emperor so that the unfriendly attitude of the nations to one another, caused by the existence of a large number of kingdoms, might not make it more difficult for Jesus's apostles to do what he commanded them when he said, 'Go and teach all nations'. It is quite clear that Jesus was born under the reign of Augustus, the one who reduced to uniformity, so to speak, the many kingdoms on earth so that he had a single empire. It would have hindered Jesus's teaching from being spread through the whole world if there had been many kingdoms, not only for the reasons just stated, but also because men everywhere would have been compelled to do military service and fight in defence of their own land. This used to happen before the times of Augustus. Accordingly, how could this teaching, which preaches peace and does not even allow men to take vengeance on their enemies, have had any success unless the international situation had everywhere been changed and a milder spirit prevailed at the advent of Jesus?" (Origen, *Contra Celsum*, 2.30, translated by H. Chadwick.)
³ Thus Melito in his argument, cited above, contends that "the greatest proof that our faith flourished for good along with the empire in its noble beginnings is the fact that is met with no persecution in the reign of Augustus, but on the contrary was thought splendid and glorious and just what men were praying for" (Eusebius, *H. E.* 4.26.8).
⁴ "Saviour of the world" and similar titles are frequent in Augustan inscriptions.
⁵ Virgil, *Eclogues* 4.6.
⁶ *Res Gestae*, 34.
⁷ *Carmen Saeculare*, 50.
⁸ *Pacato orbe terrarum, restituta re publica, quieta deinde nobis et felicia tempora contigerunt* (Dessau, *Inscriptiones Latinae Selectae*, 8393).
⁹ *Annals*, 1.9.
¹⁰ See the important article on "Roads and Travel" by W. M. Ramsay in *Hastings Dictionary of the Bible* (Extra Volume), 1904, and M. P. Charlesworth, *Trade Routes and Commerce in the Roman Empire*.
¹¹ *Corpus Inscriptionum Graecarum*, no. 3920.
¹² Horace speaks of *sermones utriusque linguae* (*Odes* 3.8.5) and the Emperor Claudius of *uterque sermo noster* (Suetonius, *Claudius* 42.1). It is clear that, even in Italy, Greek was more than on a par with Latin, whilst in the East it was *the* lingua franca.
¹³ *Institutio Oratoria*, 1.1.12.
¹⁴ Juvenal, *Satires* 6.186ff., Martial, *Epigrams*, 10.68.
¹⁵ Acts 21:37.
¹⁶ e.g. *Republic*, 376ff.
¹⁷ The critique of polytheism by Greek philosophers was carried into the Latin world through Cicero's *De Natura Deorum* and this work was greatly

exploited by Latin Christian writers, Tertullian, Minucius Felix, Arnobius and Lactantius.

[18] *Fragments* 11–16 of Xenophanes show that he was concerned to expose not only the intellectual folly of crude polytheism but also the morally degrading effects it had.

[19] Xenophanes, *Fragments*, 23.

[20] In Homer he is much stronger than all the other gods put together (*Iliad* 8.18–27). As early as Hesiod his actions are identified with those of the gods (*Works* 42, 47) and Aeschylus in the fifth century B.C. has a noble conception of Zeus as the all-powerful moral ruler of the universe (*Agamemnon* 160ff.).

[21] No doubt it is an oversimplification to equate "the Idea of the Good", "God" and "the Demiurge" in Plato's writings. They belong to rather different layers of his thought, so that they overlap rather than permit a straight identification. It was in subsequent Platonism that the more overtly religious overtones predominated, and it was against this later background that the early preaching must be seen.

[22] "He was good, and the good has never at any time a feeling of jealousy towards anything, so he wished everything to become as like himself as possible" (*Timaeus* 29e).

[23] *Metaph.* 1074b.

[24] Aristotle varies in his usage between the neuter and the masculine. The Greeks were generally not so concerned as we are about personality in the divine.

[25] Assuming this to be a genuine work of Aristotle: it is disputed.

[26] *De Praescriptione*, 7.

[27] See chapter 2 of Tatian's *Address to the Greeks*.

[28] The Areopagus Address in Acts 17 is the most notable example; so are whole areas of the Fourth Gospel and Hebrews.

[29] *1 Apology* 20.

[30] Apart from the ceremonial of the state religion, the main religious activity was concerned with the shadowy *penates*, the spirits who looked after the larder, and the *lares familiares*, originally probably farm deities which came to be thought of as the spirits of the household.

[31] "The secret of the maintenance and spread of these oriental religions is to be found in the institution of the *collegia*, which are of great importance for the private life of the slave for they extend their services beyond the province of religion, and in many cases must have furnished most of what made life worth living for him." (R. H. Barrow, *Slavery in the Roman Empire*, p. 164). However, it was not only among the common people that these oriental cults were popular, as the pages of Juvenal make clear. They travelled up the social scale fast: a *taurobolium* was a very expensive investment.

[32] and that crowning benefit, an epitaph.

[33] Aeschylus was certainly no innovator on this theme: it is prominent in Homer.

[34] See *Inscriptiones Latinae Selectae*, 4152. Though Cybele worship spread to the West in the third century B.C., it is uncertain when the *taurobolium* was introduced into the cult. It is probable that the ideas behind this late inscription were influenced by Christianity: see Prudentius, *Peristreph.*, 10.1011ff.

[35] *Metamorphoses*, 11.5.

[36] See the last two chapters of Tacitus's *Agricola*, and Horace, *Odes*, 3.30.

[37] *Metamorphoses*, 11.23.

[38] For instance, Antiochus the Great settled no less than 2,000 families in Phrygia and Lydia, (Josephus, *Antiquities of the Jews*, 12.3, 4).

[39] 1 Maccabees 15:16–23.

[40] *Bellum Judaicum* 2.20.2. Josephus is notoriously unreliable in his numbers; he makes the number 18,000 in *B.J.* 7.8.7. But in any case there must have been an enormous colony of Jews in Babylon.

[41] *B.J.*, 7.3.3.

[42] *In Flaccum*, 6.

[43] 1 Maccabees 8:17–32; 12:1–4.

[44] I.iii.2, 3.
[45] Tacitus, *Histories*, 5.9.
[46] *Legatio ad Gaium*, 23.
[47] *Antiquities of the Jews* 14.10, a chapter that makes fascinating reading.
[48] Josephus, *Antiquities of the Jews*, 14.10.8. Whether they ever served with the Roman army is disputed.
[49] See Harnack, *Mission and Expansion of Christianity*, p. 14.
[50] The evidence, however, is precarious. See E. M. Smallwood on "The alleged Jewish tendencies of Poppaea Sabina" in *J.T.S.* 1959, p. 329ff., who minimizes it. Josephus is emphatic about her Jewish leanings (*Antiquities of the Jews*, 20.8.11).
[51] *Corpus Inscriptionum Latinarum*, 10.1971.
[52] Josephus, *B.J.* 1.32.6.
[53] In *Satires*, 3, 6, and 14.
[54] *Histories*, 5.5.
[55] *Timaeus* 28 C, a passage greedily taken over by the Apologists.
[56] *B.J.*, 7.3.3.
[57] Luke, 7:5.
[58] *M. Bikkurim*, 1.4.
[59] *Satires* 1.4.142f., "and, like a Jew, will make a proselyte of you".
[60] *Satires*, 14.96–106 is a remarkably well-informed cartoon.
[61] *C. Apion*, 2.10, 39; *B.J.*, 7.3.3.
[62] Matthew 23:15.
[63] On this whole subject, see Schürer, *The Jewish People in the Time of Christ* Div. 2, Vol. 3, pp. 270–316.
[64] *M. Aboth* 1.12.
[65] *b. Pes.* 87b.
[66] Though even in the first century the school of Shammai was cool to the Gentile mission. See *b. Shabb.* 31a, and the discussion in M.-J. Lagrange, *La Messianisme*, p. 270ff.
[67] For Tiberius see Josephus, *Antiquities of the Jews* 18.83 and Suetonius, *Tiberius* 36; for Claudius see Acts 18:2 and Suetonius *Claudius* 25. Cassius Dio (specifically says the cause was their rapid growth 60.6.6).
[68] *Mission and Expansion of Christianity*, p. 15.

CHAPTER 2

[1] *M. Aboth*, 1.1.
[2] Acts 4:13.
[3] Acts 6:7.
[4] John 7:48.
[5] Deuteronomy 21:22f.
[6] I have dealt with this at some length in my *The Meaning of Salvation*, p. 145f. The Deuteronomy text underlies the argument in Acts 5:30, 10:39, 13:29, Galatians 3:13 and 1 Peter 2:24. The "stumbling-block" became, in Christian hands, a powerful explanation of the Cross and even an aid in apologetic.
[7] *Dialogue with Trypho*, 89.
[8] See for instance J. Crehan, *Early Christian Baptism and the Creed*, and O. Cullmann, *The Earliest Christian Confessions*.
[9] Philippians 2:11.
[10] On the centrality of this text in early Christian apologetic, see C. H. Dodd, *According to the Scriptures* and B. Lindars, *New Testament Apologetic*.
[11] Justin, *Dial*. 67.
[12] Isaiah 7:14. See *Dial*. 67, 84 for a discussion between Christian and Jew on the meaning of '*almah*.
[13] Celsus quotes contemporary second century Jewish propaganda as claiming that Jesus was the illegitimate son of Mary and a Roman soldier, Panthera (Origen, *Contra Celsum* 1.32).
[14] Acts 7:46ff.
[15] Acts 15:10.

[16] If it be objected that recourse is had too often to Justin's *Dialogue with Trypho*, it must be remembered that of the three examples we have of early Jewish reaction to the Christian preaching, contained in Celsus, the Talmud and Justin, Justin's material is the earliest and represents Jewish views current in the first and early second centuries. Of course, it is a propagandist work, and to some extent, no doubt, misrepresents Judaism, at times obviously so (68.9 is a case in point. See A. J. B. Higgins "Jewish Messianic Beliefs in Justin Martyr's Dialogue with Trypho" in *Novum Testamentum* 1967–8, p. 298ff.). But both Harnack, "Judentum und Judenchristentum in Justins Dialog mit Trypho" in *Texte und Untersuchungen*, 1913, p. 53ff., and H. Chadwick in *B.J.R.L.*, 1965, pp. 275–97 conclude that, given critical caution, he can be used as excellent evidence for contemporary Jewish beliefs.

[17] *Dial.* 10.

[18] Acts 8:1.

[19] Acts 9:2.

[20] Revelation 2:9, 10 and 3:9.

[21] *Mart. Polyc.* 12.

[22] The attitude of Caiaphas (John 11:48) must often have been reiterated by responsible Jews in the face of Christian disturbances.

[23] *Pap. Lond.*, 1912. See also his decrees recorded with pride in Josephus, *Antiquities of the Jews* 19.5.2, 3 and compare the edict of Augustus on the same problem nearly fifty years earlier (Josephus, *Ant.* 16.6.2).

[24] *Pap. Lond.*, 1912, lines 98–101.

[25] Suetonius, *Claudius*, 25.

[26] *Ant.* 18.4.1.

[27] The phrase is first met with in Tertullian, but the status was assured from the days of Julius Caesar. See above p. 24.

[28] See below ch. 4 note 4.

[29] *Res Gestae* 20, Suetonius (*Augustus* 30), Ovid (*Fasti* 2.63) and Virgil (*Aen.* 6.716) all emphasize the significance of this.

[30] See Horace, *Odes* 3.6.1ff. The Augustan religious policy was a return to the old attitude of bargaining with the gods, which is well illustrated for the Republican period by Plautus. He represents the man in the street's feelings, and in the *Miles Gloriosus* says humorously, "money spent on religion is always well invested." The other side of the coin appears in the prologue to the *Aulularia*, "After the father died," says a Lar (household god), "I began to see whether his son would, perhaps, show me greater devotion. Instead, he grew more and more careless about my cult. So I repaid him in kind, and he is dead."

[31] *Satires* 12.1ff.

[32] *Satires* 2.149ff.

[33] *Laws*, 10.888.

[34] At least, not officially. Of course, they suffered constantly at the hands of their pagan neighbours.

[35] "The daily ritual of Isis produced an immense effect on the Roman mind. Every day there were two solemn offices, at which white-robed, tonsured priests, with acolytes and assistants of every degree, officiated. The morning litany and sacrifice were an impressive service. The crowd of worshippers thronged the space before the chapel at the early dawn. The priest, ascending by a hidden stair, drew apart the veil of the sanctuary and offered the holy image to their adoration. He then made the round of the altars, reciting the litany and sprinkling holy water from a secret spring." Dill, *Roman Society from Nero to Marcus Aurelius*, p. 577f.

[36] Josephus, *Ant.*, 18.3.4.

[37] The actual decree survives (*C.I.L.* 1.196). Livy (39.8–18) gives a full account and stresses that prejudice to Roman religion was as much the cause of their suppression as was their criminal behaviour.

[38] Suetonius, *Tib.* 36, Dio, 57.15.8.

[39] Suetonius, *Claudius* 25. See the discussion in A. D. Momigliano, *Claudius* p. 92f.

[40] Tacitus, *Hist.* 4.54.
[41] Tacitus, *Ann.* 15.44.
[42] A. N. Sherwin-White's neat translation in *Roman Society and Roman Law in the New Testament*, p. 13. His whole treatment is most illuminating.
[43] Sherwin-White, *op. cit.* p. 14.
[44] The claim of Tertullian (*Ad Nationes* 1.7) and Melito of Sardis (in Eusebius *H. E.* 4.26.5ff.) that from the time of Nero there was an Empire-wide ban on Christianity must be rejected. If there had been, the persecution of Christians would have been less sporadic. Moreover, that well-qualified legal expert, Pliny the Younger, would not have needed to ask the Emperor Trajan what to do about the Christians in A.D. 112, nor would that prince have returned so enigmatic a reply (Pliny, *Epistles* 10.96 and 97). Tertullian's own ignorance in the matter is indicated by the fact that in *Apologet.* 5 he makes the Emperor Tiberius out to be a Christian! Neither Suetonius (*Nero* 16) nor Tacitus (*Ann.* 15.44) indicate that the Neronian attack on the Christians after the Fire of Rome was either continued later or extended beyond Rome. What is clear is that at any time after A.D. 64 there was good imperial precedent for suppressing Christians if the provincial governor concerned chose to adopt it.
[45] Many of the Apologists, it is true, went above the head of the governor, and appealed direct to the Emperor, as the second century progressed. It is difficult to know how far this was a merely literary device, and whether the Apologies were ever read by those to whom they were addressed, or were merely used as propaganda by Christians. In any event, it was with the provincial governor that they would have to deal in the first instance.
[46] *Digesta Juris Romani* 1.16.11. Augustus's Cyrene Edicts of 7 B.C., make this very plain. See Edict 4 lines 65ff. in *Documents illustrating the reigns of Augustus and Tiberius*, ed. Ehrenberg and Jones, p. 132.
[47] Edict 1 lays down the procedure to be followed.
[48] Pliny, *Ep.* 10.97.
[49] Suetonius, *Claudius* 25. "Christos" and "Chrēstos" would be indistinguishable in pronunciation, as in Modern Greek. The early Christians made play with the fancied derivation from "the best people" (*chrēstoi*). See Justin, 1 *Apol.* 4 and Tertullian, *Apologet.* 3: "Even when it is wrongly pronounced by you, 'Chrēstianus' (for you do not even know accurately the name you hate) it comes from 'sweetness and goodness'."
[50] See above, p. 33.
[51] A fragment of Tacitus recorded in Sulpicius Severus, *Chron.* 2.30.6.
[52] Juvenal also appears to confuse Christians (whom he nowhere specifically mentions) with Jews. See *Satires* 14.86ff., on which Gilbert Highet comments, "Juvenal may have been mixing up Christian converts with Jewish proselytes" (*Juvenal the Satirist*, p. 283).
[53] See Tacitus, *Hist.* 5.5, Pliny, *N.H.* 13.4.46. Caecilius, the pagan in Minucius Felix's *Octavius*, asks why Christians should oppose the conclusions of all men and rage against the gods? "They despise the temples as houses of the dead; they reject the gods; they laugh at holy things" (ch. 8). He continues, "Why do they endeavour with such pains to conceal and to cloak whatever they worship, since honourable things always rejoice in publicity, while crimes are kept secret? Why have they no altars, no temples, no acknowledged images? . . . Moreover, whence or who is he, or where is the one God, solitary, desolate, whom no free people, no kingdoms, and not even a Roman *superstitio* have known? The lonely and miserable nation of the Jews worshipped one God, and one peculiar to itself; but they worshipped him openly with temples, altars, victims and with ceremonies; and he has so little force or power that he is enslaved, with his own special nation, to the Roman gods" (ch. 10).
The Christians, who shared the quaint monotheism of the Jews, had none of the redeeming features of being a nation or possessing a visible cult. No wonder they seemed to be most dangerous atheists. See also Athenagoras, *Presb.* 2.7, 9 and 3.12f., and Tertullian, *Apologet.* 10.1, 28.2f., 35.1, 40.1ff.
[54] *Ep.* 10.96.

[55] *promiscuum tamen et innoxium.*

[56] See the whole of the third book of the *Stromateis* of Clement, and Irenaeus *Adv. Haer.* 1.23ff. Typical is the charge in Minucius Felix *Octavius* 9, "Everywhere there is mixed up among them a religion of lust, and they call one another promiscuously brothers and sisters, that even a not unusual debauchery may by the intervention of that sacred name become incestuous; it is thus that their empty and foolish superstition glories in crimes". Similarly Theophilus complains, "You falsely accuse us . . . who are Christians, alleging that the wives of all of us are held in common, and made promiscuous use of; and that we even commit incest with our own sisters, and what is most impious and barbarous of all, that we eat human flesh" (*Ad Autol.* 3.4).

[57] Minucius Felix, *Oct.* 9.

[58] They were, of course, wildly slanderous, though 2 Peter and Jude show that the Agape could get out of hand. Indeed, the nervous regulations in Hippolytus's *Apostolic Tradition* ch. 26 indicated that Christians remained very sensitive to such charges.

[59] On Tacitus's *odio humani generis conjuncti* (*Ann.* 15.44) Ramsay commented, "To the Romans *genus humanum* meant not the human race in general but the Roman world, men who lived according to Roman manners and laws; the rest were enemies and barbarians. The Christians, then, were enemies to civilized man, and to the customs and laws which regulated civilized society . . . They introduced divisions into families and set children against their parents." (*The Church in the Roman Empire*, p. 236.)

[60] *The Christian in Pagan Society*, p. 6f.

[61] Acts 24:5.

[62] *Protagoras*, 322D.

[63] Revelation 13:16f., and see E. Stauffer's perceptive if one-sided essay on "Domitian and John" in *Christ and the Caesars*, p. 147–91.

[64] *Apologet.* 42.

[65] It is notoriously difficult to separate rhetoric from fact in Christian, as in other apologetic. The problem occurs in another shape on p. 45, where Justin, in no less purple a passage, stresses the "otherness" of the Christians. No doubt the truth lay somewhere in between, and differed with different individuals and communities. Tertullian's main point here is that Christians have not contracted out of the Empire, and that remained true, although the extent of their active involvement varied greatly.

[66] *Ad. Uxorem* 2.6 and 5.

[67] *Op cit.* p. 266–78.

[68] See the definitive work of L. R. Taylor, *The Divinity of the Roman Emperor.*

[69] Even Verres, one of the most shameless sharks who ever preyed as proconsul on a Roman province, was hailed as "Saviour" (Cicero, *In Verrem Act.* 2.2.63).

[70] *The Romans*, ed. J. P. V. D. Balsdon, p. 200f.

[71] Seneca wrote a savage parody of the divinization of Claudius in the *Apocolocyntosis*, and the dying Emperor Vespasian joked, "*Vae, puto deus fio!*" (Alas, I suppose I am becoming a god!) See Suetonius, *Vesp.* 23.

[72] The denarius of Tiberius's reign which Jesus used to make this famous distinction between the realms of God and Caesar, a separation which cut at the fundamental conception of the state in the ancient world, would have read *TIberius CAESAR DIVI AUGusti Filius AUGUSTUS Pontifex Maximus.* Christology developed, to some extent, by conscious contradistinction to the claims of coinage such as this.

[73] I Peter 2:17, Romans 13:7.

[74] "*Neque enim dubitabam, qualecunque esset quod faterentur, pertinaciam certe et inflexibilem obstinationem debere puniri.*" Naturally therefore, "*perseverantes duci jussi*" (Pliny, *Ep.* 10.96).

[75] "But further, they say that our doctrine has but recently come to light" (Theophilus, *Ad Autol.* 3.4).

[76] See Justin, *1 Apol.* 31ff., 59.

[77] Justin, *2 Apol.* 13, "Whatever things were rightly said among all men are the property of the Christians." Similarly Origen, *Contra Celsum* 1.4, 5.

[78] Compare the graffito (p. 174 below) of a youth worshipping a crucified ass's head, with the inscription, "Alexamenos worships (his) God" (See O. Marruchi, *Eléments d'archéologie chrétienne* 1. p. 38) and the charge in Minucius Felix, "I hear that they adore the head of an ass, that basest of creatures—a worthy and appropriate religion for such manners. Some say that they worship the virilia of their priest . . ." (*Oct.* 9).

[79] The early Church did not tire of quoting 1 Corinthians 1:19f., 26f. The reaction against pagan culture is strong in Tertullian and Tatian. Celsus in the mid-second century asserted that Christians cried, "Do not examine, but believe", "Your faith will save you", and "The wisdom of this life is evil, but foolishness is a good thing" (Origen, *Contra Celsum* 1.9).

[80] 1 Corinthians 1:26.

[81] Origen, *Contra Celsum* 6.14, 3.18, 3.44.

[82] Romans 16:10f. See below, p. 212.

[83] See below, chapter 6.

[84] *1 Apol.* 14. The point is reiterated in the subsequent chapter.

[85] Romans 1:32.

[86] The evidence for these clubs is almost entirely epigraphic, as they were not used by the aristocratic writers whose works have come down to us. Cf. *e.g. I.L.S.* 2215, 3360 and E. G. Hardy, *Studies in Roman History*, vol. 1 on Christianity and the *collegia*. See also E. A. Judge, *The Social Pattern of Christian Groups in the First Century*, ch. 4, and A. De Marchi, *Il culto privato di Roma antica*, esp. p. 162, also W. L. Westermann, *The Slave Systems of Greek and Roman Antiquity*, esp. p. 108, 144f.

[87] Pliny, *Ep.* 10.92 and 93.

[88] Acts 18 and 19.

[89] Pliny, *Ep.* 10.33, 34.

[90] Pliny, *Ep.* 10.96, "*quod ipsum facere desiisse post edictum meum, quo secundum mandata tua hetaerias esse vetueram.*"

[91] One of the second century Oxyrhyncus Papyri (3.523) reads, "Antonius, son of Ptolemaeus, invites you to dine with him at the table of the Lord Serapis". Cf. 1 Corinthians 8:10.

[92] Juvenal had asked sourly, "At what temple does a prostitute not sit?" (*Satires* 9.24).

[93] Revelation 2 and 3.

[94] The fact that they constantly preached the end of the world in fire and judgment (*e.g.* 2 Thessalonians 1:8, 2 Peter 3:10–14, and throughout the second century) was hardly calculated to endear them either to the populace or the authorities. It gave some plausibility to Nero's suspicion that they were incendiaries: hence his vicious punishment of them after the Great Fire in A.D. 64. In a most interesting article on Tacitus, *Ann.* 15.44 where the accusation, arrest and execution of the Christians is recorded, K. F. C. Rose (*Classical Quarterly*, 1960, p. 195) suggests that the Christian community was already large enough to attract the attention of the Imperial police; that Nero had planted informers among them, and that Tacitus's much discussed phrase "*correpti qui fatebantur*" refers to them. The stool-pigeons were rounded up first, then "*indicio eorum ingens multitudo*" of genuine Christians, whose names the informers had discovered. This, moreover, would be fully in line with Nero's known practice on another occasion (*Ann.* 16.17).

CHAPTER 3

[1] See C. F. D. Moule, *The Phenomenon of the New Testament*, ch. 1, for the contention that the resurrection itself lies at the heart of the Christian movement, as the sole validation of her claims for and beliefs in Jesus. His introduction to *The Significance of the Message of the Resurrection for Faith in Jesus Christ*

has an importance out of all proportion to its length on the historicity of the resurrection event.

² The central importance of this term, is recognized by B. Rigaux. "*Euaggelion* est le premier terme, et sans doute le plus characteristique du message" (*Les Épîtres aux Thessaloniens*, p. 158).

³ The term was applied by Irenaeus to the gospel as a book (*Adv. Haer.* 3.1), and Eusebius laid great stress on the identity of the written and the preached gospel (*H.E.* 3.37.2).

⁴ Luke 4:17–21.

⁵ Romans 1:4.

⁶ 4 Maccabees 17:22.

⁷ Mark 6:14.

⁸ Mark 5:33ff., Luke 7:11ff., 22, John 11:43ff.

⁹ 1 Corinthians 15:4. See E. Schweizer in *Current Issues in New Testament Interpretation*, ed. Klassen and Snyder, p. 168.

¹⁰ Isaiah 53:12, Daniel 7:14, 2 Samuel 7:1–16. On the Nathan prophecy see O. Betz, *What do we know about Jesus?*, p. 88ff., 100f.

¹¹ Luke 3:18.

¹² Luke 3:3, 4, 16–18.

¹³ Mark 1:1.

¹⁴ Mark 1:14.

¹⁵ Luke 7:22.

¹⁶ See Isaiah 65:17ff., Isaiah 52:7 ("How beautiful upon the mountains are the feet of him who brings good tidings, who publishes peace, who brings good tidings of salvation"—a verse which is taken up and applied to the Christian gospel in Romans 10:15, and is made much of by Origen in his fascinating examination of the nature of the gospel in his *Comm. in Johann.* i., 4–11).

¹⁷ Ephesians 2:17.

¹⁸ Luke 2:10.

¹⁹ *e.g.* Acts 14:7.

²⁰ *e.g.* Romans 1:15.

²¹ *e.g.* Acts 14:21.

²² 1 Corinthians 15:1, 2 Corinthians 11:7, Galatians 1:8, 11.

²³ Galatians 1:23.

²⁴ Acts 8:12.

²⁵ Acts 17:7.

²⁶ *Comm. in Matt.* 14:7.

²⁷ Acts 13:32ff. quoting Psalm 2:7, Isaiah 55:3, Psalm 16:10.

²⁸ Acts 10:36.

²⁹ Acts 11:20.

³⁰ 1 Corinthians 15:2, 3.

³¹ Acts 17:18, 1 Corinthians 15:4.

³² Acts 8:35.

³³ Acts 8:4, 15:35.

³⁴ The following quotations are taken from chs. 5–15 of Origen's *Comm. in Johann.*, book 1.

³⁵ Acts 15:7, 20:24.

³⁶ In the LXX the noun comes only a handful of times, and always in the plural. Friedrich, in the Kittel *Wörterbuch* s.v. *euaggelion*, makes great play with this fact, but fails to notice the passage in *Ps. Sol.* 11:1, which gives the word in the singular, indicating the Messianic good news, and alluding to the passage in Isaiah 61:1 which proved so important fifty years later in Christian writing. Curiously enough, there is another allusion in the verse to a further Old Testament chapter which was to be of great significance to Christians in showing that the day of the Lord had already arrived, Joel ch. 2. *Ps. Sol.* 11.1 reads

"Blow ye in Zion on the trumpet to summon the saints,
Cause ye to be heard in Jerusalem the voice of him that bringeth good tidings:
For God hath had pity on Israel in visiting them."

As we shall see below with regard to Qumran, p. 84ff., it was much the same areas of the Old Testament that excited the hopes of various groups in Judaism as they waited for the days of salvation; and these areas were taken over by the Christians and explained with great conviction as applying to Jesus.

[37] Mark 1:14, 13:10.

[38] Mark 1:15.

[39] Mark 1:14f.

[40] Mark 1:1.

[41] Mark 8:35, 10:29 and 14:9.

[42] Stemming from Papias in Eusebius, *H.E.* 3.39, also Irenaeus *Adv. Haer.* 3. 1 and Clement of Alexandria in Eusebius *H.E.* 6.14, etc.

[43] This is not the place to go into the extremely complex and largely subjective task of attempting to ascertain the validity of particular *logia* in Mark, and assess whether or not they go back to Jesus. For our purposes, anything Mark wrote (*c.* A.D. 65) is evidence of early Christian beliefs, quite independent of the question who was the original speaker.

[44] Mark 1:1.

[45] Whether or not Mark intended to end his Gospel at this point (16:8) is highly debatable.

[46] Mark 14:8, 9.

[47] Mark 13:10.

[48] See the careful discussion in J. Jeremias, *Jesus' Promise to the Nations.*

[49] See, *e.g.* Matthew 10:5, 15:26, John 12:20–33.

[50] Matthew 8:11, Luke 13:29 and Isaiah 49:6, etc.

[51] The anonymous author (unless a note preserved by a tenth century M.S. is right in assigning it to Aristion, presumably the Aristion to whom Papias refers as an apostolic man, Eusebius, *H.E.* 3.39.15) of the longest of the three continuations to the Gospel of Mark: it was clearly regarded as unfinished in antiquity, and various attempts were made to round off its sudden ending at 16:8.

[52] Mark 1:15, 8:35.

[53] 2 Corinthians 11:7.

[54] Ephesians 6:19.

[55] 1 Corinthians 9:14.

[56] 1 Thessalonians 2:2.

[57] 1 Corinthians 15:1.

[58] Galatians 2:2.

[59] Colossians 1:23.

[60] 2 Corinthians 11:4.

[61] Galatians 1:12, 1 Corinthians 15:1.

[62] Romans 1:1, 1 Thessalonians 2:2, 8, 9.

[63] 1 Thessalonians 2:9, 12; 1 Corinthians 4:15, 20; Colossians 1:13, 23; 2 Thessalonians 1:5, 8.

[64] 2 Corinthians 2:12, 9:13, 10:14, etc. These are unlikely all to be possessive genitives.

[65] 1 Corinthians 15:3, etc.

[66] 1 Corinthians 15:4, Romans 1:4, 2 Timothy 2:8.

[67] Galatians 2:7, 8, Romans 1:16.

[68] Romans 1:16, 15:19.

[69] Romans 15:16, Galatians 2:7.

[70] See William Baird's useful discussion of this point in "What is the kerygma?" *J.B.L.* 1957, pp. 181–91, also F. F. Bruce, "Paul and Jerusalem" in the *Tyndale Bulletin*, 1968, pp. 3–15.

[71] 1 Thessalonians 1:5, 9, Romans 1:16, 3:22, etc.

[72] 1 Corinthians 9:1, 11, 14, 18, 23, Philippians 2.22, 2 Timothy 1:8.

[73] Philippians 1:5.

[74] Philippians 1:27, 4:3.

[75] 1 Corinthians 15:1ff.

[76] Mark 1:2ff.

[77] Romans 2:16, 10:16, 21, 2 Thessalonians 1:8.

[78] I Peter 4:17, Revelation 14:6 (for a quaint explanation of this verse, see Origen, *Comm. in Joann.* 1:14).

[79] See below p. 246ff.

[80] Mark 8:35f., cf. 16:16.

[81] Romans 1:16, I Thessalonians 1:5f.

[82] Notably in Romans and Galatians. See J. Jeremias, "Paul and James" *Expository Times* 1954, p. 368ff.

[83] Colossians 1:5, 23, I Thessalonians 1:5f., 2 Timothy 1:8, I Timothy 1:11.

[84] Ephesians 6:19, I Corinthians 2:4–6.

[85] 2 Corinthians 9:13f.

[86] Philippians 1:27.

[87] Plutarch, *Demet.* 17.

[88] The earliest example is Homer *Od.* 14.152f., where *euaggelion* means "reward for good news". See also Aristophanes, *Eq.* 656, *euaggelia thuein* for "to celebrate good news by sacrifice".

[89] Plutarch, *Sertorius*, 11.

[90] See Plutarch, *De Fortuna Romanorum*, 6.

[91] This dates from 9 B.C. Text in Dittenberger, *Orientis Graeci Inscriptiones Selectae*, no. 458, line 40f.

[92] See the text and discussion in *American Journal of Archaeology*, 1914, p. 323.

[93] See A. Deissman, *Light from the Ancient East*, p. 371.

[94] Justin comments acidly on this: "And what of the emperors who die among yourselves whom you deem worthy of deification, and in whose behalf you produce someone who swears he has seen the burning Caesar rise to heaven from the funeral pyre?" (I *Apol.* 21).

[95] Article *euaggelion* in Kittel's *Wörterbuch* (E.T.) vol. 3, p. 725.

[96] Article *euaggelizomai* in Kittel's *Wörterbuch* (E.T.) vol. 3, p. 709f.

[97] See Friedrich for references and further examples, *op. cit.* p. 715f.

[98] Although it occurs (rarely) in the LXX and Jewish writings, where the verb is less infrequent but is used to translate a variety of Hebrew roots, *kērux* is essentially a Greek term. We meet the herald at the dawn of Greek literature, in Homer, where he plays a most important role. Heralds in the Homeric age were "godlike men" (*Il.* 3.268, 12.343, etc.) who possessed regal dignity (*Il.* 2.277, *Od.* 2.38) and yet performed menial tasks as servants of their princes — preparing meals and serving guests (*Il.* 18.558, *Od.* 1.143f.). Later on their status declined, but heralds continued inviolable diplomatic figures as in Homer, and continued to play a part in cultic life, prayer, sacrifice, reconciliation (see *Inscriptiones Graecae*, 12. 5,647, 14). Most interesting of all from our point of view, heralds were thought of as in some way inheriting the role of Hermes as messengers of the gods: the philosophers, accordingly, were quick to call themselves heralds and to think of themselves as purveying divine revelation (Philostratus *Vit. Soph.* 2.33, 4; Epictetus, *Diss.* 3.1.36f.). Set apart from the ties of home, possessions and family (Epictetus, *Diss.* 3.22, 46ff.) they offered a peace which was supposed to surpass the *pax Romana* (Epictetus, *Diss.* 3.13.9f.). It is easy to see the parallels with Christian missionaries: it is easy, too, to see why Paul was anxious not to be confused with teachers of this type (I Thessalonians 2.3ff.).

[99] Matthew 12:41, Luke 11:32.

[100] See note 98 above.

[101] I Corinthians 1:21.

[102] I Corinthians 2:4.

[103] Titus 1:3, 2 Timothy 4:17.

[104] 2 Timothy 4:17.

[105] Romans 2:21.

[106] See above, p. 49ff. Indeed, Isaiah 61:1 itself combined concepts which had long proved important in Israel, namely the themes from Psalm 107:20 and Isaiah 52:7. This linkage of ideas is a characteristic of rabbinic exegesis (see J. W. Doeve, *Jewish Hermeneutics*, p. 89) and greatly influenced the emerging

Christian movement. Isaiah 61:1 with its multiple themes, provided the Christians with important lines of self-understanding, and was in fact widely used (Matthew 5:4, 11:5=Luke 7:22, Acts 10:38 as well as Luke 4:18f.).

[107] *Op cit.* p. 706f.

[108] So A. M. Hunter, *The Message of the New Testament, The Unity of the New Testament*, J. N. Sanders, *The Foundations of the Christian Faith*, F. V. Filson, *Three Crucial Decades*, C. S. C. Williams and F. F. Bruce in their commentaries on the Acts of the Apostles. Continental writers, too, such as O. Cullmann, O. Bauerfiend, E. Stauffer, M. Goguel and L. Cerfaux accept the theory in broad outline.

[109] See also his *Aufsätze zur Apostelgeschichte*. Dibelius, unlike Dodd, thought that the sermons were Lucan compositions, but that he availed himself of forms of gospel preaching which were, none the less, very old. Like A. Seeberg (*Der Katechismus der Urchristenheit*), to whom he was much indebted, Dibelius believed Luke to be following a traditional scheme which could be detected both in 1 Corinthians 15:1ff. and in the Gospels.

[110] A. M. Hunter, *The Message of the New Testament*, p. 29f.; C. T. Craig, *Journal of Biblical Literature*, 1952, p. 182.

[111] F. V. Filson, *Jesus Christ the Risen Lord*, p. 41ff.; T. F. Glasson, *Hibbert Journal*, 1953, p. 129ff.

[112] B. Gärtner, *The Aeropagus Speech and Natural Revelation*, p. 26ff.

[113] *Die urapostolische Heilsverkündigung nach der Apostelgeschichte*.

[114] *The New Testament in Historical and Contemporary Perspective*, ed. Anderson and Barclay, p. 1ff.

[115] *e.g. The Theology of the New Testament*, 1. p. 307, *Kerygma and Myth* (ed. Bartsch and Fuller), p. 111.

[116] *Die Missionsreden der Apostelgeschichte* and *Z.N.T.W.*, 1958, p. 223ff.

[117] *The Theology of St Luke,* and in *Studies in Luke–Acts* (ed. Keck and Martyn), p. 217ff.

[118] His approach is well represented in his *Essays on New Testament Themes*. E. Haenchen in *Die Apostelgeschichte* also adopts much the same approach.

[119] W. Baird, "What is the Kerygma?" in *J.B.L.*, 1957, p. 191.

[120] *The Background of the New Testament and its Eschatology* (ed. Daube and Davies), p. 320.

[121] *Op. cit.*, p. 168.

[122] *Australian Biblical Review*, December 1967.

[123] Schweizer defends himself against sinister interpretation of this term by pointing out that this is parallel to the royal adoption met with in the enthronement psalms (*e.g.* Psalm 2). Moreover it is not formulated in contrast to any other doctrine (*viz.* that Jesus was merely man before Easter). Rather, it asserts that the magnitude of the Resurrection and its implications overshadows all else. Furthermore, Hebrew man would be interested not so much in the nature as in the function of Jesus. And since Easter his function was to be Son of God in fulfilment of the Nathan prophecy.

[124] *Carmen Christi*, p. 287–311.

[125] W. J. Hollenweger, "Johannes Christian Hoekendijk: Pluriformität der Kirche" in *Separatdruck aus "Reformatio"*, X (1967).

[126] See his illuminating treatment in *Jesus and the Christian*, p. 199ff.

[127] Eusebius *H.E.* 3.39.

[128] In an important doctoral thesis forthcoming in print, *The Primitive Preaching and Jesus of Nazareth*, Graham Stanton has effectively demolished the view of Ulrich Wilckens in the *Z.N.T.W.* article referred to above, that the *historia Jesu* had no place in the preaching of the kerygma. As soon as the disciples passed beyond the areas of Galilee and Jerusalem where Jesus was well known, they would inevitably have had to answer the question, "Who is your Jesus? What was he like? What has he done?" It would have been absolutely impossible to preach the gospel effectively without including an answer to these very legitimate questions. The answer must surely have included material remarkably similar to the *pericopae* of the Gospels!

¹²⁹ I am grateful to Professor Henry Chadwick for directing my attention to this most interesting man. His doctrinal imprecision is matched by an evangelistic zeal which runs right through his *Homilies*. His emphasis is not very much on the sacraments: Jesus is indeed the Vine and the Bread of life to him, but not in a eucharistic context. Baptism does not ensure salvation: "All the worldly people dwelling within the pale of the Church; are their hearts spotless or pure? Do we not find that many sins are committed after baptism, and many live in sin?" (*Hom.* 15). His whole concern is Christocentric and evangelistic. Not for him the doctrinal arguments and cataclysmic church struggles that rent the fourth century. He wanted to see changed lives. "It is one thing to give descriptive accounts with a certain head knowledge and correct notions, and quite another in substance and reality, in full experience and in the inward man and the mind, to possess the treasure and the grace and taste the effectual working of the Holy Spirit." (*Hom.* 27). The *Sitz im Leben* of this sort of material must have been the market place and not the desert in the first instance. It is difficult to resist the conclusion that he was reflecting a pious individualistic type of evangelistic preaching which has never died out in Christendom but whose practitioners rarely reach official distinction in the Church. It is, accordingly, all too easy to lose in the surviving documents, all track of this type of warm-hearted direct evangelism. We are fortunate therefore that these *Homilies* of Macarius give us some fine examples of it.

¹³⁰ Macarius, *Homilies* 20.

¹³¹ So U. Wilckens, *Die Missionsreden*, p. 32–55, E. Schweizer, "Concerning the Speeches in Acts" in *Studies in Luke–Acts* (ed. Keck and Martyn), p. 208ff.

¹³² So C. F. Evans, "The Kerygma" in *J.T.S.* 1956, pp 25–41 and many others.

¹³³ "As for the speeches made by various persons either on the eve of the war, or during its actual course, it was difficult for me to remember exactly the words which I myself heard, as also for those who reported other speeches to me. But I have recorded them in accordance with my opinion of what the various speakers would have had to say in view of the circumstances at the time, keeping as closely as possible to the general gist of what was really said." (Thucydides, *Hist.* 1.22).

¹³⁴ It must be remembered that Thucydides was a participant in the Peloponnesian War which he describes with such accuracy and artistry. His standards of precision were so high, moreover, that he declined to write about some far-off event of the past, because he regarded past history as beyond the possibility of verification. That is why he chose a theme which was contemporary and in which he was personally implicated. Perhaps Luke did the same! See T. F. Glasson, "The Speeches in Acts and Thucydides", *Expository Times*, 1965, p. 165.

¹³⁵ *On Writing History*, 39 "The one task of the historian is to describe things exactly as they happened."

¹³⁶ Thucydides 1.22. He did not, however, for that reason feel free to "create" events which would make salutory reading. See F. Adcock, *Thucydides and his History*, pp. 27–42.

¹³⁷ See the Preface of his *History* where he makes it plain that he writes in the interest of national glory and morality, and is therefore not particular in distinguishing fact from fable.

¹³⁸ This was very understandable. When Cicero advanced this theme in Book Two of his *De Oratore* he was merely echoing a long line of Hellenistic historiographers between the days of Thucydides and Polybius. After the death of Thucydides, prose writing developed in three main areas: dull chronicling (practised by the lesser followers of Xenophon), oratory and philosophy. The rise of literary criticism placed a greater emphasis on style than accuracy, and history became a largely rhetorical exercise in the hands of the Peripatetics. Truth was subordinated to the purpose of creating more sophisticated prose than one's predecessors. After all, had not Herodotus, the "father of history" (Cicero, *De Leg.* 1.1.5) derived his art from the poets, and supremely Homer?

Such was his own admission (Herodotus 2.53, 2.116f., 4.32). Who could blame those who took a leaf out of his book ? It was Polybius who set historical writing back on the path of critical concern for truth which Thucydides had blazed, and he did much to discredit the Hellenistic school of orator-historians. His offensive against Timaeus of Tauromenium, the worst offender, makes powerful reading (*Hist.* 12.25k–26a). His own integrity influenced other (Latin) writers, notably Sallust, and a century later Tacitus, then Lucian and Arrian.

[139] See the judicious article "Historical Reporting in the Ancient World" by A. W. Mosley in *N.T.S.* 1965, pp. 10–26.

[140] Several shorthand manuals have come down to us. See E. G. Turner, *Greek Papyri*, p. 142.

[141] See the powerful case made by B. Gerhardsson, *Memory and Manuscript*, stressing the place of memory in Hebrew teaching and the rabbinic background which underlies so much of the New Testament.

[142] *J.T.S.*, 1956, pp. 25–41.

[143] See E. G. Selwyn, *The First Epistle of St Peter*, p. 33ff. and my *The Meaning of Salvation*, ch. 8, "Salvation in the Early Preaching".

[144] Acts 13:39, 20:28.

[145] *Die Missionsreden*, pp. 55–71.

[146] See his *Documents of the Primitive Church* and *Composition and Date of Acts*.

[147] *e.g.* M. Black, *An Aramaic Approach to the Gospels and Acts*.

[148] *J.T.S.*, 1950, pp. 16–28, "The Semitisms of Acts", where he argues that the Hebrew background is not due to Aramaisms but to the influence of Septuagintal Greek.

[149] M. Wilcox, *The Semitisms of Acts* who modifies Torrey's position and rejects that of Sparks.

[150] "Statistical Evidence of Aramaic Sources in Acts 1–15", *N.T.S.*, 1964, pp. 38–59.

[151] 2:22; 3:22, 7:37; 3:14; 3:15, 5:31. See E. Schweizer, *Erniedrigung und Erhöhung bei Jesus und seinen Nachfolgern*, p. 54.

[152] 3:20.

[153] See the assessments of this in J. C. O'Neill, *The Theology of Acts*, C. K. Barrett, *Luke the Historian in Recent Study* and Hans Conzelmann, *The Theology of St Luke*.

[154] "Die Bezeichnung Jesu als Knecht Gottes und ihre Geschichte in der Alten Kirche" in *Sitzungberichte der Preuss. Akad. der Wiss. zu Berlin*, 1926, pp. 212–38.

[155] *The Christology of the New Testament*, chapter 3.

[156] Jeremias in Zimmerli and Jeremias, *The Servant of God*. Dr M. D. Hooker's attempt to unsettle this conclusion in *Jesus and the Servant* is unconvincing. I find it intriguing that she, who can find no room for a Suffering Servant in the teaching of Jesus, should contend so valiantly for a suffering Son of Man in *The Son of Man in Mark*.

[157] *Op. cit.*, pp. 155–78.

[158] *Revue Biblique*, 1962, p. 50ff.

[159] in *According to the Scriptures*.

[160] Indeed it has been strengthened. See J. Dupont, *Études sur les Actes des Apôtres*, p. 271ff.

[161] 2 Timothy 1:13.

[162] Bo Reicke, in *The Root of the Vine* (ed. A. Fridrichsen) pp. 138–43, stresses well the variety and homogeneity of the earliest evangelistic preaching.

[163] Cf. Acts 13:22, 15:8, Romans 3:21, Hebrews 7:8, 17.

[164] Isaiah 43:10–12.

[165] Isaiah 44:8.

[166] Although the actual "witness" root is not mentioned in any of the Servant Songs, the idea is certainly prominent.

[167] The Epistle to the Hebrews often speaks of the witness of Scripture (*e.g.* 11:2, 4, 5) but uses the word in something approaching this specialized sense of

testimony to others about Christ only once, in 12.1. But even here the word has a different nuance, loyalty rather than personal testimony to Jesus being the main point.

[168] 1 Timothy 6.13.

[169] This is the only place in his Gospel where Luke uses the word in its specialized sense; needless to say it comes very frequently in Acts.

[170] Acts 1:8.

[171] Acts 1:6ff.

[172] "*My* witnesses", Acts 1:8.

[173] Acts 22:15, 26:16.

[174] Acts 10:39, 5:32f., 1:22, 2:32, 3:15.

[175] Acts 5:31f.

[176] Acts 10:39 and 41 are significant in this regard. Both the actions of the incarnate Jesus and his post-resurrection life are included in the witness which the Christians bear: the "bridge" function of the eye-witness generation could hardly be brought out more emphatically.

[177] Acts 22:20 cf. 7:56.

[178] Acts 22:15, 26:16.

[179] Not only in Germany. D. E. Nineham asserts, without a shred of evidence, "historical curiosity as such was something in which the early Church was conspicuously lacking" (*Studies in the Gospels*, ed. D. E. Nineham, p. 223f.).

[180] See his article referred to above, in *Z.N.T.W. XLIX* (1958).

[181] In his Cambridge Ph.D. thesis, *The Primitive Preaching and Jesus of Nazareth*. See n. 128 above.

[182] See also F. V. Filson, "The Christian Teacher in the First Century", *J.B.L.*, 1941, pp. 317–28. He argues for the existence of a brief outline such as Acts 10:37–43 which would be needed to show who Jesus was and why he was significant.

[183] In the writings of Luke it is the crucified and risen Christ who gives forgiveness.

[184] *e.g.* 3:19, where the *hina* stresses that without repentance there can be no pardon: 10:42, 17:31.

[185] *e.g.* 2:23, 3:13.

[186] 2:21, 9:27, 5:30f.

[187] 2:23, 3:18.

[188] 2:36, 38; 3:18, 19; 5:30, 31.

[189] 8:32f., 3:13, 26, 4:27–30.

[190] 20:28.

[191] Acts 5:30, 10:39, 13:29. Nowhere in extra-biblical Greek is *xulon* (lit. "wood") used for a cross: this makes it virtually certain that the reference is to the LXX of Deuteronomy 21:22.

[192] See further Galatians 3:10, 13 and p. 31 above. It is perhaps also noteworthy that it is the crucified and risen Christ who is the source of all man's blessings, *i.e.* the Holy Spirit (2:33), justification (13:39), peace (10:36), the inheritance (20:32), the new covenant (3:19–26) which we receive when we repent and believe (16:30, 2:38).

[193] If we ask why Luke did not make more explicit the relation between the cross of Christ and the forgiveness of sinners, at least part of the answer may lie in his emphasis on the *imitatio Christi* theme. Christian suffering is suffering with Jesus (Acts 9:4f.); the death of Jesus is deliberately depicted as parallel to that of his faithful martyr, Stephen; suffering is the path to glory for Master and disciple alike (Acts 14:22, cf. Luke 12:1–12). This stress on the similarity between Christ's death and ours would make it hard for Luke to emphasize the dissimilarity involved in his atoning death, even supposing that he had grasped the import of it as clearly as St Paul, which is most unlikely.

[194] John 17:3.

[195] John 1:7, 8, 15, 19, 32, 34; 3:26.

[196] This does not exclude the possibility of a polemical thrust in St John's Gospel. There were Baptist disciples in Ephesus (Acts 19:1ff.), and there is

evidence that some Jews regarded him as the Messiah. It was important, accordingly, for the evangelist to remind his readers that John the Baptist ranked among the witnesses to Jesus.

[197] 3:11, 32, 33; 8:13f.; 18:37.

[198] 8:17.

[199] 5:32, 36f., 8:18, etc.

[200] 7:16, 17; 8:42–7.

[201] 5:36, 9:4, 10:25.

[202] 2:22, 5:39, 8:33–58; 19:24, 28, 36, 20:9.

[203] 15:26, 16:13, cf. I John 5:10.

[204] *e.g.* 4:39–42, cf. I John 5:9, 10.

[205] 21:24.

[206] 20:31.

[207] This is brought out in any good commentary: see, for instance, C. K. Barrett, *The Gospel according to St John.*

[208] 1:1, 15, 34; I John 4:14.

[209] 14:6, 8:12, 1:1.

[210] 4:42.

[211] 1:29–34 and the whole account of the Passion.

[212] 1:33, 15:26.

[213] 1:1–14.

[214] 19:35.

[215] 21:24.

[216] 20:29.

[217] 11:40, 14:8ff., 20:29.

[218] I John 5:10.

[219] But so central is it that it enables the Christian message to be called simply "the witness to Jesus" (Revelation 1:1, 2, 9, 12:11, 17). Because faithfulness to Jesus in witness bearing may well lead to death in a world which loves neither him nor his followers, we find the later use of *martus* in the sense "martyr" beginning to make its appearance in the Book of Revelation (2:13, 12:11f., 6:9).

[220] This was also connected integrally with the *martureō–martus* group of words as W. C. van Unnik has shown so convincingly in his article, "The Book of Acts, the Confirmation of the Gospel" in *Novum Testamentum* 1960, pp. 26–59. On St Luke's answer to the question, "How can I be sure?" see my *The Meaning of Salvation*, pp. 125–31.

[221] See his "Eschatology in I Peter" in *The Background of the New Testament and its Eschatology* (ed. Daube and Davies), p. 395.

[222] Though very frequent in the New Testament, and occasionally used for "chattering the good news" it does not have any of the specific content of the three word roots we have been considering.

[223] This is a fairly colourless word, devoid of Old Testament background, which is used eleven times in Acts and seven in Paul's writings for announcing the good news of the gospel, of Jesus, or the Word of God.

[224] "The United Character of the New Testament" in *The New Testament in Historical and Contemporary Perspective*, ed. H. Anderson and W. Barclay, p. 1ff.

[225] In *The Unity of the New Testament, Paul and his Predecessors*, and *The Message of the New Testament.*

CHAPTER 4

[1] *The Fall of Jerusalem and the Christian Church.*

[2] *The Enigma of the Fourth Gospel.*

[3] *The History of Jewish Christianity, The Passover Plot* and *Those Incredible Christians.*

[4] The *Birkath-ha-minim* "heretic benediction" seems to have been directed against Jewish Christians. It required the loyal Jew to include in his prayers a

petition which ran somewhat as follows (it has been much revised, and the original form is conjectural): "Let there be no hope for the renegades, and may the arrogant kingdom soon be rooted out in our days, and the Nazarenes and the *minim* perish as in a moment, and be blotted out from the Book of Life, and may they not be inscribed with the righteous. Blessed art thou, O Lord, who humblest the arrogant." See *b. Berakoth* 28b and Justin, *Dial.* 16, and 96, and Epiphanius, *Haer.* 29.9.

⁵ Acts 14:15–17.
⁶ Mark 8:31, 9:11, 13:10.
⁷ Matthew 1:22, 2:15, 17, 23, etc. Matthew is presenting Jesus as the embodiment of ancient Israel, and his work as the antitype of earlier redemptive history. See R. H. Gundry, *The Use of the Old Testament in St Matthew's Gospel.*
⁸ Luke 4:21.
⁹ Luke 24:44.
¹⁰ John 19 and 20:9.
¹¹ John 13:18, 17:12, 18:9.
¹² John 5:39, 10:35f.
¹³ *Comm. in Joann.,* 1.14.
¹⁴ *Mysterium Christi,* p. 70f.
¹⁵ Acts 2:16. Peter adopts the fulfilment *pesher* type of exegesis familiar to us from the *Habakkuk Commentary* at Qumran. "The 'this is that' *pesher* motif, as contrasted with the 'this has relevance to that' theme of the rabbis well characterizes the distinctive treatment of Scripture by the early Jewish Christians," writes R. N. Longenecker in his 1969 Tyndale Lecture, "Can we reproduce the exegesis of the New Testament?", p. 26.
¹⁶ *The Apostolic Preaching and its Developments,* p. 38.
¹⁷ See Acts chs. 2, 4, 10, 8, 26, 28.
¹⁸ *Dial.* 1–8.
¹⁹ *Dial.* 8.
²⁰ Luke 24:26f.
²¹ Acts 6:10.
²² Acts 9:22.
²³ Acts 18:28.
²⁴ Acts 17:11.
²⁵ Acts 13:44, 28.23ff.
²⁶ *Dial.* 142.
²⁷ Origen, *Contra Celsum,* 1:55.
²⁸ *According to the Scriptures,* p. 110.
²⁹ Origen, *Contra Celsum,* 1.51.
³⁰ 4Q *Testimonia.*
³¹ He does not appear elsewhere in the Qumran writings.
³² See J. T. Milik, *Ten Years of Discovery in the Wilderness of Judaea,* p. 126.
³³ But the term "anointed" or "Messiah", although more specific than in the Old Testament, does not approximate in the Scrolls to the personal precision it acquires in the New Testament.
³⁴ Milik, *op. cit.,* p. 124. See Ezekiel 34:24, 37:25.
³⁵ Cf. Isaiah 11:1.
³⁶ Cf. *Test. Judah* 21:2: "To me God has given kingship, to him (Levi) priesthood; and he has subordinated the kingship to the priesthood".
³⁷ The speculation about two anointed ones or Messiahs goes back to Zerubbabel and Joshua (Hag. 1:12ff., Zechariah 4:14). It reappears in *Test. Reuben* 6.7–12, *Test. Sim.* 7.2, *Test. Levi* 2.11, 8.11ff., *Test. Dan.* 5.10, etc.
³⁸ *J.B.L.,* 1956, pp. 174–87.
³⁹ 1 *Apol.* 32, 54, *Dial.* 52–4, 120.
⁴⁰ See O. Betz, *What do we know about Jesus?* p. 88ff., 100f.
⁴¹ On the complicated issue of the Messianic beliefs of Qumran, see A. R. C. Leaney, *The Rule of Qumran and its Meaning,* p. 225ff., G. R. Driver, *The Judaean Scrolls,* pp. 462–86, J. F. Priest, *J.B.L.,* 1962, p. 55f., J. T. Milik, *op. cit.,* pp. 123–28, M. Black, *The Scrolls and the Christian Origins,* ch. 7, *The*

Scrolls and Christianity (ed. M. Black) ch. 4, "Eschatology in the Dead Sea Scrolls" by John Pryke, and, less reliably, *The Dead Sea Scrolls and the Early Church* by L. Mowry, ch. 7.

[42] Compare the Pharisaic method of combining texts, "pearl-stringing", which Paul adopts in Romans 3:10–18, 10:18–21, Galatians 3:10–13.

[43] The widely held view that there were no clear word and sentence divisions in pre-Massoretic texts is precarious in view of inscriptions (such as the Siloam Inscription and the Lachish ostraka) which long antedate the Massoretes.

[44] See above, p. 79.

[45] Acts 2:17–21, 25–8; 4:11, etc.

[46] I Peter 1:10–12, 2:6–8.

[47] John 2:17, 12:15, 38, 40; 19:24, 36f.; cf. 6:45, 13:18, 15:25.

[48] I Corinthians 10:1–6, 2 Corinthians 3:12–18, Galatians 3:16, Ephesians 4:8–10.

[49] I Corinthians 9:9f. and Galatians 4:21–31.

[50] *Op. cit.*, p. 18.

[51] Typology was another method used a good deal in the early Church: the *Epistle of Barnabas* and the *Dialogue with Trypho* are full of it. R. M. Grant writes: "Without the typological method, it would have been almost impossible for the early Church to retain its grasp on the Old Testament." He goes on to point out that, whilst "the Epistle to the Hebrews represents the most thorough analysis of the Old Testament in typological terms which we possess in the New Testament, there are many other examples of typology", and he concludes, not without exaggeration, that "the New Testament method of interpreting the Old was generally that of typology" (*The Interpretation of the Bible*, p. 36, 39). This approach has been investigated recently by A. T. Hanson in *Jesus Christ in the Old Testament*, and was clearly of enormous importance to the early missionaries.

The midrashic type of exegesis was an equally significant part of the Christian approach to the Jew, as they searched the Scriptures together. See, e.g. Aileen Guilding, *The Fourth Gospel and Jewish Worship* and J. W. Bowker, "Speeches in Acts: a study in proem and yelammedenu form" *N.T.S.*, October 1967. He makes out a strong case for regarding some of the evangelistic sermons in Acts as based on synagogue exegesis of Jewish lections, drawing upon the contemporary (and later) homily usual in synagogue worship to point up the instruction of Torah. This fell into two main categories, the proem type, where the homily starts with a proem or introductory text: and the yelammedenu type which is basically a response to requests for instruction from one of those present. There are traces, he concludes, of both these types of sermon in the speeches of Acts. The whole article is a mine of information, and gives an acute insight into the preacher's workshop of the early missionaries.

[52] Some were blatantly improper. For one thing, the Old Testament text was sometimes twisted to fit the Christian meaning: Isaiah 7:14 is a classic case in point. What is more, it received interpolations: a notable one is the inclusion of "The Lord reigned from a tree" into the text of Psalm 96, and the Jews are bitterly arraigned in Justin's *Dialogue 72, 73* for having excised this and other verses from their texts of Scripture. Apocalyptic books, too, received Christian glosses, and indeed this became so widespread that the Jews ceased to make much use of them. A good example is found in *Orac. Sibyll.* 5.256–9, which reads, "Then there shall come from the sky a certin exalted man, whose hands they nailed upon the fruitful tree, the noblest of the Hebrews, who shall one day cause the sun to stand still, when he cries with fair speech and pure lips." Here is a manifest Christian gloss, based on the identity in Hebrew of Jesus and Joshua: Jesus, the crucified and risen, is seen as the coming eschatological Joshua. The *Testaments of the Twelve Patriarchs*, 2 *Esdras* and the *Slavonic Josephus* received similar interpolations. Rabbinic reaction to this practice of interpolation was understandably sharp: "The margins and books of the *minim* they do not save, but these are burnt" (*b. Shabb.* 13a). R. Meir and R. Jochanan made puns on the Christian word for gospel, *euaggelion*, calling it respectively

Aven-gilyon (margin of idolatry) and *Avon-gilyon* (margin of iniquity) in allusion to this practice of glossing the Jewish Scriptures. See *b. Shabb.* 116b.

⁵³ See my *The Meaning of Salvation*, ch. 3, on this subject.

⁵⁴ *Vespasian* 4.

⁵⁵ *Hist.* 5.13. See also Josephus, *B.J.* 6.5.4.

⁵⁶ *P. Tebt.* 276, cited by C. K. Barrett in *New Testament Background: Selected Documents*, p. 13. See also the discussion in my *The Meaning of Salvation*, p. 8of.

⁵⁷ On the legend of the original Sibyl, see Virgil, *Aeneid*, bk. 6.

⁵⁸ *Orac. Sibyll.* 3.46ff.

⁵⁹ *Orac. Sibyll.* 3.632–731.

⁶⁰ *Ps. Sol.* 17 is a particularly striking example.

⁶¹ *Test. Reuben* 6.7–12, *Levi* 8.13f., *Naphtali* 8.2f, *Joseph* 19.11.

⁶² *b. Sukkah*, 52b, Midrash *Tehillin*, 43,2. etc.

⁶³ See above p. 85.

⁶⁴ He was known as the *taheb*. See Driver, *op. cit.*, p. 467 and J. Macdonald, *The Theology of the Samaritans*, p. 353.

⁶⁵ For some attempt to examine at any rate the outlines of the problem of the Son of Man in Enoch, see my *The Meaning of Salvation*, p. 57ff., and the bibliography there cited, to which there should be added the recent discussions by M. D. Hooker, *The Son of Man in Mark* and F. H. Borsch, *The Son of Man in Myth and History*, but the literature on the subject is endless.

⁶⁶ Though *2 Esdras* appears to have reached its final form early in the second century A.D., there is no certainty of Christian interpolation, least of all in the "Man" vision of chapter 13 which has close affinities with Daniel 7. The Man from the sea, who flies on the clouds of heaven, brings in the heavenly Jerusalem and slays the wicked with the fire of the Law, is an individual Messianic figure thoroughly Hebraic in character.

⁶⁷ I *Q.S.* 4.22, 8.4ff.

⁶⁸ I *Q.S.*, 4.2off. Leaney, *op. cit.*, p. 156 doubts a Messianic interpretation: Brownlee, in *B.A.S.O.R.*, 1954, p. 36ff. argues for one.

⁶⁹ I.Q.H. 9.23–7, 2.8, etc.

⁷⁰ E.g., Romans 1:3, Revelation 5:5, 22:16, Matthew 15:22, etc.

⁷¹ Psalm 110:1, the most frequently used Old Testament proof text. Its use springs from Jesus himself (Mark 12:35ff.).

⁷² Acts 2:25–36.

⁷³ The current debate concerning whether or not Jesus thought of himself in Messianic terms is, to my mind, conclusively settled by the superscription over his cross. The Messiahship was no status trumped up after his resurrection by the disciples; it was nothing less than the occasion of his death—for he died as a Messianic pretender.

⁷⁴ So Cullmann argues (more persuasively of some disciples than of others!) in *The State in the New Testament*.

⁷⁵ Acts 1:6, Matthew 19:28, Revelation 11:15.

⁷⁶ Belief in an earthly millennium seem to have been nothing short of Christian "orthodoxy" from Justin to Irenaeus, though both are aware of some Christians who spiritualize it. See Justin *Dial.* 8of., Irenaeus *Adv. Haer.* 5.35. Origen condemns such crude views of heavenly bliss (*De Principiis* 2.11).

⁷⁷ Acts 3:2off.

⁷⁸ It is highly significant that Irenaeus's conception, derived from Papias, of the Messianic kingdom is identical with that of the *Apocalypse of Baruch* (39.5). Irenaeus quotes Papias who claims that "John the disciple of the Lord; related ... how the Lord used to teach in regard to these times, and say, 'The days will come in which the vines shall grow, each having 10,000 branches, and in each branch 10,000 twigs, and in each twig 10,000 shoots, and in each one of the shoots, 10,000 clusters, and on every one of the clusters 10,000 grapes . . .'" (Irenaeus *Adv. Haer.* 5.33; see also Eusebius *H.E.* 3.39). This attribution to Jesus of this quotation from an apocryphal source which reappears in *Baruch* suggests that there was less at issue than is often supposed between zealous

nationalists and zealous Jewish Christians—apart from the great divide caused by the Christian belief that Jesus was the Messiah.

⁷⁹ See the development of this argument in 1 Corinthians 1:23ff.

⁸⁰ H. J. Schonfield makes this error in *Those Incredible Christians*, p. 80. Rightly stressing the political aspect of early Jewish Christianity, he then declares, "They (i.e. the Christians) and the Zealots stood in the same condemnation: they were different sides of the same coin."

⁸¹ *e.g.* Matthew 24:24f.

⁸² Luke 7:16, Matthew 21:46.

⁸³ John 6:14, Mark 6:15, Matthew 21:10f.

⁸⁴ Acts 3:22, 7:37.

⁸⁵ "My Son, in all the prophets I was waiting for you, that you should come and that I should find my rest in you" (*Fr.* 2 in Jerome, *Comm. in Isaiah IV* on Isaiah 11.2).

⁸⁶ This basic document underlying the Clementine romances constantly speaks of Jesus as "the true prophet", though the eschatological flavour of the title is reinterpreted in a Gnostic direction. It certainly shows the appeal of this sort of Christology for sectarian syncretistic Judaism.

⁸⁷ It has been argued credibly, e.g. by C. Spicq, that the Epistle to the Hebrews was originally addressed to a body of priests—perhaps the very men mentioned in Acts 6:7. Undeniably the Christology of Stephen's speech in Acts and that of the Epistle are very similar, as W. Manson's *The Epistle to the Hebrews* shows.

⁸⁸ Hebrews 7:4–11.

⁸⁹ Hebrews 7:1–3.

⁹⁰ Hebrews 7:21.

⁹¹ Hebrews 7:26, 24f., 27.

⁹² Hebrews 7:25, 10:12ff., 9:28.

⁹³ Cf. A. J. B. Higgins, *Jesus and the Son of Man*, R. H. Fuller, *The Foundations of New Testament Christology*, H. E. Tödt, *The Son of Man in the Synoptic Tradition*.

⁹⁴ The lynch pin of the contrary view, that Jesus in Mark 8:38 is distinguishing himself from the Son of Man, seems particularly unconvincing.

⁹⁵ The only exception is Acts 7:56 where Stephen says, "I see the heavens opened, and the Son of Man standing at the right hand of God". This is a plain allusion to Daniel 7:14 (and perhaps also Psalm 110:1) which is fulfilled by the ascension of Jesus, here seen as standing in order to welcome the proto-martyr to heaven. It may well be that this deliberate reference back to Jesus's own self-designation by Stephen had another nuance, as W. Manson has suggested in a posthumous work. Stephen, he argues, was among the first to see in Jesus more than a Jewish Messiah—the Son of Man. "His reign had a vaster compass than any kingdom restored to Israel. For did not the chapter in Daniel which spoke of the dominion given to the 'one who resembled a son of man' say that 'all peoples and nations and tongues' would serve him (Daniel 7:14)?" (*Jesus and the Christian*, p. 202).

⁹⁶ *Galiläa und Jerusalem*, p. 68ff.

⁹⁷ Mark 10:45.

⁹⁸ 'Erlöser und Erlösung im Spätjudentum' in *Deutsche Theologie*, 1929, 106ff.

⁹⁹ *Legum Allegoria* 1.31f., *De Mundi Opificio* 134ff.

¹⁰⁰ See the detailed treatment of this aspect of the subject in F. H. Borsch, *The Son of Man in Myth and History*.

¹⁰¹ See Philippians 2:4–10, Romans 5:12ff., 1 Corinthians 15:45–7. In the last passage he contests Philo's position directly: the heavenly man comes after the earthy, the ideal after the empirical, not *vice versa*.

¹⁰² John 3:13, 12:23, 31; cf. Revelation 1:13, 14:14.

¹⁰³ Hebrews 5:7ff.

¹⁰⁴ Apart from the men of Qumran, cited above, it is clear from Justin, *Dial.* 89 that the concept was not unfamiliar to Jews, though it was highly uncongenial. The Targum on Isaiah 53 does indeed identify the Servant with the Messiah, but strives hard by means of fanciful exegesis to eliminate the real

suffering from the destiny of the Servant. See Cullmann, *The Christology of the New Testament*, p. 58f.

[105] 1 *Q.S.* 8.5ff.

[106] The Jews came to attach expiatory significance to martyrdom during the Maccabaean wars (2 Maccabees 7:37, 4 Maccabees 6:27). The Covenanters thought of themselves both as suffering for the righteous and also as defeating the ungodly ("requiting the wicked with their reward") in the final battle between the Sons of Light and the Sons of Darkness. The Christians, by way of contrast, were convinced that both judgment and atonement were vested in Jesus.

[107] See Hebrews 10:1ff. The sacrificial system brought sin to remembrance, but could not remove it. How could the death of a lamb or a goat eradicate moral guilt? This could be done only by a moral agent, in solidarity both with sinful mankind and the holy God. Jesus was this agent, and has accomplished this task of reconciliation once for all. Such is the argument of Hebrews 10:1–17.

[108] Acts 8:34.

[109] 1 Peter 2:22ff.

[110] Justin, *Dial.* 89.

[111] Justin, *Dial.* 90.

[112] See above, p. 30f., 90.

[113] *e.g. Dial.* 73.

[114] 1 Corinthians 1:24.

[115] Colossians 2:15.

[116] Acts 2:23f., 31f.

[117] Philippians 2:8–11.

[118] W. A. Shotwell shows in his *Biblical Exegesis of Justin Martyr*, ch. 4, how thoroughly rabbinic Justin's method of exegesis is.

[119] Justin, *Dial.* 90.

[120] Justin, *Dial.* 91.

[121] Deuteronomy 21:22f.

[122] Acts 5:30f., 10:39, 13:29.

[123] 1 Peter 2:24.

[124] Galatians 3:10, 13.

[125] It may well underline the "tree of life" language in Revelation 22:2, 14, 19. The tree associated with man's disobedience and fall becomes the tree for the healing of the nations and their restoration.

[126] Justin, *Dial.* 95.

[127] Justin, *Dial.* 50, cf. 87.

[128] It is interesting to see how a modern Jewish writer such as H. J. Schonfield advances precisely the same arguments as Trypho against the deity of Christ. See *Those Incredible Christians*, pp. 41, 48, 56.

[129] For this, see P. Pringent, *Justin et l'Ancient Testament*, ch. 5.

[130] Thus 2:22 "a man attested to you by God".

[131] Its absence in St John's Gospel was obviously noticed by the scribe who wrote *hos egenēthē* (who was born) for *hoi egenēthēsan* (who were born) in John 1:13, in order to import the doctrine of the Virgin Birth there. I do not regard "born of a woman" in Galatians 4:4 as a cryptic reference to it, nor "son of Mary" in Mark 6:3, though it is possible that both may reflect knowledge of the tradition, in view of the great insult it was to a Jew to call him the son of his mother.

[132] It is fully set out in J. Gresham Machen, *The Virgin Birth of Christ*, and J. Klausner, *Jesus of Nazareth*. He is called Ben Panthera in the second century in a scurrilous story that his father was a Roman soldier. See Origen's handling of this story as produced by Celsus (*Contra Celsum*, 1.32), and H. Chadwick's note *in loc*. Perhaps the most significant allusion to the virgin birth in the early days is by Rabbi Eliezer, a third century rabbi of distinction. "R. Eliezer said, 'Balaam looked forth and saw that there was a man, born of a woman, who should rise up and seek to make himself God, and cause the whole world to go astray'. Therefore God gave power to the voice of Balaam that all the peoples of

the world might hear, and thus he spake: 'Give heed that you go not astray after that man, for it is written, God is not man that he should lie. And if he says that he is God he is a liar; and he will deceive and say that he departeth and cometh again at the end' '' (*Yalkut Shimeoni* 725, cited by Klausner, *op. cit.*, p. 34f). There are, of course, earlier allusions, such as the early second century statement of R. Shimeon ben Azzai, "I found a genealogical scroll in Jerusalem wherein was recorded, 'Such-an-one (commonly used of Jesus in the Talmud) is a bastard of an adulteress' '' (*b. Yeb.* 49a).

[133] Philippians 2:11, 1 Corinthians 12:2. See O. Cullmann, *The Earliest Christian Confessions.*

[134] *e.g.* Acts 2:36.

[135] 1 Corinthians 16:22, *Didache* 10.6.

[136] That a minimizing interpretation of *Mar* is impossible in the cry *Maranalha* is clear from the fact that it occurs in an invocation. Though one might address a living rabbi as *Mar*, it is an inconceivable form of address to a dead one. When Christians prayed to Jesus to be present in their midst as *Mar*, they meant nothing short of "Lord". See Cullmann, *The Christology of the New Testament*, p. 201ff.

[137] Mark 1:11.

[138] Mark 12:6.

[139] Mark 14:61f.

[140] *What do we know about Jesus?* p. 88ff.

[141] Romans 1:4, Acts 2:36. Alternatively they regarded the baptism of Jesus as authenticating his Sonship. This seems to be the standpoint of Mark and the Western Text of Luke: "Thou art my Son; this day have I begotten thee." This reading appealed to Jewish Christians, and it is produced by Trypho in argument (*Dial.* 88 and 103, the latter actually quoting Luke 3:23).

[142] Both citations come from Fragment 1, to be found in Jerome, *Comm. in Isaiah IV* on Isaiah 11:2.

[143] Fragments 1 and 4 in Epiphanius, *Haer.* 30.13, 2 and 7.

[144] This docetic tendency was almost inevitable in view of the inability of the Ebionite movement to accept Jesus as the fulness of God.

[145] John 1:33f.

[146] John 3:34.

[147] *Dial.* 48 and 87. Justin argues in the latter chapter that the Holy Spirit, who used to speak through the prophets, has ceased to do so since he rested in his fulness on Jesus. The Hebrews, accordingly, have no more prophets: but the Christians have inherited the prophetic role.

[148] See above ch. 4, note 4. The introduction of this curse on the *minim* is credited to Simeon the Small, *c.* A.D. 85. Its effectiveness in wrecking relations between Jewish Christians and Jews is clear from Justin, *Dial.* 16 and 96.

[149] Cf. 1 Peter 2:9, 10, Galatians 6:16 and the *Epistle of Barnabas, in toto.*

[150] Romans 2:28.

[151] See the course of the argument in Romans 9 and Acts 7.

[152] Galatians 6:16.

[153] Acts 2:38, 3:19, 4:10ff., Romans 9:1–3.

[154] Romans 11:15ff.

[155] See Matthew 13:14, John 9:39, 12:40, Mark 4:12, Acts 28:25–7, 2 Corinthians 3:14, 4:4, Ephesians 4:18, Justin, *Dial.* 12 (where it is wrongly attributed to Jeremiah). Isaiah 53:1 was used apologetically by Christians for the same purpose (John 12:38, Romans 10:16).

[156] *Dial.* 11.

[157] "Israel" in early Christian usage always appears to denote either Jews *in toto* (*e.g.* Acts 2:22, 3:12) or else believing Israel, in whose privileges Gentiles share (Ephesians 2:12 Luke 7:9) although there is always a residual priority to the Jew: compare, by way of contrast, 1 Corinthians 10:18.

[158] Romans 2:28, 1 Peter 2:9, 10, Hebrews 13:10.

[159] Revelation 2:9, 3:9. Compare the attitude to the Jews in the Fourth Gospel.

[160] Justin, *Dial.* 59, 60: Tertullian, *Adv. Judaeos, in toto.*
[161] *Verus Israel*, p. 104.
[162] *Dial.* 114, 97.
[163] *e.g.* Matthew 1:18, where in the Psalm it is Yahweh who saves Israel from her sin, but in the Christian application of the verse the role is applied to Jesus.
[164] *Adv. Haer.* 3.21.
[165] The whole subject of the origins and recensions of the LXX is, however, highly complex. See S. Jellicoe, *The Septuagint and Modern Study*, especially pp. 29–70.
[166] *Dial.* 29.
[167] *Barnabas* 9.
[168] *Barnabas* 8.
[169] *Apol.* 14.
[170] *Op. cit.*, p. 69.
[171] *Dial.* 10.
[172] Galatians 3:21.
[173] Galatians 3:24.
[174] in Romans and Galatians: cf. Acts 15:5.
[175] Acts 15:1.
[176] Galatians 6:13. This has been argued by Johannes Munck in *Paul and the Salvation of Mankind.*
[177] Cf. Philippians 3:2ff.
[178] *Philad.* 6.
[179] Romans 7:12.
[180] Romans 7:7.
[181] Romans 3:21, Galatians 4:21ff., 3:22.
[182] Galatians 3:17.
[183] Galatians 3:13f.
[184] Galatians 3:28.
[185] Romans 3:19, 20, Galatians 3:10.
[186] Galatians 3:11f.
[187] *e.g.* Acts 16:3, 21:24f. He refuses cultic acts of this sort if they are made criteria of salvation, but is prepared to make use of them in the interests of Christian charity where there is no question of their being regarded as essentials. His attitude to things offered to idols, as set out in Romans 14, 1 Corinthians 8 and 10 enshrines the same principle.
[188] 1 Corinthians 9:20f.
[189] Romans 7:4.
[190] See 2 Corinthians 3 *in toto.* The Spirit has replaced the Law by fulfilling it; the covenant has been interiorized.
[191] See 1 Corinthians 9:21.
[192] Romans 10:4.
[193] Galatians 5:14, 6:2.
[194] Acts 15:10ff.
[195] 1 Peter 4:8.
[196] *Barnabas* 14.
[197] *Dial.* 16, 18, 20, 30, 40–6.
[198] There was, of course, plenty of spiritualizing being done in Diaspora Judaism. But this did not assail such central features as the Christians attacked.
[199] Mark 14:58, John 2:19, cf. Acts 15:16 and 2 Samuel 7:13f.
[200] Mark 10:45.
[201] Mark 1:44.
[202] Mark 7:18ff.
[203] Acts 6:11, 13f.
[204] "Sanctuary and Sacrifice in the Church of the New Testament", *J.T.S.*, 1950, p. 29f.
[205] Romans 14:5f. On the whole subject of Sabbath keeping in Christianity see W. Rordorf, *Sunday.*
[206] Hebrews 8:13.

[207] What a lot more he could then have made of the forty years in the wilderness in ch. 3, the obsolescence theme of ch. 8, and the ineffectiveness of the priest always standing at his sacrifices in ch. 10!

[208] *Dial.* 16.

[209] *Ep. ad Diognetum*, 3 and 4.

[210] *Philad.* 6.

[211] *Barnabas* 9.

[212] *Barnabas* 4.

[213] *Barnabas* 9.

[214] *Dial.* 47.

[215] *Homily* on Psalm 36:1.

[216] Particularly in Revelation, but no less in very early parts of the New Testament such as 1 Thessalonians 2:15ff.

[217] See p. 33.

[218] Suetonius, *Claudius*, 25.

[219] Matthew 10:23, Mark 9:1.

[220] Acts 8 and 13.

[221] Acts 19:13ff.

[222] *b. Abod. Zar.* 27b.

[223] *M. Sanhedrin* 10.1.

[224] So A. H. McNeile in *J.B.L.* vol. xli, p. 122ff.

[225] See H. J. Schonfield, *The History of Jewish Christianity*, p. 79f.

[226] Acts 6:8, 10.

[227] James 2:10.

[228] *Hom. in Num.* 10:2.

[229] *R.E.J.* lxxi, p. 190.

[230] *j. Taan.* 4.2, cf *Gen. R.* 56.10.

[231] *The Conflict of the Church and the Synagogue*, p. 120, to whom I am indebted for several of the references cited above.

CHAPTER 5

[1] Chapters like Acts 15, Galatians 2, Ephesians 2 show how acrimonious this had been. On the universalism implicit in Jesus's offer of salvation, see Jeremias, *Jesus' Promise to the Nations*, and for a shrewd appraisal of the early Jewish controversy see F. V. Filson, *Three Crucial Decades*, ch. 5.

[2] Galatians 4:4, John 4:22.

[3] John 4:42, in continuation of the offer of salvation to believing Gentiles proffered in Deutero–Isaiah and exemplified in the surge of missionary activity among the Jews in the first centuries B.C. and A.D.

[4] Acts 1:8.

[5] Biography as such is as little to his purpose in Acts as it is in the Gospel.

[6] Acts 26:31.

[7] For the recognition of this pattern in Acts, see C. H. Turner's article, "Chronology of the New Testament" in Hasting's *Dictionary of the Bible* I, p. 241.

[8] Acts 11:20.

[9] See F. M. Abel, *Histoire de la Palestine* I, pp. 363–80.

[10] See Josephus, *B.J.*, 7.3.3, and Edersheim, *Life and Times of Jesus the Messiah*, vol. 1, p. 74.

[11] *Satires* 3.62ff., cf. Propertius, *Carm.* 2.21.

[12] Josephus, *B.J.*, 7.3.3.

[13] *St Paul and the Church of Jerusalem*, p. 156.

[14] *History of Antioch in Syria from Seleucus to the Arab Conquest*, and *Ancient Antioch*.

[15] G. Downey, *Ancient Antioch*, ch. 10.

[16] The *kyrios* of Acts 11:20 is probably significant. See below, p. 115.

[17] *According to the Scriptures* and *The Apostolic Preaching and its Development*. See chapter 3.

[18] *The Beginnings of Christainity*, vol. 4, p. 128f., ed. Foakes Jackson and Kirsopp Lake.

[19] Though overemphasizing the differences in these three approaches, he does not make the mistake of J. A. T. Robinson in *Twelve New Testament Studies*, ch. 10, who supposes that Acts 3 and 7 contain "the most primitive Christology of all" according to which, even after the Resurrection, Jesus is merely Christ-elect. No such Christology existed. Easter always was the key to his Lordship. "What event after Easter could have suggested the transformation of an 'embryonic' faith in Jesus into its full Messianic form?" asks Professor Otto Betz in an article on "The Kerygma of Luke" in *Interpretation*, April 1968, p. 143. See his illuminating answer in that article to the enigma of the peculiar Christology in Acts 3 and 7.

[20] See A. D. Nock in *Essays on the Trinity and Incarnation*, ed. A. E. J. Rawlinson, p. 85ff., W. Bousset, *Krios Christos*, and O. Cullmann, *The Christology of the New Testament*, pp. 195–237.

[21] 1 Corinthians 8:6.

[22] See Suetonius, *Domit.* 13 for Domitian's claim. *Mart. Polyc.* 8.2 is also significant, where Polycarp is asked, "What harm is there in saying *Kyrios Kaisar*?"

[23] So 1 Corinthians 12:3, Philippians 2:9, Romans 10:9.

[24] When Gentile readers of the Septuagint saw *Kyrios* in an Old Testament passage, they were inclined to think of Jesus. This process of reinterpreting Old Testament references to the Lord and applying them to Jesus is to be seen in the New Testament itself, e.g. Hebrews 1:8, 10, Philippians 2:10. All the functions of the Deity, in creating, judging, saving, were applied to Jesus. For "in him dwells all the fulness of the Godhead in bodily form" (Colossians 2.9).

[25] See R. P. Martin's *Carmen Christi*, where he argues that the Lordship of Jesus over Fate and demonic forces is one of the main themes of Philippians 2:4–11, and, moreover, a theme which made enormous appeal to Hellenistic man, whose problem was not so much sin as *Angst*. T. W. Manson's posthumously collected lectures, *On Paul and John*, take precisely the same view, as does O. Cullmann in his celebrated interpretation of the "powers" in Romans 13:1ff. as the demonic powers. However, the position advocated by Martin must not be taken too exclusively. It is clear enough, both from Acts and 1 Corinthians 15:1ff. that the main thrust of mission preaching to Gentiles included deliverance precisely from *sin*. Nevertheless when this has been said, his positive conclusion that the creed of Philippians 2 spoke of release from frustration and aimlessness is both true and of contemporary relevance.

[26] Acts 17:7 and 16:21. See Sherwin-White, *op. cit.* p. 75ff., who examines the charges carefully, but curiously does not connect them with the proclamation of "another king". Instead, he stresses the appeal of the Philippians to the non-Roman nature of the new religion. This seems to me to be rather thin in view of the prevalence of non-Roman religions in the first century, not least among the army; the colonists of Philippi would have been retired soldiers.

[27] Mark 10:15–26.

[28] Otto Betz sees this clearly. "Why can the apostolic message about Christ be identified with the *kerygma* of the kingdom of God? Because the kingdom is revealed through Jesus the Christ and Saviour of Mankind." ("The Kerygma of Luke" in *Interpretation*, April 1968, p. 144f.).

[29] 1 Corinthians 9:22.

[30] "All things to all men", in *New Testament Studies*, 1954, p. 261–75.

[31] Cf. 1 Corinthians 1:26ff., 7:21, Colossians 3:22ff.

[32] "A slave is a living tool, just as a tool is an inanimate slave" (Aristotle, *Nic. Eth.* viii.11). Cato's advice is "Sell worn out oxen, blemished cattle ... old tools, an old slave, a sickly slave, and whatever else is useless" (*De Agricultura*, 2.7). See also Juvenal, *Satires* 14.16–22. The papyri show that this remained the prevalent attitude to slaves. Arabarchos accepts Thermoutharion and the

maimed Heraclorus "with the future slave children that may be born from them" (*Select Papyri*, (Loeb) 1.51), while Dryton the soldier leaves to his relations "two female slaves and a cow in equal shares for their households" (*op. cit.*, 1.83). The cow and the slave are on precisely the same level!

There were, of course, shining exceptions to this gloomy picture. For a marvellous example of the love and trust that could sometimes exist between master and slave, see the Loeb, *Select Papyri*, 1.85.

[33] And the legal position gradually improved. The *Lex Petronia* forbade the sale of slaves for combat with wild beasts, whilst the *Lex Aelia Sentia* regularized the manumission situation. Hadrian and his successors did much to ameliorate the slave's lot. Much of the credit for such legislation must not go to Christians but to Stoic philosophers like Seneca and Epictetus, whose influence gradually percolated at any rate the upper échelons of society. Seneca, for instance, took over Terence's dictum in his famous *homo sum*; *humani nihil a me alienum puto* (*Epistles* 95.53), or his *homo sacra res homini* (*Epistles* 95.33).

[34] Colossians 3:11, Galatians 3:28.

[35] See Ephesians 6:5–8, cf. *Didache* 4, "Thou shalt not command in thy bitterness thy slave or thine handmaid, who hope in the same God, lest they cease to fear the God who is over you both." Ignatius (*Polyc.* 4) inculcates the same gentle (but not sentimental) attitude to slaves, with the hint that not infrequently Church funds were used to free them: they must not, however, trade on this! By the time of the *Apostolic Constitutions* the freeing of slaves was seen as a Christian virtue (4.9). See also *1 Clem.* 55, Tertullian, *Apologet*. 39. On the effect of Christianity on slave owners, see Clement of Alexandria, *Protrepticus*, 10.

[36] They ate at the same Agape, took the same elements in the Holy Communion, and bond and free faced martyrdom together: Blandina in Gaul and Felicitas in Africa were both slaves. To be sure, some pagan *collegia* made no distinction between bond and free *while at the meeting* (see Dessau, *I.L.S.* 4203, 4215), "but the majority of slaves seem to have belonged to colleges which were composed of freedmen and slaves only." (R. H. Barrow, *Slavery in the Roman Empire*, p. 166).

[37] This letter was written by one Aurelius Sarapammon to his friend *c*. A.D. 298. It is a graphic example of how the inhuman attitude to slaves lived on in the pagan world outside Christian circles. See also similar injunctions in *Pap. Par.* 10, the text of which is given in C. F. D. Moule's *Colossians and Philemon* (Cambridge Greek Testament), p. 34ff.

[38] See my discussion in *The Meaning of Salvation*, p. 167f.

[39] *The Greeks* (esp. p. 220ff.).

[40] *Roman Women*.

[41] See above, p. 26.

[42] Luke 23:49, 8:3, John 19:25.

[43] Acts 18:2, 26, Acts 16:14ff., Romans 16:1, Philippians 4:2, 3, Origen, *Contra Celsum* 3.55.

[44] Acts 6:7, Luke 8:3, Acts 13:1. See Deissmann, *Bible Studies*, p. 301ff. for the significance of this formal relationship.

[45] "The phrase 'strangers of Rome' is found in epigraphic parallels as a technical term of constitutional affairs for the Roman citizens resident in a particular place and acting corporately in concert with the local public bodies." (E. A. Judge, *op. cit.* p. 55).

[46] Sergius Paullus, the proconsul of Cyprus, believed the preaching of Paul. His daughter seems also to have become a Christian. See the inscription and comment in W. H. Ramsay, *The Bearing of Recent Discovery on the Trustworthiness of the New Testament*, pp. 150–73. It is highly probable that the wife of the proconsul of Asia who condemned Ignatius to the beasts was a Christian. He sends his greetings to *tēn tou epitropou*, which can only mean "the wife of the governor" if Epitropus is not the name of an individual (*Polyc.* 8).

[47] *Epistles* 10.96.

[48] This seems fairly conclusive from the combined testimony of Dio, Suetonius, and archaeology. Dio writes (67:14), "And the same year (A.D. 95)

Domitian slew, along with many others, Flavius Clemens the consul, although he was a cousin and had to wife Flavia Domitilla, who was also a relative of the emperor's. The charge brought against them both was that of atheism, a charge on which many others who drifted into Jewish ways were condemned. Some of these were put to death and the rest were at least deprived of their property. Domitilla was banished to Pandateria, but Glabrio, who had been Trajan's colleague in the consulship was put to death, having been accused of the same crime as most of the others, and in particular of fighting as a gladiator with wild beasts." He then proceeds to tell the story of Acilius Glabrio's lion fight and its sequel. See below, p. 212f. Suetonius's account is as follows. "Lastly, there was Flavius Clemens, his own cousin, a man of most despicable sloth, whose sons, while still of tender age, he had openly designated to succeed him . . : him of a sudden, when his consulship had barely expired, Domitian put to death on the most shadowy suspicion" (*Domit.* 15).

The combination of references to the "laziness" of Clemens (*i.e.* his unwillingness to enter fully into the public affairs of the pagan Roman state), with the charge of "atheism and Jewish ways" makes it almost certain that Christians are meant. See the indignant repudiation of such charges in Minucius Felix (*Oct.* 8) and Tertullian (*Apologet.* 42), and the important notes on the passage in G. W. Mooney, *Suetonius*, p. 580f. It is to be noted that Dio never differentiates Christians from Jews, and may well be mistaken in assigning Pandateria, rather than Pontia (see Eusebius, *H.E.* 3.18) as the place for Domitilla's exile. Eusebius is explicit that she was exiled for her "testimony to Christ". This draws confirmation from the fact that within the Cemetery of Domitilla was discovered a remarkable inscription, still preserved there, which reads, *Flaviae Domitillae Vespasiani neptis eius beneficio hoc sepulchrum meis libertus libertabus posuit.* See the full discussion in G. Edmundson's Bampton Lectures, *The Church in Rome in the First Century*, Appendix F.

⁴⁹ See Tacitus, *Annals*, 13.32 and below p. 211.

⁵⁰ Suetonius, *Domit.* 10 and Mooney's note.

⁵¹ *Mand.* 10.1.

⁵² The nobler the Stoic, the more he recognized his inability to live the good life: Seneca realized that "evil has its seat within us, in our inward part", and Ovid's whimsical *video meliora proboque, deteriora sequor* ("I see the better course, and I approve it—but I follow the worse") must have been echoed in all sincerity by earnest men who knew that their lives did not and could not match up to their ideals.

⁵³ Acts 13:12.

⁵⁴ A. D. Nock comments, "Christianity satisfied both the religious and the philosophic instincts of the time. It offered a cultus which . . . shared with others the merit of giving the realization of the means of salvation. It was superior in that the Saviour was not merely a figure of unique attraction, but also a recent historical figure invested with deity. It was superior in that the salvation involved was salvation from forces of moral evil . . . He (i.e. Jesus) was not limited by any over-emphasis on his home in Judaea. Mithras was and remained Persian: Jesus was universal. Again, the new faith satisfied the desire for . . . *gnōsis*, special knowledge, union with deity, illumination and the like, and succeeded in combining with this a personal conception of God often lacking in Hellenistic analogues" (*Essays on the Trinity and Incarnation*, ed. A. E. J. Rawlinson, p. 154).

⁵⁵ Thus Tertullian claims, "It is our care for the helpless, our practice of loving kindness, that brands us in the eyes of many of our opponents. Only look, they say, look how they love one another (they themselves being given over to mutual hatred). Look how they are prepared to die for one another (they themselves being readier to kill each other). Thus had this saying become a fact, 'Hereby shall all men know that ye are my disciples, if ye have love one to another' " (*Apologet.* 29).

⁵⁶ 1 Corinthians 1:18–31.

⁵⁷ But a wisdom which is a *mustērion* and has a givenness about it (1 Corin-

thians 2:6ff.), a wisdom which cannot be pierced by human cleverness but only received humbly by faith in the crucified. Justin, for all his emphasis on Christianity as the true philosophy, knows that it is recognized by a God-given faculty. He therefore combined prayer that God would open blind eyes with his intellectual arguments and his scriptural proofs. He "does as much as he can" in apologetics, but "adds the prayer that all men everywhere may be counted worthy of the truth" (*2 Apol.* 15). He makes the point abundantly plain in *Dial.* 7, where he writes, "Pray that, above all things, the gates of light may be opened to you; for these things cannot be perceived or understood by all, but only by the man to whom God and his Christ have imparted wisdom."

[58] See Andresen, *Z.N.T.W.*, 1952–3, pp. 157–95.

[59] See G. Bardy, "Saint Justin et la philosophie stoicienne", *Revue des sciences religieuses*, 1923, p. 493ff.

[60] See E. R. Goodenough, *The Theology of Justin Martyr.* Middle Platonism included as much Stoicism as it could accommodate. On Philo's possible influence on Justin, see H. Chadwick in the *B.J.R.L.*, March 1965, p. 275ff. The parallels are not compelling.

[61] *I Apol.* 5.

[62] *Dial.* 8.

[63] *Dial.* 1.

[64] *Dial.* 8.

[65] One suspects that the latter were more numerous than the former. It could be an expensive matter to belong to a mystery cult.

[66] *De Morte Peregrini* 11.

[67] Apuleius *Met.* 11.23, *Pap. Par.* 43.

[68] *Pap. Oxyr.* 110, 523. See A. B. Cook, *Zeus* i. p. 651ff., and the careful discussion in A. D. Nock's article in *Essays on the Trinity and Incarnation*, ed. A. E. J. Rawlinson, pp. 120–38.

[69] The Corinthian Christians certainly were not! See 1 Corinthians 3:1ff., cf. 11:27.

[70] Tatian is an interesting example of a man who was admitted to the Mysteries but was disgusted by their obscenities: in the Eleusinian Mysteries, for example, the initiate was obliged to have contact with a representation of the genitals of Demeter.

[71] See Juvenal, *Satires* 13.46–52, 15.36–8, 2.149–59, 1.85f.

[72] The prosperity of the community was deemed to depend on the performance of sacrifice to the state gods. See Horace, *Od.* 4.15 and Virgil, *Ecl.* 4. The refusal of the Christians to take part in this activity was naturally enough regarded as seditious. See p. 34f. above.

[73] See Juvenal, *Satires* 13.90–96, 6.489, 9.22–4, 6.536–41.

[74] See Juvenal, *Satires* 9.137ff., 2.124f., 6.445f.

[75] *Satires* 4.71, 6.115.

[76] *C.I.L.* 10.5382, whose translation reads, "This offering to Ceres Junius Juvenalis . . . priest of the deified Vespasian, vowed and dedicated at his own expense."

[77] *Satires* 3.143f., 10.23f., 295ff., 12.48ff., 13.130ff., 14.173ff. The extent of Juvenal's treatment of the subject, confirmed by the excavations at Antioch, show how widespread was this tendency to venerate ideals and moral qualities instead of the old gods who so imperfectly embodied them. It is easy to see how Christian evangelism flourished in such a climate. All these qualities and more were realized in the historical person of Jesus of Nazareth.

[78] *Satires* 3.318ff., 12.1–9.

[79] Acts 14:8ff.

[80] Peter Green, in his Penguin Translation of Juvenal, comments justly, "In the famous Sixth Satire against women, what Juvenal really objects to is not so much licentiousness *tout court*, as the breaking of class and convention . . . One gets the impression that he would have no particular objection to a little in-group wife-swapping, provided it was done discreetly" (*Juvenal, the Sixteen Satires*, p. 25).

[81] *e.g.* 1 Timothy 2:2.

[82] 2 Peter 1:3.

[83] *Ibid.*, 2 Timothy 3:5.

[84] Titus 1:1.

[85] 2 Peter 1:7.

[86] See below, p. 180ff.

[87] See Justin, *1 Apol.* 14, for instance, or *Epist. ad Diogn.* 10, Athenagoras, *Presb.* 35.

[88] See the cohesion and love which characterized the Jerusalem church or the Antioch church, poised for advance (Acts 2:41–7, 13:1ff.), also 1 Corinthians 13, and 14:24f.

[89] This was always an important part of the message—cf. Acts 17:31, 24:25, Romans 2:4f., etc. But it became a major emphasis in the second century, and was backed by the uncanny other-worldliness of the Christian confessors in their complete mastery of fear. See *Mart. Polyc.* 11, Justin, *1 Apol.* 68, *2 Apol.* 11, 14, Athenagoras, *Presb.* 12, *Ep. Barn.* 21, etc.

[90] Mark 1:34, 39, 3:15, etc. Luke 8–11 *passim.*

[91] See Origen's *Contra Celsum* edited by H. Chadwick, especially the Introduction, pp. xvi–xxii.

[92] See T. R. Glover, *Conflict of Religions in the Early Roman Empire*, p. 95ff., for an illuminating study of demons in Plutarch.

[93] Tatian, *Orat.* 29.

[94] Tatian, *Orat.* 9, taking *planēton* in the sense of "deceiving", not "wandering".

[95] *Dial.* 30.

[96] *Dial.* 30.

[97] Colossians 2:15. Indeed, St Paul is convinced that had the evil spirits known the power Christ would exercise through the apparent failure of his crucifixion, they would never have combined their forces to put him on the cross. See 1 Corinthians 2:8 and the discussion in O. Cullmann, *The State in the New Testament*, p. 62ff.

[98] It was closely related to the demons. See Tatian, *Orat.* 9, "Such are all the demons; these are they who have laid down the doctrine of Fate."

[99] The Emperor Tiberius is said to have given up worship of the gods for this reason (Suetonius, *Tib.* 69): "He lacked any deep regard for the gods or other religious feelings, his belief in astrology having persuaded him that the world was wholly ruled by Fate.

[100] See R. P. Martin, *Carmen Christi*, p. 308 for details, and P. Wendland, "Hellenistic Ideas of Salvation in the Light of Ancient Anthropology" in *A.J.T.* 1913, p. 345ff.

[101] Cf. Revelation, ch. 5.

[102] *Op. cit.*, p. 310f.

[103] Ignatius, *Ephesians*, 19.

[104] See above, p. 114.

[105] We see the dominance of the risen Christ over magic in Acts 19:13ff., and 8:18ff. The magicians realized they had met their match. Here was something in every way superior to magic. Instead of attempting to dominate the powers of the unknown by the discovery of the right spells, Christians submitted themselves in prayerful trust to the Lord of the universe, to be his agents in healing. So great was the power of Jesus's name seen to be, that even Jews used it as a spell. See above, p. 109f. What is more, it occurs in the Paris Magical Papyrus, which contains a fantastic amalgam of Jewish, Greek and Egyptian elements. So great was the impact of the Christian gospel that men were converted in Ephesus, extolled the name of Jesus as Lord, gave up their magic arts, and burnt their books of spells—a bonfire that cost them some 50,000 pieces of silver. "So the word of the Lord grew and prevailed mightily" (Acts 19:20). On the other hand, it was not long before magic exercised its own impact on Christianity. A magical attitude to the sacraments appears as early as Ignatius and the attitudes of magic frequently persisted in peasant superstitions and the *sortes biblicae* against which

Augustine inveighed (*Ep.* 55.37)—forgetful that his own conversion ("*tolle, lege*") was based on this very thing!

[106] *Ephesians* 19.

[107] Irenaeus, *Adv. Haer.* 2.32.

[108] This deliverance became a very prominent feature of second century apologetic. Tertullian treats it fully in his *Apologeticus*, ch. 22–6, concluding that many people have become Christians because of the manifest superiority of Christ's power over any other. In *Ad Scapulam*, 2, he claims, "We do more than repudiate the demons; we overcome them. We expose them daily to contempt, and exorcize them from their victims, as is well known." See also Tertullian, *De Corona* 11, *Clem. Hom.* 9.19, Theophilus, *Ad Autol.* 2. Celsus regards Jesus as a master magician, and Origen has no difficulty in refuting the charge (*Contra Celsum* 1.68).

[109] Acts 14:11.

[110] Lystra was made a Roman *colonia* for retired veterans in A.D. 6.

[111] Such is the meaning of Acts 14:13, in the light of epigraphic evidence, set out by W. M. Calder, *Classical Review*, 1910, pp. 67–81. Artemis Propolis (before the city) occurs in *C.I.G.*, 2963.

[112] See the evidence in F. F. Bruce, *The Acts of the Apostles*, p. 281, Cadbury and Lake, *The Beginnings of Christianity*, iv, p. 164.

[113] Ovid *Metamorph.* 8.626ff.

[114] This is, of course, hotly contested, in particular by Barthian scholars, but it seems to me to be clearly supported by the texts in Acts and Romans, and is undeniably present in second century preaching.

[115] "Who made the heaven and the earth and the sea and all that is in them" comes from Exodus 20:11 (significantly enough in the context of ethical commands); "food and gladness" recalls Ecclesiastes 9:7; the reference to crops and rainfall suggests Jeremiah 5:24, Genesis 8:22, Psalm 147:8, etc.

[116] Isaiah 44:9–20, Psalms 115:4–8, 135:15–18.

[117] Acts 17:16.

[118] Acts 17:18.

[119] Altars to "unknown gods" (in the plural) are attested for Athens by an inscription (see B. Gärtner, *The Areopagus Address and Natural Revelation*, p. 242 for details) and by references in Pausanias (1.1.4), Diogenes Laertius (1.110), and Strabo (3.16).

[120] It most probably alludes to an occasion when Epimenides of Crete (quoted in Acts 17:27), is said to have put an end to a plague in Athens by sending out black and white sheep from the Areopagus to wander at will before being sacrificed at various spots to the appropriate god. He then commemorated the whole affair by setting up altars to unknown gods. John Chrysostom, Isho'dad, and other writers, however, have different accounts.

[121] Gärtner, *op. cit.* p. 245.

[122] There are echoes of Isaiah 42:5, 55:6, Psalms 50:12, 145:18, Jeremiah 23:23, Deuteronomy 32:8.

[123] Psalm 50:9–12.

[124] F. F. Bruce, *The Book of the Acts*, p. 336. See also his *Apostolic Defence of the Gospel*, ch. 2.

[125] They liked to think of themselves as *autochthones*, original inhabitants (a conceit for which there was no historical justification!) and thus superior to other Greeks who had migrated, and of course to barbarians. What the implications are of Paul's assertion that all men spring from a single stock may be seen in Romans 5:12ff.; there is indeed a human unity, but it is one of sin and failure.

[126] The poem of Epimenides on the tomb of Zeus is probably cited here, as also in Titus 1.12. It became a commonplace, however: Aratus, *Phaenomena* 5, Cleanthes, *Hymn to Zeus*, 4.

[127] The Stoicism here is more apparent than real: the background is predominantly that of the Old Testament, as is shown by the phrase "made by man" (v. 24), which has roots in Old Testament polemic against all idolatry as "the work of men's hands".

[128] Romans 1:19f.

[129] Romans 1:21, 25.

[130] Romans 1:24, 26, 28.

[131] *De Ira Dei*, 2.

[132] "Stoic, Sceptic and Cynic philosophers (in part the Epicureans also) had preceded Christianity along this line, and satires upon the gods were as cheap as blackberries in that age" is Harnack's splendid comment (*op. cit.* p. 292).

[133] See Schürer, *Jewish People in the Time of Christ* 2. iii. 262ff.

[134] No philosopher would refuse to make sacrifice to the gods, if it came to the pinch. He would not dream of dying for the sceptical position about the gods he often advocated. For such men their attacks on the gods was a matter of purifying common superstition: for the Christian it was a matter of conviction, opposing fundamental error.

[135] *Dialexeis*, 2.5. See H. Chadwick's Introduction to Origen's *Contra Celsum*, p. xvii. He compares *Dio Chrys.* 31.11, "Some say that Apollo, Helios and Dionysus are the same god, as indeed you also think: and many maintain that all the gods are simply one particular force and power, so that it makes no difference whether one worships this one or that one."

[136] Celsus, who made this point strongly (as did Julian after him), was merely reiterating the traditional Roman view that the prosperity of the Empire depended in no small measure upon the maintenance of the *religio* with the gods.

[137] This, of course, they strenuously denied, and drew analogies with Socrates who rejected the polytheism then current but had a strong belief in the Divine. On this, see Justin, *1 Apol.* 5. Nevertheless an international society with no national gods appeared to be a very queer anomaly on the religious scene of the ancient world.

[138] The writings of Tertullian are more concerned with this problem than any other.

[139] 1 Corinthians 8:4.

[140] 1 Corinthians 10:19, 20.

[141] *Contra Celsum*, Book viii.

[142] *Ep. ad Diogn.* 2.

[143] *Contra Celsum*, 3:29, 37.

[144] *Apologet.* 22.

[145] Thus Isis worship imposed some restrictions on Lucius's sexual adventures, as the eleventh book of the *Metamorphoses* makes plain, nevertheless the notorious sexual licence of the Isis cult was a commonplace in antiquity. Juvenal, *Satires* 6.35ff. refers to the rule that there should be abstention from sexual intercourse for a few days before engaging in the Isis cult, or for nine days before the feast of Ceres, but he also makes it abundantly plain that this regulation was shamelessly flouted. Nock is over-influenced by the ritual requirements of a Lydian inscription of the second century B.C., and rather naïvely assumes that ethics and religion were more closely intertwined in antiquity than in fact they were. See his *Conversion*, p. 217.

[146] For details, see my *Commentary on 2 Peter and Jude*, p. 48ff., 177ff.

[147] *2 Apol.* 5.

[148] Athenagoras, *Presb.* 24–8.

[149] *De Principiis*, 3.2.1 and 4. Contrast with this, Origen's warning to the *more* intelligent that they should take note of Scripture, and not suppose that they can discount the possibility of evil arising from demons! (*Comm. in Joann.* 20.4).

[150] *1 Apol.* 14.

[151] Tertullian, *De Idol.* 1.

[152] The strands of sacramental realism and Logos Christology show a particularly close affinity in the two writers.

[153] *The Doctrine of Grace in the Apostolic Fathers.*

[154] *The Divine Apostle* and *The Spiritual Gospel*. The sensitivity of Professor

Wiles's approach is clear from the following warning against supposing that we have a final interpretation of the meaning of the apostles. "We as much as they (the subapostolic interpreters of the apostles) are children of our own times, and there may well be aspects of Pauline thought to which we are blinded through the particular presuppositions and patterns of theological thinking in our own day" (*The Divine Apostle*, p. 132).

[155] Ch. 8.
[156] Ch. 7.
[157] Ch. 9.
[158] Ch. 10.
[159] Ch. 9.
[160] Ch. 8.
[161] Ch. 10.
[162] especially in Luke, Paul and 1 Peter.
[163] Ch. 10.
[164] Ch. 11.
[165] Ch. 7.
[166] Ch. 5.
[167] especially 2 Corinthians 4:12, 6:9, 10.
[168] The date is much in doubt. Westcott placed it as early as A.D. 117, Lightfoot and most scholars about A.D. 150. See the discussion in H. G. Meecham, *The Epistle to Diognetus*.
[169] P. Andriessen in *Rècherches de Théologie, ancienne et medievale*, 1946, has argued that it is in fact the lost *Apology* of Quadratus, addressed to the Emperor Hadrian (under the honorific pseudonym of Diognetus) in the first quarter of the second century. See the discussion in Meecham, *op. cit.* pp. 148-52.
[170] The first quotation comes from his *Spiritual Homilies* no. 20 and the second from no. 30.
[171] In *Ephesians*, 12, he addresses "fellow-initiates of the Mysteries".
[172] *Ephesians*, 20.
[173] *Ephesians*, 18. The meaning of *pathei* is uncertain.
[174] See especially *Sim.* 9.16.
[175] 1 Corinthians 1:10-17.
[176] 1 Corinthians 10:1ff.
[177] 1 Corinthians 15:29.
[178] Particularly John 6:51ff.
[179] 1 Corinthians 10:1-5 and 21ff.
[180] Sometimes, as at Corinth, both attitudes were found in the same community (chs. 6 and 7 of 1 Corinthians). The same seems to have been true at Colossae (see Colossians 2:16-3:11).
[181] It was almost the only word to express Christian tenets to outsiders. *Superstitio* would have played down the intellectual basis of Christianity: *religio* would have been both impossible (for it denoted a *national* faith) and ridiculous (for to the uninitiated they appeared to be atheists, since they denied the state gods). In any case, a *religio* which had no altar, no temple, no sacrifice would have been quite incredible, as Celsus pointed out.
[182] See J. Munck, *Paul and the Salvation of Mankind, passim.*
[183] This, though carefully avoided in the New Testament, soon crept in. It is to be found as early as Ignatius, *Philad.* 9, *1 Clem.* 40, 41, *Didache* 13.
[184] See Hermas, *Sim.* 8.3.2, where the law is described as the proclamation of salvation which goes out to man. Thus the law possesses a soteriological function integrated with the Son of God in whom men believe. My friend the Rev. George Carey points out to me that Nomos (Law) in Hermas has a somewhat analogous function to Logos (Word) in John, and that both derive, in all probability, from the Wisdom speculation of later Judaism. See also Justin, *Dial.* 43.1 who speaks of Christ as "he who was proclaimed as about to come to all the world, to be the everlasting law and everlasting covenant". It is not right to speak of this tendency deprecatingly as mere moralism, as Moody does. There is

nothing necessarily disloyal to the New Testament revelation in this identifying Christ with the New Torah. It is done both by Matthew and by Paul: undeniably, however, it opens the door to mere moralism once the personification of Torah in Christ is lost sight of.

[185] This is particularly the case in Hermas.

[186] Hermas, *Vis.* 1.2. Hermas, already baptized, asks, "How can I be saved? How shall I propitiate God for the full tale of my sins?", cf. *Sim.* 9.28.6. The same attitude is evident in *Did.* 4.6, "If you can afford it, you shall give the ransom for your sins", and it recurs in the *Apostolic Constitutions* 7.12. This was a most disastrous declension from the New Testament concept of grace, and it bedevilled Western Christendom for centuries.

[187] So J-P Audet, *La Didache*, pp. 187-219. He ascribes the work to Antioch, and dates it A.D. 50-70.

[186] Cf. the "Matthaean Exception", 5.32, 19.9.

[189] Origen, in his *Letter to Gregory*, 2, is well aware of this danger. He is advocating the risky procedure of "spoiling the Egyptians", taking from pagan thought and culture all that is good and true, and using it in the interests of Christian truth. But he continues, "I may tell you from my own experience that not many take from Egypt only the useful, and go away and use it in the service of God . . . There are those who, from their Greek studies, produce heretical notions, and set them up, like the golden calf, in Bethel, which signifies 'God's House'."

[190] Another interesting contrast is that whereas Jewish Christianity always tended to be weak on the deity of Jesus, Gentile Christianity erred in the opposite direction. Jesus was so manifestly divine, in their eyes, that only with difficulty could they think of him as human. The stir which J. A. T. Robinson's *Honest to God* caused is partly, at least, due to this subconscious antagonism among Christians to take the humanity of Jesus as a prime category in understanding him.

[191] *2 Apol.* 12. In the context he goes on to say that he understood from the way they met their deaths that the Christians could not be, as they were accused of being, living in wickedness and vice. But the impact of these deaths on him as a vindication of the doctrines they espoused, is obvious.

[192] *Acta Justin.* 4.

[193] See H. Rahner, *Die Griechischen Mythen in Christlicher Deutung*. Recently a mosaic pavement has been discovered in Hinton St Mary, Dorset, dating from the fourth century, which shows this very characteristic still prevailing. The central figure of this magnificent pavement is manifestly Christ: not only is the XP symbol placed behind the head, but the whole portrait brings immediately to mind the *Christos Pantokrator* of Daphní. However, the adjoining mosaic is of Bellerophon slaying the dragon. No doubt this was rationalized to mean the dragon of evil, now overcome by the victor Christ. See J. M. C. Toynbee, "A New Mosaic Pavement found in Dorset", *J.R.S.*, 1964, p. 7ff.

[194] *1 Clem.* 25. Once again, this pagan symbol of resurrection lived on in the Christian Church. A sixth century mosaic in Sabrotha, Tripolitania, shows clearly the Christian use made of the phoenix.

[195] Herodotus, *Hist.* 2.73, cf. Pliny, *N.H.* 10.2. Hence the wistful mosaic found at Pompeii, and now preserved in the *Museo Nazionale* at Naples, depicting the phoenix, with the inscription, "*Phoenix, felix et tu*" (facing p. 209).

[196] Paul did not like the methods and motives of some who preached Christ at Rome(?) during his imprisonment; but he still rejoiced that, however inadequately, Christ was preached (Philippians 1.14-18).

[197] This unquestionably applies to preaching. See E. Schweizer in *Current Issues in New Testament Interpretation* (ed. Klassen and Snyder), p. 177, "We have to dare to be one-sided, and to make a choice. Otherwise we preach to men of yesterday instead of men of today. At the same time we have to keep the old formulations, even if we do not understand them, as guardians to remind us of parts of our faith which may not be important or even understandable at present, but which may become of first importance in a new situation."

CHAPTER 6

[1] *La conversion au Christianisme*, p. 1.

[2] *Conversion*, chs. 8, 9, 10. Nock was over-influenced by the *Religionsgeschichte* school, and Bardy has little difficulty in showing more clearly the uniqueness of Christianity. Many of the examples Nock chooses are either isolated instances or have particular causes to explain them. See below, n. 4, and p. 145f.

[3] The formalism of ancient religion is hard to exaggerate. "Sanctity," said Cicero (*De Natura Deorum* 2.41) "consists in the knowledge of ritual" ("*sanctitas est scientia colendorum deorum*"). On the Greek side, Plato had said much the same. "What would you say is the essence of holiness and being holy? Is it not the knowledge of how to sacrifice and make prayers?" (*Euthyphro* 14c: see also *Republic* 290d.).

[4] True, here and there you find real ethical piety being stressed in pagan religion. But it is the exception, not the rule. The Philadelphian inscription quoted by Nock, *Conversion*, pp. 216–18, is almost unique for pre-Christian times, though by the late second century A.D. ethical demands are being made for entry into the mystery cults, no doubt under the influence of Christianity. See Origen, *Contra Celsum*, 3.60.
Furthermore, even in the inscription Nock cites, prohibition of robbery, murder and sexual offences are a far cry from the Christian conception of holiness: they are, moreover, all offences which involve ritual impurity, recognized in most societies as a taboo on worship of the gods.
The other passage with which Nock makes play is contained in Apuleius, *Metamorphoses* 11.22.6, the injunctions laid on Lucius when he becomes a priest of Isis after his transformation back to human shape again subsequent to his adventures as an ass. However this, too, is an imperfect parallel. In the first place it is unique. Secondly, it is not holiness but ceremonial correctness which is enjoined on Lucius: his vows to Isis, involving fasts, special foods, and sexual purity are not to be compared with Christian ethics. Even if they were, the exceptional nature of the story must be taken into account; this is the very special response of one who has been rescued from being an animal through the intervention of the goddess Isis, and the vows are his thank-offering as he becomes a priest in her service. Finally, it must not be forgotten that the story is an imaginary one, dating from the latter part of the second century. What pagans of that date could postulate for an imaginary hero had in fact been accomplished for many real people throughout more than a century by the Christian gospel!

[5] Cicero, *De Finibus*, 14.

[6] *Baptism and Conversion*, p. 56.

[7] *Meditations*, 12.28.

[8] At the end of his treatise *De Natura Deorum*.

[9] *Epist.*, 88.

[10] *Epist.*, 45.

[11] The same might be said of Marcus Aurelius, the philosopher-emperor who mercilessly liquidated Christians.

[12] *Op. cit.*, p. 182.

[13] *De Vita Beata*, 20.

[14] Tacitus, *Ann.*, 13.42, 14.52. See also Dio, 61.10 for a list of Seneca's vices. Some of these may be imaginary, but the consensus of ancient sources indicates that when every allowance has been made for malicious gossip, Seneca's life was far from exemplary. S. Dill, in *Roman Society from Nero to Marcus Aurelius*, makes the most of the case in his defence.

[15] *Ad Polyb.*, 6.

[16] *Epist.*, 45.

[17] *Op. cit.*, p. 59.

[18] Josephus, *Antiq.*, 17.5.7, *B.J.*, 1.33.7.

[19] Josephus, *Antiq.*, 19.5.1.

[20] Josephus, *Antiq.*, 20.8.11, *Vita*, 3.

[21] Harnack has an excellent description of the growth of this self-consciousness in his *Mission and Expansion of Christianity*, p. 240ff.

[22] See the discussion in J. Jeremias, *Infant Baptism in the First Four Centuries*, p. 24f, where the evidence is cited.

[23] In his book, *Dialogue with the World*.

[24] So does Lesslie Newbigin in his penetrating book, *The Finality of Christ*, especially chapter five on 'Conversion'.

[25] Page 178.

[26] It is noteworthy that it is the Holy Spirit, not the apostles, who extends the Church's frontiers at points the early Church's leaders would scarcely have considered—Samaritans (ch. 8), eunuchs (ch. 8), Godfearers (ch. 10), and complete Gentiles (ch. 13).

[27] 2:4, 33; 4:8; 6:10; 8:29.

[28] 9:17, 16:6.

[29] 10:45ff., 13:2.

[30] *Essays on New Testament Themes*, pp. 89–91.

[31] *Church Order in the New Testament*, p. 75.

[32] 15:26f.

[33] There is a remarkable recognition of this in Origen, *Contra Celsum* 1.46.

[34] This is a fluid expression which can mean either the Scriptures, or the apostolic proclamation of the Good News with particular emphasis on the resurrection of Jesus. A Turck, writing on the primacy of the Word in evangelism, has this to say: "Toute vie chrétienne commence, d'une façon ou d'une autre, par l'acceptation d'une Parole, qui est l'Évangile du Salut, Parole proposée dans ce qu'on a appelé le Kérygme, et qui porte essentiellement sur le Christ crucifié et ressuscité, Sauveur et Seigneur". (*Évangelisation et Catéchèse*, p. 62.)

[35] Ephesians 6:17.

[36] *Op. cit.* p. 68. He points out that mention of preaching or receiving this Word comes no less than thirty-two times in the Acts.

[37] Thus it was in Judaea (6:7), Samaria (8:4–7, 14), on the First Missionary Journey (13:49), and in Asia (19:20).

[38] Acts 8:35, 5:42, 28:31.

[39] Acts 2:22ff., 3:13ff., ch. 7.

[40] Acts 14:16, 17:30.

[41] It is, however, all too easy to suppose that they had no interest in the historical Jesus. Theophilus, after all, had the whole of Luke's Gospel to read before he got on to the missionary preaching of Acts. He was assuredly not confined to what he could glean from the Acts sermons for his knowledge of the historical Jesus.

[42] Acts 2:38, Romans 8:15, 2 Corinthians 5:19ff.

[43] Acts 13:39.

[44] Acts 14:3, 15:11, 13:46f., 4:12, 13:39.

[45] Jeremiah 31:35f, Ezekiel 36:25ff.

[46] 22:16, 9:17. No less than seven times in Acts is the Holy Spirit described as a gift to be received.

[47] Both repentance and faith, the main elements in the response, are seen as divine gifts, so great is the emphasis on the initiative of God in salvation (5:31, 11:18, 18:27).

[48] Indeed, they counted them! See 2:41, 4:4.

[49] Acts 26:20.

[50] Acts 17:30, 3:26.

[51] The New Testament writers have different ways of expressing the immediacy of faith. To Mark it means "touching" Jesus, to John "seeing" him, to Paul "being in Christ". On any showing, faith is far more than assent to propositions about Christ, though it involves this. It means encounter with Christ arising from commitment on the strength of certain propositions. It is nothing less than self-surrender to the One who surrendered himself for us.

[52] *e.g.* Acts 2:44, 4:4, 11:21, etc. It is hardly surprising that the Christians became known simply as "believers" (5:14, etc.).

[53] Acts 10:43, 14:23, 24:24, etc.

[54] *Op cit.*, p. 14.

[55] On the whole subject of baptism as the "seal" of Christian initiation, see G. W. H. Lampe, *The Seal of the Spirit.*

[56] Genesis 17:9ff.

[57] Colossians 2:11 brings the two sacraments of circumcision and baptism together. The language of Romans 4:1–12 uses language highly significant in this context.

[58] Galatians 3:26, 27.

[59] This does not mean that baptism was inevitably and invariably effective as a sacrament in uniting a man to Christ, if his own attitude was not right. Simon Magus remains the standing example that it was—and is—possible to be still "in the gall of bitterness and the bond of iniquity" after having professed faith and received baptism. G. R. Beasley-Murray's point is a fair one: "Oepke warned us long ago that whoever would rightly evaluate the New Testament teaching on baptism and salvation must keep steadily before him the fact that criticism of any purely external materialistic estimate of religious objects and actions is constitutive for the Bible from the days of the prophets." (*Baptism in the New Testament*, p. 300). Incidentally, Simon Magus provided an invaluable reminder of the importance of baptismal preparation (Cyril, *Procatechesis* I.2).

[60] I Corinthians 12:13.

[61] 2 Peter 1:9.

[62] I Corinthians 6:11.

[63] Titus 3:5.

[64] See the whole cumulative argument in chapter four of Lampe's *Seal of the Spirit.*

[65] Ephesians 1:13, 14.

[66] Romans 6:1ff., 1 Peter 3:21–4.3.

[67] *Polyc.* 6.2.

[68] *Smyrn.* 8.2.

[69] *Sim.* 9.16.3–4.

[70] *Mand.* 4.3.

[71] *The Epistle of Barnabas* links baptism with circumcision (ch. 9) as the New Testament does, and interprets the river of Ezekiel 47:1–12 as the baptismal water into which "we descend laden with the filth of sins" and from which we arise "bearing fruit in our hearts and resting our fear and hope on Jesus in the Spirit", assured of life with Christ for ever (11:11).

[72] See below, p. 154.

[73] Hippolytus, *The Apostolic Tradition*, and Tertullian, *De Baptismo*, at the beginning of which Tertullian speaks of Christians as "little fishes born in water, after the example of our ΙΧΘΥΣ, Jesus Christ."

[74] Justin, *1 Apol.* 61, Tertullian, *De Baptismo* 1.

[75] Acts 16:33, 9:18, 1 Corinthians 1:14f., Acts 8:37. This, of course, does not preclude the probability that careful instruction frequently preceded baptism. Perhaps the reason why Paul did little baptizing may, at least partly, have been due to the fact that he did not normally stay long enough in one place to undertake such instruction, but was always pressing on. At all events, the lack of mention of any catechesis in these New Testament examples was a singular embarrassment to Tertullian (*De Baptismo* 18).

[76] *Baptism in the New Testament*, p. 71ff.

[77] This makes an especially interesting contrast with Acts 8:37, if, as seems quite possible, the *Didache* springs from the first century. If so, it would demonstrate the variety of practice in the matter which would in any case seem probable *a priori* in a rapidly developing and expanding church.

[78] *Didache* 7.1. J.-P. Audet contests the authenticity of the phrase, "Having rehearsed all these things", i.e. the teachings recorded in the first six chapters. But even if he is right, the baptismal context of the Two Ways holds good. See A. Turck, *op. cit.* p. 47f.

[79] P. Carrington, *The Primitive Christian Catechism*, and E. G. Selwyn, *The First Epistle of St Peter*, Essay I.

[80] See Selwyn, *loc. cit.*, C. H. Dodd, *Gospel and Law*, p. 20f., and A. M. Hunter, *Paul and his Predecessors*, pp. 52–7, 128–31. Selwyn points out that these four injunctions always come after some allusion to baptism or the new birth. This strengthens his case that here we have to do with an early baptismal catechesis, but it does not actually demonstrate it.

In 1962 André Turck took matters further than Carrington or Selwyn had done, or for that matter A. Seeberg in *Der Katechismus der Urchristenheit* or J. N. D. Kelly in *Early Christian Creeds*. He maintained that a two-pronged catechesis was used in the Church from the days of the apostles. The one was ethical, with strong Jewish antecedents, and appears in characteristic form in "The Two Ways", as reflected in the *Didache*, *Barnabas*, *Hermas*, *1 and 2 Clement*, the *Clementine Homilies*, and the *Apostolic Constitutions*. This ethical instruction was not, he thinks, necessarily linked very closely with baptism, which it may have preceded or followed in different areas of the Church. It represented *"l'instruction commune aux chrétiens et aux catéchumènes"* (*op. cit.* p. 141).

The other prong of early catechesis was dogmatic, kerygmatic and thoroughly Christocentric, incorporating credal affirmations and demanding a response. It was specifically baptismal in character: here Turck draws heavily on the work of Selwyn. The source of this double catechetical tradition was, he thinks, none other than Jesus himself, in Matthew 7; the apostles followed it up. He points out what an admirable precedent there was for all this in Qumran, where the eschatological and ethical sides of the community's teaching and life went hand in hand. Turck's work is careful and balanced: it may prove to be a decisive contribution to the debate on this perplexing issue.

[81] *1 Apol.* 61.

[82] *Mission and Expansion of Christianity*, p. 228f., where he pens a splendid purple passage against what he takes to be the sacramentalist distortion of Christianity.

[83] This period might be shortened for good conduct!

[84] *Adv. Haer.* 1.10.

[85] Acts 2:41–47.

[86] Acts 9:2, 19.9, 23, 22:4, 14, 22.

[87] and from the ethical implications of the *halak* root which lay behind it in Jewish thought.

[88] Acts 2:43, 5:5, 11, 9:31.

[89] 2:44, 4:32–35, 6:1–6, 10:27–30.

[90] 2:42–46, 20:7.

[91] This statement needs considerable modification in church situations where infant baptism is the norm. The extent of the modification is the subject of extensive contemporary debate. Typical Continental examples are the discussions between Barth and Cullmann, Jeremias and Aland. In England A. Gilmore has edited *Christian Baptism*, and G. R. Beasley-Murray written *Baptism in the New Testament*, both of which question the early use of infant baptism. It is true that the first explicit mention of it comes in Tertullian, but there are plenty of allusions prior to that. Considerations of the attitude of Jesus towards children, the parallel of proselyte baptism (which was applied to all members of the family), the baptism of households in the New Testament, and the absence of any hint of division in the second century over so momentous a subject as the proper recipients of Christian baptism, have combined to convince most Christians that infant baptism probably was practised from apostolic days, as Origen specifically claims. Certainty in the matter cannot be arrived at unless fresh evidence comes to light. But even supposing paedobaptism was practised from the dawn of the Church, it must be understood in the light of the adult rite, as was infant circumcision. Like circumcision, baptism was the covenant seal on God's grace meeting man's response. For adults, the expression of faith was prior to reception of the sacrament: for children it followed later (thus, inci-

dentally, serving to underline the important truth of the priority of God's initiative over man's responsive faith). Failure to repent and believe in those baptized (as infants and as adults alike) indicates that although they possessed the promise of God's salvation they failed to appropriate it personally. The early Christians were well aware of the perils of nominal Christianity, and longed to be Christians not only in name but in reality. See Ignatius, *Rom.* 3.2, *Magn.* 4.1, Polyc. *Phil.* 2.2, *2 Clem.* 14.1, Justin, *1 Apol.* 4.7f, 16.8.

[92] John 8:56, Romans 4:2, 6f.
[93] *Apologet.* 17.
[94] *1 Apol.* 5.
[95] *2 Apol.* 10.
[96] e.g. Tertullian, *Apologet.* 46.
[97] In the context he is bringing a stinging indictment against "the crowning guilt of men, in that they will not recognize One of whom they cannot possibly be ignorant."
[98] *Apologet.* 40.
[99] *Apologet.* 18.
[100] 1 Corinthians 12:13, Romans 6:4, 1 Peter 3:21, John 3:5.
[101] 1 John 2:19.
[102] 1 Corinthians 10:1–11, 11:20.
[103] Acts 8:23.
[104] *Rom.* 3.2, *Magn.* 4.1.
[105] *Phil.* 2.2.
[106] *2 Clem.* 14.1.
[107] Acts 28:23.
[108] Acts 20:7–11.
[109] Acts 13:42.
[110] 17:17, 24:10, 26:1ff.
[111] J. R. W. Stott draws attention to this variety of language used to denote their preaching, *op. cit.* p. 8.
[112] 2:40, 8:25, 10:42, 18:5, 23:11, etc.
[113] 4:2, 13:5, 38, 15:36, etc.
[114] 17:2, 17, 18:4, 19, 19:8, 9, 24:25.
[115] 18:28.
[116] 5:42, 8:4, 12, 25, 35, 40, etc.
[117] 9:29.
[118] 17:3.
[119] 9:22.
[120] 9:22.
[121] 5:28.
[122] 5:21, 25, 28. 5:42 combines both in the phrase "preaching and teaching the Lord Jesus". See F. V. Filson, *Three Crucial Decades*, ch. 2, and the wholesale assault on Dodd's dichotomy in R. C. Worley, *Preaching and Teaching in the Earliest Church.*
[123] *Op. cit.* p. 87.
[124] See A. J. Festugière, "L'éxperience réligieuse du médecin Thessalos", *Revue Biblique*, 1939, p. 57ff.
[125] *Dial.* 1–8. See above, p. 81.
[126] *Orat.* 29.
[127] According to Philip of Side, he was reading the Scriptures in order to confute them—a delightful example of the converting power of the Word of God.
[128] *Ad Autol.* 1.14.
[129] *Strom.* 1.1.
[130] Tatian (*Orat.* 29) and Clement of Alexandria (*Strom.* 1.2) both wax eloquent on this point.
[131] *Orat.* 29.
[132] *Protrep.* 2.
[133] *Barnabas* 2.6.
[134] *Ephesians* 19. See above, p. 124f.

[135] *Clem. Recogn.* 1.1–10. See below, p. 198f., 208.
[136] *2 Apol.* 2.
[137] *Ad Donatum* 3, 4. Somewhat surprisingly, Professor Wiles does not "sense the personal anguish of soul which so clearly shines through the also highly rhetorical account of the conversion of the later North African Bishop, Augustine". He doubts whether the record of Cyprian's conversion suggests any deep transformation of personal life and moral ideals. Yet as he recognizes, the change consequent on Cyprian's transition from paganism to Christianity was so marked that he gave away a large proportion of his possessions and made such a radical break with pagan practices and culture that he refused even to quote pagan literature in his writings. Moreover, it would be difficult to imagine a more deeply moving and genuine way of speaking about his sense of sin and release than Cyprian in fact gave in this letter to Donatus. See "The Theological Legacy of St Cyprian" by M. F. Wiles, in *J.E.H.* xiv. 2, pp. 139–49.
[138] Galatians 2.20.

CHAPTER 7

[1] Mark 3:14.
[2] Matthew 10.
[3] Acts 6:4.
[4] *H.E.* 2.3.1f.
[5] *H.E.* 3.1.1.
[6] Mid-third century.
[7] Eusebius, *H.E.* 5.10. Professor H. Chadwick, citing two articles by A. Dihle, writes of the Pantaenus story, "In view of the trade between the Red Sea and Malabar during the first and second centuries A.D., there is no *a priori* improbability in the story." (*Early Christian Thought and the Classical Tradition*, p. 138.)
[8] J. N. Farquhar, *B.J.R.L.* 1926 and 1927, "The Apostle Thomas in North India" and "The Apostle Thomas in South India". See also ch. 10 n. 4.
[9] Matthew 28:18–20, Mark 13:10, Acts 1:8.
[10] *I Apol.* 39.
[11] See Rengstorf's article "Apostolos" in Kittel's *Theologisches Wörterbuch zum N.T.*
[12] He had to fight hard for recognition of his position as an "apostle of Jesus Christ". The Epistles to Galatia and Corinth shows that there were plenty in the early Church who refused to credit it: he did not, after all, fulfil the conditions of apostolate indicated by Mark 3:10, Acts 1:21ff. By the time of *I Clem.* 47.4, Ignatius, *Rom.* 4.3, his claim was not seriously questioned, though continued rumblings in the pseudo-Clementines seem to show that some Jewish Christians remained unconvinced.
[13] Thus possibly James (Galatians 1:19), Barnabas (1 Corinthians 9:4), Silvanus (1 Thessalonians 2:7), Andronicus and Junia or Junias (Romans 16:7), though all of these can be disputed.
[14] 2 Corinthians 8:23, Philippians 2:25.
[15] 2 Corinthians 11:5, 13, 12:11.
[16] Galatians 1:1ff.
[17] 2:2.
[18] *Vis.* 3.5.1, *Sim.* 9.15.4, 16.5.
[19] *Op. cit.* p. 352–66.
[20] Though bishops and presbyters are equivalent in the New Testament. For a discussion of the evidence, see my *Called to Serve*, p. 42f.
[21] 3 John 6, 7.
[22] *Didache* 4.
[23] *Didache* 13.
[24] *Didache* 11.
[25] On Christian prophecy, see below, p. 200ff.
[26] *Contra Celsum*, 3.9.
[27] Eusebius, *H.E.* 5.10.2.

[28] Eusebius, *H.E.* 3.37.2.
[29] Mark 1:38.
[30] 2 Timothy 4:2, 5.
[31] Ephesians 4:11.
[32] Acts 20:18–28.
[33] 1 Timothy 3:1–7.
[34] Ignatius, *Polyc.* 1.
[35] *Mart. Polyc.* 12.
[36] *Preface* to *Adv. Haer.* 1.1.
[37] Thus Cyprian, of whose conversion we read in the last chapter, was actually brought to faith through the agency of a presbyter. "Caecilianus brought Cyprian from pagan error and led him to the knowledge of the true God" (Pontius, *Vit. Cypr.* 1).
[38] *Ap. Const.* 2.6.
[39] Eusebius, *H.E.* 5.10. See note 7 above.
[40] *Contra Celsum*, 3.50–8.
[41] *Act. Just.* 2.
[42] Irenaeus, *Adv. Haer.* 1.28.
[43] Eusebius, *H.E.* 5.13.
[44] Origen, *Contra Celsum*, 3.52. This policy was, of course, potentially (and actually) explosive.
[45] Origen, *Contra Celsum*, 3.54.
[46] Eusebius, *H.E.* 6.3.
[47] Eusebius, *H.E.* 6.21.
[48] Harnack, *op. cit.*, p. 368.
[49] Acts 8:4.
[50] Acts 11:19–21.
[51] *Contra Celsum*, 3.55.
[52] See above, ch. 2, n. 78, and G. Highet, *Poets in a Landscape*, p. 231f.
[53] 1 Peter 3:15.
[54] Phoebe in Romans 16:1f. occupies an official position. She is *patrona* of the Church, her home its headquarters, her status that of an accredited deaconess. On this office, see the *duae ministrae* of Pliny, *Ep.* 10.96; 1 Timothy 3:11 also probably denotes this office.

It is possible that the Junia of Romans 16:7 is a woman (the accusative case, *Junian*, in which it occurs here would be the same for a man and a woman), and that "apostles" there indicates "apostles of Jesus Christ", particularly as Paul says they were Christians before he was.
[55] Philippians 4:2, 4.
[56] *Contra Celsum*, 3.55.
[57] 1 Peter 3:1f.
[58] *Ap. Const.* 1.10.
[59] *Ad Uxorem*, 2.3–7.
[60] and nerve-racking as well. As Tertullian remarks, at any moment the husband could denounce his wife to the authorities as a Christian, and unless she recanted she would face execution. We have already seen this very thing taking place in Rome when an aristocrat's denunciation of his Christian wife was the main cause for the writing of Justin's *Second Apology*.
[61] *Ad Uxorem*, 2.7.
[62] *De Praescr.* 41.
[63] See W. H. Ramsay, *The Church in the Roman Empire*, p. 375ff.
[64] *Dio.* 67.14, cf. Suetonius, *Domit.* 15, and ch. 5, n.48 above.
[65] Eusebius, *H.E.* 5.1–61.
[66] 1 Peter 3:15f.
[67] 1 Thessalonians 2:1–14.
[68] 1 Thessalonians 2:15, cf. Philippians 4:9.
[69] 1 Thessalonians 1:7, 8.
[70] 2 Corinthians 4:1–5.
[71] Theophilus, *Ad. Autol.* 4.

[72] *Ad. Autol.* 9.
[73] *Ad. Autol.* 13.
[74] *Ad Autol.* 15.
[75] *Ad Autol.* 6.
[76] *Ad Autol.* 5.
[77] *Ad Autol.* 3, 7, 8.
[78] *Ad Autol.* 14.
[79] *Presb.* 11.
[80] Acts 2:42.
[81] Acts 13:1ff.
[82] 1 Thessalonians 1:3.
[83] 1 Thessalonians 3:12.
[84] 1 Thessalonians 4:9ff.
[85] 1 Thessalonians 5:13.
[86] 1 Corinthians 11:20ff.; chs. 12–14.
[87] Philippians 1:15, 3:15–19, 4:2f., Romans 14:1–15:3.
[88] Jude 1 and 2 Peter 2.
[89] James 2:1ff.
[90] Mark 3:32ff. cf. John 7:5.
[91] Later, of course, James achieved leadership in the Jerusalem Church, and was in fact succeeded by another of the Lord's relatives.
[92] See on this term, A. R. George, *Communion with God*.
[93] 1 Corinthians 14:23ff.
[94] *1 Apol.* 9.
[95] The descriptions which follow are all taken from Tertullian, *Apologet.* 39. See, however, above, ch. 2, n. 65.
[96] *Epi.* 10.96.
[97] 2 Corinthians 3:18, cf. Romans 12:1, 2.
[98] Galatians 4:19.
[99] *1 Apol.* 14.
[100] Pliny, *Ep.* 10.96, Lucian, *De Morte Peregrini*, *passim*.
[101] *Med.* 11.3; Galen, *De Sententiis Politiae Platonicae*.
[102] *Ephes.* 10.
[103] *2 Clement* 13.3. While *2 Clement* contains much preaching material, it is designed for use in church, at worship. Consequently, Conzelmann's astounding statement, "No primitive Christian preaching has been transmitted to us ... The oldest is *2 Clement*" (*The Theology of the New Testament*, p. 88) is as misleading about *2 Clement* as it is libellous about Acts.
[104] Sadly, the variety of Christian good works (cf. Titus 2.7 Gk) tended to become fossilized as time went by into the more obvious categories of sexual continence and abstinence from anything cruel or idolatrous. But these short-hand pointers to Christian ethic never entirely supplanted the flowering of true Christian *agapē*.
[105] Harnack (*Mission and Expansion*, p. 208f.) has pointed out the curious paradox in Christian moral theology at this point. On the one hand they assumed that pagans knew, almost intuitively, what virtue was: in that respect Christian morality was not new. It was professed, if not kept, by the philosophers. On the other hand, they argued that the quality of their Christian living was a demonstration of the supernatural life at work within them, and in this sense, therefore, it was entirely new. If a Celsus had to confess that "nobody could entirely change people who sin by nature and habit, not even by punishment, much less by mercy" (Origen, *Contra Celsum* 3.65) the writer of the *Epistle to Diognetus* could point to Christian lives and say, "This does not look like the work of man: this is the power of God" (*Diogn.* 7).
[106] *Oct.* 22.8, Tertullian, *Apol.* 15.
[107] *Martyrdom and Persecution in the Early Church*, p. 330ff.
[108] Acts 4:12.
[109] John 15:11, 16:22.
[110] Acts 16:25.

[111] Cf. Philippians 3:1, 4:4.
[112] Acts 8:8, 13:52, 15:3.
[113] 1 Thessalonians 1:6.
[114] Acts 5:41.
[115] Romans 5:2.
[116] Romans 5:3.
[117] Romans 5:11.
[118] Hebrews 13:5.
[119] Hebrews 12:2.
[120] Acts 20:24.
[121] Romans 8:34–9.
[122] *Apologet.* 21.
[123] ch. 5.
[124] Psalm 16:11, Philippians 1:23.
[125] Acts 8:5, 6, 26ff.
[126] 1 Peter 1:8, Tacitus, *Ann.* 15.44.
[127] It is not improbable that Flavius Sabinus, the elder brother of the Emperor Vespasian, who perished in the year of the four emperors, A.D. 69, was a Christian, and owed his conversion to the events he had witnessed in A.D. 64 when, as *Praefectus Urbi*, he was in charge of the execution of Christians for supposed arson. He had been a man of action throughout his distinguished career, in the course of which he had served the State in thirty-five campaigns and had been the Governor of Moesia. Surprisingly, therefore, we read that he became "a gentle man who abhorred slaughter and bloodshed" at the end of his life. "Some thought had had got lazy, but others believed that he had mellowed, and was anxious to spare the blood of his fellow citizens" (Tacitus, *Hist.* 3.65 and 75). The latter estimate proved the more just, it would seem, for he died, when the Vitellians stormed the Capitol, "unarmed and showing no thought of flight" (Tacitus, *Hist.* 3.73). All of this does not prove he was a Christian. But when taken alongside the fact that his niece Domitilla and others in the family were Christians, the sudden transformation of a man of action into a man of peace, of a soldier into a martyr, of a man whose trade was arms into one who hated bloodshed, then the probabilities are that he did come under Christian influence, to rate it no higher. The most probable cause was the wholesale slaughter of Christians, which disgusted Roman society, and in which Sabinus was officially implicated. It may well be that the entry of Christianity into the imperial family in this way was the direct result of the faithful testimony of the Christian martyrs of A.D. 64.
[128] *Apologet.*, 50.
[129] Acts 4:23ff.
[130] Galatians 6:17.
[131] Philippians 1:29.
[132] Colossians 1:24.
[133] Acts 12:1–6.
[134] *1 Clem.* 5.
[135] Recorded in Eusebius, *H.E.* 2.8.
[136] 1 Thessalonians 1:5.
[137] *Op. cit.*, p. 131.
[138] G. B. Caird, *Principalities and Powers*, H. Schlier, *Principalities and Powers in the New Testament*. See also K. E. Koch, *Between Christ and Satan*.
[139] *The Significance of Satan* and *Essentials of Demonology*.
[140] Mark 6:12, 13.
[141] Luke 10:17.
[142] Mark 16:15ff.
[143] Hebrews 2:4.
[144] Acts 3:1ff.
[145] Acts 5:14.
[146] Acts 8:13.
[147] Acts 8:6f.

[148] Acts 19:1–12.
[149] I Corinthians 12:9, 10, James 5:14f.
[150] *2 Apol.* 6.
[151] *Adv. Haer.* 2.32.
[152] *Ibid.*
[153] *Adv. Haer.* 2.31, 32.
[154] *Contra Celsum*, 2.51.
[155] *Contra Celsum*, 1.6, 7.4. Origen's words clearly refer to recounting some stories about Jesus.
[156] *Contra Celsum*, 7.4.
[157] *Dial.* 85.
[158] *Apol.* 23.
[159] Ch. 2.
[160] *Oct.* 27.
[161] *Orat.* 12–19.
[162] *Contra Celsum, passim.*
[163] *Ad Demetr.* 15, *Ad Donat.* 5.
[164] 8:1.
[165] See above, p. 109ff., also the Paris Magical Papyrus, and, of course, Acts 19:13ff.
[166] 8:1.
[167] The same chapter of the *Constitutions* points this out. Precisely the same thing happened in Jesus's own day. His mighty works could either be shrugged off by persistent unbelief, or assigned to Beelzebub.
[168] Origen, *Contra Celsum*, 8.36.
[169] In his massive book *Possession, Demoniacal and Other.* See, for instance, p. 389: "The purely negative reply [*i.e.* to the question of "parapsychic phenomena"] which so greatly facilitated for rationalism the historical criticism of all these accounts is frankly no longer possible today."
[170] *After the Apostles*, pp. 61–71. His opinion is particularly weighty as he was not only a Professor of Church History but also a missionary. He gives records of both exorcisms and healings on the contemporary mission field.
[171] Thus the head of the Overseas Missionary Fellowship writes, in a personal letter, of scores of such instances in South East Asia, referring to such written documentation as *Borneo Breakthrough* by S. Houlison, and *Demons Despoiled* by N. M. Nordmo. He continues, "What is called 'demon possession' seems to relate chiefly to dramatic manifestations of demon possession or demon influence. But in our thinking this is the sign and symptom, whereas the crux of the matter is submission to demons, the manifestations of which, in addition to demon possession, include service as spirit mediums, trance activities such as fire walking, having swords thrust through cheeks and tongue, and so forth, and also manifestations of demonic violence and wickedness quite apart from the usual evidences of trances or 'possession'." Foster's conclusion (see previous Note), is this. "This Younger Church is repeating the experience of the Early Church and is true to the tradition both of apostolic and post-apostolic preaching." (*op. cit.* p. 71). See also C. N. Moody, *The Mind of the Early Converts*, p. 105f., "Joy in redemption from bondage to idols and demons, joy in the great Creator and Preserver, is a prominent feature in the Christianity of many peoples. Among converted savages it is sometimes the whole of religion." He proceeds to give specific examples.
[172] See, e.g. Dr K. E. Koch, *Between Christ and Satan.*
[173] Page 224.

CHAPTER 8

[1] *Worship in Ancient Israel*, ch. 7, "The Synagogue".
[2] Acts 13:16, 26, 38.
[3] ch. 4.
[4] *Missionary Methods*, p. 62ff.

⁵ On the place of healing in the total context of salvation preaching, see my *The Meaning of Salvation*, p. 218ff., and Dorothee Hoch, *Healing and Salvation*.
⁶ Israel Levinthal, *Problems of Jewish Ministry*, p. 17, citing *Koheleth Rabba* 11.2.
⁷ John Peterson, *Missionary Methods of Judaism in the Early Roman Empire*, p. 155ff. See also R. C. Worley, *Preaching and Teaching in the Earliest Church*, p. 64ff.
⁸ See above, p. 170.
⁹ *Ad Demetr.* 13.
¹⁰ *H.E.* 1.13.18.
¹¹ *H.E.* 1.13.20f. See further, ch. 10, n. 3 and 4.
¹² *Clem. Recogn.* 1.7. On the value that may attach to the *Grundschrift* of the Clementine romances, see O. Cullmann, *Le Problème Literaire et Historique du Roman Pseudo-Clementin*, and G. Strecker, *Das Judenchristentum in den Pseudoklementinen*.
¹³ See Suetonius, *Vespasian* 4, Tacitus, *Hist.* 5.13 and Josephus, *B.J.* 6.5.4.
¹⁴ *Clem. Recogn.* 1.9.
¹⁵ See Acts 11:27, 13:1, Romans 12:6, 1 Corinthians 12–14, 1 Thessalonians 5:20, Revelation 1:3, 22:18. One category in which Christians saw the newness of their religion was that of prophecy. Jesus was *the* eschatological prophet, promised long ago in Deuteronomy 18:18, who revived and brought fulfilment to Israel's long line of prophets (Matthew 5:19, Acts 3:22, 7:37, 17:37 cf. John 4:44). In succession to Jesus, Christian prophecy was born on the Day of Pentecost (Acts 2:18). And its content was none other than *the* prophet, Jesus himself. Once again the proclaimer had become the proclaimed.
¹⁶ 1 Corinthians 12:29. However, Revelation 10:7 (cf. 11:10, 16:6) seems to indicate that the gift was open to all: "prophets" seems to be synonymous with "servants of Christ".
¹⁷ It was also prized, of course, because it was so valuable to the community bent on discerning the will of the Lord. See 1 Corinthians 14:1.
¹⁸ Ephesians 2:20, 3:5.
¹⁹ 1 Corinthians 14:3, 32.
²⁰ Acts 11:28.
²¹ 1 Timothy 4:14.
²² Revelation 19:10.
²³ 1 Corinthians 14:24f.
²⁴ 1 Corinthians 14:3f., and the probable implication of Acts 13:1 is that the prophets are also teachers.
²⁵ 1 Corinthians 14:29f.
²⁶ 1 Corinthians 14:37–9.
²⁷ e.g., *Didache* 11.
²⁸ *Adv. Prax.* 1.
²⁹ *Contra Celsum* 7.9.
³⁰ So Harnack, *op. cit.*, p. 353, n. 3, Reitzenstein, *Hellenistische Mysterienreligionen*, p. 143f.
³¹ So, for instance, Ritsch in *Die Entstehung der altkatholischen Kirche*, p. 506. As, however, P. de la Labriolle has observed in *La Crise Montaniste*, p. 95f., Origen knew too much about the Montanists not to mention them in his reply to Celsus's charge, if it was indeed they who were meant.
³² W. K. Knox, *Hellenistic Elements in Primitive Christianity*, p. 83, n. 2.
³³ The text appeared in *Papyrus Bodmer* 13, and is edited by M. Testuz, *Méliton de Sardes, Homélie sur la Pâque*, 1960. A little of it is to be found in the recently identified Latin of Melito. See H. Chadwick, "A Latin Epitome of Melito's Homily on the Pascha" in *J.T.S.* April 1960.
³⁴ Eusebius, *H.E.* 5.24.5.
³⁵ *Philad.* 7.1.
³⁶ *Pap. Bod.* 13, para. 100ff.
³⁷ *Pap. Bod.* 13, para. 9.
³⁸ This was professedly based on the style of Gorgias in the fifth century B.C.,

as Michel Testuz points out in his Introduction, p. 20f. There are traces of this style of writing in the New Testament: Ephesians 1:3–14, 1 Timothy 3:16, and, he might have added, 2 Peter and Jude, where it is particularly marked. See my *Commentary on 2 Peter and Jude*, p. 18f., E. Norden, *Die antike Kunstprosa*, pp. 126–52. Sherman Johnson agrees, and points out in his Essay on "Christianity in Sardis" (*Early Christian Origins*, ed. Allen Wikgren, p. 84) that both Melito and Ignatius were influenced by this "florid Asian style which arose in the Maeander valley before the Christian era, and at this time was gradually being superseded among pagan *literati* by the sober Atticistic fashion."

[39] 1 Corinthians 14:24f.
[40] *The First Five Centuries*, p. 117.
[41] Origen, *Comm. in Ps. 36*, 3.3 (my translation).
[42] Eusebius, *H.E.* 6.3.
[43] *Ibid.*
[44] Eusebius, *H.E.* 6.4.
[45] *Act. Just.* 1, 2.
[46] Acts 19:31.
[47] Acts 19:8.
[48] Acts 24:12.
[49] "If the custom of the country was the same as it is now, the period almost exactly covers the time devoted to the midday meal and the siesta. At one p.m. there were probably more people sound asleep than at one a.m." (*Beginnings of Christianity*, iv. p. 239.).
[50] *The Book of Acts*, p. 389.
[51] 2 Corinthians 9:15.
[52] 1 Timothy 1:15.
[53] Romans 7:23–5.
[54] *Act. Just.* 3.
[55] *Protrep.* 12.
[56] *Orat.* 42.
[57] *Ibid.* 29.
[58] *Contra Celsum*, 3.55.
[59] *Clem. Recogn.* 1.12–16.
[60] *Clem. Hom.* 8.38. A further example is provided by *Clem. Recogn.* 10.71, which tells us that Theophilus (? supposedly the man mentioned in Luke 1.1) "with all eagerness of desire made over the great palace of his house as a church . . . and the whole multitude, assembling daily to hear the Word, believed."
[61] Acts 17:5.
[62] Acts 18:7.
[63] Acts 21:8.
[64] Acts 16:15, 32–4.
[65] 1 Corinthians 1:16.
[66] 1 Corinthians 16:15.
[67] Acts 1:13f., 12:12.
[68] *Infant Baptism in the First Four Centuries*, ch. 1, and *The Origins of Infant Baptism*, ch. 2.
[69] "Zur Kindertaufe in der Urkirche", in *Deutsches Pfarrerblatt*, 1949, p. 152ff.
[70] See H. Mattingly, *The Emperor and his Clients*.
[71] Acts 13:1.
[72] John 19:12.
[73] K. Aland, *Did the Early Church Baptize Infants?*
[74] Assuming, as is highly likely, but not as yet conclusively demonstrable, that the practice of Jewish proselyte baptism goes back to pre-Christian days.
[75] Acts 10:24.
[76] Acts 10:27.
[77] Acts 10:48.
[78] Acts 16:15.
[79] Acts 16:33.
[80] *Ad Uxorem* 2.

[81] *2 Apol.* 2.

[82] 2 Corinthians 6:14.

[83] 1 Corinthians 7:14.

[84] Tacitus *Ann.*, 13.32. The verdict was proper enough. At that date Christianity was undifferentiated from the *religio licita* of Judaism in Roman eyes.

[85] See H. Leclerq, "Aristocratiques: Pomponia Graecina" in *Dictionaire d'archaeologie Chrétienne et de liturgie*, i. 2847f., and G. Edmundson, *The Church in Rome in the First Century*, p. 85f.

[86] Philippians 4:22.

[87] Philippians 1:13. I do not regard the arguments of G. S. Duncan in *St Paul's Ephesian Ministry* as persuasive, let alone conclusive. The oft-repeated claim that there is inscriptional evidence for the presence of a detachment of the Praetorian Guard at Ephesus is a gross blunder. The inscription, "*T. Valerio T. F. Secundo Militis Cohortis VII Praetoriae*" belongs to the time of Septimius Severus, not Nero! In any case, it need mean no more than that proud relatives in Ephesus set up this memorial to Valerius Secundus, the local boy who had made good and had had the honour of serving in the Praetorian Guard at Rome.

[88] Duncan presses the claims of Ephesus hard, but there are strong reasons against it. The *Aristobuliani* and *Narcissiani* both suit Rome better (16:10f.). So does the greeting, "The churches of Christ greet you" (16:16). Moreover Paul's policy seems to have been to include large numbers of personal greetings in a letter only when he had *not* visited the place. Many noses would have been put out of joint at Ephesus if Paul had sent his love to only twenty-six people after having laboured in their midst for upwards of three years.

[89] See his Excursus, "Caesar's Household" in his *St Paul's Epistle to the Philippians*.

[90] Romans 16:10.

[91] Romans 16:11.

[92] The date of his death is uncertain. He was still alive in A.D. 45 (Josephus, *B.J.* 2.11.6, *Ant.* 20.1.2).

[93] A. N. Sherwin-White, in private correspondence, writes, "I suspect the method of contact for upper class Roman families was through their freedmen", a judgment in which Professor Jocelyn Toynbee concurs.

[94] Dio 67.14. It is a curious fact, which Fergus Millar notes in his book, *A Study of Cassius Dio* (pp. 108, 179) that Dio nowhere mentions Christians, though he must have been well aware of their existence and rapid growth. His silence, no doubt, was induced by disapproval.

[95] Suetonius, *Domit.* 13. The Christian reaction comes through loud and clear in the Book of Revelation.

[96] Suetonius, *Domit.* 13.

[97] Eusebius, *H.E.* 3.20.1ff.

[98] L. Hertling and E. Kirschbaum, *The Roman Catacombs*, p. 40. For detailed discussion see Marruchi's *Éléments d'archéologie chrétienne*, ii. p. 422ff.

[99] Acts 18:1, Suetonius, *Claudius* 25. The date is supplied by Orosius.

[100] Even this is not necessary. She, too, may have been a freedwoman, who took the feminine *nomen gentile* of Prisca. See the careful note by Sanday and Headlam, *Romans*, pp. 418–20, and Pauly-Wissowa, *Real-Encyclopädie* s.v. "Acilius".

[101] Sanday and Headlam comment, "If this suggestion be correct, then both the names of these two Roman Christians and the existence of Christianity in a leading Roman family are explained."

[102] See J. Daniélou, *Primitive Christian Symbols*, p. viiif., and 138f. He draws attention to the work of B. Bagatti and E. Testa on these Jewish Christian symbols of an early date. The evidence is set out in Testa's *Il Symbolismo dei Giudei Christiani*, published in 1962 after their finds in Hebron, Nazareth and Jerusalem in 1960, to which I have not had access.

[103] This is all the more probable in view of the centrality of the cross to Christian preaching and living from the earliest days (1 Corinthians 1:18, 2:2). So central was it that "Barnabas" could read it back into the enumeration of

Abraham's servants, and Justin could argue that the shape of the plough, the ship's mast, or the legionary standard bore unconscious testimony to the Christian symbol of the cross (*Barnabas* 9, Justin, *1 Apol.* 55). Moreover, charcoal crosses were found on the Talpioth ossuaries, which are apparently Christian burial caskets coming from an undisturbed tomb on the outskirts of Jerusalem and datable numismatically to *c.* A.D. 50. See E. L. Sukenik in *A.J.A.* 1947, pp. 351–65, and B. Gustafsson's partial reassessment of the significance of the graffiti (though not of the crosses) in *N.T.S.* 1956, p. 65ff. These discoveries call in question the oft-repeated claim that the cross was not used as a Christian symbol in the early days, and that it appears to have come in from Gnostic sources in the third century (see the discussion and illustrations of the cross found in the Christian-Gnostic hypogaeum of the Aurelii dating from before A.D. 270 in Jerome Carcopino, *De Pythagore aux Apôtres*).

[104] Indeed, one might hazard the guess that just as the heathen *lararia* housed replicas of their gods, so the Christian chests may have contained the Communion vessels and a copy of the Septuagint. It may well be to a chest of this sort, rather than to the oblong object we would otherwise envisage, that the proconsul of Africa Proconsularis referred in A.D. 180 when he asked the Scillitan martyrs what they had in their box (*capsa*); to which they replied, "Books, and the letters of Paul, a good man." It is very interesting indeed to note that in the fifth century mosaic at Ravenna in the Mausoleum of Galla Placidia there is a chest of almost exactly the same shape as the one at Herculaneum, showing St Lawrence by it, and enabling one to read the names of the books within: Matthew, Mark, Luke and John! See Plates 2 and 3.

[105] André Grobar in his massive book, *Christian Iconography*, is unfortunately rather slight on the earliest period. He maintains (p. 32) that there is no difference between the Christian and the pagan *oranti*. However, the illustrations he gives (plates 59 and 60) show precisely the difference I am maintaining. cf. Plate 1.

[106] The scene is unmistakable. The two women, the child, the king on his *tribunal*, and the crowd of fascinated sightseers awaiting the verdict, all make the subject beyond dispute.

[107] See note 108 below, and the account of M. Della Corte, *Nota degli Scavi*, vol. v. 449, no. 112, and his *Renconditi Pontif. Acc. di Archaeologia*, vol. xii, pp. 397–400. A further example of the *Rotas–Sator* square was found in the *palaestra* at Pompeii, and survives. The excavators say that it was discovered in a layer of thick and undisturbed ash (I owe this observation to Professor J. M. C. Toynbee) which makes nonsense of the desperate expedient of arguing that the magic square was put there by investigators long after the destruction of the city, like the interpretative graffito, *Sodoma*! The square has now been found in either certain or probable Christian contexts, as far apart as Dura-Europus on the Euphrates and Cirencester in England. Its importance at Pompeii lies in the fact that it indicates that some Italian Christians in the first century spoke Latin in preference to Greek.

[108] Two other discoveries at Pompeii seem to be straws in the wind pointing in the same direction, particularly when attention is paid to the spots where they were unearthed.

It was not unusual for Romans to mark the very centre of a cross-roads with a small cross, each arm of which pointed exactly along the appropriate road. There are some examples at Pompeii. But at the junction of the Via di Stabia and the Via di Nola there is a cross of a different design, which looka a more amateur and unofficial mark on the pavement and is certainly not in the centre of the cross-roads. This place was a very crowded thoroughfare, at the exit from the Central Baths. Could this cross be some early Christian's way of alluding to his faith in the streets of the city by means of an ambivalent symbol, at once like the official cross-roads mark and unlike?

The other scrap of evidence concerns the famous *Rotas-Sator* square (see note 107 above). The present state of the discussion is well summarized by H. Last in *J.T.S.* 1952, p. 92ff. See also F. V. Filson in the *Biblical Archaeologist*, 1939, p. 14f. The square is as follows:

```
R  O  T  A  S
O  P  E  R  A
T  E  N  E  T
A  R  E  P  O
S  A  T  O  R
```

At first sight its meaning is obscure: perhaps "Arepo the sower holds the wheels with care". But a deeper meaning must have made it congenial to the Christian community. As A. R. Smith suggests to me in a personal letter, it could be translated thus: "The God who sows the seed (i.e. of the Gospel) holds the spheres (i.e. of the universe) with care." This assumes that AREPO can be a concealed way of alluding to God. This is not impossible: *Alpha Rex Et Pater Omega*. Certainly the Alpha and Omega motif attracted them strongly. The letters of the square can be rearranged in the following anagram which gives us both a double *Pater Noster* in the shape of a cross and also a repetition of the A and O, as if to stress that Christ crucified is the alpha and omega of human history. Indeed, the T (an early Christian symbol for the cross: *Epistle of Barnabas* 9.8) lies between the A and O on all four sides of the square, as if to reiterate the message. The rearranged square reads as follows:

```
              A

              P
              A
              T
              E
              R
A  PATERNOSTER  O
              O
              S
              T
              E
              R

              O
```

It would not be difficult for a Christian to expound his faith on the basis of a crossword puzzle of this sort to an enquiring friend. It is not without significance, therefore, that this *Rotas-Sator* square was found in the *palaestra* at Pompeii. After his athletic practice some Christian apparently sat down with a friend to share with him in this way the good news of Jesus.

These are, of course, tenuous enough pieces of evidence to go on. They are unfortunately all we have. We know that we cannot be far astray in our estimate of their significance, for whether we look to Philip bearing testimony to the Ethiopian eunuch in the open air in the first century, or to Octavius, in the late second century account of Minucius Felix, enjoying his early morning swim at Ostia and talking about his Lord with Caecilius, the Serapis worshipper, we find the same answer. This is the way the gospel spread. And we are fortunate to have even such meagre evidence as we have surveyed of specific instances when the home, the roadside and the sports arena seem to have been used for this allusive, indirect evangelism.

[109] Acts 12:12.
[110] Acts 21:7.
[111] Acts 2:46.
[112] Acts 20:7.
[113] Acts 16:32.
[114] Acts 10:22.
[115] Acts 18:26.
[116] Acts 5:42.

[117] Acts 28:17f.
[118] Acts 20:20f.
[119] *The Reformed Pastor*, p. 10.
[120] He was able to say before his execution, "For eighty-six years I have served him, and he never did me any wrong. How can I blaspheme my king who has saved me?" (*Mart. Polyc.* 9.3, Eusebius, *H.E.* 4.15.20).
[121] His father was Bishop of Sinope in Pontus (Hippolytus, *Syntagma*, cited in Epiphanius, *Haer.* 42).
[122] *Act. Justin.* 3.
[123] *I Apol.* 15.
[124] Pliny, *Ep.* 10.96.
[125] Ephesians 6:1, 2.
[126] Ephesians 6:4.
[127] Matthew 18:2–4, Mark 9:33–6, Luke 9:46–8.
[128] Acts 21:5.
[129] *Barnabas* 19.10.
[130] Philippians 4:2.
[131] *I Clem.* 21.6–8.
[132] Mark 10:14.
[133] *Mand.* 12.3.6, *Sim.* 5.3.9, 7.6.
[134] *Vis.* 2.2.3.
[135] *Vis.* 1.1.9.
[136] *Vis.* 2.2.3f.
[137] *Vis.* 1.3.1.
[138] *Vis.* 2.2.2.
[139] *Vis.* 2.2.3, 4.
[140] *Vis.* 1.3.1, 2.
[141] *Vis.* 2.3.1.
[142] This record all comes from Eusebius, *H.E.* 6.2. A different, and hostile, account is given by the anti-Christian writer, Porphyry, quoted in Eusebius, *H.E.* 6.19.7, but Eusebius's own account is to be preferred. See H. Chadwick, *Early Christian Thought and the Classical Tradition*, p. 67f. (and notes).
[143] Acts 18:3.
[144] Acts 18:26.
[145] See the discussion in E. Käsemann, *Essays on New Testament Themes*, p. 136ff.
[146] Acts 18:26, 2 Timothy 4:19, 1 Corinthians 16:19, Romans 16:5.
[147] Acts 19:27.
[148] 1 Corinthians 16:19.
[149] Acts 18:26.
[150] Such is, perhaps, fair inference from 1 Corinthians 1:18ff., coupled with his initial inactivity at Corinth, but it has been grossly exaggerated, by writers like W. L. Knox, until it has been built up without any substantial evidence into one of the great turning points of Paul's life.
[151] Acts 18:4.
[152] Acts 18:5., reading *tō logō*.
[153] Romans 16:4.
[154] John 1:37.
[155] John 1:41.
[156] John 1:43.
[157] John 1:45.
[158] See C. F. D. Moule, "The Individualism of the Fourth Gospel" in *Novum Testamentum* 1962, pp. 171–90.
[159] Justin, *Dial.* 1.3.
[160] *Octavius*, 1.
[161] Acts 8:5, 6, 26–40.
[162] Acts 8:26.
[163] "Arise and go. And he arose and went" (8:26f. See too 8:39).
[164] Acts 9:10–18.

[165] 1 Thessalonians 2:7, 11.
[166] Philemon 10.
[167] 1 Corinthians 4:15.
[168] *Panegyr.* 5.
[169] All the above citations come from *Panegyr.* 5.
[170] *Panegyr.* 6.
[171] See above, p. 203 and Origen, *Commentary on Psalm 36.*
[172] *Panegyr.* 7.
[173] Origen reckons that between one and two hours of Bible reading daily is barely adequate for the individual Christian (*Homily 2 on Numbers,* 10.19).
[174] *Letter to Gregory,* 3.
[175] The variant reading *pistuesēte* for *pisteuēte* would strengthen the argument that the main purpose of the book is evangelistic, for the aorist subjunctive might be held to stress the initial act of faith to which it is the writer's aim to bring his readers. The reading *pisteuete* could mean that the Gospel was written to confirm the readers in the faith they already had. This is, however, unlikely to have been the author's main concern, though no doubt it was a subsidiary aim. The Gospel was written in the first instance from faith to unbelief. It selects the signs which attest Jesus's status and work in order to induce faith in the readers rather than strengthen it.
[176] Part of the genius of this Gospel is the way in which its leading themes, bread, vine, shepherd, light, life and so forth, were as evocative in Greek as in Jewish thought.
[177] See his essay, "The Intention of the Evangelists" in *New Testament Essays,* ed. A. J. B. Higgins, p. 176.
[178] *The Gospel according to Saint Matthew,* p. 21.
[179] Thus Horace dedicated his *Odes* to Maecenas, and Virgil his *Aeneid* to Augustus himself.
[180] See my *The Meaning of Salvation,* pp. 125–30.
[181] C. K. Barrett, *Luke the Historian in Recent Study,* p. 68f.
[182] *The Birth of the New Testament,* p. 92f.
[183] *The Theology of Acts,* pp. 166–77.
[184] "The Book of Acts, the Confirmation of the Gospel", in *Novum Testamentum,* 1960, pp. 26–59.
[185] In *New Testament Essays,* ed. A. J. B. Higgins, p. 175.
[186] A strong link exists between Luke and the Apologists. He was, in fact, the first of them, and as I have pointed out elsewhere, Luke is the first to employ the three classic arguments for the truth of Christianity so common among the Apologists in the second century, namely the argument from miracle, the argument from fulfilled prophecy, and the argument from the success and spread of the Christian movement. For an examination of the evangelistic aims of the Apologists, see J. Daniélou, *Message Évangélique et Culture Héllenistique aux II et III Siècles,* pp. 11–19.
[187] "The Work of St Luke" in *Studies in the Gospels and Epistles* by T. W. Manson, pp. 46–67.
[188] On this see E. P. Sanders, *The Tendencies of the Synoptic Tradition;* J. Rohde, *Rediscovering the Teaching of the Evangelists.*
[189] He claims to "know it all" (*Contra Celsum* 1.12) but only specifically refers to the lost *Dialogue of Jason and Papiscus* (*Contra Celsum* 4.52).
[190] Justin, *2 Apology,* 15.
[191] See p. 162f. Tatian's celebrated testimony to the converting power of the Scriptures (*Orat.* 29) stresses several points which made a great impression on him. He was moved by their directness and simplicity, the manifest honesty of their writers, their immense antiquity, their intelligible and intelligent account of the creation of the world, their stress on the unity and providential government of God, the moral precepts they inculcated, and the astonishing fact of fulfilled prophecy. Justin, too, was deeply impressed by the fulfilment of the prophecies (*Dial.* 7) and he made great play with this fact in his discussions with Trypho.

[192] Hebrews 4:12.
[193] 2 Timothy 3:15.
[194] Ch. 38.
[195] Ch. 1.
[196] Ch. 2.
[197] Ch. 5. There is an ambivalence between the Scriptures and Christ in his use of "the Word".
[198] Jerome, *Adv. Rufin.* 1.9.
[199] Philostorgius, *H.E.* 2.3.
[200] For the text, see G. Waitz, *Über das Leben und die Lehre des Ulfilas*, p. 20.
[201] Acts 4:31f.
[202] Ephesians 6:20.
[203] 2 Corinthians 1:11. Such is the force of the Greek, *sunhupourgountōn humōn*.
[204] *Dial.* 7.
[205] *Ephes.* 10.

CHAPTER 9

[1] Galatians 2:20.
[2] Romans 5:5.
[3] 1 John 4:10–12, 14, 19.
[4] 2 Corinthians 5:14.
[5] This legend is old enough to have influenced the *Acts of Paul*, and can therefore scarcely have originated later than A.D. 180.
[6] *Acta Petri* 35 (= *Mart. Petri* 6).
[7] *De Monarchia* 1.
[8] Clement, *Protrep.* 11.
[9] *Ibid.* 12.
[10] John Foster, *After the Apostles*, p. 82.
[11] See the interesting discussion of this Great Commission in J. Blauw, *The Missionary Nature of the Church*, p. 83ff., and the extensive bibliography he cites. He quotes with approval Otto Michel's exegesis which relates this passage to Daniel 7:14. The Son of Man has gone to the place of authority in the clouds of heaven, and the service rendered to him by all the nations is an aspect of his enthronement, as Son of Man—for "to him was given dominion and glory and a kingdom, that all peoples, nations and languages should serve him". Christ now calls on his disciples to proclaim his Lordship to the nations. "The proclamation of the Gospel is thus the proclamation of the Lordship of Christ among the nations. Matthew means that since Easter the Gospel has taken on a new form, like the Lord himself . . . Here we have a Christology similar to the one we meet in Philippians 2.5–11." (O. Michel, *Evangelische Missionszeitschrift*, 1941, p. 261f.). See also Karl Barth's exegesis of these verses in *The Theology of the Christian Mission*, ed. G. H. Anderson, pp. 55–71, which concludes: "Because of Jesus's presence, the sum and substance of our text, the Great Commission of the risen Lord to baptize and evangelize is valid throughout the days of this 'last' age."
[12] *Philad.* 9 in the Syriac.
[13] Irenaeus, *Adv. Haer.* 3.18.
[14] See Roland Allen, *Missionary Principles*, ch. 1.
[15] *Op. cit.* p. 25.
[16] *Op. cit.* p. 31.
[17] Ephesians 3:1, 2 Corinthians 5:20, 1 Corinthians 3:9, 1 Corinthians 4:1, 2 Timothy 2:2.
[18] 1 Peter 4:11, 5:2–4.
[19] 3:15.
[20] 2 Corinthians 4:1.
[21] There seems to be a gradual progression in humility to be discerned in these three references, which would be spread out over the years if St Paul is in fact the author of all three documents. This characteristic would be thoroughly

consonant with a unity of authorship: it is not unusual for a saint of God to grow in humility as the years go by. If, however, Ephesians and 1 Timothy should prove to have been written by a later Paulinist, that would only serve to strengthen the present argument. Instead of being restricted to St Paul himself, this motive of responsible ministry in the light of mercy received would be shared, on this view, by two of his associates or imitators. But whilst the question of authorship bristles with problems, it cannot be said at present that conclusive reasons have been adduced for regarding either the Pastorals or Ephesians as pseudonymous.

[22] Ephesians 3:7f.

[23] 1 Timothy 1:2ff.

[24] Philippians 2:4ff. For a justification of this exemplarist view of the verse, see I. H. Marshall, "The Christ Hymn in Philippians 2:5–11", *Tyndale Bulletin* (1968), pp. 104–27, and R. Deichgräber, *Gotteshymnus und Christushymnus in der frühen Christenheit.*

[25] Acts 13:46.

[26] *Contra Celsum* 6.79.

[27] *Hom. in Rom.* 9.1.

[28] Acts 4:20.

[29] John 8:29.

[30] Colossians 1:10.

[31] 1 Timothy 1:20.

[32] 1 Corinthians 9:25–7.

[33] 1 Corinthians 9:20f.

[34] 1 Corinthians 4:3–5.

[35] The emphasis placed by Jesus on the free and unmerited grace of God in his parabolic teaching has been well brought out in J. Jeremias's great book, *The Parables of Jesus.*

[36] See Romans 4:1–25, Galatians 3:6–29.

[37] So T. W. Manson, *On Paul and John*, p. 56f.

[38] Romans 4:25.

[39] Romans 5:1, reading *echomen.*

[40] Romans 6:1ff.

[41] Acts 20:21–4.

[42] This still seems to me to be the meaning of these words, despite the ingenious argument of my friend, Professor E. Earle Ellis to the contrary in *New Testament Studies*, April 1960, p. 211ff.

[43] 2 Corinthians 5:9–11.

[44] 2 Timothy 4:8.

[45] 2 Timothy 4:17.

[46] 1 Corinthians 4:11–15.

[47] A. N. Wilder, *Eschatology and Ethics in the Teaching of Jesus*, ch. 5.

[48] See *ta mē anēkonta* and *ta mē kathēkonta* in Ephesians 5:3, 8, etc.

[49] *To sumpheron*, 1 Corinthians 6:12, 10:23.

[50] Ephesians 5:17, Corinthians 14:20.

[51] Colossians 1:10, Ephesians 5:1ff.

[52] 1 Corinthians 14:40, Romans 13:13, 1 Corinthians 7:35, where *to euschēmon* is used.

[53] *1 Apol.* 8.

[54] *Barnabas*, 19.

[55] *Barnabus*, 21.

[56] Polycarp, *Ep.* 1, 2.

[57] *Ibid.* 5.

[58] *Presb.* 12.

[59] Justin, *2 Apol.* 12.

[60] Thus the Scillitan martyrs, executed in A.D. 180 in Carthage, made statements like this at their trial. "Cittinus said, 'We have none other to fear, save only our Lord God, who is in heaven' and Donata said, 'Honour to Caesar as Caesar; but fear to God'." (*Passion of the Scillitan Martyrs.*)

[61] Tertullian, for instance, gives the matter undue proportion as an incentive to holy living, in *Apologet.* 45. "No doubt about it, we who receive our awards under the judgment of an all-seeing God, and who look forward to eternal punishment from him for sin—we alone make real effort to attain a blameless life under the influence of our ampler knowledge, the impossibility of concealment, and the greatness of the threatened torment, not merely long-enduring, but everlasting." To be sure, Tertullian tempers this motive with others elsewhere, but the fact remains that this unhealthy preoccupation with rewards and punishments tended to make men lose hold of the great truths of justification through grace, as we have seen in the case of Hermas above. It also tended to make holy living and evangelistic effort into meritorious actions whose primary end was to benefit the agent. In course of time, this led to a developed doctrine of merit.

[62] I Corinthians 9:16f.
[63] Luke 19:10.
[64] Luke 11:13.
[65] John 2:25.
[66] Mark 7:22ff.
[67] Mark 10:18.
[68] John 14:6.
[69] Matthew 7:13.
[70] Matthew 6:24.
[71] John 5:40, 17:3.
[72] Matthew 25:31ff., 13:36ff., 25:1ff., 22:1–13.
[73] Matthew 6:21ff., 26ff.
[74] See Mark 10:15, 21, 24, 26.
[75] Romans 3:19, 23, Ephesians 2:1f., 2:12f.
[76] Ephesians 2:3.
[77] Acts 20:19–24.
[78] Acts 20:26.
[79] Ezekiel 3:17f.
[80] Romans 1:14f.
[81] 2 Corinthians 4:4.
[82] Matthew 4:8–10, John 14:30.
[83] 2 Corinthians 4:6.
[84] 2 Corinthians 4:5.
[85] I Corinthians 1:21.
[86] Romans 1:16.
[87] *Apologet.* 47.
[88] *2 Apol.* 9.
[89] *Apologet.* 48.
[90] *I Apol.* 19.
[91] *Mart. Polyc.* 11.
[92] *2 Apol.* 15.
[93] *Ibid.* 14.
[94] *Ibid.* 13 and 10.
[95] *Ibid.* 13.
[96] *2 Apol.* 15, *Dial.* 7.
[97] *Ad Scapulam* 3 and 4.
[98] *Ad Scapulam* 1.
[99] *Protrep.* 9.
[100] *Ibid.*
[101] *Protrep.* 10.
[102] *Ibid.*
[103] *Ibid.*
[104] *Ibid.*
[105] *Ibid.*
[106] *Protrep.* 12. See above, p. 200ff., on Melito and other Christian prophets.
[107] *Protrep.* 10.

[108] *Ibid.*
[109] *Protrep.* 12.

CHAPTER 10

[1] The archaeological evidence in these towns sufficiently answers Tertullian's rhetorical statement to the contrary in *Apologet.* 40.

[2] The evidence is conveniently gathered in J. G. Davies's, *The Early Christian Church* and Harnack's *The Mission and Expansion of Christianity*, as well as in the larger Church histories. There is a useful collection of coloured maps illustrating the expansion of the faith in F. van der Meer's *Atlas of the Early Christian World*.

[3] Nevertheless these exceptions were few in the first two centuries, so far as we can tell. Tertullian claims (rhetorically?) that there are Christians beyond the Roman Wall in Britain: the gospel can penetrate further than the legions (*Adv. Jud.* 7). Even if this were true, however, it would scarcely alter the main contention of this section that the gospel spread along the lines of communication within provinces of the Empire. The "overspill" is a natural result of the importance attached to their faith by the converts, and their desire to share it with all and sundry.

Nor does the acceptance of Christianity in Osroëne at an early date invalidate this geographical factor in evangelism. F. C. Burkitt placed great stress on the strength of Christianity here, and though he overstates his case when he describes it as the only region outside the Empire where early Christianity was to be found (*Early Christianity outside the Roman Empire*, p. 87), his exaggeration serves to underline the paucity of evidence there is for the spread of the faith beyond the confines of the Roman world. Even Osroëne could hardly be described in these terms. This tiny kingdom, situated just outside the Empire in northern Mesopotamia, played an important part in the struggle between Rome and Parthia. It was taken over for Rome by L. Verus in A.D. 164. Prior to that it had been an independent buffer state, though a titular dependency of Parthia. During that period it had accepted Christianity as its religion, as the apocryphal story of the correspondence between Jesus and King Abgar and the subsequent conversion of the king at the preaching of Thaddaeus indicates (Eusebius, *H.E.* 1.13). The strongly Semitic character of the country, coupled with its proximity to the zealous missionary centre of Antioch, make its early evangelization readily comprehensible. The capital, Edessa, became one of the earliest homes of Syrian Christianity. Her bishops traced their descent to Serapion, bishop of Antioch from A.D. 190–203, thus confirming the *a priori* likelihood that they owed their evangelization to Antiochene missionaries.

[4] The King of Armenia, Tiridates (*c.* A.D. 238–314) was converted to Christianity through the ministry of Gregory the Illuminator, a nobleman of the country who had himself found faith while he was an exile in Cappadocia. With the king's conversion, the official religion of the country became Christianity.

The legend of Thomas and his visit to India is set out in the third century *Acts of Thomas*. That a substratum of truth may well underlie the legend has been demonstrated by the discovery that the King Gundaphorus whom he is said to have evangelized was a real person who lived in the first century A.D. and reigned in north-west India. His Greek name was Hyndopheres (emphasizing his cultural and trade links with the West) and some of his coinage survives. See C. P. T. Winckworth in *J.T.S.* 1929, pp. 237–44 and L. W. Brown, *The Indian Christians of St Thomas*, and above, ch. 7, n. 8.

[5] John 4:38.
[6] F. J. A. Hort, *The First Epistle of St Peter*, p. 17.
[7] Acts 19:10.
[8] W. M. Ramsay, *The Letters to the Seven Churches*, p. 183.
[9] *H.E.* 3.1.1.
[10] *Acta Thom.* 1.1.
[11] Galatians 2:9.

[12] Romans 15:20.
[13] *Op. cit.* p. 16.
[14] 2 Timothy 2:2.
[15] Acts 19:10.
[16] Colossians 1:5f., 2:1.
[17] L. Newbigin, *The Finality of Christ*, p. 113.
[18] Romans 15:19, 23.
[19] Romans 15:20f.
[20] *Mission in the New Testament*, p. 97.
[21] *Op. cit.* p. 99.
[22] Justin, *Dial.* 42 and cf. *1 Apol.* 39.
[23] Origen, *Contra Celsum* 8.68.
[24] *Op. cit.* 8.69.
[25] *Op. cit.* 8.70.
[26] *Op. cit.* 8.68.
[27] *Op. cit.* 8.70.
[28] *Op. cit.* 8.72.
[29] It is fascinating to reflect on how nearly this happened at the end of the first century. Had the two sons of the Christian family of Flavia Domitilla and Flavius Clemens (ch. 5, n. 48) lived, they might have anticipated Constantine by two centuries: for they had been openly designated by the Emperor Domitian as his successors (Suetonius, *Domit.* 15).
[30] Jude 23.
[31] *1 Clement* 23.
[32] *2 Clement* 11.
[33] *Barnabas* 19. The significance of this reference is enhanced when one recalls that it forms part of the very early catechism, "The Two Ways", which is incorporated into the latter part of the *Epistle of Barnabas*.
[34] Theophilus, *Ad Autol.* 1.13, 14, and 2.38.
[35] Clement, *Protrep.* 9 and 10.
[36] Ignatius, *Ephesians* 11.
[37] Justin, *1 Apol.* 17f.
[38] Tatian, *Orat.* 5 and 6.
[39] Irenaeus, *A.H.* 5.27ff.
[40] Indeed, so cardinal is this assumption to a scholar like Conzelmann that he makes the whole theme of his *Die Mitte der Zeit* depend on it.
[41] 1 Thessalonians 1:10, 3:11f.
[42] 2 Thessalonians, ch. 2.
[43] 1 Thessalonians 4:15, 17. The repeated "we who are alive and remain" is surely significant. Paul seems to be writing not only to comfort those who had lost dear ones and were wrongly bemoaning their supposed missing of the parousia and its joys; he also writes to correct those who were rejoicing that they were still alive and ready for the great event, as if they would thereby get the better of those who had fallen asleep. Paul as so often reverses their assumption, while quoting their war-cry. The "we who remain" (among whom he naturally classes himself. He could scarcely have done otherwise!) will not be at any advantage compared with their dead brethren when the parousia comes. Indeed, if there is to be any priority, it lies with the deceased, who not only possess a depth of intimacy with Christ now, expressed by "with Christ" and "in Christ" in these verses, but it is they who will rise first. Only thereafter shall "we who remain" be caught up to share their company with the Lord at his return. See further my article in *Expository Times*, 1958, p. 285f.
[44] 1 Thessalonians 5:1.
[45] Matthew 24:43f., Luke 12:39f., Revelation 3:3, 16:15.
[46] Luke 17:24.
[47] Luke 12:35–48, Luke 17:24, Mark 13:32, Acts 1:7.
[48] See the most careful working out of this thesis in A. L. Moore, *The Parousia in the New Testament*. He shows how the characteristic attitude of the New Testament is to regard the End as "indeed near, ready to break in at any

moment, held back only by the merciful patience of God who wills that men should repent while there is time" and at the same time to refuse any attempt to calculate dates or to bring it about by social action, recognizing that "it is for God only to decide" (*op. cit.* p. 218).

[49] *Twentieth Century Theology in the Making*, ed. Jaroslav Pelikan (a translation of *Die Religion in Geschichte und Gegenwart*), p. 258.

[50] Ephesians 1:14, 4:30.

[51] *Twentieth Century Theology in the Making*, ed. by Jaroslav Pelikan, p. 263.

[52] *Op. cit.* p. 291f.

[53] Acts 2:16f.

[54] Romans 8:19–23.

[55] Acts 1:6–8.

[56] Many scholars believe, with Conzelmann, that Luke was the first to develop a theology of history; the first to realize that the awaiting of the parousia was a blind alley, and that the culmination was to be achieved through a historical process of evangelism.

[57] Mark 13:9f., Matthew 24:14.

[58] John 15:26f.

[59] 2 Peter 3:12.

[60] See Strack-Billerbeck, vol. 1, p. 163ff, for several such texts.

[61] 2 Peter 3:9, and cf. my *2 Peter and Jude*, pp. 133–36.

[62] Matthew 8:10f., 28:19, Mark 13:10, etc. See Jeremias *op. cit.* pp. 46–54.

[63] Cf. F. Hahn, *Mission in the New Testament*, p. 107f., K. F. Nickle, *The Collection*, p. 130ff. Hahn gives an extensive bibliography on this subject on p. 18f. of his book.

[64] *Op. cit.* p. 60.

[65] He battles with the problem of Israel and the Gentiles in relation to the mission in Romans 9–11. The commentaries by C. K. Barrett and F. J. Leenhardt are perceptive on this section: that of C. H. Dodd is strangely lacking in sensitivity and insight at this point.

[66] It was, of course, no pragmatic consideration such as the comparative success of the Gentile mission that induced Paul to prosecute it with such dedication; rather, it was the conviction that he was obedient to the purpose of Jesus, and carrying on the work of the Servant of Yahweh whose role was declared by the prophet to be a light to the Gentiles.

[67] Romans 11, especially v. 25f.

[68] Nickle, following Munck in the last two chapters of his *Paul and the Salvation of Mankind* (but without the bizarre features of the latter's hypothesis, which have been well criticized by W. D. Davies in his review article in *N.T.S.* 1955, pp. 60–72) sets out the position well and cites the literature in full (*op. cit.* p. 138ff.).

[69] Hence his agitation lest the gift should be refused (Romans 15:30f.) and his determination to present it in person, no matter what dangers lay in his way (Acts 20:22f., 21:11–14).

[70] See further on the link between eschatology and mission O. Cullmann, "Eschatology and Missions in the New Testament" in *The Theology of the Christian Mission* (ed. G. H. Anderson), pp. 42–54. J. Blauw has a valuable chapter on "Towards a Theology of Mission" in *The Missionary Nature of the Church*, ch. 7.

[71] *International Review of Missions*, 1953, p. 225. The two articles by William Manson in this journal for 1953 (pp. 257–65 and 389–96) are exceptionally suggestive. He develops some of his thought further in a posthumous book, *Jesus and the Christian*, p. 199ff.

EPILOGUE

[1] "Origen does not affirm universal salvation as something we can all comfortably take for granted, and it is more his hope than his assured certitude." So

H. Chadwick assesses Origen's attitude in *Early Christian Thought and the Classical Tradition,* p. 119.

[2] 2 Corinthians 4:4f.

[3] I have attempted to develop this theme in the contemporary context in *Runaway World,* pp. 64–70.

[4] Anne Ross, *Pagan Celtic Britain,* p. 5f.

[5] I owe this quotation from Gregory of Nyssa's panegyric on Gregory Thaumaturgus to J. G. Davies, *The Early Christian Church,* p. 128.

SELECT SUBJECT INDEX

SELECT SUBJECT INDEX

Index

Messianic,
salvation: 48–52, 57, 60, 80f., 87–99, 290, 298–300
speculation: 87–99, 291f., 296–300
Moralism, 140, 185
Monotheism, 17–20, 23–5, 97ff., 119–21, 126–32, 163, 179, 191, 284, 287, 311
Montanists, 200f., 325
Mystery Cults, 20–2, 36, 114, 121f., 138, 146, 155, 163, 284, 309, 313, 315

Nathan Prophecy, 50, 62, 85, 97, 290
New Birth, 121, 137, 153–6, 161–5, 226, 253

Obedience, 157, 161, 220f., 239, 246, 330
Open Air Preaching, 81, 170f., 196–9
Orante, 216–18, 328
Osroëne, 258, 335

Paganism, 122f., 126–32, 286–9, 315, 320, 322, 328
Pagan motifs, 215, 314
Pantaenus, 163, 167, 171, 205, 224
Pax Romana, 13ff., 256ff., 292
Perpetua, 177
Persecution, 33, 264f., 287–9
Pesher, 86, 208, 298
Peter, St, 104, 187, 210
Philosophy, 17, 25, 43f., 58, 120f., 139, 145, 162, 171f., 199, 204f., 227f., 239, 292, 309, 311f., 315
Phoenix, 142, 314
Pomponia Graecina, 119, 211, 327
Poppaea Sabina, 24, 147, 285, 381
Post-baptismal sin, 140, 153, 156, 221
Power, 55, 90, 95, 109f., 119, 202ff., 250f., 310f., 331
Praeparatio Evangelica, 13ff., 106, 120, 252, 283
Prayer, 162, 180, 187, 190, 235, 252, 309, 315
Priscilla, 118, 213f., 222f., 327
Prophets,
Old Testament: 80–4, 106, 162f., 234, 325, 331
New Testament: 168f., 176, 200–2, 254, 325, 334
Proselytes, 25–7, 112f., 147f., 285
Punishment, 140f., 245ff., 267, 289, 334

Qumran, 84–6, 88, 93, 291, 298, 300, 301f., 318
Quo Vadis, 237f., 332

Religio, religion, 33, 34–6, 144f., 210, 284, 286f., 309, 312f., 327
Repentance, 60, 126f., 151f., 153, 188, 198, 235, 271, 296, 337
Responsibility, 240–8
Resurrection, 49f., 73, 94f., 97, 120, 127, 129, 137, 142, 150, 159, 197, 202, 289, 293, 306
Reward, 140f., 245–8, 334
Roads, 15f., 256, 258f., 283, 335
Rotas-Sator Square, 218, 328f.

Sabinus, Flavius, 323
Scriptures, 25, 49, 69, 70, 78–87, 100–2, 128, 139, 148–52, 162f., 171, 195, 222ff., 228f., 233–5, 292f., 295f., 298ff., 304f., 306, 319, 331
Security, 21, 116
Servant of Yahweh, 71, 73, 79, 82f., 88f., 92f., 95f., 110, 241f., 295f., 301f.
Slaves, 117f., 146, 209, 212, 284, 289, 306f.
Social Groupings, 44ff., 118ff.
Son of Man, 88, 92f., 109, 295, 300f., 332
Spirit, Holy, 60, 71f., 81, 90, 98, 104, 148–53, 155, 159, 165, 182ff., 186, 200f., 240, 268f., 270f., 303f., 316
Superstitio, 34–7, 40, 44, 210, 215f., 287f., 313
Synagogues, 25, 81, 105, 194–6
Syncretism, 34–7, 41–3, 158

Talpioth ossuaries, 328
Testimonia, 69, 83–7, 100, 298
Testimony, 163–5, 196, 206f.
Thirteenth Benediction, 34, 99, 105, 297f., 303

Universalism, 27, 53, 54, 112ff., 148ff., 231f., 256, 264f., 277, 283, 288, 301, 305, 308, 337

Virgin Birth, *see* 'Jesus, virgin born'
Visiting, 225–9

Wisdom, 43f., 120, 141, 308
Witness, 70–7, 109, 199, 229, 295ff.
Women, 41, 118f., 169, 175–8, 210f., 307

SELECT AUTHOR INDEX

SELECT AUTHOR INDEX

This index includes ancient and modern authors mentioned in the text, but not in the footnotes.